PUBLISHING

2003

NARSIDASS

WARSAW INDOLOGICAL STUDIES

VOLUME 2

Essays in Jaina Philosophy and Religion

Editors:

PIOTR BALCEROWICZ

&

MAREK MEJOR

WARSAW 2002

LALA SUNDARLAL JAIN RESEARCH SERIES

General Editor
PROF. SATYA RANJAN BANERJEE

VOLUME XX

चतुररनयचक्रम्

Essays in Jaina Philosophy and Religion

Edited by
PIOTR BALCEROWICZ
MAREK MEJOR

MOTILAL BANARSIDASS PUBLISHERS
PRIVATE LIMITED • DELHI

First Indian Edition: Delhi, 2003

Cover design and photograph: Piotr Balcerowicz

Devanāgarī text typeset with
Amrita © *The Amrita Package—A Devanâgarî Sanskrit Keyboard Program developed by Piotr Balcerowicz*

ISBN: 81-208-1977-2

Also available at:

MOTILAL BANARSIDASS

41 U.A. Bungalow Road, Jawahar Nagar, Delhi 110 007
8 Mahalaxmi Chamber, 22 Bhulabhai Desai Road, Mumbai 400 026
236, 9th Main III Block, Jayanagar, Bangalore 560 011
120 Royapettah High Road, Mylapore, Chennai 600 004
Sanas Plaza, 1302 Baji Rao Road, Pune 411 002
8 Camac Street, Kolkata 700 017
Ashok Rajpath, Patna 800 004
Chowk, Varanasi 221 001

Printed in India
BY JAINENDRA PRAKASH JAIN AT SHRI JAINENDRA PRESS,
A-45 NARAINA, PHASE-I, NEW DELHI 110 028
AND PUBLISHED BY NARENDRA PRAKASH JAIN FOR
MOTILAL BANARSIDASS PUBLISHERS PRIVATE LIMITED,
BUNGALOW ROAD, DELHI 110 007

TABLE OF CONTENTS

तृतीयारनयविवरणम्
ETHICS AND MONASTIC DISCIPLINE

चतुर्थारनयविवरणम्
MEDIAEVAL MYSTICISM AND SECTARIAN DIVISIONS

FOREWORD

It is a pleasure to write a Foreword to the book *Essays in Jaina Philosophy and Religion* edited by Piotr Balcerowicz and Marek Mejor. The book has four sections which describe the Jain Philosophy and *Anekānta* as well as the historical development of Jainism together with its relation to Buddhism and the *Ājīvikas*. The book also deals with the Jaina system of ethics and conduct including social life, monastic rules and rituals along with the mediaeval Jaina Literature. It is a collection of articles written by acclaimed Jaina scholars of the world.

Though all the articles are written from a different angle, the articles on *Anekānta* are somewhat striking. It explains how an object or idea can be judged from all possible angles of vision. It is a fact worth noting that according to the Jains a substance has two opposite characters—permanence and change, universality and particularity, similarity and dissimilarity. Jaina authors like Samantabhadra, Akalaṅka, Vidyānanda and Yośovijaya laid a firm foundation of *Anekāntavāda* and established a grand superstructure of *Anekānta* doctrine. The *Anekānta-jaya-patākā* of Haribhadra Sūri is a standard work of the subject and is the most solid contribution to the treasure-house of Jain Philosophy.

I believe that Professors Balcerowicz and Mejor's book *Essays in Jaina Philosophy and Religion* will earn name and fame for the subject, because the style of the book is simple and lucid, and the exposition of the subject is clear and crystal. It is, therefore, quite in the fitness of things that Shri N.P. Jain of Motilal Banarsidass Pvt. Ltd. has published such an important treatise for the benefit of the scholars. I can unhesitatingly recommend this book to the reading public.

SATYA RANJAN BANERJEE
Quondam Professor of Linguistics
Calcutta University

Dated: 15 June 2003

Message to the International Seminar on Jainism
'Aspects of Jainism'

श्री ऋषभदेवस्वामिने नमः।

श्री शङ्खेश्वरपार्श्वनाथाय नमः।

श्री सद्गुरुदेवेभ्यो नमः।

अयि जैनदर्शनरहस्यजिज्ञासवो महानुभावा जगतो विद्वांसः, विभिन्नदेशनिवासिनां भवतां महानुभावानां विदुषां संमीलनं वोर्सो (Warsaw) नगरे 2000 September 8–9 दिनयोः भविता इति विज्ञाय परमं प्रमोदमनुभवामि।

भवतां द्वारा जैनदर्शनस्य यथातथं स्वरूपं जगति ज्ञातं भवेदिति नितरामाशंसे।

सर्वेऽपि विश्वस्य जीवाः शान्तिं सुखं समाधिं चेच्छन्ति। 'सर्वेऽपि सुखिनः सन्तु' इति जैनदर्शनस्य परमं रहस्यम्।

परमात्मनः कृपया अस्मिन् कार्ये भवन्तो वयं च संमीभ्य सहभागिनो भवेम इति परमात्मानं प्रार्थये।

इति पूज्यपादगुरुदेवमुनिराजश्रीभुवनविजयान्तेवासी मुनि जम्बूविजयः।

6th September, 2000
India

PREFACE

Modern Indological scholarship still suffers dearth of thorough and critical research in the field of Jaina studies as such, and likewise adequate exploration of the history and background of the exchange of ideas between the Jainas and other systems of thought in India is imperative.

It is our hope that the present volume will contribute to our knowledge and understanding of Jaina philosophical, historical, religious, literary and social aspects, and will, at least to a certain degree, be a meaningful advancement in Indological research, deepening our understanding of Indian intellectual heritage and culture in general.

The present collection of *Essays in Jaina Philosophy and Religion* contains contributions of world-acclaimed scholars who specialise in Jaina studies.

Some of these papers were directly presented by the authors (Nalini Balbir, Colette Caillat, Christoph Emmrich, Peter Flügel, Jayandra Soni, Luitgard Soni, Kenji Watanabe and Albrecht Wezler) at the International Seminar 'Aspects of Jainism', held at Warsaw University, Poland, 8–9 September, 2000. The Seminar was one of the most important Indological events in Poland and the first opportunity in the history of Polish Indology for scholars to meet and debate on issues pertaining to the field of Jaina and related studies. The honorary president of the Seminar was Muni Jambūvijayajī, the advisor and consultant was Professor Albrecht Wezler, and the Seminar was organised by Professor Marek Mejor and Piotr Balcerowicz.

Each of the four main sections of the present volume is an 'exposition' of a different 'viewpoint-spoke' (अरनयविवरणम्), and pertains to an important aspect within Jaina studies. Thus, such vital branches are comprised as (1) philosophy, with the emphasis on epistemology and the theory of the multiplexity of reality (*anekânta-vāda*), (2) historical development of Jainism and its origins, with special consideration of its relation to Buddhism and Ājīvikism, (3) Jaina system of ethics and conduct, including rituals, social life, monastic rules and regulations, and

(4) Jaina mediaeval literature as an expression of mysticism and sectarian background. Thus, the four 'viewpoint-spokes' make up चतुरस्नयचक्रम्, or 'The Wheel of Modes [of Considering Jainism] which has Four Spokes', which is the subtitle of the *Essays in Jaina Philosophy and Religion*.

As the organisers of the International Seminar 'Aspects of Jainism', Professor Marek Mejor and myself wish to express our deepest gratitude to Professor Albrecht Wezler, without whose invaluable advice, consulting voice as well as his passionate support and stimulating involvement the seminar would not only have been far less productive and noteworthy, but probably would not have taken place at all. Our thanks are also proffered to Śrī Muni Jambūvijaya, who so kindly agreed to become the Honorary President of the Seminar on Jainism.

The present edition appears as Volume Two of the Series *Warsaw Indological Studies* by the arrangement with Motilal Banarsidass Private Limited, Delhi. Our thanks are due to Messrs Jain, the Directors, for their kind co-operation.

We wish to extend our most sincere thanks to Mr. Vijay Tyagi (T&T Julida Co.) for his financial support, without which the present publication would not be possible.

Last but not least, I would like to gratefully acknowledge the immense help and valuable suggestions given by Professor Marek Mejor to the completion of this work.

Piotr Balcerowicz

प्रथमारनयविवरणम्

Philosophy and Anekânta

Studien zum *Dvādaśâra-naya-cakra* des Śvetāmbara Mallavādin. II:*
The Twelve *Ara*s of the *Dvādaśâra-naya-cakra* and their relation to the Canon as seen by Mallavādin
First Part

ALBRECHT WEZLER

For Muni Jambūvijayajī
as a token of my deep respect and gratitude

– 1 –

MUNI JAMBŪVIJAYAJĪ's richly annotated critical edition of Siṁhasūri Gaṇivādin Kṣamāśramaṇa's *Nyāyâgamânusāriṇī* (NĀA) is a most remarkable achievement: A highly impressive specimen of Jaina monastic erudition, and the continuation of this tradition on to the present age, an absolutely convincing example of a really happy marriage between traditional Indian learning in general and philology in particular and Western scientific methods (blessed by the angel of sharp intelligence), an outstanding contribution to our knowledge of Jaina philosophy as well as of the history of Indian philosophy and, so one has to add, world philosophy. Although the MUNI was also not able to conjure up (a) manuscript(s) of the *mūla* text, Ācārya Śrī Mallavādin Kṣamāśramaṇa's *Dvādaśâra-naya-cakra* (DNC), he has penetrated the commentary so deeply and presents it in such a lucid manner that the loss of the DNC itself is almost compensated for: It is reconstructed by the learned editor to such an extent, and in such reliable a manner that by and large it can be made the object of scholarly studies. (The earlier similar attempts[1] have not only been eclipsed, but practically turned into waste paper (if the historical point of view may be disregarded for the sake of rhetorical effect).) This holds good in particular for the internal structure of Mallavādin's work which is announced

* For the first article of this series see WEZLER (1981).

[1] Viz. Vijayalabdhi Suri (1948–1960) und Caturvijayaji and Gandhi (1952) (cf. POTTER (1970: 47 f.)).

Essays in Jaina Philosophy and Religion.
Warsaw Indological Studies, Volume 2 (2002), pp. 13–23.

already by its title: 'The Wheel of Modes [of Considering Things] which has Twelve Spokes'.[2] And it is on this structure that attention is focused in my paper, the second problem to be addressed being its relation to, or justification by, canonical texts.

– 2 –

As 'it was mainly one aspect of the Jain doctrine with which Mallavādin 'was occupied, viz. the doctrine of the Naya, the various possibilities to consider things', to quote from FRAUWALLNER's 'Introduction', it is little wonder that the work as such was given a title which contains this term. And, to be sure, there can, as was also underlined by the MUNI,[3] be hardly any doubt that at least *Naya-cakra* is in fact the title given to this his work by its author, the prior member (*Dvādaśâra-*) being a little less certain. Yet the image itself, its motive(s) and aim(s), is obviously not made clear by Mallavādin. Intuitively however, it is understood—even by us who are not any longer familiar with bullock carts—(1) that a wheel basically consists of a circular ring, the rim, connected by spokes to a hub, (2) that the number of spokes may vary, (3) but that twelve is by itself a plausible number, also technically, in that it arises if the circle is divided first into four sectors, and each of them in order to strengthen the support then into three, and (4) finally, that it is designed to turn around an axle passed through the centre.[4] And this is also the picture we are shown of this particular wheel on the dust jackets of MUNI JAMBŪVIJAYAJĪ's edition (see ill. 1): a clear, beautiful and symmetrical geometrical figure. In passing only—for it would in fact call for a separate, comprehensive and necessarily detailed study—I should like to draw attention to the fact that Indian philosophers seem to share with their European colleagues the susceptibility to concrete images illustrating the doctrinal structure of their systems, or even vindicating their correctness.

Leaving aside, for the time being, the question addressed by FRAUWALLNER ('Introduction', p. 1 f.) of how Mallavādin's 'doctrine of the Naya' is related to the older one put forward by Siddhasena Divākara in his *Saṁmati-tarka-prakaraṇa*,[5] and the even more intricate problem of the origins of the *naya* theory as such, i.e.

---

[2] Cf. *Ṭippaṇāni* (henceforth Ṭipp.), at the end of the first part, on *pṛ*° 1 *paṁ*°12, i.e. p. 1 f.

[3] Cf. the reference given in n. 2.

[4] I follow here closely the definition found in WEBSTER's *New Encyclopedic Dictionary* (All new edition of 1994).

[5] Which was commented upon by Mallavādin himself; cf. FRAUWALLNER (1966: 'Introduction', p.1).

confining myself to a closer examination of Mallavādin's own conception, or should I say: scheme of *naya*s, 'partial expressions of truth' (JAINI 1979: 93), I think it is but fair to quote from MUNI JAMBŪVIJAYAJĪ's *Prāk-kathana*. After describing the older—and historically dominant—theory of the seven *naya*s called *naigama*, *saṅgraha* etc. and the relation in which they are said to stand to the two *naya*s called *dravyârthika* and *paryāyârthika*[6] he explains:

> '"*Naya-cakra*", this is an appropriate name: Like in the wheel of e.g. a chariot here too there are twelve treatises (*prakaraṇa*) called "Spokes"; in [these] 12 treatises the 12 *naya*s [called] "*vidhi*" etc. are set forth here one after the other; under the pretext of expounding the *naya*s [called] *vidhi* etc. all philosophical doctrines without exception, which follow one or the other of [these] *naya*s and belong to his period, are described minutely by Mallavādin; and just as in the case of the wheel of e.g. a chariot the spokes are separated from each other, so here too the 12 spokes are separated from each other by that part (*aṁśa*) which consists in the refutation of the opponent's position (*para-pakṣa*) because the spokes [called] "*vidhi*" etc. are put forward in order to establish one's own position (*sva-pakṣa*) immediately after first refuting the opponent's position; and just as there (i.e. in the case of a wheel) [there is] a rim made up of several parts (*avayava*), so [there is] here a rim made up of three parts,[7] because each part of the rim is completed in four spokes and just as there (i.e. in a wheel) [there is] a hub which is also called "gourd" (*tumba*)[8] which forms the support of all the spokes—because otherwise if they were not connected to it they would fall apart / off and because they would lack the capacity to perform their function—, so here too there is the hub of the *syād-vāda* which forms the support of all the 12 spokes of *naya*s called *vidhi* etc. because it renders stability to all the *naya*s connected with it and because for this reason they would otherwise fall apart / off. For all the twelve *naya*s stand in contradiction to each other and would hence be destroyed; but when they have the *syād-vāda* as their basis, then they refer to each other as being connected with

[6] Note that the second part of these two—originally Prakrit—compounds is also rendered by Sanskrit *-astika*; cf. FRAUWALLNER's 'Introduction' and e.g. Ill. 1.

[7] Cf. *Prāk-kathana* p. 9, f. 1.

[8] On the word *tumba* see now GHOSH (2000: 64 f.). As for the drinking vessel made out of a 'gourd', M. Mejor kindly drew my attention to verse 86ab of Rājaśekhara's *Ṣaḍ-darśana-samuccaya*: *dormūle tumbaka-bhṛtaḥ prāyeṇa vana-vāśinaḥ* / .

> the hub of the *syād-vāda*, as forming one textual unit,[9] as representing one exposition and become hence firmly established as truth (*satyârtha*). In this way *Naya-cakra* is an appropriate title.
> Since all *naya*s are here described in form of the shape of a wheel, the [philosophical] position of the twelfth spoke is in its turn again contradicted by the first *naya*, etc. And thus this wheel of *naya*s moves forward/revolves incessantly.'[10]

Not a few questions the title of Mallavādin's *magnum opus* is likely to raise, including that whether the wheel is also conceived of as rotating or not, are thereby conveniently answered. And it should now also be clear that what lies at the foundation of the 'Twelve-Spoke-Wheel' is—not as implied by my earlier (above p. 14) description a 4 times 3 scheme, but—a 3 times 4 scheme—as is also explained by FRAUWALLNER in his 'Introduction' (p. 2), who states that

> 'Mallavādin teaches three fundamental modes of considering things: general affirmation (*vidhiḥ*), affirmation and restriction (*vidhiniyamam*), pure restriction (*niyamam*). In addition hereto each of these modes of consideration can be subject of the same three viewpoints, so that finally a total of twelve modes of consideration is brought about.'[11]

---

[9] ... *syād-vāda-nābhi-pratibaddhatvenâika-vākyatayā eka-prabandhena* ...

[10] The Sanskrit original (*Prāk-kathana* p. 18 f.) reads as follows:

"*Naya-cakram*" *iti cânvarthikâivēyaṁ saṁjñā. rathâdi-cakravad atrâpi* "*ara*"-*saṁjñakāni dvādaśa prakaraṇāni vidyante. dvādaśasu prakaraṇeṣu kramaśo dvādaśa vidhyâdayo nayā atra nirūpyante. vidhy-ādi-naya-nirūpaṇa-vyājena tat tan nayânusāriṇas tat-kālīnāḥ sarve 'pi dārśanika-vicārā Mallavādi-sūribhir atrôpanyastāḥ. yathā ca rathâdi-cakre 'rāṇāṁ parasparato 'ntaram evam atrâpi ādau parapakṣaṁ nirasyânantaraṁ sva-pakṣa-sthāpanāya vidhy-ādi-nayānāṁ pravṛttatvāt para-pakṣa-nirasanâtmako yo 'ṁśas tad dvādaśānām arāṇāṁ parasparato antaram. yathā ca tatra nānâvayava-ghaṭito nemir evam atrâpi try-avayava-ghaṭito nemiḥ, caturṣu caturṣu areṣu ekâikasya nemeḥ parisamāptatvāt. yathā ca tatra sarveṣām apy arāṇām ādhāra-bhūtas tumbâpara-paryāyo nābhir anyathā tad-asambaddhānāṁ teṣāṁ visaraṇāt sva-kārya-karaṇâsamarthyāc câivaṁ atrâpi vartate sarveṣām api vidhy-ādi-dvādaśa-nayârāṇām ādhara-bhūtaḥ syād-vāda-nābhiḥ, tat-pratibaddha-sarva-nayâvasthānād ato 'nyathā viśaraṇāt. ete hi dvādaśâpi nayāḥ paraspara-virodhena pravartamānā vighaṭante, yadā tu ta eva syād-vādam āśrayante tadā syād-vāda-nābhi-pratibaddhatvenâika-vākyatayā eka-prabandhenânyonyâpekṣayā pravartamānāḥ satyârthatvena pratiṣṭhitā bhavanti. evaṁ cânvarthakam idaṁ* "*Naya-cakram*" *iti nāma.*

cakrâkāra-rūpeṇa sarveṣāṁ nayānām atra niveśitatvād dvādaśasyâpy arasya mataḥ punaḥ prathamâdi-nayena niṣidhyate. evaṁ cânavaratam idaṁ Naya-cakram kramate.

[11] On the tripartite *nemi*, i.e. on *tri-mārga* cf. *Prāk-kathana* p. 2 together with n. 1.

Both these explanations of the title and thus of the structure of the DNC ultimately go back to a corresponding explicit statement by Mallavādin himself, viz. the Āryā,[12] significantly called *gāthā-sūtra*:

> 'The [formulation of the inference] by the dissimilarity[13] of the properties [of the probans from that of the probandum][14] is as follows: A[ny philosophical] teaching different from that of the Jina is false (i.e. not true) because it lacks the function[15] of *vidhi*, *niyama* and [their] various logically possible alternations[16], like the statement of a mad person[17] (or rather: like a senseless statement[17]).'[18]

What is meant by *tayor bhaṅgāḥ*, the various logically possible modifications of *vidhi* and *niyama*, is in fact also made clear by Mallavādin himself, almost immediately after the verse quoted just now, viz. DNC 10.1–4:

1) *vidhiḥ*, 2) *vidhi-vidhiḥ*, 3) *vidher vidhi-niyamam*, 4) *vidher niyamaḥ*[19],
5) *vidhi-niyamam*, 6) *vidhi-niyamasya vidhiḥ*, 7) *vidhi-niyamasya vidhi-niyamam*, 8) *vidhi-niyamasya niyamaḥ*,
9) *niyamaḥ*, 10) *niyamasya vidhiḥ*, 11) *niyamasya vidhi-niyamam*, 12) *niyamasya niyamaḥ*.

Quite evidently what is meant by *bhaṅga* (*bhaṅgāḥ*) here is, if the various steps of the process in deriving them may be separated from each other and each stated explicitly, firstly, the combination of *vidhi* (= A) and *niyama* (= B) so as to generate the *samāhāra-dvandva*-compound[20] *vidhi-niyama* (= AB), secondly, the application of these three 'modes' to each of them so as to generate *vidhi-vidhiḥ*, *vidher vidhi-niyamam* and *vidher niyamaḥ*, etc. (= AA, AAB, AB etc.), and, finally, the addition of these 3 times 3 'modes' to the basic 'modes' so as to arrive at the result of *vidhiḥ*,

---

[12] Cf. DNC p. 9.6–7 and Ṭipp. p. 13, on *pr̥*° 9 *paṁ*° 6.

[13] Cf. NĀA p. 9.22 f.

[14] Cf. Ṭipp. p. 13, on *pr̥*° 9 *paṁ*° 6.

[15] Cf. NĀA p. 10.21 f.

[16] Cf. the expression *vikalpa* used NĀA e.g. p. 10.20.

[17] For both interpretations cf. Ṭipp. 12 (see n. 14).

[18] DNC 9.6–7

vidhi-niyama-bhaṅga-vr̥tti-vyatiriktatvād anarthaka-vacovat /
jaināḍ anyac chāsanam anr̥taṁ bhavatîti vaidharmyam //

[19] The sequence of the last two members is just the other way round in NĀA p. 10.16 ff.

[20] Cf. NĀA p. 10.18.

vidhi-vidhiḥ, *vidher vidhi-niyamam*, *vidher niyamaḥ*, etc. (= A, AA, AAB, AB etc.) the total being 3 times 4, i.e. twelve.

I wonder what a mathematician's comment would be, but pass over the problem of the mathematical structure of this 'combination' (if this is the right word) to the remark that if one wants to try to trace back Mallavādin's *Dvādaśâra-naya-cakra*, the expression / term *bhaṅga* would certainly be a promising keyword.

Even more fundamental for the full understanding of this peculiar 'wheel', however, is the question—which for that very reason should have been asked already before—what the meanings of the expressions *vidhi* and *niyama* used by Mallavādin actually are. I deliberately avoided the use of 'term' with regard to them; for Siṁhasūri expressly states that *vidhi* and *niyama* are explained by Mallavādin by 'uttering immediately after them synonyms (*paryāya-śabda*) in order to prevent the opponent from forming the wrong idea that the words *vidhi* and *niyama* are *alaukika* (i.e. not used by him with the meaning they have in everyday language).'[21] In other words, they are *laukika* and not *śāstrīya* words which would later call for a definition (*lakṣaṇa*).

Now, the synonyms mentioned by Mallavādin can unfortunately be reconstructed only in part, viz. two of *vidhi*[22] and none of *niyama* although there must have been at least three of the latter (in the lost original).[23] The two synonyms of *vidhi* are *ācāra* and *sthiti*.[24] The former is explained by Siṁhasūri (NĀA 10.9 f.) in terms of its linguistic formation as *ādāna-maryādayā*[25] *cāra(ḥ)*, 'moving within the boundary of taking for oneself'; and conceptionally[26] it is said by him to mean 'not entirely abandoning one's own form irrespective of the form of other [things]' (*ātma-rūpâparityāgaḥ para-rūpânapekṣaḥ*). The word *ācāra* appears to be taken in its basic etymological meaning which can approximately be rendered as 'conduct = way of acting / behaviour'. Similarly *sthiti*, the second synonym—which is not explained by Siṁhasūri—is most probably used in its basic meaning of 'staying / remaining / being (in a state of condition).'

[21] The Sanskrit original reads thus (NĀA 10.6 f.): *tad-vyācakṣāṇaḥ sūriḥ "niyama-vidhi-śabdāv alaukikau" iti paro mā maṁsteti tat-paryāya-śabdān uccārayati — vidhir ācāra iti*.

[22] The expression (*evaṁ*) *sthity-ādiṣu* (*yojyam*) used by Siṁhasūri (NĀA p. 10.10) seems to indicate that Mallavādin mentioned more than just two synonyms.

[23] Evidence is, among others, the final remark of Siṁhasūri (NĀA 10.13 f.): *paryāya-śabdānāṁ śeṣāṇām api ayam artho yathâkṣaraṁ yojyaḥ*.

[24] Cf. also Ṭipp. p. 13 on *pr̥*° 10 *paṁ*° 1.

[25] This explanation seems to be based on Pāṇ. 2.1.13.

[26] Cf. NĀA p. 10.9: *lakṣaṇatas* (*tu*) …

Of *vidhi* itself Siṁhasūri explicitly states that it denotes, in terms of Pāṇini's *kāraka*-theory, the *bhāva*[27]—and not, to be sure, the means of performing the action denoted by the verb *vi√dhā*, i.e. that it does not mean 'rule'—; and immediately afterwards he explains that the agent which performs the action of *vi√dhā* is the *dravyârtha*, 'the entity / object which is a substance'[28], and that it is (the) clay which produces / brings about things such as a lump, and [then] a *śivaka*[29], etc.[30] He adds the reason: 'for by the clay these *śivaka* etc. are produced.'[31] Yet this semantic analysis is, again, followed by an explanation of the characteristics of the denotatum, viz. that *vidhi* is equivalent to 'an entity / object that is a substance' ('ein substanzhaftes Ding', in German), 'an entity / object in regard to which that which distinguishes it [from other entities / objects] is disregarded.'[32]

Turning a little later to the next expression, *niyama*, Siṁhasūri first explains that this now refers to the mode of consideration called *paryāyârtha*, 'the entity which consists in the [various] states [of an object]';[33] again he offers an explanation based on the analysis of the derivation of the word,[34] and then of the conceptual content of the notion, by stating:

> '[*Niyama*] is a particular state determined each moment [and] characterised by the properties of becoming etc. distinguished from each other, such as form (*rūpa*) etc. and a *śivaka* etc. which either exists at the same time or does not exist at the same time; that which [a thing] is [at a particular moment] that is [its *niyama*] [at this moment].'[35]

---

[27] NĀA 10.7: *vidhīyata iti vidhir bhāva-sādhano 'dhyāhṛta-kartr-arthaḥ.*

[28] Com. STP p. 271.15 and DNC (2. Part) p. 454.6 ff.

[29] *Śivaka* quite clearly refers to the second stage in the production of e.g. a *ghaṭa* from a lump (*piṇḍa*) of clay: the lump is made into a—necessarily slightly longer—cylindrical 'small *śiva*', i.e. 'small *liṅga*' (cf. also KAPADIA 1940-47: 268 [Notes]). A somewhat similar expression (used in Kashmirian texts?) is *stūpaka*.

[30] NĀA 10.7 f.: *yo vidadhāti sa kartā dravyârthaḥ. ko vidadhāti? piṇḍa-śivakâdi-bhāvān mṛd vidadhāti.*

[31] NĀA 10.8 f.: *tayā hi mṛdā, śivakâdayo vidhīyante.*

[32] NĀA 10.9: *lakṣaṇas tu anapekṣita-vyāvṛtti-bhedârtho dravyârtho vidhiḥ, loke dṛṣṭatvāt.*

[33] Cf. STP (see n. 28).

[34] Viz. (NĀA p. 10.11): *nir ādhikye ādhikyena yamanaṁ niyamaḥ.*

[35] NĀA 10.11 f.: *... paraspara-prativivikta-bhavanâdi-dharma-lakṣaṇaḥ pratikṣaṇa-niyato 'vasthā-viśeṣo yugapad-bhāvy ayugapad-bhāvī vā rūpâdiḥ śivakâdiś ca yo yo bhavati sa eva sa evêti.*

Therefore I hesitate to follow FRAUWALLNER and to render *niyama* by 'restriction'; in my view a more literal rendering is strongly recommended such as 'determining / regulating [the manner of being of an object] to a high degree / fully.'[36] [I approach the problem very cautiously, but I think such caution is really called for in the case of Mallavādin's highly abstract and at least for the newcomer evasive way of thinking.] Yet particularly unhappy I am about FRAUWALLNER's rendering of *vidhi* by 'general affirmation'. For, as has been shown by me just now, both these basic 'modes' do not refer to classes of propositions, or statements, if you prefer this expression, but to aspects of, or perspectives of, perceiving (real) objects. The 'scheme' of the twelve *ara*s of Mallavādin is, at least first of all, basically of an ontological character, albeit combined with a logically grounded combinatory system of differentiation (*bhaṅga*). As far as I can see, MUNI JAMBŪVIJAYAJĪ refrains from explaining the two basic expressions himself, but confines himself to referring to the relevant passages in Mallavādin's work itself.[37]

I disagree even more with FRAUWALLNER about the categorisation and origin of the expression *vidhi* and *niyama*: In my view—the evidence on which it is based has been presented in the foregoing—they are not 'terms'; and it does, already for this very reason, not make any sense to say 'that the terminology applied here', viz. as regards *vidhiḥ / utsargaḥ*, 'corresponds to the terminology of grammar'. Grammar is indeed concerned with 'rules' (*vidhi*), 'general rules' (*utsarga*) and 'exceptions' (*apavāda*), but not so Mallavādin, at least not as regards the fundamental structure of the DNC.[38]

FRAUWALLNER is, however, right when he points out ('Introduction', p. 1) that grammar has 'according to Mallavādin been recognised by all systems (*sarva-tantra-siddhâṇtaḥ*[39]), and its views are binding for them all.' Indeed, especially the NĀA abounds in references to or quotations from Pāṇini, Kātyāyana and Patañjali, the *muni-traya* of Vyākaraṇa. Of even greater significance, however, is the relation in which the DNC stands to Bhartṛhari's *Vākyāpadīya*, or more correctly: *Tri-kāṇḍī*[40]. This is clear already from a corresponding passage in MUNI JAMBŪVIJAYAJĪ's *Prāk-kathana* (26.3–7) which reads thus in translation:

> 'The following, however, should be noted: At the beginning [of the exposition of each *naya*] the opponent's position is refuted, thereafter one's own position is established, [and] then that meaning-of-a-word and

[36] I follow Siṁhasūri's explanation of the meaning of *ni-*.

[37] Cf. *Prāk-kathana* p. 18.

[38] Except for cases where he refers to the Mīmāṁsā.

[39] Cf. FRAUWALLNER, 'Introduction', p. 1.

[40] Cf. AKLUJKAR (e.g.) 1993: 11 and 33.

that meaning-of-a-sentence are shown as approved which [correspond] to the [particular] *naya*, among the meanings-of-a-word and meanings-of-a-sentence expounded in the *Vākya-padīya* and similar treatises, and, finally, after showing in which of the [seven] *naya*s [called] *naigama*, etc., [the particular *naya* dealt with in this part (*prakaraṇa*) of his work] is contained and after explaining the meaning of [the terms] *dravya*, etc.[41] it is made clear what the source (literally the 'basis / foundation') of the particular *naya* in the sacred tradition of the Jina is because all *naya*s are grounded in that which was propounded by the Jina. This is the characteristic manner of exposition of the author with regard to all the twelve spokes consisting in the *naya*s called "*vidhi*", etc.'[42]

Quite to the point what the learned editor says, a correct and exact description, albeit by and large an description only. For, one should, of course, wish to know why Mallavādin chose this particular procedure, i.e. w h y he correlates each and every *naya* to theories about the *padârtha* and the *vākyârtha* as covered by *kārikā*s in the *Vākya-padīya*, w h y he determines each of his *naya*'s relation to the seven traditional *naya*s and especially Siddhasena Divākara's dichotomy of *dravyârtha* and *paryāyârtha* and, finally, w h y he quotes passages from the 'scripture'. In some of these cases the answer may in fact be patent, but in others it is certainly not.

The final quotations from the *jina-pravacana*, i.e. the explicit statements of the *nibandhana* of a *naya*, or—as Mallavādin expresses himself at other places[43]—of that passage in canonical texts 'from which the particular *naya* has come forth' (*nirgama-sūtra*, °*visarga-sūtra*), all quite evidently meant to vindicate the contention, i.e. Mallavādin's own conviction, that all the various philosophical positions dealt with by him are indeed found in the *ārṣa*, that is to say, are in fact a constituent element of the all encompassing Jaina doctrine. Nevertheless it is, I think, important to note that Mallavādin is not by any chance concerned here, at the end of each *prakaraṇa*, with tracing back his 'scheme' of *naya* to the Canon, but each individual *naya* in terms of its doctorial contents. And it is, of course, necessary to closely examine these quotations, and the relation in which they

[41] Cf. e.g. DNC p. 114.5 and p. 244.2.

[42] The original reads as follows: *idaṁ punar avadheyam—ādau para-pakṣa-nirasanaṁ tataḥ sva-pakṣa-sthāpanaṁ tato Vākyapadīyâdi-pratipāditeṣu śabdârtha-vākyārtheṣu yasya nayasya yau śabdârtha-vākyārthāv abhimatau tayor upadarśanam ante ca yathā-yogaṁ naigamâdy-anyatame naye 'ntar-bhāvaṁ dravyâdi-śabdârthaṁ ca prādarśya jina-pravacana-nibandhatvāt sarva-nayānāṁ nayasya yad nibandhanaṁ jinâgameṣu tasyôpardarśanam iti dvāsaśasv vidhy-ādi-nayâreṣu grantha-kārasya pratipādana-śailī.*

[43] Cf. e.g. DNC (II) p. 450.1, p. 415.2, and p. 736.4.

allegedly stand to the philosophical position of the *naya*, etc., etc.; but this I have to postpone to another occasion or rather the second part of my paper.

Similarly, it is absolutely clear that Mallavādin wants to closely connect his own 'scheme' of the 12 *naya*s with the older one of the 7 *naya*s and of the 2 modes of the *Saṁmati-tarka-prakaraṇa*; yet, again, the problem of how precisely this 'connection' is conceived of and described by Mallavādin, i.e. his self-perception within the framework of this particular part of the Jaina tradition, deserves our full attention.

The situation is different in the case of the—equally stereotypical—discussion of the corresponding *padârtha* and *vākyârtha*, and in general Mallavādin's relation to the *Vākya-padīya*, the most significant work of the Indian philosophy of language. I must confess that I myself don't think that I have already fully grasped the motive behind, or reason for this part of his procedure. But I am at least able—and with these remarks I come to the end of my paper—to say something about the relation to the *Vākya-padīya* in general.

This work is quite evidently highly respected by Mallavādin and treated as an authority; but at the same time it is equally evident that Mallavādin disagrees with Bhartṛhari as regards a central, in fact vital point of his doctrine, or rather presupposition. According to Bhartṛhari all *pravāda*s, all the various philosophical doctrines—systems, if you like—[44] are based on *artha-vāda*s found in Vedic texts, *Brāhmaṇa*s or *Brāhmaṇa*-like portions, that is to say, ultimately on the (Vedic) *śruti*. For Mallavādin this is, it need hardly be stated, absolutely unacceptable; his own position—and in this regard he is but a pious follower of the Jaina tradition itself—all philosophical doctrines, all the *naya*s expounded and dealt with by him, as also the many more he cannot pay equally attention to,[45] are without exception derived from, nay practically clearly stated in the Jaina canon. It is the *Jina-pravacana* which forms the true *nibandhana* of Indian philosophy, including that of the Veda. The Veda of the Brahmins is in reality but one of the necessarily one-sided *naya*s contained in and comprised by the all-encompassing perspectivistic *śāsana* of the Jina. The Jaina canon is the true Veda.

---

[44] Cf., however, WEZLER (1999).

[45] In reality there are a 'hundred', i.e. many, many subvarieties of each *naya*; see e.g. NĀA p. 115.18.

BIBLIOGRAPHY

AKLUJKAR 1993 = Aklujkar, Ashok: 'An introduction to the study of Bhartṛhari,' *Asiatische Studien* XLVII.1 (1993) 7–36 [= *Proceedings of the First International Conference on Bhartṛhari*, ed. by J. Bhate and J. Bronkhorst, P. Lang, Bern (etc.) 1993].

DNC = Mallavādin Kṣamāśramaṇa: *Dvādaśâra-naya-cakra. Dvādaśāraṁ Nayacakraṁ of Ācārya Śrī Mallavādī Kṣamāśramaṇa. With the commentary Nyāyāgamānusāriṇī of Ācārya Śrī Siṁhasūri Gaṇi Vādi Kṣamāśramaṇa.* Ed. with critical notes by Muni Jambūvijayajī. Pt. I (1–4 Aras): Bhavnagar 1966 [Reprinted: Bhāvnagar 2000]; Pt. II (5–8 Aras): Bhavnagar 1976; Pt. III (9–12 Aras): Bhavnagar 1988.

FRAUWALLNER 1966 = 'Introduction' to the volume of DNC, ed. by Muni Jambūvijayajī.

GHOSH 2000 = Ghosh, Abhijit: *Non-Aryan Linguistic Elements in the Atharvaveda. A Study of some words of Austric Origin.* Sanskrit Pustak Bhandar, Calcutta 2000.

JAINI 1979 = Jaini, Padmanabh S.: *The Jaina Path of Purification.* University of California Press, Berkeley 1979.

KAPADIA = Kāpadīā, H.R.: *Anekāntajayapatākā by Haribhadra Sūri with his own commentary and Municandra Sūri's supercommentary.* Vol. 1 & 2, Ed., *Gaekwad's Oriental Series* 88 & 105, Oriental Institute, Baroda 1940 & 1947.

Pāṇini = Pāṇini: *Aṣṭādhyāyī.*

POTTER 1970 = Potter, Karl H.: *Encyclopedia of Indian Philosophies.*—Vol. I: *Bibliography.* Compiled by .... Third Revised Edition. Princeton University Press, Princeton–New Jersey 1970. [= Indian edition: Motilal Banarsidass, Delhi 1970].

STP = Siddhasena Divākara: *Saṁmati-tarka-prakaraṇa* with Abhayadevasūri's *Tattva-bodha-vidhāyinī.* Ed. by Sukhlāl Saṅghavi and Becardās Dośi; Vol. I & II, RBTS VI–1,2; Kyoto 1984. [Reprinted from the original edition published in 5 vols., *Gujarāt-purā-tattva-mandir-granthāvalī* 10, 16, 18, 19, 21, Gujarāt-purā-tattva-mandir, Amdāvād, 1924–1931].

WEZLER 1981 = Wezler, Albrecht: 'Studien zum Dvādaśāranayacakra des Śvetāmbara Mallavādin. I. Der *sarvasarvātmakatvavāda.*' In: K. Bruhn und A. Wezler (eds.), *Studien zum Jainismus und Buddhismus, Gedenkschrift für Ludwig Alsdorf. Alt- und Neu-Indische Studien* 23, Franz Steiner Verlag, Wiesbaden 1981: 359–408.

WEZLER 1999 = Wezler, Albrecht: 'On the origin(s) of the *guṇa*-theory. Struggling for a new approach (I): Wrestling with Frauwallner,' *Asiatische Studien* LIII.3 (1999) 537–551.

Kundakunda and Umāsvāti on *Anekânta-vāda*

JAYANDRA SONI

The two revered thinkers Kundakunda and Umāsvāti in Jainism are unique figures in the sense that both have laid the foundation for most of the issues that have emerged gradually in the history of Jaina philosophy. There is no doubt that in several cases the source of their ideas are taken from the canonical literature, e.g., the emphasis on *ahiṁsā* and the view of different standpoints from which an object of inquiry may be undertaken. However, it is well-known that Mahāvīra's philosophical ideas in the canonical literature are scattered all over and one needs to read a vast amount of material to extract the essence of his teaching. Moreover, one needs a fine sieve to filter out the crucially significant philosophical issues from among long and repeated descriptions of rules for ascetics and the Jaina religious code of conduct in general. These two thinkers have done this for us, each in his own way, whilst at the same time indirectly telling us how they understand Mahāvīra's teaching.

One of the significant differences between the two is that Kundakunda wrote in Prakrit and Umāsvāti in Sanskrit. This is significant for two reasons: on the one hand, Kundakunda has clearly shown how the Prakrit language can also be used for philosophical ideas (and not only for beautiful Prakrit poetry) and Umāsvāti, on the other hand, was the first Jaina thinker to have written a philosophical work in the *sūtra* style. It is unfortunate that we hardly have any biographical information about these two giants in Jainism and hence we do not know when exactly they lived.

If, however, recent research is correct then Kundakunda lived in the second or third century CE and this would make him the first significant and independent thinker of the post-canonical period whose views are accepted as representing the essence of Jaina thought.[1] Moreover, it is generally believed that he was a

[1] See A.N. UPADHYE (1935: 5), who first published his views in 1935. His dating of Kundakunda was, however, not left uncontested, especially by contemporary Śvetāmbara scholars and there ensued a great deal of debate regarding this early date. See DHAKY (1991: 193) where he also suggests that Kundakunda's date 'can only be the latter half of the 8th cent. CE.' See also JOHNSON (1995: 95): 'early fifth century or later,' and its review by DUNDAS (1997: especially 507 f.).

Essays in Jaina Philosophy and Religion.
Warsaw Indological Studies, Volume 2 (2002), pp. 25–35.

pioneering Digambara thinker who probably lived in the South, with appreciation for his views also coming from the Śvetāmbaras. It seems certain that he was also known as Padmanandin. A.N. UPADHYE has shown that possibly apart from the name Elācārya, all the other names ascribed to Kundakunda or Padmanandin (Vakragrīva, Gṛdhrapiccha or Mahāmati) go against the tradition of the early epigraphic records.[2] The name Gṛdhrapiccha erroneously used for him since about the fourteenth century has led to confusion because this name is also an alias for Umāsvāti.

Umāsvāti, on the other hand, is said to have lived in the North. His dates vary from the second to the fifth centuries CE with recent preference for the fourth or fifth centuries. Also in his case biographical details are scanty and both the sects of Jainism claim him as one of their own (with the Digambaras also calling him Umāsvāmin), and both regard his work, in traditional Indian manner, as an authority on Jaina thought. His name too is indelible in history of Jaina philosophy, especially for the pioneering work of the now famous *Tattvârtha-sūtra* (TS). If there is anything anyone knows about Jaina philosophy then it is certainly from this work. The problem concerning the first commentary on TS seems to be irreconcilable, namely whether Umāsvāti wrote an auto-commentary, the *Svopajña-bhāṣa*, as the Śvetāmbaras say, or whether Pūjyapāda's *Sarvârtha-siddhi* ('Attainment of the Meaning of Everything') is the first commentary, as the Digambaras say, written in the fifth or sixth century. In any case both commentaries are available and the comment by Suzuko OHIRA (1982: 42) is relevant here: 'The prime contribution of the *Sarvârtha-siddhi* is that it revised and improved the *Bhāṣya* by way of clearly elucidating its general contents in the current language and concept of the time.'

There are at least three crucial areas in Jaina thought for which a comparison of the views of Kundakunda and Umāsvāti may be fruitfully undertaken: *anekânta-vāda*, *pramāṇa* and *upayoga*. To this may also be added an observation about the number and exact sequence of the basic Jaina categories (*tattva* / *padârtha*).[3] In this paper I am concerned with only the first in which the terms *naya* and *syāt* play key roles. In other words what I am attempting here is to collect together the most significant references to *naya* and/or *syāt* that can be found in the important works of these two thinkers and to compare the ways in which they use (or do not use) them.

---

[2] See UPADHYE (1935: 5) where he draws his conclusions after discussing the various names.

[3] I have hinted at this in the conclusion below. A slightly more detailed account, using the same biographical information given above, can be found in SONI (2001).

1. Kundakunda on *anekânta-vāda*

Three works by Kundakunda are especially praised as philosophical masterpieces: *Pañcâstikāya-samaya-sāra* (PSSā), *Pravacana-sāra* (PSā), and *Samaya-sāra* (SSā). These works are all in Prakrit and they contain not only one of the earliest interpretations of *syād-vāda* but also give one a good impression of how the Prakrit language was used to express philosophical ideas. For his ideas related to *anekânta-vāda* reference will be made only to Kundakunda's PSā and PSSā.

In PSā 2.22–23 Kundakunda says:[4]

davvaṭṭhieṇa savvaṁ davvaṁ taṁ pajjayaṭṭhieṇa puṇo /
havadi ya aṇṇam aṇaṇṇaṁ takkāle tammuyattādo // 22 //

[*dravyârthikena sarvaṁ dravyaṁ tat paryāyārthikena punaḥ /*
bhavati cânyad anyat tat-kāle tan-mayatvāt // — p. 144]

'All substances are non-different from the substantial view-point, but again they are different from the modificational view-point, because of the individual modification pervading it for the time being' [p. 394].

atthi tti ya ṇatthi ya havadi avattavvam idi puṇo davvaṁ /
pajjāyeṇa du keṇa vi tad ubhayam ādiṭṭham aṇṇaṁ vā // 23 //

[*astîti ca nâstîti ca bhavaty avaktavyam iti punar dravyam /*
paryāyeṇa tu kenâpi tad ubhayam ādiṣṭam anyad vā // — p. 146]

'According to some modification or the other it is stated that a substance exists, does not exist, is indescribable, is both or otherwise' [p. 394].

The last point is repeated in Kundakunda's PSSā 14:

siya atthi ṇatthi uhayaṁ avvattavvaṁ puṇo ya tattidayaṁ/
davvaṁ khu sattabhaṁgaṁ ādesa-vaseṇa saṁbhavadi //14 //

[*syād asti nâsty ubhayam avaktavyaṁ punaś ca tat-tritayam /*
dravyaṁ khalu sapta-bhaṅgam ādeśavaśena saṁbhavati // — p. 9]

'According as *Dravya* is viewed from different aspects of reasoning it may be described in the following propositions: 1) Perhaps it is; 2) Perhaps it is not; 3) Perhaps it is both (is and is not); 4) Perhaps it is

[4] For both texts I am supplying the Prakrit text, with the Sanskrit translation (in brackets) from the commentary by Amṛtacandra (tenth century), with UPADHYE's English translation.

indefinable; 5) Perhaps it is and is indefinable; and 6) Perhaps it is not and is indefinable; and 7) Perhaps it is and is not and is indefinable' [p. 9].

Although Kundakunda does not use the word *anekânta-vāda*, two points are noteworthy here: the word *naya* is used with reference to an object depending on the standpoint which emphasises it as a substance (*dravya*) or a mode (*paryāya*). Secondly, Kundakunda explicitly mentions the sevenfold predication (*sapta-bhaṅgī*) in PSSā 14, and again in PSSā 72 where it is stated that the soul (*jīva*) 'is capable of admitting the sevenfold predication' (p. 61), namely that the soul is capable of grasping the nature of an object in all its aspects at once. On the basis of what Kundakunda says above, it cannot be decided whether *naya* or *syāt* has priority. Hence, it seems they would have to be taken together, as the one being implicit in the other.

2. Umāsvāti on *anekânta-vāda*

It is noteworthy that although the word *syāt* appears in the canonical literature, and Kundakunda uses it too, it does not feature in the first Sanskrit work presenting Jaina philosophy in the traditional *sūtra* style, namely, in TS. Commentators to TS regard *syād-vāda* as being 'implied'[5] in TS 5.32 (or 5.31 in the Śvetāmbara version): *arpitânarpita-siddheḥ*—'[The contradictory characteristics are established] from different points of view'[6] (*vide infra*, p. 29). In TS 1.33 (or 1.34 in the Śvetāmbara version) Umāsvāti mentions only the standpoints (*naya*s), and they are not statements or assertions that may be made about an object of investigation, each of which is qualified by the word *syāt*. They are the standpoints which reflect the common or non-distinguished (*naigama*), general or collective (*saṅgraha*), practical (*vyavahāra*), etc., positions from which an object may be ascertained. The word *naya* in the canonical literature also refers to two other contexts, with reference to *vyavahāra-naya* and/or *niścaya-naya*,[7] or to the two standpoints with reference to *dravya* and *paryāya* mentioned above. In other words, when dealing with the word *naya*, one has to distinguish three contexts in which it is used: (1) with reference to *dravya* and *paryāya*; (2) with reference to *vyavahāra-naya* and/or *niścaya-naya* (the

[5] A.N. UPADHYE (1935: 83).

[6] TATIA's (1994: 136) translation: 'The ungrasped [unnoticed] aspect of an object is attested by the grasped [noticed] one.'

[7] See BHATT (1974).

latter being synonyms of the *śuddha* or *paramârthika-naya*); and (3) with reference to *naya* in the context of *naigama, saṅgraha*, etc.

In order to better understand the difference between Kundakunda and Umāsvāti on *anekânta-vāda* we have also to take recourse to the commentaries on TS, because the *sūtra* alone is too brief for any comparison.

3. *Anekânta-vāda* in two Commentaries on TS

Pūjyapāda, also called Devanandin, is generally believed to have belonged to the fifth or sixth century and to have been a renowned grammarian.[8] His philosophically celebrated work is the *Sarvârtha-siddhi* which is—for the Digambaras—the first commentary on TS. The following are references to the problem under discussion, taken from S.A. Jain's translation of the work.[9] S.A. JAIN (1960: 157–158) translates Pūjyapāda's commentary to TS 5.32(31) *arpitânarpita-siddheḥ*—'[The contradictory characteristics are established] from different points of view'—in the following way[10]:

> 'Substances are characterised by an infinite number of attributes [*anekântâtmakasya vastunaḥ*]. For the sake of use or need, prominence is given to certain characteristics of a substance from one point of view. And prominence is not given to other characteristics, as these are of no use or need at the time. Thus even the existing attributes are not expressed, as these are of secondary importance (*anarpita*). There is no contradiction in what is established by these two points of view. For instance, there is no contradiction in the same person Devadatta being a father, a son, a nephew and so on. For the points of view are different. From the point of view of his son he is a father, and from the point of view of his father he is a son. Similarly with regard to his

[8] He wrote the *Jainendra-vyākaraṇa* (JV). On p. 32 Nāthūrāmjī Premī comes to the conclusion that 'Samantabhadra and Devanandi belong to the sixth century and were contemporaries.'

[9] For the Sanskrit text see the reference given under SSi. In some cases I am supplying the Sanskrit words in square brackets from the Sanskrit original. All references to Pūjyapāda are from S.A. JAIN's translation of TS which he supplies.

[10] Here the key word to be noticed is *anekânta*—it has already been stated that *syād-vāda* is regarded as being implicit in this *sūtra*, since Umāsvāti does not mention it anywhere in TS.

other designations. In the same manner, substance is permanent from the point of view of general properties. From the point of its specific modes it is not permanent. Hence there is no contradiction. These two, the general and the particular, somehow, are different as well as identical [*kathaṁcid bhedâbhedābhyām*]. Thus these form the cause of worldly intercourse…'

Although Pūjyapāda uses the word *anekânta* here in the commentary, the sevenfold statements with the word *syāt* are not given as we find them in Kundakunda. Even though it is important that the word is explicitly used, it is puzzling that he does not make any reference to the use of *syāt*. Pūjyapāda belongs to the Digambara tradition and certainly lived after Kundakunda whom all Digambaras revere profoundly. If indeed this *sūtra* of TS really 'implies' *syād-vāda*, one would have expected Pūjyapāda to have clinched the opportunity to mention the *sapta-bhaṅgī*, easily taking it over from Kundakunda (as he does so in the case of *dravyârthika-naya* and *paryāyârthika-naya*, see n. 11).

With regard to the word *naya*, Pūjyapāda explains it in his commentary on TS in two places (TS 1.6 and in TS 1.33/34). TS 1.6 (p. 9) says: *pramāṇa-nayair adhigamaḥ*—'Knowledge [of the seven categories] is attained by means of *pramāṇa* and *naya*.' A part of his commentary to this *sūtra* reads in the translation of S.A. Jain (1960: 10):

> '…it has been said that "*pramāṇa* is a comprehensive view, whereas *naya* is a partial view." *Naya* is of two kinds, *dravyārthika* and *paryāyārthika*. The former refers to the general attributes of a substance, and the latter to the constantly changing conditions or modes of a substance. *Bhāva nikṣepa* must be ascertained by the standpoint of modes, and the other three by the standpoint of substance.[11] For the latter refers to general characteristics. That which has the substance as its object is the standpoint of substance. That which has the mode as its object is the standpoint of modes. Both the substance and the mode are ascertained by *pramāṇa* (comprehensive knowledge).'

---

[11] This refers to the previous *sūtra*, TS 1.5: *nāma-sthāpanā-dravya-bhāvatas tan-nyāsaḥ*—'These [categories, *jīva*, etc., given in TS 1.4] are installed (in four ways) by name, representation, substance (potentiality) and actual state.' *Nyāsa* is a synonym for *nikṣepa*, which is a typical Jaina way of presenting a topic of discussion. *Bhāva* is a synonym for *paryāya* which refers to the object as it is at a particular moment, i.e. the mode or modification (*paryāya*) taken on by a particular substance (*dravya*).

The other place where Pūjyapāda has to comment on *naya* is at TS 1.33. In the Digambara version this closes the first chapter of TS, whereas it represents TS 1.34 of the Śvetāmbara version, with the difference that the Śvetāmbara version has only the first five *naya*s, omitting *samabhirūḍha-naya* and *evaṁ-bhūta-naya*. The Śvetāmbara version closes the chapter with *sūtra* 35, which, for the full understanding of *naya*s according to the Śvetāmbaras, has to be read together with 1.34 which merely enumerates the five *naya*s.[12] In the Digambara version Umāsvāti enumerates the seven *naya*s in TS 1.33: *naigama, saṅgraha, vyavahāra, ṛju-sūtra, śabda, samabhirūḍha, evaṁ-bhūta*, namely, the standpoints which are generally discussed in Jainism.

Referring to TS 1.33, where the seven *naya*s are enumerated, Pūjyapāda says, see JAIN (1960: 41 f.):

> 'The general and specific definitions (*sāmānya-viśeṣa-lakṣaṇam*) of these [seven *naya*s] must be given. First the general definition. Objects possess many (*anekânta*) characteristics. *Naya* is the device which is capable of determining truly one of the several characteristics of an object (without contradiction) from a particular point of view. It is of two kinds, namely statements which refer to general attributes of a substance and those which refer to the constantly changing conditions or modes of a substance. *Dravya* means general or common, a general rule or conformity. That which has these for its object is the general standpoint (*dravyārthika naya*). *Paryāya* means particular, an exception or exclusion. That which has these for its object is the standpoint of modifications (*paryāyārthika naya*).
>
> Their specific definitions are given now. The figurative standpoint (*naigama naya*) takes into account the purpose or intention of something which is not accomplished. …'

The commentary then goes on to explain each of the *naya*s, and thereby ends the chapter. From this it seems that Pūjyapāda is the only one who uses the word *anekânta* with a clear hint of the sense in which the term came to be applied as a synonym for the Jaina approach with its epistemological significance. The word *naya* is used both with reference to *dravya* and *paryāya* and with reference to the seven beginning with *naigama, saṅgraha*, etc.

As already stated, the Śvetāmbaras believe that Umāsvāti himself wrote a commentary to his TS and it is now necessary to see what, if any, reference to

[12] For the different traditions of the types of *naya*s see Pt. SUKHLALJI (1974: 56).

anekânta there is in Umāsvāti's commentary to the *sūtra*s which Pūjyapāda commented on above.[13]

TS 5.32 (*arpitânarpita-siddheḥ*) corresponds to TS 5.31 of the Śvetāmbara version, for which SUKHLALJI (1974: 211, 212) gives two interpretative translations: 'Each thing is possessed of a number of properties; for as viewed from the standpoint adopted and as viewed from another standpoint it proves to be something self-contradictory' and 'Each thing is liable to be a subject matter of usage in various ways; for usage is accounted for on the basis of *arpaṇā* and *anarpaṇā*—that is, on the basis of a consideration of chief or subordinate status depending on the desire of the speaker concerned.' The context here is existence (*sat*) which has already been defined as being characterised by origination, destruction (or disappearance) and permanence (TS 5.30(29): *utpāda-vyaya-dhrauva-yuktaṁ sat*). In his commentary Umāsvāti begins by saying that there are three kinds of existence, namely, as characterised in the *sūtra*, all of which are eternal in so far as they occur continually. Each of these may be established through *arpita* or *anarpita*, which he equates with the practical (*vyavahārika*) and the non-practical (*avyavahārika*). The commentary continues with an explanation of what existence means on the basis of this classification, in which he mentions, for example, *dravyâstika, utpannâstika* and *paryāyâstika*, viz. existence as a substance, as origination (i.e. as a particular object), and as a modification. Although Umāsvāti neither uses the word *naya* nor *anekânta* here, it is clear that the idea is intended, namely, that the nature of an object or existence as such can be ascertained depending on the standpoint from which one approaches the subject, i.e. on the basis of what is given a primary or secondary significance.

Umāsvāti's commentary on TS 1.6 is relatively short, in which *pramāṇa* is said to be of two kinds, indirect (*parokṣa*) and direct (*pratyakṣa*) and that the *naya*s (seven for the Digambaras and five for the Śvetāmbaras), such as *naigama*, etc., will be discussed later, i.e. in TS 1.33 (34 in the Śvetāmbara version, see above).[14] There is

[13] I am consulting the following two editions of TS from the same publisher: *Sabhāṣya-tattvârthâdhigama-sūtram* Rāyacandra Jaina Śāstramālā, published in śrīvīra-nirvāṇa-saṁvat 2432 (CE), and the one published in śrīvīra-nirvāṇa-saṁvat 2458 (CE 1932).

[14] It is interesting to note that Pūjyapāda says the following about *pramāṇa* at TS 1.6 (tr. JAIN (1960: 10)): '*Pramāṇa* is of two kinds, namely for oneself (*svârtha*) and for others (*parârtha*). All kinds of knowledge except scriptural constitute *pramāṇa* for oneself. But scriptural knowledge is of two kinds, namely for oneself and for others.' Moreover, Umāsvāti does not mention *dravyârthika-naya* and *paryāyârthika-naya*, as Pūjyapāda does.

nothing else significant for the context under discussion here. In Umāsvāti's commentary to the *sūtra* mentioned above the word *anekânta* does not appear, although it seems easy to read this into it. Hence, although neither Kundakunda nor Umāsvāti uses the word *anekânta* explicitly, it is evident that the theory is implicit in their ideas.

4. Differences between Kundakunda and Umāsvāti

The significant difference between these two thinkers lies in detail: (1) Kundakunda explicitly uses the word *syāt* in the context of the five statements given in PSā 2.23 and seven in PSSā 14 above (p. 27 f.) that can be made about an entity, and Umāsvāti on the other hand, does not use the word *syāt*; (2) the word *naya* is used in different contexts by them: Kundakunda uses *naya* with reference only to *dravya* and *paryāya* in the stanzas considered above (and these are also used by Pūjyapāda in his *Sarvârtha-siddhi* on TS 1.6), whereas Umāsvāti uses it in the context of the well-known *naya*s (*naigama*, etc., either 7 or 5). In the context of *pramāṇa* in TS 1.6 there is no reference to *dravya* nor *paryāya* in Umāsvāti's commentary, although it is found in Pūjyapāda's *Sarvârtha-siddhi*.

As for the word *anekânta* itself, in the sense in which it can be associated with the theory of manifoldness unique to the Jainas, it seems that Pūjyapāda was the first person to explicitly use it. By the eighth century, however, the theory was undoubtedly already established in this sense, as is evident in Akalaṅka's works.

In conclusion it is noteworthy to mention one more point of difference between Kundakunda and Umāsvāti, not directly related to *anekânta-vāda*, but significant because it concerns the enumeration of the basic categories in Jainism:[15] in his PSSā 108 (and SSā 1.13) Kundakunda explicitly mentions *puṇya* and *pāpa* as the third and fourth *padârtha*s (*jīvâjīva-puṇya-pāpâsrava-saṁvara-nirjarā-bandha-mokṣāḥ*). Umāsvāti enumerates not only seven of these, omitting *puṇya* and *pāpa*, but the sequence is slightly different in TS 1.4 (*jīvâjīvâsrava-bandha-saṁvara-nirjarā-mokṣāḥ*): in the TS *bandha* is number four (after *āsrava*) and in PSSā 108 it is number eight (before the last, *mokṣa*). Here Umāsvāti's enumeration seems more logical if one takes into account the role of *karman* as soon as *jīva* becomes associated with *ajīva*. The association is responsible for an inflow of matter which then binds the soul (the *karman* can be stopped and gradually completely obliterated). On the other hand, without explicitly mentioning *puṇya* and *pāpa* in the *sūtra* itself Umāsvāti leaves little room for the ethical role of these categories in the

[15] See footnote 3 above.

context of the ascetic discipline. Perhaps Umāsvāti does not mention *karman* explicitly in the *sūtra*, because it may be regarded as being implicit in *āsrava*. But then these would be implicit also in Kundakunda's *gāthā*, who also does not mention *karman* explicitly, but instead *puṇya* and *pāpa*. Furthermore, Kundakunda mentions *bandha* and *mokṣa* together at the end, one after the other in that sequence, perhaps in order to highlight the soul's liberation from the bondage of *karman*, i.e. to emphasise that without *bandha* there cannot be *mokṣa*.

BIBLIOGRAPHY

BHATT 1974 = Bhatt, Bansidhar: 'Vyavahāra-naya and Niścaya-naya in Kundakunda's Works.' In: Wolfgang Voigt (ed.): *XVIII. Deutscher Orientalistentag vom 1. bis 5. Oktober 1972 in Lübeck, Vorträge. Zeitschrift der Deutschen Morgenländischen Gesellschaft, Supplement II*, Franz Steiner Verlag, Wiesbaden 1974: 279–91.

DUNDAS 1997 = Dundas, Paul: 'The Laicisation of the Bondless Doctrine: A New Study of the Development of Jainism.' In: *Journal of Indian Philosophy* 25 (1997) 495–516. [This is a review of JOHNSON (1995)].

DHAKY 1991 = Dhaky, M. A.: 'The Date of Kundakundācārya.' In: M.A. Dhaky and Sagarmal Jain (eds.): *Aspects of Jainology Vol. III: Pt Dalsukhbhai Malvania Felicitation Volume I*. P.V. Research Institute, Varanasi 1991: 187–206.

JAIN 1960 = Jain, S.A. (tr.): *Reality: English Translation of Pūjyapāda's Sarvārthasiddhi*. Vira Sasana Sangha, Calcutta 1960. [Reprinted: Jwalamalini Trust, Madras 1992].

JOHNSON 1995 = Johnson, W. J.: *Harmless Souls. Karmic Bondage and Religious Change in Early Jainism with Special Reference to Umāsvāti and Kundakunda*. Motilal Banarsidass, Delhi 1995.

JV = Pūjyapāda Devanandin: *Jainendra-vyākaraṇa*, ed. Śambhunātha Tripāṭhī and Mahādeva Caturvedī, Bhāratīya Jñānapīṭha, Kāśī 1956.

PSā = Kundakunda: *Pavayaṇa-sāra* [*Pravacana-sāra*]. A.N. Upadhye (ed.): *Śrī Kundakundācārya's Pravacanasāra (Pavayaṇasāra), a Pro-Canonical Text of the Jainas, the Prakṛit Text critically edited with the Sanskrit Commentaries of Amṛtacandra and Jayasena*. Parama-Śruta-Prabhāvaka Mandal, Shrimad Rajachandra Ashrama, Agās–Gujarat 1984. [First edition: Bombay 1935].

PSSā = Kundakunda: *Pañcâstikāya-samaya-sāra*. A. Chakravartinayanar and A.N. Upadhye (eds.): *Pañcāstikāyasāra. The Building of the Cosmos*. Prakrit text, Sanskrit *chāyā*, English commentary etc. Bharatiya Jnanpith Publication, Delhi 1975.

SSā = Kundakunda: *Samaya-sāra. Āchārya Kundakunda's Samayasāra*, with English translation and commentary based upon Amṛtacandra's *Ātmakhyāti* by A. Chakravarti, Bharatiya Jnanpith, New Delhi 1989.

Ohira 1982 = Ohira, Suzuko: *A Study of the Tattvārthasūtra with Bhāṣya with Special Reference to Authorship and Date*. L.D. Series 86, L.D. Institute of Indology, Ahmedabad 1982.

SSi = Pūjyapāda: *Sarvârtha-siddhi*. 5th ed., Bhāratīya Jñānapīṭha Prakāśana, Delhi 1991.

SONI 2001 = Soni, Jayandra: 'A Note on the Jaina *tattva / padārtha*' in *Vasantagauravam. Essays In Jainism Felicitating Professor M. D. Vasantha Raj of Mysore on the Occasion of his Seventy-fifth Birthday*, ed. Jayandra Soni. Vakils, Feffer and Simons Ltd., Mumbai 2001.

SUKHLALJI 1974 = Sukhlalji, Pandit: *Commentary on Tattvārtha Sūtra of Vācaka Umāsvāti*. L.D. Series 44, L.D. Institute of Indology, Ahmedabad 1974.

TS = Umāsvāti: *Tattvârtha-sūtra. Sabhāṣya-tattvârthādhigama-sūtram*. Rāyacandra Jaina Śāstramālā, published in (1) Śrīvīra-nirvāṇa-saṁvat 2432 (CE 1906), and (2) Śrīvīra-nirvāṇa-saṁvat 2458 (CE 1932).

TATIA 1994 = Tatia, Nathmal (tr.): *Tattvārtha Sūtra: That Which Is. Umāsvāti / Umāsvāmī; with the combined commentaries of Umāsvāti / Umāsvāmī, Pūjyapāda and Siddhasensgaṇi*. The Sacred Literature Series, Harper Collins Publishers, San Francisco—London—Pymble 1994.

UPADHYE 1935 A.N. Upadhye: 'Introduction,' See: PSā.

Some Remarks on the *Naya* Method*

PIOTR BALCEROWICZ

The most significant and intriguing Jaina contribution to Indian philosophical heritage is beyond doubt the theory of the multiplexity of reality (*anekânta-vāda*), that trifurcates into the method of the four standpoints (*nikṣepa-vāda*, *nyāsa-vāda*), the method of the seven-fold modal description (*sapta-bhaṅgī*[1], *syād-vāda*) and the doctrine of viewpoints (*naya-vāda*), or the (usually) sevenfold method of conditionally valid predications. At the same time no other Jaina concept bred so much controversy as the idea that one and the same sentence can be either true or false, which seems implied by the admission of the multiplexity.

In the present paper, instead of dealing with the historical development of the concept of the *naya*s,[2] I wish to clarify the ramifications that were instrumental in moulding the concept and to analyse internal dependencies within the framework of the seven viewpoints (*naya*), and, finally, to briefly propose a certain interpretative basis for the *naya-vāda*. A closer look at a sample textual material is imperative, in

---

* The main ideas found in this paper appeared for the first time in a succinct form in Polish in BALCEROWICZ (1994).

[1] The term *sapta-bhaṅgī* (lit. 'seven-angled', 'seven-twister') usually refers to *syād-vāda*, cf. e.g. SVM 24.2–3 (p. 148.2–3): *anekântâtmakatvaṁ ca sapta-bhaṅgī-prarūpaṇena sukhôpanneyaṁ syād iti sâpi nirūpitā*. However, it may occasionally in mediaeval period also refer to *naya-vāda* itself, etc. Thus we can eventually speak of *pramāṇa-sapta-bhaṅgī* (which is *syād-vāda*), *naya-sapta-bhaṅgī* (which is *naya-vāda*) and *duraya-sapta-bhaṅgī*; comp. e.g. SBhT, p. 16.1: *iyaṁ ca sapta-bhaṅgī dvividhā: pramāṇa-sapta-bhaṅgī naya-sapta-bhaṅgī cêti*, and ṆC 254ab (p. 128): *sattêva huṁti bhaṅgā pamāṇa-ṇaya-duṇaya-bheda-juttāvi* / —'There are as many as seven conditional perspectives with divisions with respect to cognitive criteria, viewpoints and defective viewpoints.'

[2] The term is well-attested not only in Jaina *Āgama*s, but is also well known—in its not strictly technical meaning—from Pāli commentaries as 'a method of interpretation' (e.g. *aparo nayo*, *evam-ādinā nayena*, *ti-ādinā nayena*) and other Buddhist sources (e.g. AN 2.193: *naya-hetu*). Interestingly enough, in Buddhist sources we also come across its opposite *durnaya*, 'the improper application of exposition' or 'misinterpretation' (e.g. AN 3.178 or *Jātaka* 4.241: *dunnaya*).

Essays in Jaina Philosophy and Religion.
Warsaw Indological Studies, Volume 2 (2002), pp. 37–68.

so far as it should help the reader assess whether my understanding based on these passages is correct. Otherwise, to indiscriminately speak of the general concept of the Jaina doctrine of viewpoints would, in its hollowness, resemble investigation of a crow's teeth (*kāka-danta-parīkṣā*).

The textual point of reference will be provided by Umāsvāti's[3] *Tattvârthâdhigama-bhāṣya*, Siddhasena Divākara's[4] *Saṁmati-tarka-prakaraṇa*, Akalaṅka's works (*Rāja-vārttika* and *Laghīyas-traya*), Siddharṣigaṇi's *Nyāyâvatāra-vivṛti* and Malliṣeṇa's *Syād-vāda-mañjarī*; only occasionally I shall take recourse to some other Jaina works; and the focus will be more textual-philological, rather than formal-logical.

An ontological assumption underlying the theory of the multiplexity of reality (*anekânta-vāda*) in general, and the doctrine of viewpoints (*naya-vāda*) in particular, consists in the belief which is supposed to defy all simplistic concepts ranging from monism and eternalism (*advaita*) to pluralism and momentariness (*kṣaṇika-vāda*). In other words, the world forms a multifaceted structure, every part of which enters into specific relations and inter-dependencies with other parts of the whole. Its make-up is complex enough to allow for a vast range of statements that can be asserted from various standpoints. The ontological framework is provided by the concept of substance (*dravya*), which is characterised simultaneously by origination (*utpāda*, *udaya*), continued existence (*sthiti*, *dhrauvya*) and annihilation (*bhaṅga*, *vyaya*, *apavarga*), insofar as it is endowed with qualities (*guṇa*) and transient modes (*paryāya*) as well as with directly experienced, though verbally inexpressible momentary occurrences (*vivarta*, *vartanā*). Any truth-conducive analysis, which is supposed to map the ontological structure onto epistemological-conceptual framework, should therefore take into account the individual ontological context and accompanying circumstances of any phenomenon or entity under examination. The maxim provides that truth should only be complete truth, whereas incomplete truth would be but a misnomer for utter falsehood. However, limitations of practical dealings and verbal communication by necessity abstract any given thing or facet of reality from all its temporal, spatial, causal and other relations, and emphasise but one aspect, relevant in a given moment.

---

[3] Since there is some controversy as to whether TBh is the auto-commentary of the author of the *Tattvârtha-sūtra*, I tentatively— not to predetermine the issue—take TS as a work by Umāsvāmin and TBh as a commentary by Umāsvāti.

[4] Not to be confused with the author of the *Nyāyâvatāra*, Siddhasena Mahāmati, who flourished after Dharmakīrti, see: BALCEROWICZ (2000), BALCEROWICZ (2001a: xxxiv–xxxvii), BALCEROWICZ (2001c) and BALCEROWICZ (forthcoming).

Due to this infinite manifoldness of inter-dependencies, including various temporal and spatial perspectives as well as either universal or particular reference, a vast range of properties, each of them being equally justified, could be predicated of a given entity with equal right. And that might even lead eventually to seeming contradictions. The Jainas maintain that such contradictions that ensue from unconditional assertions standing in opposition to one another can easily be resolved when individual points of reference for each and every assertion are taken into consideration.[5] Given such ontological presuppositions, the description on the epistemological level becomes equally complex: each of such dichotomic categories as big–small, good–bad, existent–nonexistent, true–false, etc., that are mutually related, when dissociated from its opposite, is false. In other words, each thesis automatically entails its antithesis, but the model is not dialectical, in so far as the synthesis remains integrated with the very same scheme and thus contingent upon its corollaries. To correlate such individual, partial standpoints is the task of the *syād-vāda* method, which systematises possible arrangements of seemingly contradictory statements. This is evident from such Malliṣeṇa's statements as 'the method of modal description … consists in all viewpoints'[6].

Interestingly enough, it is the *naya* model which the Jainas used to interpret and incorporate various philosophical theories or worldviews into a consistent holistic framework, instead of the doctrine of the seven-fold modal description (*sapta-bhaṅgī*, *syād-vāda*). Numerous Jaina authors such as Akalaṅka, Siddhasena Divākara in STP, Siddhasena Mahāmati in his NAV 29, Malliṣeṇa in SVM 28 correlate particular theories and views represented by particular thinkers and philosophical schools o n l y under the *naya* scheme.

On the other hand, 'the doctrine of the seven-fold modal description' (*sapta-bhaṅgī*) is primarily discussed in three contexts: that of the triple nature of reality, which is believed to consist of 'origination, continuation and decay', that of the relation between the universal and the particular (e.g. RVār 4.42, p. 258–259), and that of the relationship between the substance and its properties / modes. Essentially, all the examples of the application of 'the doctrine of the seven-fold modal

---

[5] TBh 1.35: *yathā vā pratyakṣânumānôpamānâpta-vacanaiḥ pramāṇair eko 'rthaḥ pramīyate sva-viṣaya-niyamān na ca tā vipratipattayo bhavanti tadvan naya-vādā iti.*— 'Or else, just the way one object is cognised by [various] cognitive criteria—such as perception, inference, analogy and testimony [imparted] by an authoritative person—and they become no contradictories (*sc.* they are not at variance with each other), because [each of them is] circumscribed to its own province, similar to them are expositions [by means] of [every conditionally valid] viewpoint.'

[6] SVM 19.76, p. 128.24: *sarva-nayâtmakena syād-vādena…*

description' pertain to one and the same problem: how to relate the whole and its parts, the problem entailed by the question of the relation between permanence and change. This finds corroboration in Hemacandra's *Anya-yoga-vyavaccheda-dvātriṁśikā* 25 and in Malliṣeṇa's *Syād-vāda-mañjarī* (SVM 25.31–36, pp. 152.34–153.4).

Occasionally, to illustrate the principle how such conditionally valid viewpoints (*naya*) apply to the real world and how differences between descriptions of one and the same phenomenon by means of different predications are possible, the Jainas resort to the simile, well-known in India, the elephant and the blind men, well known from *Udāna* 4.4 (pp. 66–69).[7] When such partial views are taken unconditionally (e.g. *sad eva*[8]), they are instances of a defective viewpoint (*durnaya*) and instantiation of 'the maxim of the blind people and the elephant' (*andha-gaja-nyāya*), known also as 'the maxim of people who are blind from birth and the elephant' (*jāty-andha-hasti-nyāya*). Also the maxim as an illustration of philosophical-religious views accepted unconditionally is, as a rule, used in the context of (*dur*)-*naya-vāda*, not *syād-vāda*. It occurs twice in Malliṣeṇa's *Syād-vāda-mañjarī* (14.103–104 and 19.75–77), and in both cases in the same context of *durnaya*. The first instance is rather obvious: '...Simply by force of extreme disorientation produced by a d e f e c t i v e v i e w p o i n t, foolish people deny one [aspect] and establish the other one. This is the maxim of the blind [people] and the elephant.'[9] Malliṣeṇa's second instance seems equivocal at first, because both the notions of *naya* and of *syād-vāda* are found there: '...Because no entity, which consists in infinite properties cannot be grasped properly without the method of modal description which consists in all viewpoints, for otherwise that would lead to the undesired consequence of seizing [merely] sprouts (sc. superficial,

[7] It is quite remarkable how widespread in other philosophical and religious schools than Buddhism the maxim became. Comp. JACOB (1907–1911: I: 3).

[8] The gist of the defective viewpoint is its unconditionality, expressed by *eva* (*sad eva*), the proper viewpoint (*naya*) is indeterminate and 'open', non-exclusive (*sat*), whereas the modal description expressly avails itself of the modal functor 'in a certain sense' (*syāt*), or 'somehow' (*kathaṁcit*). Cf. SVM 28.10–12, p. 159.14–16: *durnītayaś ca nayāś ca pramāṇe ca* ***durnīti-naya-pramāṇāni*** *taiḥ. kenôllekhena mīyetêty āha sad eva sat syāt sad iti.*—'Defective opinions, viewpoints as well as both cognitive criteria are [the members of the compound in Hemacandra's aphorism AYVD 28]; [they are used there in the instrumental case]. "By what manner of description [a thing] is cognised [through them]?" It is replied: (1) x is nothing but existent, (2) x is existent, (3) x is in a certain sense existent.'

[9] SVM 14.103–104, p. 88.9–10: *kevalaṁ durnaya-prabhāvita-mati-vyāmoha-vaśād ekam apalapyânyatarad vyavasthāpayanti bāliśāḥ. so 'yam andha-gaja-nyāyaḥ.*

deficient cognition) following the maxim of the blind [people] and the elephant.'[10] In the latter quotation we encounter, as a matter of fact, a triple-level parallelism: *dharma* – *vastu*, *naya* – *syād-vāda*, and *andha-gaja-nyāya* – *pallava-grahitā-prasaṅga*; in other words, an entity pertaining to its properties, the modal description pertaining to viewpoints, and the undesired consequence (*prasaṅga*) pertaining to the maxim (*nyāya*). Accordingly, a complex entity as a whole (*vastu*) is the scope of the comprehensive modal description (*syād-vāda*), the defective form of which is the superficial, deficient cognition (*pallava-grahitā*) that grasps only 'undeveloped' sprouts, or scanty, partial data. Furthermore, a single property (*dharma*) is the scope of an particular viewpoint (*naya*), the defective form of which is exemplified by the maxim of 'the maxim of the blind people and the elephant', which is tantamount to *durnaya*. Thus, Malliṣeṇa's both illustrations are consistent in referring to the idea of the unconditional, defective viewpoint. This additionally supports the contention that only the (*dur*)*naya* model is employed to map philosophical opinions.

Due to multifaceted circumstances, all assertoric sentences can only be relatively true:

> 'Therefore all viewpoints with no exception are false views [when strictly] related to their respective spheres (*pakṣa*); however, [when understood] as mutually dependent, they become [viewpoints] conducive to truth.'[11]

This relativity, however, is not eventually tantamount to professing scepticism, and the Jainas are quite explicit about that.

The possibility of a t t a i n i n g truth is ensured jointly by the concept of comprehensive and consistence-based cognitive criteria (*pramāṇa*) and partial, aspect-qualified viewpoints, as instruments of detailed examination.[12] However, the existence of truth a s s u c h and the possibility that it can become the contents of cognition is eventually warranted, according to Jaina beliefs, by omniscience

[10] SVM 19.75–77, p. 128.23–25: *ananta-dharmâtmakasya sarvasya vastunaḥ sarva-nayâtmakena syād-vādena vinā yathāvad grahitum aśakyatvāt. itarathândha-gaja-nyāyena pallava-grahitā-prasaṅgāt.*

[11] Cf. Siddhasena Divākara's statement in STP 1.21:
tamhā savve vi ṇayā micchā-diṭṭhī sapakkha-paḍibaddhā /
aṇṇoṇṇa-ṇissiā uṇa havaṁti sammatta-sabbhāvā //

[12] TS 1.6: *pramāṇa-nayair adhigamaḥ*—'The comprehension of [the categories representing reality, mentioned in TS 1.4,] is [accomplished] through cognitive criteria and [conditionally valid] viewpoints'. See also n. 19.

(*kevala*). The latter assumption led to such paradoxical contentions that ultimately truth consists of all false statements taken together:

> '[Let there be] prosperity to Jina's words that are made of an amassment of false views, that are conducive to immortality, that are venerable, and lead to the salvific happiness.'[13]

This relativity of every predication and the impossibility of uttering an unconditionally valid statement about the reality could theoretically lead to two more—beside scepticism—different approaches. On the one hand, it could be a reason good enough to dispense with the soundness of the discursive thinking altogether and, in this way, it would embrace the negative approach of Nāgārjuna and be reflected in the structure of the tetralemma (*catuṣ-koṭi*). The dependent character of every notion and conceptual representation, the ineffable and complex structuring of reality (*prapañca*), as it is reflected in the rational and dichotomic mind, inescapably involves real contradictions (*virodha*) and antinomies (*prasaṅga*). On the other hand, the result could as well be an all-inclusive, positive approach. Two contradictory conclusions derived from one and the same thesis do not have to falsify the initial thesis, e.g., 'things arise from a cause' and 'things do not arise from a cause' do not have to unconditionally negate the discourse about causality; 'there is motion' and 'there is no motion'; 'there is time,' 'there is a part and the whole,' etc. Such two seemingly contradictory conclusions should make us only perceptive of the fact that they may—and indeed do—pertain to different contexts. This would be the Jaina approach. Despite this, the Jaina theory of *anekânta-vāda* has frequently, and undeservedly, been blamed to disregard the law of the excluded middle[14] or the law of non-contradiction in stronger or weaker sense[15]. However,

---

[13] Siddhasena Divākara's concluding verse of STP 3.69:
baddaṁ micchā-daṁsaṇa-samūha-maiyassa amaya-sārassa /
jiṇa-vayaṇassa bhagavao saṁvigga-suhâhigammassa //

[14] The criticism concerns especially the conjunction of the first two figures (*syāt*-descriptions) of the *sapta-bhaṅgī* that refer to the predicated object: (1) *syād asti*: 'from a certain viewpoint, *x* exists,' and (2) *syād nâsti*: 'from a certain viewpoint, *x* does not exist.'

[15] Notably, the violation of the law of contradiction is said, mistakenly as it were, to be involved in either or both the third and fourth figures of the *sapta-bhaṅgī*: (3) *syād asty eva syān nâsty eva*: 'from a certain viewpoint, *x* exists and, from a certain viewpoint, *x* does not exist' (wherein two predicated features are claimed to be taken subsequently), and (4) *syād avaktavyam*: 'from a certain viewpoint, *x* is inexpressible,' (two contrary features are believed to be predicated of a thing in question jointly and simultaneously). Comp. PANDEY (1984: 163): '[O]nly that logic is indicated by *syādvāda* which challenges the law

one and the same sentence (p), when negated conditionally (i.e. with the particle *syāt*—'from a certain point of view'), yields not a contrary statement ($\neg p$) in the sense that when combined with the initial statement p is an application of the law of the excluded middle ($p \vee \neg p$), but refers to a different context, viz., its point of reference of two conjuncts is different.[16]

---

of contradiction and gives some truth value to contradictory statements'; BHARUCHA–KAMAT (1984: 183); MATILAL (1991: 10–11 [13–15]) or GANERI (2002: 9): 'When talking about the "law of non-contradiction" in a deductive system, we must distinguish between two quite different theses: (a) the thesis that "$\neg (p \,\&\, \neg p)$" is a theorem in the system, and (b) the thesis that it is not the case that both "p" and "$\neg p$" are theorems. The Jainas are committed to the first of these theses, but reject the second. *This* is the sense in which it is correct to say that the Jainas reject the "law of non-contradiction".'

16 GOKHALE (1991: [77]) was right to point out that in case of *anekânta-vāda* 'both p and not-p are true in some respect. But of course the respect in which p is true is different from the one in which not-p is true. In this way the role of the term *syāt* in *syāt*-statements is to dissolve the apparent contradiction between statements by pointing out that the truth of apparently contradictory statements is relative to the respective standpoints'. The seeming inconsistency between, or contradictoriness of two sentences, e.g. 'it (some object) exists' and 'it (some object) does not exist'—that are symbolised as p and $\neg p$—is due to the fact that what we have is an incomplete statement. To cite an example attested by textual sources (e.g. JTBh 1.22 § 63):

—'with respect to substance (***S***), a given pot x exists as being made of clay' ($A^{S}_{1}x$) and 'with respect to substance (***S***), a given pot x does not exist as something made of water' ($\neg A^{S}_{2}x$),
—'with respect to place (***P***), a given pot x exists in the city of Pāṭaliputra' ($B^{P}_{1}x$) and 'with respect to place (***P***), a given pot x does not exist in the city of Kānyakybja' ($\neg B^{P}_{2}x$),
—'with respect to time (***T***), a given pot x exists in the autumn' ($C^{T}_{1}x$) and 'with respect to time (***T***), a given pot x does not exist in the spring' ($\neg C^{T}_{2}x$),
—'with respect to condition (***C***), a given pot x exists as something black' ($D^{C}_{1}x$) and 'with respect to condition (***C***), a given pot x does not exist as something red' ($\neg D^{C}_{2}x$).

Accordingly, the first two conditional statements, as well as their conjunction should be analysed as a range of indexed predicates:

(1) $A^{S}_{1}x$, $B^{P}_{1}x$, $C^{T}_{1}x$, $D^{C}_{1}x$, …, and
(2) $\neg A^{S}_{2}x$, $\neg B^{P}_{2}x$, $\neg C^{T}_{2}x$, $\neg D^{C}_{2}x$, …

Here *A*, *B*, *C*, *D*, … are predicates indexed with the set of parameters of substance (*dravya*) = ***S***, place (*kṣetra*) = ***P***, time (*kāla*) = ***T***, and condition (*bhāva*) = ***C***.

In this way, we neither have the case of two inconsistent statements (the adjunction of) p and $\neg p$ that are both theorems of the system, nor their conjunction $p \wedge \neg p$, but

Jaina realism has it that even images in a dream are not purely figments of our conceptualisation but have some kind of objective basis and rational justification. By the same token, our statements pertaining to reality are claimed by the Jainas to possess some truth; however, the infinity of ontological correlations can in no way be reflected in our language due to its inherent limitations (*avadhāraṇa*)[17]. That is why a range of utterances articulated about one and the same object, seemingly standing in contradiction to each other, may take its various contexts and ramifications into consideration. Likewise, different points of reference and time of expression, different intentions and context of apparently one and the same sentence on the verbal level make it h o m o n y m i c .

The way we deal with cognised objects is reflected in the Jaina scheme of *naya*s, and this takes place on the conceptual (*svâdhigama*, *jñānâtmaka*), verbal (*parâdhigama*, *vacanâtmaka*) and practical (*vyavahāra*) level,[18] since all these three are interconnected. A set of conditionally valid viewpoints was not only considered an ancillary theoretical device, subordinate to the theory of multiplexity of reality, and was

---

rather two related statements expressed under different circumstances or with relation to different parameters.

Furthermore, the conjunction of two apparently contradictory statements p & $\neg p$ is in fact a conjunction, which, having been disambiguated, yields no real contradiction:

(3) $A^{S}{}_{1}x \ \& \ \neg A^{S}{}_{2}x,\ B^{P}{}_{1}x \ \& \ \neg B^{P}{}_{2}x,\ C^{T}{}_{1}x \ \& \ \neg C^{T}{}_{2}x,\ D^{C}{}_{1}x \ \& \ \neg D^{C}{}_{2}x, \ldots$

[17] Cf. NAV 1.9 (p. 17) and NAV 29.28 (p. 472): 'every sentence functions with a restriction'—*sarvaṁ vākyaṁ (vacanaṁ) sâvadhāraṇaṁ*.

[18] This is implied in the passage of RVār 1.6 (p. 33.11–13): ***4. adhigama-hetur dvividhaḥ***. [*adhigama-hetur dvividhaḥ*] *svâdhigama-hetuḥ parâdhigama-hetuś ca. svâdhigama-hetur jñānâtmakaḥ pramāṇa-naya-vikalpaḥ, parâdhigama-hetur vacanâtmakaḥ. tena śrutâkhyena pramāṇena syād-vāda-naya-saṁskṛtena pratiparyāyaṁ sapta-bhaṅgīmanto jīvâdayaḥ padârthā adhigamayitavyāḥ.*—'The cause of comprehension [of the categories representing reality] is two-fold: the cause for one's own comprehension and the cause for the other's comprehension. The cause for one's own comprehension consists in cognition [and] is divided into cognitive criterion and viewpoint, [whereas] the cause for the other's comprehension consists in statements. Entities such as living elements etc. that are amenable to the seven-fold description should be comprehended from every angle by means of the cognitive criterion called testimony, refined through [the method of the] modal description and through [the method of] viewpoints.' Clearly, the idea of *svâdhigama-hetu* and *parâdhigama-hetu* directly corresponds to Siddhasena Mahāmati's distinction between 'the sentence for oneself' (*svârtha-vākya*) and 'the sentence for others' (*parârtha-vākya*) in NA 10, which was in its turn influenced by Diṅnāga's and Dharmakīrti's well-known division of *svârthânumāna* and *parârthânumāna*.

supposed to corroborate the latter, but, from the very beginnings of Jaina epistemology, it coexisted with cognitive criteria (*pramāṇa*) as an alternative epistemic instrument:

> 'All states of [all] substances, that are comprehended by means of all cognitive criteria, are [equally] capable of being predicated of by means of all [conditionally valid] viewpoints in a detailed manner.'[19]

Here, we clearly find a conviction that any given utterance functions within its given individual context and it is only within the confines delineated by this context that the sentence retains its veracity. The viewpoints (*naya*) organise the world of things of our practical dealings, and within their sphere of practical application they help us determine the truth-value of a proposition by way of its contextualisation within a given universe of conceivable points of reference. They are not supposed to contribute anything new to our knowledge,[20] as Akalaṅka declares: 'Application of viewpoints with regard to things cognised by means of cognitive criteria is the basis of everyday practice.'[21] Accordingly, the *naya*s only s e l e c t i v e l y (*vikalâdeśa*) arrange comprehensive data material already acquired[22]. In the same spirit, Yaśovijaya defines conditionally valid viewpoints as 'particular varieties of cognitive activity that grasp one facet of a real thing, which by its nature has infinite

---

[19] Uttar 28.24:

davvāṇa savva-bhāvā savva-pamāṇehi jassa uvaladdhā /
savvāhi naya-vihīhiṁ vitthāra-rūi tti nāyavvo //

[20] Interestingly, the idea that *naya*s are clearly distinguished from cognitive criteria, precisely because they avail themselves of the knowledge already acquired by a *pramāṇa*, complies with the Mīmāṁsaka's idea that cognitive criterion (*pramāṇam*) contributes a new element to our cognition, or 'comprehends a not [yet] comprehended object' (*anadhigatârthâdhigantṛ*), see ŚBh 1.1.5: *autpattikas tu śabdasyârthena sambandhas tasya jñānam upadeśo 'vyatirekaś cârthe 'nupalabdhe tat pramāṇaṁ bādarāyaṇasyânapekṣatvāt*; ŚDī, p. 45: *kāraṇa-doṣa-bādhaka-jñāna-rahitam agṛhīta-grāhi-jñānaṁ pramāṇam*; MŚV 5.(*Vṛtti-kāra*).11ab: *sarvasyânupalabdhe 'rthe prāmāṇyam smṛtir anyathā /*

[21] RVār 1.6 (p. 33.6–7): *pramāṇa-prakāśiteṣv artheṣu naya-pravṛtter vyayahāra-hetutvād abhyârhaḥ. yataḥ pramāṇa-prakāśiteṣv artheṣu naya-pravṛttir vyavahāra-hetur bhavati ato 'syâbhyarhitatvam.*

[22] Comp. the unidentified quotation in RVār 1.6 (p. 33.9–10): *sakalâdeśaḥ pramāṇâdhīno vikalâdeśo nayâdhīnaḥ*—'Complete account rests on cognitive criteria, [whereas] incomplete account rests on viewpoints', as well as LT 62 and LTV ad loc. (*Pravacana-praveśa*), pp. 686.2–688.2:

upayogau śrutasya dvau syād-vāda-naya-saṁjñitau /
syād-vādaḥ sakalâdeśo nayo vikala-saṁkathā //

properties [and] which has been discerned by cognitive criterion, [and that] do not disprove [facets] others than this [one].'[23]

Thus, *pramāṇas* serve as criteria of validity and reliability of our cognition and are expected to ensure the acquisition of truth, whereas the viewpoints are an attempt to contextualise any given utterance and determine in which sense it asserts truth.

The process of arrangement and selection is accomplished with the help of progressive indexation, in which each viewpoint (*naya*) delimits the context by introducing indices of spatial co-ordinates, temporal factors, linguistic convention, etc. The idea of the viewpoint (*naya*) as a device to single out a particular aspect of an object, viz. its point of reference, is underscored, for instance, by Siddhasena Mahāmati[24] in NA 29: 'The real thing, whose essence is multiplex, [forms] the domain of all acts of awareness; an object qualified by [only] one facet is known as the province of the viewpoint.'[25]

The assumption of the manifold character of reality in which things relate to each other by an infinite number of relations finds its expression in the conviction that every situation can be both viewed from infinite angles as well reflected in our language: infinity of interrelations corresponds to a theoretically infinite number of predications, each retaining its validity only conditionally, viz. restricted to its particular perspective.[26]

Usually, but not always, conditionally valid predications are divided into two major classes: substantial (*dravyâstika-naya*), or substance-expressive

---

[23] JTBh 2.1: *pramāṇa-paricchinnasyânanta-dharmâtmakasya vastuna eka-deśa-grāhiṇas tad-itaraṁ sāpratikṣepino 'dhyavasāya-viśeṣā nayāḥ.*

[24] See n. 4.

[25] NA 29:

anekântâtmakaṁ vastu gocaraḥ sarva-saṁvidām /
eka-deśa-viśiṣṭo 'rtho nayasya viṣayo mataḥ //

Cf. STP 1.22–25.

[26] This idea is explicitly stated by Siddharṣigaṇi in NAV 29.12 (p. 440): *saṁkhyayā punar anantā iti, ananta-dharmatvād vastunas, tad-eka-dharma-paryavasitâbhiprāyāṇāṁ ca nayatvāt, tathâpi cirantanâcāryaiḥ sarva-saṅgrāhi-saptâbhiprāya-parikalpanā-dvāreṇa sapta nayāḥ pratipāditāḥ.*—'According to the number, however, [viewpoints are] infinite, because the real thing is endowed with infinite properties and because [various] outlooks confined to [one] property of this [real thing] are viewpoints. Nevertheless, ancient preceptors taught that there are seven viewpoints, by means of assuming seven outlooks that collect together all [possible viewpoints].' The passage is quoted and elaborated in SVM 28.56–60 (p. 161.11–15): *nayāś cânantāḥ. ananta-dharmatvād vastunas tad-eka-dharma-paryavastitānāṁ vaktur abhiprayāṇāṁ ca nayatvāt tathā ca vṛddhāḥ. jāvaiyā vayaṇa-vaha tāvaiyā ceva hoṁti ṇaya-vāyā /* [STP 3.47ab] *iti.*

(*dravyârthika-naya*), and attributive (*paryāyâstika-naya*), or mode-expressive (*paryāyârthika-naya*)[27]. Whereas the former emphasises continuity and essential identity of evolving things, the latter predominantly deals with the mutable character of phenomena and their transient manifestations and accentuates the attributive side of reality. Most commonly these two classes of conditionally valid viewpoints are further subdivided into seven following types[28]:

[27] Cf., e.g., STP 1.3. Akalaṅka (RVār 1.33, p. 94) has substantial (*dravyâstika-naya*) and attributive (*paryāyâstika-naya*). Kundakunda, e.g. in PSā 2.22, has: *davvaṭṭhieṇa* (*dravyârthika*) and *pajjayaṭṭhieṇa* (*paryāyârthika*), without any further subdivision. It is well known that Kundakunda (e.g. in SSā 353) uses also another two-fold classification of viewpoints, viz. *vavahāra* (*vyavahāra-naya*), or empirical, and *ṇicchayu* (*niścaya-naya*), or ultimate, the former not be confused with the *vyavahāra-naya* of the sevenfold '*naigamâdi*' classification. This classification in its import goes back to the earlier Buddhist distinction of the empirical truth (*saṁvṛti-satya, vyavahāra, laukika-satya*) and the ultimate truth (*paramârtha-satya*), which is already attested in *Kathā-vatthu* and *Milinda-pañha*, finds its classical expression with Nāgārjuna (e.g. MMK 24.8–9) and is taken over in such Yogâcāra works as *Mahāyāna-sūtrâlaṅkāra* (MSA 11.3) and *Uttara-tantra* (UtT 1.84). On Kundakunda's *vavahāra– ṇicchaya* division see in this volume Jayandra Soni's 'Kundakunda and Umāsvāti on *Anekânta-vāda*' (pp. 25–35, esp. p. 28 ff.), and Christoph Emmrich's 'How many times? Pluralism, dualism or monism in early Jaina temporal description' (pp. 69–88, esp. p. 71 f.).

[28] Cf. STP 1.4–5:

davvaṭṭhiya-naya-payaḍī suddhā [(1)] *saṁgaha-parūvaṇâvisao* /
paḍirūve [(2)] *puṇa vayaṇa-ttha-nicchao tassa vavahāro* //
mūla-nimeṇaṁ [(3)] *pajjava-ṇayassa ujjusuya-vayaṇa-vicchedo* /
tassa tu saddāiā sāha-pasāha [(4)] *suhuma-bheyā* [(4)] //

—'The pure nature of the substance-expressive viewpoint is the province of the description [by means] of the collective [viewpoint]. As regards [its] countertype, in its turn, the empirical [viewpoint] of this [substance-expressive category consists in] the determination of the meaning of an utterance. The prime support of the mode[-expressive] viewpoint is the division of the utterance [expressing] the direct viewpoint. Of this, the verbal and other [viewpoints] are subtle[r] divisions, [like] branches and twigs.'

[[(1)-(4)] Abhayadevasūri's relevant glosses in STPṬ. *ad loc.* are quite useful: [(1)] [p. 315.9–10:] ***suddhā*** *ity asaṅkīrṇā viśeṣâsaṁsparśavatī*. ('"Pure" means not mingled, having no association with the particular.'), [(2)] [p. 316.11–12:] [*a*]*śuddhaṁ* ***paḍirūvaṁ*** ... ***pratirūpaṁ*** *pratibimbaṁ pratinidhir iti yāvat* (countertype = impure), [(3)] [p. 317.12, 349.2–3:] ***mūlam*** *ādiḥ ne(**ṇi)meṇaṁ*** *ādhāraḥ*, [(4)] [p. 349.5–6:] ***śākhā-praśākhā*** *iva sthūla-sūkṣmatara-darśitatvāt* ***sūkṣmo bhedo*** *viśeṣo yeṣāṁ te tathā*.]

substance-expressive (*dravyârthika*)	mode-expressive (*paryāyârthika*)
1. comprehensive (*naigama*)	4. direct (*ṛju-sūtra*)
2. collective (*saṅgraha*)	5. verbal (*śabda*)
3. empirical (*vyavahāra*)	6. etymological (*samabhirūḍha*)
	7. factual (*evaṁ-bhūta, itthaṁ-bhāva*)

Table 1

This scheme, found also in Akalaṅka's *Rāja-vārttika*, is not universally followed in Jaina literature. For certain reasons (*vide infra* n. 80) STP does not distinguish separately *naigama-naya* and speaks of only six viewpoints.

Furthermore, we find the divisions of *dravyârthika-naya* and *paryāyârthika-naya* neither in the canonical works such as *Aṇuoga* or *Ṭhāṇaṁga*, nor in such relatively late treatises as TS, TBh, NA or NAV. As against the frequently quoted opinion (e.g. JAINI (1920: 45 ff.), SCHUBRING (1978: 161, § 76)), they are entirely absent from TS and TBh. Thus, for instance, TS in TBh-recension subsumes the varieties of (5), (6) and (7) under the head of *śabda-naya* (*vide infra*).

NAV 29 classifies the seven viewpoints into two main divisions slightly differently:

object-bound, operating by means of object (*artha-dvāreṇa* [*pravṛtta*])	speech-bound, operating by means of speech (*śabda-dvāreṇa* [*pravṛtta*])
1. comprehensive (*naigama*)	5. verbal (*śabda*)
2. collective (*saṅgraha*)	6. etymological (*samabhirūḍha*)
3. empirical (*vyavahāra*)	7. factual (*evaṁ-bhūta*)
4. direct (*ṛju-sūtra*)	

Table 2

See also PALV 6.74, p. 54.7–9: *tatra mūla-nayau dvau dravyârthika-paryāyârthika-bhedāt. tatra dravyârthikas tredhā naigama-saṅgraha-vyavahāra-bhedāt. paryāyârthikaś caturdhā ṛju-sūtra-śabda-samabhirūḍhâivaṁ-bhūta-bhedāt.* For the purely sevenfold division see: AṇD 606 (*satta mūla-ṇayā paṇṇattā. taṁ jahā—ṇegame saṁgahe vavahāre ujjusue sadde samabhirūḍhe evaṁbhūte*) = Ṭhāṇ 552, as well as TBh 1.35, SSi 1.33, NAṬ 29, etc. Umāsvāmin's tradition of TS enumerated only five major types. The comprehensive viewpoint was divided into two subtypes, viz. selective (*deśa-parikṣepin*) and all-inclusive (*sarva-parikṣepin*), even though Umāsvāti does not explicate them further in TBh, whereas the verbal viewpoint was further subdivided into three viewpoints (*tiṇṇi sadda-nayā*): accurate (*saṁpai-sadda-naya, sāmprata-naya*), etymological (*samabhirūḍha*) and factual (*evaṁ-bhūya*). See TS 1.34,35: /34/ *naigama-saṅgraha-vyavahāra-rju-sūtra-śabdā nayāḥ*, /35/ *ādya-śabdau dvi-tri-bhedau.* (This is according to the reading preserved in TBh 1.34–35). SSi 1.33 offers a *varia lectio* of TS: *naigama-saṅgraha-vyavahāra-rju-sūtra-śabda-samabhirūḍhâivam-bhūtā nayāḥ.*

A scheme rather similar to that of Table 2 is apparently followed also by TS in view of the explicit mention (TS 1.34) of the group *naigama-saṅgraha-vyavahāra-ṛju-sūtra* appended by the uniform *śabda* subcategory, which is subdivided only in the following aphorism of TS 1.35—this would correspond to *śabda-dvāreṇa* [*pravṛtta*] of NAV.

Also TBh seems to share a similar model not only because of the absolute absence of *dravyârthika-naya* and *paryāyârthika-naya*, but also because, in the introductory part[29], the viewpoints 5–7 are singled out by a special preliminary description of their common feature under the head *śabda* (*yathârthâbhidhānaṁ śabdam*), and because, in the four recapitulatory verses on p. 35.4–36.2, the stress is specifically laid on the comprehensive *śabda* category[30]:

1. comprehensive (*naigama*)	2. collective (*saṅgraha*)	5. verbal (*śabda*)
a. partially inclusive (*deśa-parikṣepin*)	3. empirical (*vyavahāra*)	a. present (*sāmprata*)
b. all-inclusive (*sarva-parikṣepin*)	4. direct (*ṛju-sūtra*)	b. etymological (*samabhirūḍha*)
		c. factual (*evaṁ-bhūta*)

Table 3

Let us have a closer look at the character of each of the viewpoints in order to examine exact relationship between them.

The comprehensive viewpoint (*naigama-naya*) grasps a given phenomenon in a most general way and takes recourse to a possibly most extensive, all-inclusive context, which is referred to by a particular utterance. From the perspective of the comprehensive viewpoint, what is taken into account is a complex of meanings and connotations evoked by an utterance, irrespective of either distinctive features of individuals or of constitutive characteristics representative of a given class: 'Speech elements that are expressed in inhabited localities (*sc*. colloquially) [have] their meaning; and the comprehension of [such a] meaning of speech elements [is what] the comprehensive viewpoint, which grasps collectively partial [denotations of a

---

[29] TBh 1.35 (p. 32.13–17): *nigameṣu ye 'bhihitāḥ śabdās teṣām arthaḥ śabdârtha-parijñānaṁ ca deśa-samagra-grāhī naigamaḥ. arthānāṁ sarvâika-deśa-saṅgrahaṇaṁ saṅgrahaḥ. laukika-sama upacāra-prāyo vistṛtârtho vyavahāraḥ. satāṁ sāmpratānāṁ arthānām abhidhāna-parijñānam ṛju-sūtraḥ. yathârthâbhidhānaṁ śabdam. nāmâdiṣu prasiddha-pūrvāc chabdād arthe pratyayaḥ sāmprataḥ. satsv artheṣv asaṁkramaḥ samabhirūḍhaḥ. vyañjanârthayor evaṁ-bhūta iti.*

[30] Esp. in verse 4cd (p. 36.2): *vidyād yathârtha-śabdaṁ viśeṣita-padaṁ tu śabda-nayam* / —'One should understand the verbal viewpoint as [consisting of] words in distinguished (*sc*. analysed) [meaning] in accordance with a speech element [denoting] an object.'

speech element, consists in].'[31] Clearly, what is meant here is a colloquial, unreflected usage of an unspecified reference, which comprises indiscriminately both the particular and the universal: 'When one says "pot" what [is meant] is this particular substance (*sc.* thing) produced by the effort [of a pot-maker], with a rounded, elongated neck [and] a rounded edge at the top [as well as] with a spherical container below, [which is] suited for fetching and carrying water etc., [and has been] finished off by secondary operations [like baking]. [Accordingly,] the comprehensive viewpoint [consists in] the comprehension without [making] any distinction between such an individual [thing] furnished with particular features or [things] belonging to its class.'[32] Conspicuously, the category of comprehensive viewpoint is absent from STP.

---

[31] TBh 1.35 (p. 32.13–14): *nigameṣu ye 'bhihitāḥ śabdās teṣām arthaḥ śabdârtha-parijñānaṁ ca deśa-samagra-grāhī naigamaḥ.*

[32] TBh 1.35 (p. 33.9–12): *ghaṭa ity ukte yo 'sau ceṣṭâbhinirvṛtta ūrdhva-kuṇḍalâûṣṭhâyata-vṛtta-grīvo 'dhastāt parimaṇḍalo jalâdīnām āharaṇa-dhāraṇa-samartha uttara-guṇa-nirvartanânirvṛtto dravya-viśeṣas tasminn ekasmin viśeṣavati taj-jātīyeṣu vā sarveṣv aviśeṣāt parijñānaṁ naigama-nayaḥ.* Cf. the exposition in the same spirit in NAV 29.13 (p. 441), e.g.: *tatrâpi ye paraspara-viśakalitau sāmānya-viśeṣāv icchanti tat-samudāya-rūpo naigamaḥ.*—'And out of these [four object-bound varieties], the comprehensive [viewpoint] consists in an aggregate of such [outlooks] that consider [jointly] the universal and the particular as being disconnected from each other;' as well as NAV 29.23 (p. 455): *vyavahāro 'pi sarvaḥ pradhānôpasarjana-dvāreṇa kathañcid itarêtarâvinirluṭhita-sāmānya-viśeṣa-sādhya eva; na hi sāmānyaṁ doha-vāhâdi-kriyāyām upayujyate, viśeṣāṇām eva tatrôpayogān, nâpi viśeṣā eva tat-kāriṇaḥ, gotva-śūnyānāṁ teṣāṁ vṛkṣâdy-aviśiṣṭatayā tat-karaṇa-sāmarthyâbhāvāt. ... tasmāt kathañcid bhedâbhedināv evâitau, tad-anyatara-samarthakaḥ punar nirālambanatvād durnayatāṁ svī-karotîti sthitam.*—'Also the whole everyday practice can only be effected [with regard to] the universal and the particular, which are somehow mutually not detached, by means of the main [import] and the subordinate [level], for neither the universal [alone] can be employed in such actions like milking, carrying [commodities], etc., because only the particulars are employed in these [actions], nor the particulars alone accomplish these [actions] because these [particulars] void of [the universal] cow-ness would lack the efficacy to accomplish these [actions], inasmuch as they would not be distinguished from tress, etc. ... Therefore, it is established that these two, [i.e. the universal and the particulars], are somehow truly [both] different and not different from each other. [Such a viewpoint], however, which corroborates [only] one of these [two, i.e. either the universal or the particular], appropriates the status of a defective viewpoint, because [it is] void of [any] objective substratum.' See also RVār 1.33 (p. 95.12 ff.): *artha-saṁkalpa-mātra-grāhī naigamaḥ. ... tad yathā: kaścit pragṛhya paraśuṁ puruṣaṁ gacchantam abhisamīkṣyâha 'kim arthaṁ gacchati bhavān' iti? sa tasmai ācaṣṭe prasthârtham iti*, etc.—

The collective viewpoint (*saṅgraha-naya*) pertains cumulatively to a whole class of individuals, which constitutes the denotation of a given utterance, and thereby it forms a basis for any taxonomy. In fact, Umāsvāti defines it briefly as 'the synthesising of one facet out of all [possible facets] of things'[33] and further explicates: 'The collective viewpoint [consists in] the comprehension of, [say,] present, past and future pots, distinguished by the name and other [standpoints (*nikṣepa*)], whether with regard to one [individual] or to many [things belonging to its class].'[34] At first glance, one might consider the wording *ekasmin vā* to refer to a particular, but in fact the phrase *ekasmin vā bahuṣu vā* links the whole statement to the previous section explaining the character of the comprehensive viewpoint and the phrase: *tasminn ekasmin viśeṣavati taj-jātīyeṣu vā sarveṣv aviśeṣāt*. Accordingly, the idea of the universal is indicated here in the phrase 'present, past and future pots' (*sāmpratâtītânāgateṣu ghaṭeṣu*). Akalaṅka likewise explicitly refers to the idea of the class, or the universal: 'The collective viewpoint grasps everything as a whole by referring to oneness without contradicting (viz. without relinquishing, *apracyavana*) its own class.'[35] In other words, the scope of the comprehensive viewpoint (*naigama-naya*) is narrowed down by excluding the particular and laying stress on the universal alone.[36]

When only a particular specimen of the whole class of objects—that has previously been defined from the perspective of the collective viewpoint—is selected for practical purposes and directly referred to by an utterance, or becomes

---

'Comprehensive [viewpoint] grasps only the general idea of the purpose. ... For instance someone notices a man walking, who has taken an axe [with him], and asks: "For what reason are you going, Sir"? He replies to him: "[I'm going] my way",' etc. Here in RVār, Akalaṅka generally follows the examples taken from SSi 1.33.

[33] TBh 1.35 (p. 32.14): *arthānāṁ sarvâika-deśa-saṅgrahaṇaṁ saṅgrahaḥ*.

[34] TBh 1.35 (pp. 33.12–34.2): *ekasmin vā bahuṣu vā nāmâdi-viśeṣiteṣu sāmpratâtītânāgateṣu ghaṭeṣu sampratyayaḥ saṅgrahaḥ*.

[35] RVār 1.33 (p. 95.12 ff.): *sva-jāty-avirodhenâikatvôpanayāt samasta-grahaṇaṁ saṅgrahaḥ*.

[36] Cf. NAV 29.13 (p. 441): *punaḥ kevalaṁ sāmānyaṁ vāñchanti tat-samūha-sampādyaḥ saṅgrahaḥ*.—'The collective [viewpoint], in its turn, is produced out of an amassment of such [outlooks] that affirm solely the universal.' See also NAV 29.23 (p. 462): *tad-apalāpī kevala-sāmānya-pratiṣṭhāpakaḥ kad-abhiprāyaḥ saṅgraha-durnaya-vyapadeśaṁ svī-kurute, viśeṣâpekṣayâiva sāmānya-sthāpakasya saṅgraha-nayatvād iti.*—'[Such] a defective outlook which denies that [multifarious object and] which determines the universal alone appropriates the designation of the defective collective viewpoint because [only such a viewpoint which] determines the universal precisely with regard to the particulars is the collective viewpoint [proper].'

an object of one's action, we have an instance of the empirical viewpoint (*vyavahāra-naya*). It is especially in early analyses that the commonplace aspect (*laukika*) and the conventional practice prevalent among people (*lokôpacāra*) is said to be emphasised in this case.[37] Clearly, the point of reference is further limited[38] to such individual things, or elements of a class, that can become directly subject to practical activity: 'The empirical viewpoint consists in the comprehension of precisely such [present, past and future things like pots, grasped by the collective viewpoint,] comprehensible to common people and experts, [and] accessible to the conventional practice just as they are gross objects.'[39] This clearly nominalist perspective reflects an aspect of speech commonly encountered in linguistic usage: most frequently we refer to particular things, viz. to individuals, by means of linguistic units of general denotation that correspond to respective classes: 'The empirical viewpoint [consists in] appropriating [a thing], which is preceded by practical application [of the thing] from this [class of things embraced by the collective viewpoint] (*atas* = *etasmāt*).'[40] Akalaṅka proceeds to illustrate the rule: 'When one admits that "[any] healing decoction is a medicine", then— insofar as the universal has the nature of the particular—[one knows] healing efficacy of a particular fig etc. (i.e. one grasps [the universal] through the efficacy of the particular).'[41]

However, a relevant statement of NAV 29, taken at its face value, seems to contradict the contention that the scope of the empirical viewpoint is the particular: 'The empirical [viewpoint], on the other hand, is produced out of a complex of such [outlooks] that intend an entity, like a pot, etc.—[when it] enters into people's everyday practice—in case of which [both] the universal and the

[37] TBh 1.35 (p. 32.15): *laukika-sama upacāra-prāyo vistṛtârtho vyavahāraḥ.*—'The empirical viewpoint has an extended meaning, similar to [the way] common people [understand it], like in the conventional practice.' Cf. TBh 1.35 (p. 35.9, verse 3cd): *lokôpacāra-niyataṁ vyavahāraṁ vistṛtaṁ vidyāt* /—'One should understand the empirical [viewpoint in an] extended [way] as confined to the conventional practice [prevalent] among people.'

[38] PALV 6.74 p. 54.11: *saṅgraha-gṛhīta-bhedako vyavahāraḥ.*—'The empirical viewpoint differentiates what has been grasped [in a general way] by the collective viewpoint.'

[39] TBh 1.35 (p. 34.2–3): *teṣv eva laukika-parīkṣaka-grāhyeṣûpacāra-gamyeṣu yathā-sthūlârtheṣu sampratyayo vyavahāraḥ.*

[40] RVār 1.33 (p. 96.20): *ato vidhi-pūrvakam avaharaṇaṁ vyavahāraḥ.*

[41] RVār 1.33 (p. 96.25–26): *'kaṣāyo bhaiṣajyam' ity ukte ca sāmānyasya viśeṣâtmakatvān naiyagrodhâdi-viśeṣa-sāmarthyam (viśeṣasya sāmarthyena grahaṇam).*

particular, being of philosophic pertinence, are disregarded.'[42] The context for this statement is a discussion with the Buddhist. What the term *viśeṣa* in this particular case is supposed to mean is 'the ultimate particular', viz. the momentary, insubstantial entity (*viśeṣāḥ paramâṇu-lakṣaṇāḥ kṣaṇa-kṣayiṇaḥ*). Clearly, the author differentiates here between *svalakṣaṇa* (the ultimate individual) and *vastu*, or the real, non-momentary, gross thing.[43] Consequently, what constitutes the point of reference for the empirical viewpoint also in NAV is indeed the particular understood as a real entity, that is graspable in daily experience, that retains its individual character but at the same time is made up of atoms, not the particular as a momentary, imperceptible atom: 'Such a [real thing,] like a pot, etc., which lasts for some time, which possesses grossness, which is instrumental to people's everyday practice [and] which is intended by you as really existing, is not accidental, but rather [it is] combined of permanent infinitesimal atoms...'[44] Thus, what is meant by *laukika* and *lokôpacāra* in TBh (above p. 52, n. 37) clearly corresponds to *yathā loka-grāha* (' just the way people take', n. 43) and *loka-vyavahāra-kāritva* of NAV ('accomplishing of the people's everyday practice', n. 44). Eventually, the practical aspect means the feasibility, on the part of an object, to become the object of human activity.

---

[42] NAV 29.13 (p. 441): *ye punar anapekṣita-śāstrīya-sāmānya-viśeṣaṁ loka-vyavahāram avatarantaṁ ghaṭâdikaṁ padârtham abhiprayanti tan-nicaya-janyo vyavahāraḥ.*

[43] NAV 29.16 (p. 445): *yathā loka-grāham eva vastv astu ... na hi sāmānyam anādi-nidhanam ekaṁ saṅgrāhâbhimataṁ pramāṇa-bhūmiḥ. ... nâpi viśeṣāḥ paramâṇu-lakṣaṇāḥ kṣaṇa-kṣayiṇaḥ pramāṇa-gocaras, tathā pravṛtter abhāvāt. tasmād idam eva nikhila-lokābādhitaṁ pramāṇa-prasiddhaṁ kiyat-kāla-bhāvi-sthūratām ābibhrāṇam udakâharaṇâdy-artha-kriyā-nirvartana-kṣamaṁ ghaṭâdikaṁ vastu-rūpaṁ pāramārthikam astu.*— 'Let the real thing be exactly just the way people take [it] ... For the universal—with no beginning nor end, [numerically] one, considered by the collective [viewpoint]—[does] not [constitute] the scope of a cognitive criterion ... The particulars—[which are] characterised by infinitesimal atoms [and which are] perishing in a moment (*sc.* momentary)—[do] not [constitute] the domain of cognitive criterion, either, because [they do] not occur in that manner. Therefore only this [what is] not subverted by opinions prevalent among people, [what is] well-known due to cognitive criterion, [what] possesses grossness lasting for some time, [what is] capable of executing efficient action such as fetching water, etc., [and what] consists in the real thing, like a pot, etc., must be ultimately real.'

[44] NAV 29.25 (p. 463): *yad idaṁ kiyat-kāla-bhāvi sthūratām ābibhrāṇaṁ loka-vyavahāra-kāri ghaṭâdikaṁ bhavatas tāttvikam abhipretaṁ tan nâkasmikaṁ...*

The last one in the quadruple classification of the 'object-bound' viewpoints that 'operate by means of an object' (*artha-dvāreṇa* [*pravṛtta*]) is the direct viewpoint (*ṛju-sūtra*). It is defined as 'the comprehension by way of the denotative acts concerning the existent and present objects'[45] and its province is the present point of time[46], viz. particular things that have already been pointed out by the empirical viewpoint[47], which are being perceived here and now. Accordingly, the direct viewpoint narrows the point of reference down to the present manifestation of an individual (*vartamāna-kṣaṇa-vivarti-vastu*), and puts aside its past and future facets (*atītânagata-vakra-parityāga*).[48] At the same time, the direct viewpoint opens up—according to the other tradition—the fourfold catalogue of mode-expressive viewpoints (*paryāyârthika-naya*), or conditionally valid attributive predications, which view things according to their transitory properties and modes and neglect their incontrovertible substantial nature and existence as substrata of those properties and modes. From such an angle, in this viewpoint, which 'grasps pure modes with regard to their antithesis (*sc.* substance)'[49], the substantial and non-momentary character of an entity is entirely ignored and merely its transient aspects (generally the present moment) are taken into account: 'it neglects previous[ly mentioned] objects belonging to the three times [and] embraces the object belonging to the present time.'[50] Here, it is irrelevant which linguistic expressions we choose to refer to one and the same individual.

---

[45] TS 1.35 p. 32.15–16: *satāṁ sāmpratānām arthānām abhidhāna-parijñānam ṛju-sūtraḥ.*

[46] TS 1.35 p. 36.1, verse 4ab:

sāmprata-viṣaya-grāhakam ṛju-sūtra-nayaṁ samāsato vidyāt /

[47] TS 1.35 p. 34.3–4:

teṣv [= *vyavahṛteṣv*] *eva satsu sāmprateṣu saṁpratyaya ṛju-sūtraḥ.*

[48] NAV 29.17 (p. 446): *tatra ṛju praguṇam akuṭilam atītânagata-vakra-parityāgād vartamāna-kṣaṇa-vivarti-vastuno rūpaṁ sūtrayati niṣṭaṅkitaṁ darśayatîty ṛjusūtraḥ.*—'In this case, the direct [viewpoint is explained as follows]: [it] draws out, [i.e.] plainly demonstrates—directly, [i.e.] in a straight manner, [or] not crookedly, [viz.] by evading past and future bends [of the real thing]—the form of the real thing, whose transient occurrence [falls to] the present moment.'

[49] PALV 6.74 p. 54.11–12: *śuddha-paryāya-grāhī pratipakṣa-sāpekṣa ṛju-sūtraḥ.*

[50] RVār 1.33 (p. 96.31): *pūrvāṁs tri-kāla-viṣayān atiśayya vartamāna-kāla-viṣayam ādatte.* Cf. NAV 29.26: *tasmāt tiro-hita-kṣaṇa-vivartam alakṣita-paramâṇu-vaiviktyaṁ vastu sarva-sāṁvyavahārika-pramāṇair gocarī-kriyata iti tat-tiras-kāra-dvāreṇâdṛṣṭa-kṣaṇa-kṣayi-paramâṇu-pratiṣṭhāpako 'bhiprāya ṛjusūtra-durnaya-saṁjñām aśnute, tad-upekṣayâiva tad-darśakasya nayatvād iti.*—'Therefore, the real thing becomes the

The three remaining viewpoints operate on the speech level and, in addition, analyse the verbal structure of an utterance, the domain for them being external objects that are nameable within a strictly limited range of verbal expression. What is common for the three varieties of the verbal viewpoint is declared (which in itself is not a very revealing observation) by Umāsvāti to be 'the denoting according to the meaning.'[51] The proper point of reference for the speech-bound viewpoints is therefore the thing as it enters the linguistic practice. Accordingly, all they are about is rather the Austinian *how to do things with words*, not *how to do things with things*.[52]

---

domain [of cognition] through all cognitive criteria, that are of importance in practical life, as something whose momentary transient occurrences are ruled out (*sc.* neglected) [and] in which the fact that it is differentiated into infinitesimal atoms is not [directly] observable. Thus, the outlook that determines invisible infinitesimal atoms which perish in a moment (*sc.* are momentary) by means of ruling out (*sc.* neglecting) this [persistence] receives the denotation of a defective direct viewpoint, because [such an outlook alone] which demonstrates these [momentary invisible infinitesimal atoms] only by putting aside this [persistence] is the [direct] viewpoint [proper].'

[51] TBh 1.35 (p. 32.16–17): *yathârthâbhidhānaṁ śabdam.*

[52] The following passage of NAV 29.15 (p. 450) delineates the character of the three verbal viewpoints: *tasmān na paramârthato 'rthaḥ śabdâtirikto 'sty, upacārataḥ punar laukikair aparyālocita-paramârthair vyavahriyate. asāv apy aupacārikaḥ śabdâtmako vârthaḥ pratikṣaṇa-bhaṅguraḥ svī-kartavyo, varṇānāṁ kṣaṇa-dhvaṁsitā-pratīteḥ* ... — 'Consequently, on the level of the ultimate truth there is no [external] object in addition to speech elements, whereas, metaphorically, [object] is used practically by common people, who do not reflect upon the ultimate truth. Also this object, either the metaphorical one or the one having speech element as its essence, should be held to be momentary (lit. perishable at every moment), because phonemes are known to be annihilated after a moment (*sc.* to be momentary) ...' As a matter of fact, the preceding is incorporated in an account of a fallacious viewpoint (*nayâbhāsa*), nevertheless it is quite an accurate description of how the verbal viewpoint operates, with the proviso that the proper viewpoint (*naya*) does not deny the existence of an external object, but takes the real thing and the word denoting it to point to each other: NAV 29: *ato 'mī śabdâdayo yadêtarêtarâbhimata-śabdârthôpekṣayā svâbhimataṁ śabdârthaṁ darśayanti, tadā nayās, tasyâpi tatra bhāvāt.*—'Consequently, when these [viewpoints like] the verbal [viewpoint], etc., demonstrate an object (denotatum) [denoted by a particular] speech element, which is intended by a respective [viewpoint], putting aside (*sc.* neglecting) [the fact that] object (denotatum) and [respective] speech elements are intended by (*sc.* point to) each other, then they are [proper] viewpoints, because also this [object (denotatum)] exists in (*sc.* is related to) these [speech elements].'

What the majority of Jaina epistemologists named simply the verbal viewpoint (*śabda-naya*), Umāsvāti called the accurate (or: present) verbal viewpoint (*sāmprata-śabda-naya*) and defined it as 'the cognition of an object through a speech element already well-known on [account of] such [categories like] name etc.'[53] and as 'the comprehension of precisely those [objects, grasped by means of the direct viewpoint, like] pots, that are present, that comprise one of [such categories like] name etc. [and] that are already well-known'[54]. Two things in these passages are conspicuous: the further diminishing of the scope (*teṣv eva*) to present (*sāmprateṣu*) phenomena and the verbal reference. The verbal viewpoint (*śabda-naya*) was interpreted variously by the subsequent Jaina tradition, but one thing remained common: the verbal point of reference and the role of verbal (or grammatical) means of expression relevant for the interpretation.[55] Applying the verbal viewpoint is tantamount to the recognition of the prevalent linguistic convention and to the overlooking of fine differentiation between meanings of synonymical expressions, etc., that may go back to different derivation, grammatical construction etc.: 'the verbal [viewpoint] intends, as they say, by the force of understanding, one object (denotatum) for all such linguistic units, like *Indra*, *Śakra*, *Purandara*,[56] etc., that are used—in accordance with the usage—to denote [one and

[53] TBh 1.35 (p. 32.17): *nāmâdiṣu prasiddha-pūrvāc chabdād arthe pratyayaḥ sāmprataḥ*.

[54] TBh 1.35 (p. 34.4–5): *teṣv eva sāmprateṣu nāmâdīnām anyatama-grāhiṣu prasiddha-pūrvakeṣu ghaṭeṣu saṁpratyayaḥ sāmprataḥ śabdaḥ*.

[55] Just to mention two Digambara opinions: SSi 1.33 (§ 246, p. 102): *liṅga-saṁkhyā-sādhanâdi-vyabhicāra-nirvṛtti-paraḥ śabda-nayaḥ. tatra liṅga-vyabhicāraḥ: puṣyas tārakā nakṣatram iti* ... —'[The verbal viewpoint] aims at removing discrepancy [in meaning] due to gender, number, case etc. Among these [various factors], the discrepancy [among synonyms] due to gender is e.g.: *puṣyas* (masc., "constellation"), *tārakā* (fem., "cluster of stars"), *nakṣatram* (n., "asterism"), etc.,' and PALV 6.74 p. 54.12–13: *kāla-kāraka-liṅgānāṁ bhedāt śabdasya kathañcid artha-bheda-kathanaṁ śabda-nayaḥ.*—'the verbal viewpoint speaks somehow of [various] differences between meanings of [one and the same] speech element depending on difference in tense, contributory factors [of an action] (semantic categories) and gender.'

[56] The above series of various names of a Vedic god has surprisingly become the standard sequence in Jaina literature. The idea may go back to Patañjali's *Vyākaraṇa-mahā-bhāṣya* (MBhā under sūtra 1.3.1, vol. II, p. 117): *bahavo hi śabdā ekârthā bhavanti. tad yathā—indraḥ śakraḥ puruhūtaḥ puraṁdaraḥ. kantu koṣṭhaḥ kusūla iti. ekaś ca śabdo bahv-arthaḥ. tad yathā—akṣāḥ pādāḥ māṣā iti*.

the same] specific object (denotatum).'[57] As Akalaṅka put it: 'It primarily overrides any difference [in meaning] due to gender, number, case etc.'[58] In other words, the users of the language agree upon a conventionally determined selection of verbal expressions that denote a particular individual.

If one further limits the context of an utterance and draws a distinction among synonyms which is based on their divergent derivation, viz. if one sticks to a viewpoint which, 'denies any equivalence among existing meanings'[59], we have the case of the etymological viewpoint (*samabhirūḍha-naya*). Thus, two expressions, for instance, 'contemplation, speculation' (*vitarka*) and 'meditation, reflection' (*dhyāna*), that are [generally] considered synonymous, may refer to different phenomena in some particular contexts[60]. To cite another example (NAV 29), although three epithets in an undiscriminating commonplace usage pertain to one and the same god, nonetheless the name 'Indra' refers in fact to a divine sovereign, the appellation 'Śakra' describes a being possessed of might and the epithet

---

[57] NAV 29.19 (p. 450): *rūḍhito yāvanto dhvanayaḥ kasmiṁścid arthe pravartante; yathêndra-śakra-purandarâdayaḥ, teṣāṁ sarveṣām apy ekam artham abhipraiti kila pratīti-vaśād*. See also NAV 29.13 (p. 441): *tathā ye rūḍhitaḥ śabdānāṁ pravṛttiṁ vāñchanti tan-nivaha-sādhyaḥ śabda iti.*—'Similarly, the verbal [viewpoint] is established by a collection of such [outlooks that] affirm that the usage of speech elements [complies] with the linguistic convention;' and NAV 29.27 (p. 471): *tataś ca kvacid anapekṣita-vyutpatti-nimittā rūḍhitaḥ pravartante ...*—'And therefore, they are used to denote certain [objects (denotata)] in accordance with the usage [when] the factors [accountable for their] grammatical formation [are] disregarded...'

[58] RVār 1.33 (p. 98.12): *sa ca liṅga-saṁkhyā-sādhanâdi-vyabhicāra-nivṛtti-paraḥ*.

[59] TS 1.35 p. 32.18: *satsv artheṣv asaṁkramaḥ samabhirūḍhaḥ*. See also NAV 29.13 (p. 441): *ye tu vyutpattito dhvanīnāṁ pravṛttiṁ vāñchanti nânyathā tad-vāra-janyaḥ samabhirūḍha iti.*—'Further, the etymological [viewpoint] is produced out of the multitude of such [outlooks] that affirm that the usage of a linguistic units [complies] with the grammatical formation, and not otherwise.' and NAV 29.27 (p. 471): *...kvacit sāmānya-vyutpatti-sāpekṣāḥ ...*—'...[they are used to denote] certain [other objects (denotata)] depending on the grammatical formation [based on] the universal...'

[60] TS 1.35 (p. 34.5–6): *teṣām eva sāmpratānām* [=*arthānām*] *adhyavasāyâsaṁkramo vitarka-dhyānavat samabhirūḍhaḥ*. Cf. JTBh 2.6: *paryāya-bhede bhinnârthān abhimanyate.*—'If there is any difference among synonyms, one means different objects,' as well as PALV 6.74 p. 54.14: *paryāya-bhedāt padârtha-nānârtha-nirūpakaṁ samabhirūḍhaḥ.*—'Due to the difference in synonyms, the etymological viewpoint describes diverse objects [following diverse] meanings of words.'

'Purandara' denotes a destroyer of strongholds etc., in the same manner as words like 'Indra', 'pot' or 'man' have different denotata[61].

The issue is further elaborated by Pūjyapāda Devanandin (SSi 1.33 § 247, p. 103) who takes the etymological viewpoint to deal, firstly, with homonyms: out of several possible meanings of one and the same expression, in a given context we select the meaning which is current and widely accepted in the society. For instance, the word '*go*' denotes a cow in accordance with the convention, even though it might theoretically refer to any 'walking creature', as a derivative of √*gam*, or 'speech', as a derivative of the root √*gai*, etc. When differentiating between various synonyms denoting a cow, we use the term '*go*' of the derivation that corresponds to popular usage[62]. Furthermore, what is crucial, this viewpoint forms a basis for distinguishing among a range of synonyms in correspondence to their etymologies.[63] Thirdly, out of several meanings a word could hypothetically convey in accordance with its etymology, only the well-known conventional meaning of an expression is selected.[64] Irrespective of minor interpretative differences, Pūjyapāda Devanandin agrees that the etymological viewpoint distinguishes between meanings on the basis of etymology or convention.[65]

---

[61] See NAV 29.20 (p. 451): *paryāya-śabdā vibhinnârthāḥ, prativibhakta-vyutpatti-nimittakatvād, iha ye ye prativibhakta-vyutpatti-nimittakās te te bhinnârthāḥ, yathêndra-ghaṭa-puruṣa-śabdā vibhinnârthā[ḥ].*—'Speech elements that are synonyms have different objects (denotata), because they have the factor [accountable] for their grammatical formation individually (*sc.* in every individual case) distinct. In this world, whatever [speech elements] have the factor [accountable] for their grammatical formation individually distinct, they have [also] different objects (denotata), [for instance such] speech elements like "Indra", "pot", "man" have different meanings.'

[62] SSi 1.33 § 247, p. 103.4: *gaur ity ayaṁ śabdo vāg-ādiṣv artheṣu vartamānaḥ paśāv abhirūḍhaḥ.*—'The term "*go*" applicable to (lit. present in) [various] things such as speech [derived from the root √*gai*] is conventionally applied to an animal.'

[63] SSi 1.33 § 247, p. 103.4–6: *athavā artha-gaty-arthaḥ śabda-prayogaḥ. tatrâikasyârthasyâikena gatârthatvāt paryāya-śabda-prayogo 'narthakaḥ. śabda-bhedaś ced asti artha-bhedenâpy avaśyaṁ bhavitavyam iti.*—'Or else, the use of words aims at (*sc.* leads to) the understanding of the meaning. Since one meaning has its meaning understood through [only] one word, the use of synonymous words is meaningless. If there is difference in words, there must also be necessarily the difference in meaning.'

[64] SSi 1.33 § 247, p. 103.77–8: *athavā yo yatrâbhirūḍhaḥ sa tatra sametv abhimukhyenârohaṇāt samabhirūḍhaḥ.*

[65] Cf. the exposition in the same spirit in TBV 1.3 (*Naya-mīmāṁsā*), p. 313.15–21: *eka-saṁjñā-samabhirohaṇāt samabhirūḍhas tv āha—yathā hi viruddha-liṅgâdi-yogād bhidyate vastu tathā saṁjñā-bhedād api. tathā hi—saṁjñā-bhedaḥ prayojana-vaśāt*

The factual viewpoint (*evaṁ-bhūta, itthaṁ-bhāva*) functions with reference to the narrowest possible context in case of any expression. It lies down the rule according to which, out of a series of synonyms, we select such a term in a given context which describes its denotatum in the p r e s e n t state in the closest possible way, for instance, the appellations 'Indra', 'Śakra' and 'Purandara' can be applied to the god only when he either is actually displaying his sovereign authority (*indana*), or is exhibiting his might (*śakana*) or is destroying a stronghold, respectively.[66] In other words, according to this viewpoint we may apply only such a term with regard to a phenomenon which describes this phenomenon in its present condition most adequately or the etymology or grammatical derivation of which corresponds most closely to the present state of an object it refers to: 'the factual [viewpoint] means the grasping of the meaning mutually dependent on subtle momentary manifestation [of an object] and the meaning [of the word denoting it, but] only [in case] of these [present objects grasped by the etymological viewpoint]'[67].

---

saṅketa-kartṛbhir vidhīyate na vyasanitayā anyathā anavasthā-prasakteḥ tato yāvanto vastunaḥ svâbhidhāyakāḥ śabdās tāvanto 'rtha-bhedāḥ pratyarthaṁ śabda-niveśāt nâikasyârthasyânekenâbhidhānaṁ yuktim iti 'ghaṭaḥ' 'kuṭaḥ' 'kumbhaḥ' iti vacana-bhedād bhinna evârthaḥ, kriyā-śabdatvāt vā sarva-śabdānāṁ sarve 'py anvarthā eva vācakāḥ tato 'ghaṭate' 'kuṭite' 'kau bhāti' iti ca kriyā-lakṣaṇa-nimitta-bhedāt naimittikenâpy arthena bhinnena bhāvyam iti 'ghaṭaḥ' ity ukte kutaḥ 'kuṭaḥ' iti pratipattiḥ tena tad-arthasyânabhihitatvāt.

[66] Cf. SSi 1.33 and NAV 29. Similarly, the word '*go*' (as the derivative of √*gam*) may be used—in consonance with the factual viewpoint—with reference to a cow only when the animal is actually walking.

[67] TS 1.35 p. 34.6–7: *teṣām eva* [=*sāmpratānām arthānām*] *vyañjanârthayor anyonyâpekṣârtha-grāhitvam evaṁ-bhūta iti.* In the same spirit TS 1.35 p. 32.18: *vyañjanârthayor evaṁ-bhūta iti.*—'The factual viewpoint [refers] to the momentary manifestation [of an object] and to the meaning [of the word denoting it];' and NAV 29.13 (p. 442): *ye tu vartamāna-kāla-bhāvi-vyutpatti-nimittam adhikṛtya śabdāḥ pravartante nânyathêti manyante tat-saṅgha-ghaṭitaḥ khalv evaṁ-bhūta iti.*—'The factual [viewpoint], however, as one should realise, is combined out of a conglomeration of [outlooks that] maintain that speech elements function by taking account of the factor [accountable] for the grammatical formation [and] existing in the present point of time, not otherwise;' as well as NAV 29.27 (p. 471): *...kvacit tat-kāla-varti-vyutpatti-nimittâpekṣayêti.*—'...[they are used to denote] certain [other objects (denotata)] depending on the factors [accountable for their] grammatical formation that occur at their [point of] time (*sc.* when the speech elements are uttered).'

These seven conditionally valid viewpoints are boldly maintained by Siddharṣigaṇi to exhaust all possibilities of the predicating of an object and to make use of all conceivable optional perspectives an object could be viewed from: 'Thus, it has been established in the above manner that these [seven viewpoints listed above] collect together all [possible] outlooks, because there is not any other alternative referring to the real thing that does not count among this septuplet of the viewpoints.'[68] It is emphasised by the Jainas that contradictions involved in this theory are only apparent,[69] in so far as each of the utterances has a different point of reference. What is significant is that not some abstract, eternal sentences are dealt with in the method of conditionally valid predications, but particular concrete utterances pronounced in a particular situation.

Even though only the seven-staged method of description is as a rule mentioned, the Jainas admitted a theoretical possibility of infinite number of thinkable viewpoints. Some instances, which are usually not mentioned in secondary literature, are to be found, e.g., in the *Tattvârthâdhigama-bhāṣya* itself. While discussing the nature of liberated beings (*siddha*), Umāsvāti avails himself of two viewpoints, which he contrasts with each other, viz. the one revealing the previous existence (*pūrva-bhāva-prajñāpanīya-naya*), during which the particular liberated being destroyed the bondage of transmigration, and the other one revealing the present existence (*pratyutpanna-bhāva-prajñāpanīya-naya*), viz. the condition of being emancipated[70]. Here two different perspectives are assumed with respect to time, and one could easily add another viewpoint predicating a property or a condition of a being in next existence (**uttara-bhāva-prajñāpanīya-naya*). Naturally, Umāsvāti does not do that with regard to liberated beings, for the liberated being is beyond any contingencies and dependencies, also temporal, and any discussion of the future existence in this particular case does not apply. However, in the commentary on the same *sūtra* the author does speak about other properties of a liberated being, taking the viewpoint of 'the existence directly

---

[68] NAV 29.13 (p. 441): *tad evaṁ na kaścid vikalpo 'sti vastu-gocaro yo 'tra naya-saptake nântar-yātîti sarvâbhiprāya-saṅgrāhakā ete iti sthitam.*

[69] TS 1.35 p. 38.3–4, verse 5:

iti naya-vādāś citrāḥ kvacid viruddhā ivâtha ca viśuddhāḥ /
laukika-viṣayâtītās tattva-jñānârtham adhigamyāḥ // —

—'Such are the variegated expositions [by means] of conditionally valid predications, that seem contradictory with regard to something (*sc.* one thing), nevertheless they are subtle, transcend the province of common people [and] should be understood in order to know the truth.'

[70] TBh 10.7.

preceding the moment of liberation' (*anantara-paścāt-kṛta-gatika-naya*) and the viewpoint of 'the last but one rebirth before the liberation' (*ekântara-paścāt-kṛta-gatika-naya*). Other instances are to be found in the *Āgamas*.

What is conspicuous in this method of description by way of applying seven conditionally valid predications is the gradual limitation of the context: from the most general one, viz. the comprehensive viewpoint (*naigama*), down to the most specialised, context-restricted factual and qualified viewpoint (*evaṁ-bhūta*) of narrowest extension. At the same time the informative contents gradually and cumulatively increases from the most undistinguished and 'contextless' *naigama* viewpoint to the most circumstantial and semantics-laden *evaṁ-bhūta* viewpoint with most complex point of reference. Thus every subsequent viewpoint is directly related to the one preceding it and it represents a further restriction of the point of reference. This hierarchical arrangement is apparent from the expressions used by various authors that explicitly indicate that the extension of successive viewpoints is included in that of their antecedents.[71] This twofold subordinating relation is stated by Akalaṅka: 'There is [such] an arrangement of these [viewpoints] because each and every subsequent [viewpoint] has more and more refined scope and is grounded in every preceding [viewpoint].'[72] The same idea, viz. that every subsequent viewpoint is hierarchically related to the preceding one, is expressed by many other Jaina authors including Malliṣeṇa[73] and Yaśovijaya[74].

These findings are crucial for any further analysis of the logical structure of the doctrine of viewpoints (*naya-vāda*). They also help us to evaluate such misconstrued conjectures that rest on the alleged presence of contradiction embedded in the *naya*-structure or claims, such as that of PANDEY's (1984), that all *naya*s can bee assigned the third truth-value I (indeterminate) of Łukasiewicz's three-valued system S3.

In[75] view of the multiplex character of all phenomena and due to limitations of verbal means of expression at our disposal, it is a practical impossibility to express

---

[71] E.g. in TBh 1.35 (*teṣv eva, teṣv eva satsu, teṣv eva sāmprateṣu, teṣām eva teṣām eva sāmpratānām*, etc.) or RVār 1.33 (p. 95 ff.): 1. (*naigama* as most general): *artha-saṁkalpa-mātra*, 3. (*vyavahāra* as included in *saṅgraha*): *atas* = *etasmāt, saṅgraha-gṛhīta-bhedakaḥ*, etc.

[72] RVār 1.33 (p. 99.17): *uttarôttara-sūkṣma-viṣayatvād eṣāṁ kramaḥ pūrva-pūrva-hetukatvāc ca*.

[73] SVM 28.204–213 (p. 167.9–18).

[74] JTBh 2 § 9, p. 14.1 ff.

[75] For the sake of completeness, on the subsequent pages I shall very briefly recapitulate the findings of a detailed logical analysis in BALCEROWICZ (2001b).

the homogeneous 'whole truth' about an object. Even though we may be aware of many other features and circumstances thanks to cognitive criteria (*pramāṇa*), we refer to any object or situation by way of an arbitrarily selected set of features which distinguish it from all other objects or phenomena in a particular situation in compliance with our practical demands.[76] How such various modes of reference operate is precisely what the *naya*-theory attempts to formalise. The general, *pramāṇa*-based knowledge of an object is thus a prerequisite for any *naya*-based reference to the same object.[77]

Since every statement is uttered in a particular situation, its does communicate truth as long as we keep in mind its particular context. In other words the relation between a statement and its referent is not a one-to-one relation of the sort 'utterance to truth-value', e.g. 'the relation characterised by the association of the denotatum and the denoter' (*vācya-vācaka-bhāva-lakṣaṇa-sambandha*). As a matter of fact, we are forced to use incomplete statements that are correctly understood by others, provided we are able to apply them to their particular context. Since the process of interpretation is not a simple binary function (utterance → truth-value), a simple statement 'Devadatta is' can trivially be either true or false depending on the context.[78] Siddharṣigaṇi explicitly states that to determine the truth-value of an utterance we have to take into account at least the intention of the speaker and the linguistic convention,[79] beside the denoter-denotatum relation. Thus, the simple relation 'utterance–truth-value' is intermediated by a range of additional parameters. Altogether the Jainas distinguish seven major parameters, or interpretative factors, comprised within the consistent scheme of the *naya*s (see p. 58 and n. 68). For the sake of simplicity, we can subsume all such parameters, or context-indicators, under an index as follows:

---

[76] NAV 29.10 (p. 438): *tasya viṣayo gocaro mato 'bhipreta eka-deśenânityatvâdi-dharma-lakṣaṇena viśiṣṭaḥ para-rūpebhyo vibhinno 'rthaḥ prameya-rūpaṁ.*

[77] NAV 29.10 (p. 438): *pramāṇa-pravṛtter uttara-kāla-bhāvī parāmarśa[ḥ]*.—'[Viewpoint is] the reflection which arises in the point of time posterior to the operation of cognitive criterion.'

[78] NAV 29.28 (p. 472): *yathâneka-puruṣa-sampūrṇe sadasi dvārâdau sthitasya kim atra devadattaḥ samasti nâstîti vā dolāyamāna-buddheḥ kenacid abhidhīyate—yathā devadatto 'stîti.*

[79] NAV 29.28 (p. 473): ... *tad-vyavacchedâbhiprāyeṇa prastuta-vākya-prayogāt, prayoktṛ-abhiprāyâdi-sāpekṣatayâiva dhvaneḥ svârtha-pratipādana-sāmarthyāt*, and NAṬ 29 *ad loc.*: ***prayoktṛ-abhiprāyâdîti****. ādi-śabdāt saṅketâd-grahaḥ.*

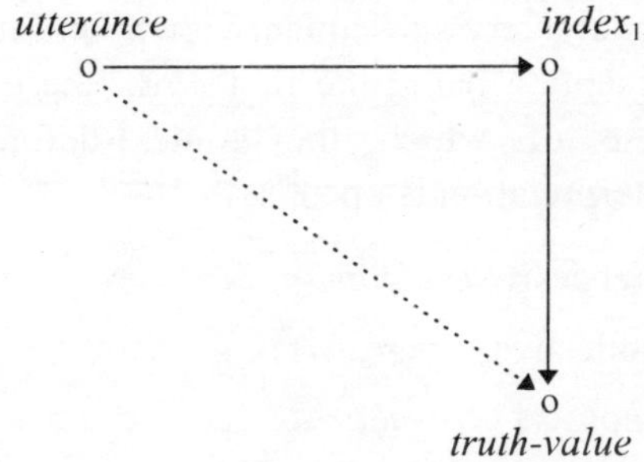

No utterance is simply either true or false. In order to ascertain its truth-value one has to ascribe it to its specific viewpoint type, that supplies the contextual information which is lacking. In this model all meaningful context-indicators (intermediary parameters) are comprised under the index *i*. The utterance yields truth or falsehood depending on the adequate interpretation of its context which is determined by means of indexation.

Accordingly, we have the following model of the context-based interpretation $\mathcal{I}$ of the utterances α, β, γ... that belong to a class $\mathcal{F}$ of formulas:

$$\mathcal{I} = < D, I, \mathbf{A} >$$

In the model, *D* is the domain of admissible interpretations, i.e. a class of conceivable individuals denotable by the utterances α, β, γ ... ; *I* is a class of indices *i*, or context-indicators; **A** comprises *i*-indexed classes of actual denotata.

The truth-value of any *i*-interpreted utterance α depends on the a c t u a l context represented by indices, or *naya*s, of the class *I* in the interpretation $\mathcal{I}$, and the paradigm index comprises the following co-ordinates:

$$i = < c, a, t, l, e, s >$$

In the formula, the variable *c* designates the subsets of meanings belonging to the general class $C \in D$ of all possible denotata of utterances α, β, γ... The variable *a* is an element of the class *C* (viz. a particular individual of the class *C*). The variable *t* is the point of time of reference (usually the present moment of 'now', which is steadily changing along the time axis). The variable *l* is the prevalent linguistic convention in accordance with which utterances α, β, γ... are pronounced and understood. The variable *e* indicates etymology and other verbal means of expression, such as prevalent convention, relevant for the proper understanding both of apparent synonyms α, β, γ... and of the difference between them based on etymology etc. The variable *s* stands for the present status of the individual that is the denotatum of α, β, γ...; in other words, *s* refers to present condition in which the referent a c t u a l l y manifests the quality by which it is being referred to by α, β, γ...

In this hierarchical model every subsequent viewpoint introduces a new indexical co-ordinate; the only exception being the first *naya*, the comprehensive viewpoint (*naigama*), in the case of which the context-defining parameters remain indeterminate and the interpretation is open[80]:

1. the comprehensive (*naigama*) : $i = < \ >$
2. the collective (*saṅgraha*) : $i = < c >$
3. the empirical (*vyavahāra*) : $i = < c, a >$
4. the direct (*ṛju-sūtra*) : $i = < c, a, t >$
5. the verbal (*śabda*) : $i = < c, a, t, l >$
6. the etymological (*samabhirūḍha*) : $i = < c, a, t, l, e >$
7. the factual (*evaṁ-bhūta*) : $i = < c, a, t, l, e, s >$

Thus, the truth-value of the utterance α is not simply $||\alpha|| = 1$ for truth or $||\alpha|| = 0$ for falsity, but rather $||\alpha||_i^{\mathcal{I}} = 1$ or $||\alpha||_i^{\mathcal{I}} = 0$, in so far as the utterance α is by necessity always understood according to the interpretation $\mathcal{I}$ at a particular point of reference *i*. Accordingly, the domain *D* of possible interpretations of the utterances $\alpha, \beta, \gamma \in \mathcal{F}$ is mapped onto the class **A** of actual denotata *via* the context delimited by $i \in I$.

That is why one may consistently express both 'Devadatta is' and 'Devadatta is not,' or 'hedgehog is' and 'hedgehog is not' in one breath without involving any contradiction. What one actually expresses is not $\alpha \wedge \neg\alpha$, but rather, for instance, $\alpha_{i1}^{\mathcal{I}} \wedge \neg\alpha_{i4}^{\mathcal{I}}$ ('There are hedgehogs in the world, but there is no hedgehog here and now'), or $\alpha_{i3}^{\mathcal{I}} \wedge \neg\alpha_{i7}^{\mathcal{I}}$ ('I have a pet hedgehog but it is *not* a hog that is presently in the hedge'), etc.

Thus, at least as far as the theory of the *naya*s is concerned, the claim of multi-faceted reality (*anekânta*) not only does not involve any contradiction but it also does not necessitate any admission of multi-valued logic and can be understood with the classical interpretation of the law of non-contradiction or the law of the excluded middle.

[80] This 'contextlessness' (the empty contents of $i = < \ >$) of the *naigama-naya* may be the reason why Siddhasena Divākara in his STP does not include the comprehensive viewpoint (*naigama*) in his classification of the *naya*s at all.

BIBLIOGRAPHY

AN = *Aṅguttara-nikāya*. 5 Vols., ed. R. Morris & E. Hardy, Pāli Text Society, London 1885–1900.

AṇD = *Nandi-suttaṁ* and *Aṇuoga-ddārāiṁ* (*Nandi-sūtra* and *Anuyoga-dvārāṇi*). Ed. Muni Puṇyavijaya, Dalsukh Mālvaṇiā, Amritlāl Mohanlāl Bhojak. *Jaina-Āgama-Series* No. 1, Shri Mahāvīra Jaina Vidyālaya, Bombay 1968.

AYVD = Hemacandra: *Anya-yoga-vyavaccheda-dvātriṁśikā*. See: SVM.

BALCEROWICZ (forthcoming) = Balcerowicz, Piotr: 'On the Relationship of the *Nyāyâvatāra* and the *Saṁmati-tarka-prakaraṇa*,' a paper delived at the *XIth World Sanskrit Conference*, Turin, April 3rd - 8th, 2000. to be published in: *Indologica Taurinensia*, Turin 2002.

BALCEROWICZ 1994 = Balcerowicz, Piotr: 'Zarys dżinijskiej teorii poznania' (The Outline of Jaina Epistemology), *Studia Indologiczne* 1 (1994) 12–67. [Warsaw].

BALCEROWICZ 2000 = Balcerowicz, Piotr: 'On the Date of the *Nyāyâvatāra*,' in: *On the Understanding of Other Cultures. Proceedings of the International Conference on Sanskrit and Related Studies to Commemorate the Centenary of the Birth of Stanislaw Schayer (1899–1941). Warsaw University, Poland, October 7–10, 1999*. Ed. by Piotr Balcerowicz and Marek Mejor. *Studia Indologiczne* 7 (2000) 17–57. [Warsaw].

BALCEROWICZ 2001a = Balcerowicz, Piotr: *Jaina Epistemology in Historical and Comparative Perspective. Critical Edition and English Translation of Logical-Epistemological Treatises: Nyāyâvatāra, Nyāyâvatāra-vivṛti and Nyāyâvatāra-ṭippana with Introduction and Notes*. 1–2 Vols., Alt- und Neu-Indische Studien 53,1–2, Franz Steiner Verlag, Stuttgart 2001.

BALCEROWICZ 2001b = Balcerowicz, Piotr: 'The logical structure of the *naya* method of the Jainas,' *Journal of Indian Philosophy* 29/3 (2001) 379–403.

BALCEROWICZ 2001c = Balcerowicz, Piotr: 'Two Siddhasenas and the Authorship of the *Nyāyâvatāra* and the *Saṁmati-tarka-prakaraṇa*'. *Journal of Indian Philosophy* 29/3 (2001) 351–578.

BHARUCHA–KAMAT 1984 = Bharucha, F. and Kamat, R.V.: '*Syādvāda* theory of Jainism in terms of devial logic', *Indian Philosophical Quarterly* 9 (1984) 181–187.

GANERI 2002 = Ganeri, Jonardon: 'Jaina Logic. A 7-Valued Paraconsistent System', *History and Philosophy of Logic*, typescript, forthcoming.

GOKHALE 1991 = Gokhale, Pradeep P.: 'The logical Structure of *Syādvāda*', *Journal of Indian Council of Philosophical Research* 8 (1991) 73–81. [Reprinted: SHAH (2000: 75–86)].

JACOB 1907–1911 = Jacob, [Colonel] G.A.: *A Handful of Popular Maxims Current in Sanskrit Literature* (*Laukika-nyāya-mañjaliḥ*). Vol. 1–3, Tukārām Jāvajī's Nirnaya-Sagara Press, Bombay 1907–1909–1911. [Reprinted: Chaukhamba Sanskrit Pratishstan, Delhi 1995].

JAINI 1920 = Jaini, J.L.: *Tattvārthādhigama-sūtra (A Treatise on the Essential Principles of Jainism). Sacred Books of the Jainas* 2, Arrah 1920.

Jātaka = *The Jātaka together with its commentary being Tales of the anterior births of Gotama Buddha.* For the first time edited in the original Pāli by V. Fausbøll, Vols. 1–6. London 1877–96. [Reprinted: Luzac and Company, London 1963].

JSK = *Jainendra Siddhānta Kośa.* ed. by Jinendra Varṇī, Parts 1–5, *Jñānapīṭha Mūrtidevī Jaina Granthamālā, Saṁskṛta Granthâṅka* 38, 40, 42, 44, 48, Bharatiya Jnanapith, Delhi 1997, 1999, 2000.

JTBh = Yaśovijaya: *Jaina-tarka-bhāṣā.* (1) Dayanand Bhargava (ed., tr.): *Mahopādhyāya Yaśovijaya's Jaina Tarka Bhāṣā With Translation and Critical Notes.* Motilal Banarsidass, Delhi–Varanasi–Patna 1973. (2) *Mahôpādhyāya-Śrī-Yaśovijayagaṇi-racitā Jaina-tarka-bhāṣā.* Ed. by Sukhlāljī Saṅghavī, Mahendra Kumār and Dalsukh Mālvaṇiyā, Sarasvatī Pustak Bhaṇḍār, Ahmedabad 1993. [first edition: 1938].

LT = Akalaṅka: *Laghīyas-traya.* In: *Nyāya-kumuda-candra of Śrīmat Prabhācandrācārya. A Commentary on Bhaṭṭākalaṅkadeva's Laghīyastraya.* Ed. by Mahendra Kumār Nyāya Śāstri, Vol. 1–2, *Sri Garib Dass Oriental Series* 121, Sri Satguru Publications, Delhi 1991. [1st ed. Bombay 1938–1942].

LTV = Akalaṅka: *Laghīyas-traya-vivṛtti.* See: LT.

MATILAL 1991 = Matilal, Bimal Krishna: '*Anekānta*: both yes and no?', *Journal of Indian Council of Philosophical Research* 8 (1991) 1–12. [Reprinted: J. Nagin SHAH (2000)].

MBhā = Patañjali: *Vyākaraṇa-mahā-bhāṣya. Śrīman-maharṣi-Patañjali-nirmitam Vyākaraṇa-mahā-bhāṣyam, śrīmad-upādhyāya-Kaiyaṭa-praṇīena Bhāṣya-pradīpena śrīman-Nageśabhaṭṭa-viracita-Bhāṣyapradīpôddyotôdbhāsitena Samullasitena.* Ed. Bhārgava Śāstri Bhikājī Jośi, Śivadatta Śarman, Raghunāth Kāśīnāth Śāstri, 6 Vols., Chaukhamba Sanskrit Pratishthan, Delhi 2000 [reprinted].

MMK = *Madhyamakavṛttiḥ Mūlamadhyamaka-kārikās de Nāgarjuna avec la Prasannapadā Commentaire de Candrakīrti.* Ed. Louis de la Vallée Poussin, *Bibliotheca Buddhica* 4, Pétersbourg 1913. [Reprinted: Osnabrück 1970].

MSA = Asaṅga (Maitreyanātha?): *Mahāyāna-sūtrâlaṅkāra.* (1) *Mahāyāna-sūtrâlaṅkāra of Asaṅga.* Ed. by S. Bagchi, *Buddhist Sanskrit Texts* 13, Mithila Institute of Post-Graduate Studies and Research in Sanskrit Learning, Darbhanga 1970. (2) *Mahāyānasūtrālaṅkāra.* Ed. and transl. Surekha Vijay Limaye, *Bibliotheca Indo-Buddhica Series* 94, Sri Satguru Publications / Indian Books Centre, Delhi 1992.

MŚV = Kumārila Bhaṭṭa: *Mīmāṁsā-śloka-vārttika. Ślokavārttika of Śrī Kumārila Bhaṭṭa with the Commentary Nyāya-ratnâkara of Śrī Pārthasārathi Miśra.* Ed. Dvārikādāsa Śāstrī, *Ratnabharati Series* 3, Tārā Publications, Varanasi 1978.

NA = Siddhasena Mahāmati: *Nyāyâvatāra*. See: BALCEROWICZ (2001/a).

NAṬ = Devabhadra: *Nyāyâvatāra-ṭippana*. (1) *Mahāvādi-śrī-Siddhasena-Divākara-praṇīta-Nyāyâvatāraḥ śrī-Rājaśekharasūri-viracita-Ṭippana-samalaṅkṛta-ācārya-Siddharṣi-viracita-Vivṛti-sahitaḥ*. Ed. by Bhagavāndās Harṣacandra (Harakhchand), Hemācāndrâcārya-Jaina-sabhā, Ahmedabad–Patan 1917. (2) *Nyāyāvatāra of Siddhasena-Divākara with The Vivṛti of Siddharṣigaṇi and with The Ṭippana of Devabhadra*. Ed. by P. L. Vaidya, Shri Jain Shwetamber Conference, Bombay 1928. [Reprinted: *Vaishali Institute Research Bulletin* 1 (1971) 1–95].

NAV = Siddharṣigaṇi: *Nyāyâvatāra-vivṛti*. See: BALCEROWICZ (2001a).

ṆC = Māilla-dhavala-[deva]: *Ṇaya-cakko* [*Dravya-svabhāva-prakāśaka-naya-cakra*]. *Ṇayacakko* [*Nayacakra*] *of Śrī Māilla-dhavala*. Ed. and transl. by Kailash Chandra Shastri, *Mūrtidevī Jaina Granthamālā* 12, Bharatiya Jnanapith, Delhi 1999. [1st ed.: 1971].

PALV = *Parīkṣāmukha-sūtram (A Digambara Jaina Work on Logic (Nyāya)) by Māṇikya Nandi Together with the Commentary Called Parīkṣāmukha-laghu-vṛttiḥ by Ananta Vīrya*. Ed. by Satis Chandra Vidyābhūṣaṇa, *Bibliotheca Indica* 1209, Calcutta 1909.

PANDEY 1984 = Pandey, S.L.: 'Naya-vāda and Many-valued logic', in: M.P. Marathe, Meena Kelkar and P.P. Gokhale: *Studies in Jainism*, Indian Philosophical Quarterly Publication, Pune 1984: 156–166.

PSā = Kundakunda: *Pavayaṇa-sāra* [*Pravacana-sāra*]. A.N. Upadhye (ed.): *Śrī Kundakundācārya's Pravacanasāra (Pavayaṇasāra), a Pro-Canonical Text of the Jainas, the Prakrit Text critically edited with the Sanskrit Commentaries of Amṛtacandra and Jayasena*. Parama-Śruta-Prabhāvaka Mandal, Shrimad Rajachandra Ashrama, Agās–Gujarat 1984. [First edition: Bombay 1935].

RVār = *Tattvārtha-vārttika* (*Rāja-vārttika*) *of Śrī Akalaṅkadeva*. Edited with Hindi Translation, Introduction, appendices, variant readings, comparative notes etc. by Prof. Mahendra Kumar Jain. Parts I–II. First edition, *Jñānapīṭha Mūrtidevī Jaina Granthamālā: Sanskrit Grantha* No. 10, 20, Bhāratīya Jñānapīṭha, Delhi 1953–1957. [Second edition: Delhi 1982].

SCHUBRING 1978 = Schubring, Walter: *The Doctrine of the Jainas*, Motilal Banarsidass, Delhi, 1978.

SBhT = Vimaladāsa: *Sapta-bhaṅgī-taraṅgiṇī*. Ed. Manoharlāl, Paramaśruta Prabhāvaka Maṇḍala, Śrīmad Rājacandra Āśrama, Agās 1995. [1st edition: 1913].

SHAH 2000 = Shah, J. Nagin (ed.): *Jaina Theory of Multiple Facets of Reality and Truth*, Bhogilal Leherchand Institute of Indology, Delhi 2000.

SSā = Kundakunda: *Samaya-sāra*. (1) *Parama-pūjya-śrīmat-Kunda-kundâcārya-devena praṇīta*[*ḥ*] *Samaya-sāra*[*ḥ*], *parama-pūjya-śrīmad-Amṛtacandrasūri-viracita-saṁskṛta-ṭīkā Ātma-khyāti*, *Sapta-*

daśāṅgī-ṭīkā. Ed. Manohar Varṇī Sahajānand, Mantrī Sahajānand Śāstramāla, Raṇajītapurī Sadar Meraṭh 1977. (2) *Śrīmad-bhagavat-Kundakundâcārya-viracitaḥ Samaya-sāraḥ Ātma-khyāti-Tātpārya-vṛtti-Ātma-khyāti-bhāṣā-vacanikā iti Ṭīkā-trayôpetaḥ*. Ed. Pannālāl Jain, Śrī Paramaśruta Prabhāvaka Maṇḍala, Śrīmad Rājacandra Āśrama, Agās 1997. (3) *Āchārya Kundakunda's Samayasāra*, with English translation and commentary based upon Amṛtacandra's *Ātmakhyāti* by A. Chakravarti, Bharatiya Jnanpith, New Delhi 1989.

SSi = Pūjyapāda Devanandin: *Sarvârtha-siddhi*. *Ācārya Pūjyapāda's Sarvârthasiddhi [The commentary on Ācārya Griddhapiccha's Tattvârtha-sūtra]*. Edited and translated [into Hindi] by Phoolchandra Shastri. Varanasi 1934. [Reprinted: tenth ed., Bhāratīya Jñānapīṭha, New Delhi 2000].

STP = Siddhasena Divākara: *Saṁmati-tarka-prakaraṇa* with Abhayadevasūri's *Tattva-bodha-vidhāyinī*. Ed. by Sukhlāl Saṅghavi and Becardās Dośi; Vol. I & II, RBTS VI–1,2; Kyoto 1984. [Reprinted from the original edition published in 5 vols., *Gujarāt-purā-tattva-mandir-granthāvalī* 10, 16, 18, 19, 21, Gujarāt-purā-tattva-mandir, Amdāvād, 1924–1931].

SVM = *Syād-vāda-mañjarī* of Malliṣeṇa with the *Anya-yoga-vyavaccheda-dvātriṁśikā* of Hemacandra. Ed. by A. B. Dhruva, Bombay Sanskrit and Prakrit Series No. 83, Bombay 1933.

ŚBh = Śabarasvāmin: *Mīmāṁsā-śābara-bhāṣya*. Ed. by Yudhiṣṭhira Mīmāṁsaka. Vols. 1–6, Śrī Śāntisvarūp Kapūr, Rāmalāl Kapūr Trust Press, Bahālgaḍh Sonīpat – Haryāṇā I: 1987, II: 1990, III: 1980, IV: 1985, V: 1986, VI: 1990.

ŚDī = Pārthasārathi: *Śāstra-dīpikā*. *Tarka-pāda Section edited with Ramakṛṣṇa's Yukti-sneha-prapūraṇī*. Ed. by L. S. Dravid, Chowkhamba Sanskrit Series 43, Benares 1916.

TBh = Umāsvāti: *Tattvârthâdhigama-bhāṣya*. See: TS.

TBV = Abhayadevasūri: *Tattva-bodha-vidhāyinī*. See STP.

Ṭhāṇ = *Ṭhāṇaṁga-suttaṁ* and *Samavāyaṁga-suttaṁ* (*Sthānâṅga-sūtra* and *Samavāyâṅga-sūtra*). Ed. Muni Jambūvijaya, *Jaina-Āgama-Series* 3, Shri Mahāvīra Jaina Vidyālaya, Bombay 1985.

TS = *Tattvârtha-sūtra* of Umāsvāmin, ed. together with *Tattvârthâdhigama-bhāṣya* by M.K. Mody, the Asiatic Society, *Bibliotheca Indica* No. 1044, Calcutta 1903–5.

Udāna = *Udāna*. ed. P. Steinthal, Pāli Text Society, London 1885.

UtT = Maitreya: *Uttara-tantra* (*Ratna-gotra-vibhāga*). *The Uttaratantra of Maitreya containing Introduction, E.H. Johnston's Sanskrit Text and E. Obermiller's English Translation*, ed. by H.S. Prasad, *Bibliotheca Indo-Buddhica* 79, Sri Satguru Publications, Delhi 1991.

Uttar = *Uttarajjhayaṇasutta* (*Uttarâdhyayana-sūtra*). Ed. Charpentier, *Archives d'Etudes Orientales* Vol. 18:1,2. Upsala 1921.

How Many Times? Monism and Pluralism in Early Jaina Temporal Description

CHRISTOPH EMMRICH

– 1 –

By temporal description I refer not only to the way in which in this case early Jaina texts deal with the phenomenon of time, both as a philosophical and soteriological problem, but also to the way in which they describe temporal phenomena in general. Additionally, description may refer to the methodological question of how to speak about time in Jaina texts, on what to focus on, what to exclude and why.

By posing the question that concerns 'the number of times' in early Jainism I want to ask the following: How did the relevant texts try to find a systematic approach in dealing with temporal questions either by isolating specific aspects of time according to various functions or by summarising its functions under general headings, and how, where and at what stage did they refrain from summarising and analysing?

If we take a short look at the current state of research in the field of the so-called 'time studies' in relation to Jainism, we come across a relatively short list of articles. This stands in contrast to the conspicuous bibliography on the same subject regarding e.g. Buddhist or Brahmanical temporal speculation.

At first glance, we see that the rather small number of Indological studies on this subject, regardless of how groundbreaking and important they have doubtlessly been in a certain sense, covers a very limited section of the question of how time is treated in Jaina texts; limited methodologically, chronologically and topically. Many studies which speak about 'time in Jainism' can be regarded as general introductions to some basic tenets and features of some Jaina positions concerning *kāla*, often contrasted to similarly general positions of competing *darśana*s.[1] They focus almost exclusively on the commentaries, or generally later works, and as the earliest limit

[1] PADMARAJIAH (1946), PRASAD (1982: 48–62), BALSLEV (1983: 73–79), BHARUCHA (1984), BHATTACHARYA (1992), but also, though to a lesser extent, classics like SCHRADER (1902: 17–30), von GLASENAPP (1964) and STCHERBATSKY (1926: 12–39).

Essays in Jaina Philosophy and Religion.
Warsaw Indological Studies, Volume 2 (2002), pp. 69–88.

on the standard dogmatic works by Umāsvāti and Kundakunda.[2] They cover roughly three topics, namely (1) the difference between *niścaya-* and *vyavahāra-kāla*, (2) the classification of *kāla* regarding *asti-kāya* and *dravya* and (3) the concept of *samaya*. So far, research concerning time has concentrated on a rather late phase, without considering earlier developments. There are, however, some significant contributions to this topic which do consider earlier and heterogeneous material and deal with questions of systematisation. Satkari MOOKERJEE[3] has done some important work as have FRAUWALLNER[4], SCHUBRING[5], METTE[6] and, comparatively recently, OHIRA[7], though, rather perfunctorily and from a broader perspective or raising simply different questions. Finally, one must not forget to recognise the great value of the *Jainendra Siddhānta Kośa* (JSK) in presenting an impressive list of passages concerning *kāla* in Jaina literature.

The question of how time, mainly under the leading term *kāla*, has been systematically analysed will lead us through all three topics, starting with the first of *niścaya-kāla*, *paramârtha-kāla* or *dravya-kāla*[8] in contrast to *vyavahāra-kāla*, opposition which confronts us with the puzzle of two times, or rather, time understood in two ways: one, *niścaya-kāla*, i.e. ascertained, determined, underlying, basic, elementary, and the other, *vyavahāra-kāla*, for common usage, derivative, secondary. Underlying this subtle differentiation is, of course, the concept of one time (*kāla*), or the intention of grappling with the variety of temporal abstractions or manifestations by subsuming them under one concept.[9] Looking into the difference of *niścaya* and *vyavahāra* also means looking at this particular expression '*kāla*' in search for alternative, possibly even earlier terms.

The central role attributed to this model of inquiry in modern Indological studies such as PRASAD (1982), BALSEV (1983), SHAH (1968) and SHAH (1978) or BHATTACHARYA (1992) goes back to and draws heavily from later works or

[2] Special credit for extensively considering the commentarial tradition and trying to define Śvetāmbara and Digambara positions on the matter goes to SHAH (1968) and SHAH (1977–78: 21–31).

[3] MOOKERJEE (1961).

[4] FRAUWALLNER (1953–1956: II: 256–257 and notes 326–327).

[5] SCHUBRING (1935).

[6] METTE (1973), METTE (1991).

[7] OHIRA (1994).

[8] In the Digambara tradition we additionally find the term *mukhya-kāla,* e.g. RVār 222, 482.

[9] This has even been done explicitly by commentators, who assume an underlying unity of its discrete constituents. See SHAH (1968: 28).

commentarial literature, especially to literature which documents the rich discussion of philosophical issues within the context of other systems. We find these concepts applied to time in terms of definition in SSi 5.7, in the commentary to *Gommaṭa-sāra-jīva-kaṇḍa* 569, in the *Tattvârtha-vārttika*,[10] in the commentary of Brahmadeva on *Dravya-saṅgraha* 21[11] and throughout Brahmadeva's commentaries as well as in Akalaṅka's, such as the *Tattvârtha-rāja-vārttika*.[12]

The method of inquiry proposed in this article is therefore to refrain from constructing a coherent 'theory of time' and, on the contrary, to try to identify at least heterogeneous contexts—if not diachronic layers—which document different strategies of explanation and varying degrees of integration of more or less coherent aspects of time into a dogmatic whole.

– 2 –

Let us first give a short look at the concepts themselves and how they appear in earlier literature: The concept of *vyavahāra* (Pkt. *vavahāra*) itself is, of course, early. We find it in mathematics as the application of a law[13] and in epistemology in relation to the third *naya* of the seven *mūla-naya*s, which denotes the empirical knowledge of the *guṇa*s of the present object.[14] The complete pair of *niścaya-naya* and *vyavahāra-naya*, which comes close to the one applied to *kāla*, is found already in the *Bhagavatī-sūtra* (*Viyāha-pannatti*): Viy 748a mentions *necchaiya-naya* and *vāvahāriya-naya* as the knowledge according to theory and practice. The example is given of a certain kind of bee which in theory has all five colours, two smells and so on, but in practice is black and has the smell of a certain flower. Definition is here understood as a method of exclusion[15] and shows how all 20 sensory properties can prevail in practical consideration. With Kundakunda we find this difference in *Pañcâstikāya-samaya-sāra* (PSSā), the work itself ending with the discussion of *niścaya-mārga* and *vyavahāra-mārga*.[16] But in all these cases, despite usage for

---

[10] RVār 477, 11: *sā ānumānikī vyavahārika-darśanāt*.

[11] *vartanā-lakṣaṇaś ca paramârtha-kālaḥ*, DS 569.

[12] *dvividhaḥ kālaḥ paramârtha-kālo vyavahāra-rūpaś cêti. tatra paramârtha-kāla [...] vartanāyā upakārakaḥ*, RVār 482.

[13] Ṭhāṇ 263a, 496a.

[14] AṇD 264 ff.; Ṭhāṇ 390.

[15] Cp. SCHUBRING (1935: 104) and, in this volume, BALCEROWICZ (37–68).

[16] PSSā 1667–168. Cp. also in this volume J. SONI (25–35).

epistemological questions, no allusion or application of this conceptual pair to the question of time is found.

– 2.1 –

Whereto now are they applied and do we find correspondences in the material of Umāsvāti and Kundakunda? Umāsvāti's discussion of *kāla* is a discussion concerning *dravya*. TS 5.22 has *vartanā pariṇāmaḥ kriyā paratvâparatve ca kālasya*, defining *kāla* as that which has the functions of 'setting in motion' (*vartanā*), change (*pariṇāma*), motion (*kriyā*) and 'the before-and-after' (*paratvâparatve*).[17] In reference to the *dravya*s we have the famous passage of TS 5.38: *kālaś cêty eke*, which is explained as 'also *kāla* is *dravya*,[18] some say.' Or in a different reading given in the Digambara *Sarvârtha-siddhi* 5.39: *kālaś ca*—'and *kāla*.' The Śvetāmbara commentary *Svopajña-bhāṣya-ṭīkā* (TSṬ) quotes Viy 109 with Mahāvīra counting six *dravya*s, including *kāla* as the sixth one, and referring to time as a mode of sentient and non-sentient beings, which undergoes change within one time unit. The time (*kāla*) as *dravya-kāla* is explained in the commentaries to be *niścaya-kāla*. To this TS 5.39 adds: *so 'nanta-samayaḥ*—'This [i.e. *kāla*] is [or consists of] endless *samaya*s.' This, too, is generally referred to by the commentaries as *niścaya-kāla*. In the light of the commentaries, its difference from *vyavahāra-kāla* is found only when we contrast this verse with another one from the same work, though from a quite different context. TS 4.15 (SSi 4.14) has *tat-r̥taḥ kāla-vibhāgaḥ*—'*kāla* is measured by the movement [of the vehicles of the luminous gods, *jyotiṣkā*], i.e. by sun, moon, stars and planets.' The *Svopajña-bhāṣya-ṭīkā* (TSṬ), in relating this same passage to the one before, adds directly that the smallest unit of time is called *samaya* and defines it as the time it takes for an atom to move from one space unit (*padesa*) to another, duration too small to be measured, the smallest time unit, one *āvaliā* (*āvalikā*) consisting of innumerable (*asaṁkhejja*) *samaya*s. The description in TS which refers to time measurement by astronomical means is called *vyavahāra* and is contrasted with that in time which lies beyond measurement, the *samaya*. Here we have a classical contraposition

---

[17] FRAUWALLNER (1953–1956: 335, n. 327) suggests to isolate *vartanā* as the original definition, regarding the subsequent expressions as later additions, a position which is supported by his interpretation oriented on Kundakunda. OHIRA (1994: 76) points to a similar direction concerning *paratvâparatve* and suggests an exposure to Vaiśeṣika influence in this regard.

[18] See the definition in TS 5.37.

which tries to answer the question: Is *kāla* measured by *samaya*s or by the movement of the stars? Is *kāla* discrete, momentary or extended, durational? The answer of the commentary to the implicit question is the *niścaya* /*vyavahāra* model: The *niścaya*-aspect of *kāla* consists in the incommensurability of *samaya*. The *vyavahāra*-aspect is the language of measuring.

We shall pursue the question of time divisions and duration further later on. Let us first look at the way Kundakunda deals with the definition of *kāla*.

– 2.2 –

Kundakunda is more explicit and systematic in his dealing with *kāla* and its relation to *samaya*. Especially in his PSa there is a sequence of verses dealing with this subject. Like Umāsvāti, he introduces *kāla* as having the quality of setting in motion (*vaṭṭaṇā*), see PSā 2.42a:

> *kālassa vaṭṭaṇā se guṇovaogo tti appaṇo bhaṇido* /
>
> —'The quality of *kāla* is setting in motion.'

Additionally, *kāla* is an entity which, being *dravya*, fills the world (*loka*), see PSā 2.44:

> *logâlogesu ṇabho dhammâdhammehi ādado logo* /
> *sese paḍucca kālo jīvā puṇa poggalā* //
>
> —'[The quality of] *ākāśa* [= *ṇabho*] applies to *loka* and *aloka*, *loka* is filled by *dharma* and *adharma*, by *kāla*, by *jīva* and by *pudgala*.'

Further (PSā 2.43b) he tries to categorise *kāla* in relation to the *asti-kāya*s:

> … *sapadesehiṁ asaṁkhā ṇatthi padesa tti kālassa* /
>
> —'… These [*jīvā poggala-kāyā dhammâdhammā puṇo ya āgāsaṁ*] have uncountable *pradeśa*s, but *kāla* does not have *pradeśa*.'

On this point Kundakunda's *Pañcāstikāya-samaya-sāra* in 23–26 concludes the *pīṭhikā* with a discussion on *kāla* being *dravya* but not *asti-kāya* and, as Amṛtacandra's commentary insists, from both the *niścaya* and the *vyavahāra* point of view, whereas these terms are absent in Kundakunda's text. The fact that *kāla* is a *dravya* is given a closer look in PSā 2.49, where the text continues:

> *ekko va dugo bahugā saṁkhātīdā tado aṇantā ya* /
> *davvāṇaṁ ca padesā santi hi samaya tti kālassa* //

—'All the substances have one, two, many, innumerable, infinite *pradeśas*, but *kāla* has *samaya*.'[19]

The text then positions *kāla* in relation to the atomistic model, which presupposes that 'a *paramâṇu* has no *pradeśa*, because it gives rise to a *pradeśa*' (PSā 2.45):

jadha te ṇabhappadesā tadhappadesā havanti sesāṇā /
apadeso paramâṇū tena padesubbhavo bhaṇido //

Thereon the text continues in relation to *kāla* (PSā 2.46):

samao du appadeso padesamettassa davvajādassa /
vadivadado so vaṭṭadi padesamāgāsadavvassa //

—'*samaya* is without *pradeśa*, it is equal to the duration of that unit of *dravya* which has the measure of one *pradeśa* to traverse one space point in *ākāśa*.'

In other words (PSā 2.47):

vadivadado taṁ desaṁ tassam samao / tado paro puvvo /
jo attho so kālo samao uppaṇṇa-paddhasī //

—'That much duration required for crossing from one to the other *deśa* is known as *samaya*, that being before or beyond is *kāla*, or *samaya*, undergoing origination and destruction.'[20]

As these texts show that, wherever the line of argument is rather straightforward, we can hardly detect any dichotomy of *niścaya* and *vyavahāra* or any imminent logical compulsion from within the text to introduce such a differentiation, Kundakunda's intention lying safely within the domain of what the commentators

---

[19] AṇD 134–135 already has this model, which performs the analysis of *kāla* by tying the concept of *pradeśa* to that of *samaya*: *se kiṁ taṁ kālappamāṇe?, duvihe paṇṇatte, taṁ jahā—paesa-nipphaṇṇe a vibhāga-nipphaṇṇe a // se kiṁ taṁ paesa-ṇipphaṇṇe? ega-samayaṭṭhiīe du-samayaṭṭhiīe ti-samayaṭṭhiīe jāva dasa-samayaṭṭhiīe asaṁkhijja-samayaṭṭhiīe, se taṁ paesa-nipphaṇṇe //*

[20] There is a similar passage in Viy 6.4, where it is said, that *jīva* (individual) and *jivā* (collective) are called *sapaesa kālâ[d]esaṇaṁ* (divisible from the viewpoint of *kāla*), because they pass through *paesas* of time, i.e. *samayas*. *jīvas*, of course, depending on to which class they belong, are either *sapaesa* or *apaesa*. Abhayadeva in his *Vṛtti* on Viy 6.4 notes that incarnate *jīvas* are only *apaesa* in the first *samaya* of their existence, whereas this distinction does not apply to *jīvas* as such which are without end or beginning.

would call *niścaya-kāla* and beyond the field of practical measurement.[21] Yet, e.g. *Rāja-vārttika* 222, referring thematically to Kundakunda, goes even further in elaborating the possibly underfocussed notion of measurement (*mātra*). Not only practical measurement by means of planetary movements, but also the theoretical measurement by movement or atoms is termed *vyavahāra*, reducing the semantic range of *niścaya-kāla* even further. The intention behind this move may be to categorically separate *kāla* from *kriyā* (motion) in order to extend the ontological range of the former to spheres of the world which are without motion and to subordinate motion (*kriyā*) to *kāla*, in short, to confer to *kāla* possibly the full status of *dravya*, which is in turn supposed to offer a common binding ground to the discrete and disconnected *samaya*s.

Kundakunda's objectives of systematisation seem slightly different. The problem with him seems to be the question how *kāla* can be related to the *dravya*s, i.e. to space and to the spatially described world. The solution seems to have been found in a spatialisation of time that was made possible through the atomistic model, i.e. by equalling points of space and matter with points of time and setting both in relation to each other. This is done by introducing motion, which however seems to be secondary. The primary force of this model is the spatial form given to the time unit (*samaya*) in analogy to *pradeśa*s and *paramâṇu*s.[22] In fact, the Digambara tradition will favour a more disintegrative time model, metaphorically describing *kāla* as consisting of jewels (*ratna*) lying next to each other and forming a heap, a

[21] As far as I can see, FRAUWALLNER (1953–56: 335, n. 326) has more than just strong motives to doubt, 'ob die Unterscheidung zwischen *vyavahārakāla* und *niścayakāla* schon auf Kundakunda zurückgeführte werden darf.' To identify first perceptible developments of this model one must look at the corresponding passages in GJK 568–591 where we find *vyavahāra-kāla* with just *kāla* as its counterpart and the later definitions clearly on their way, yet still no clear-cut terminological differentiation. See esp. GJK 589–590.

[22] For a more in-depth treatment of the passages concerning *kāla* in *Pavayaṇa-sāra* (PSā) and *Pañcâstikāya-samaya-sāra* (PSSā) see EMMRICH (2001). Further research, especially in the development of the *niścaya-* / *vyavahāra-kāla*, may be done on the passages GJK 538, 551–554, 568–582, 585, 588–590. They come very close to the above passages of PSSā. The usage of *vyavahāra-kāla* contrasted to *kāla*, still without attribute, e.g. GJK 572 and 580 (cp. PSSā 108), though *pajjāyāvaṭṭhāṇaṁ suddhaṇaye*, GJK 571, which conspicuously has *khaṇa-mettaṁ* instead of *samaya*, could be already regarded a proto-definition of *niścaya-kāla*, constituting a first important stage in the terminological development.

heterogeneous whole. The Śvetāmbaras instead favour the notion of a cohesive time behind the *samaya*s, paying the price of its temporal commensurability.[23]

The difference *niścaya-* / *vyavahāra-kāla* in Jainism seems to have evolved out of the necessity to adapt the atomistic model—which may have been developed and expanded in competition with other systems of thought—to earlier Jaina concepts and models of world description, already established and fixed in the *Āgama*s. Additionally, it was used by the commentators and apologetics to systematise and harmonise certain fields of argument like time analysis or durational description, which would not fit so tightly into the atomistic model when referring to the *Āgama*s or to the texts of Umāsvāti and Kundakunda, especially in the discussion with rival schools or systems.

At this point it would be interesting to broaden the perspective even further in order to investigate the possibility whether the evolution of the *niścaya-* / *vyavahāra-*difference concerning *kāla* may have gone hand-in-hand with, or even had preceded, the overarching development of *anekânta-vāda*. But this would lead our enquiry into a rather different direction. In this limited context let me just note that the *anekânta-vāda* background should remind us that the basic monism of *kāla* is retained throughout the dogmatic and commentarial texts and that the very distinction of *niścaya* and *vyavahāra* is intended to avoid any kind of theoretical divergence, not to speak of dualism.

We run into the question of systematising temporal concepts as soon as we move our attention towards *Āgamic* material, e.g. the *Bhagavatī-sūtra* (*Viyāha-pannatti*), where the establishment or a coherent atomistic doctrine is on its way, but where firstly we find descriptions which, as we said, may have prompted the *niścaya-* / *vyavahāra-kāla* distinction, and secondly, models to differentiate aspects of *kāla* which might have been predecessors of the later development leading to a monistic solution.

– 3 –

Viy 207b gives the names of spaces of time in reference to the structure of the world. It starts with stating that when it is day in the North and South, it is night in the East and West, that the duration of a day over a year is inversely proportional to a night as to the amount of *muhūrta*s, that the night starts lengthening as the day

[23] For the later discussion between Śvetāmbaras and Digambaras see SHAH (1968) and SHAH (1977–78: 20–31).

becomes shorter[24] until both last 15 *muhūrtas*. It mentions the three seasons and their subdivisions starting from a *samaya* and an *āvaliyā* (*āvalikā*), mentioning *uū* (*ṛtu*, season), *ayaṇa* (*ayana*, half year), *saṁvacchara* (*saṁvatsara*, year) and its multiples *jua* (*yuga*, here 5 years)[25] and *osappiṇī* (*avasarpiṇī*) and *ussappiṇī* (*utsarpiṇī*) respectively.[26] The largest unit[27] being the *sīsa-pahelia* (*śīrṣa-prahelikā*,[28] 8,400,000 years). Beyond this time is measured in so-called *paliovama*s (*palyôpama*, 'receptacle-like') and further in *sāgarovama*s (*sāgarôpama*, 'ocean-like'), temporal measures or periods, i.e. by the simile of a receptacle or container one *yojana* in breadth and in depth tightly filled with hair, one *palyovama* being the time it would take one man to empty that huge container pulling out one hair at a time. The *sāgaropava* is the same image, yet applied to the volume of the ocean or, in figures, multiplied by 1015.[29] All these divisions of time[30] apply to the regions of Lavaṇa, Dhāyaīsaṇḍa, Kāloda and Abbhintara-Pukkhar'addha. The innermost of the Pukkhar'addhas is located on the fringe of the so-called *Samaya-khetta* (146b) which is the range within which time is measured[31] and beyond which there is none (210a),[32] because of the lack of suns or planets to supply rhythmical and constant

---

[24] Viy 207b: *aṭṭhārasa-muhuttâṇantare divase* [...] *sāiregā duvālasa-muhuttā rāī*.

[25] We find differences in the highly elaborate systematisation of the time divisions especially beyond the *yuga*- or the *pūrvâṅga*–range, esp. in e.g. RVār 3.30 on the one hand and the Digambara *Trailokya-dīpikā* 5a ff. and *Trailokya-sāra* 3a ff. on the other.

[26] For an in-depth analysis of Jaina description of world ages and the decay of cosmos and mankind see especially the study of the relevant passage in the *Āvaśyaka-cūrṇi* in METTE (1973: 7–24).

[27] Uttar 10.5 and 36.14–15 have the term *asaṁkhya* and *asaṁkhya-kālaṁ* respectively. The first designates the enormous time span until the single event of liberation may take place, in contrast to the shortness of the human life span (Uttar 10.1–3), whereas *saṁkhyijja* (*saṁkhyeyya*) designates the countable time a *jīva* may stay in the body of a *tri-*, *catur-* and *pañca-indriya* (Uttar 10.10–12). The second measures the longest duration (*sthiti*) and interruption (*antara*) of the existence of *ajīva*s, *samaya* being the shortest. We find this term within a fourfold model including end, viz. endlessness, and beginning, viz. beginninglessness, as a fourfold division regarding time (here: *addhā-samaya*).

[28] According to the tradition followed by *Trailokya-dīpikā* (TrD) and *Trailokya-sāra* (TrS) the name is *acalappa* (*acalātmaka*).

[29] Viy 535; JDP 92b; Ṭhāṇ 90b, 430b.

[30] See also Viy 275a, 887b; JDP 89a; Ṭhāṇ 158; AṇD 136. Cp. von GLASENAPP (1964: 154–155) and the classic compilation by KIRFEL (1920: 337–339).

[31] With ref. to JA 179a ff.

[32] Cp. *cāraṭṭhitiyā no gairaiyā*, SP 282b, 282a; JA 345b.

movement. In order to accommodate models like this into a coherent concept of time and to harmonise it especially with a fully developed theory of *samaya*, which categorically excludes temporal measurement on the fundamental ontological level, the construct of *vyavahāra-kāla* at a later point in commentarial history must have been extremely helpful. Interestingly, time in this context as in many others in Viy is not called *kāla* but *addha-samaya*, being the composite of the Skt. *adhvan* (way), Pāli *addhan*, Pkt. *addhā* (way, stretch of time) and *samaya*.

This leads us to the question as to whether other forms of classification and terminology might have preceded the term *kāla*, which became later dominant. We find one good example of an earlier classification, a quadruple definition, still, of *kāla*, in Viy 11.11 with a parallel reading at Ṭhāṇ 201a, on the occasion of a question dealing also with time divisions. The merchant Sudaṁsana, a *samaṇovāsaya* from *Vāṇiyamāma*, questions Mahāvīra about whether the above mentioned periods *palyôpama* and *sāgarôpama* eventually come to an end. Mahāvīra tells the story of Sudaṁsana's past life when he was Mahabbala initiated into the ascetic order by a disciple of Arhat Vimala, 13th Tīrthaṅkara, reborn in Brahmaloka and arriving at his present birth after ten *sāgarôpama*s. This gives the author the occasion to consider *kāla* from four perspectives: (1) *pamāṇa-kāla* (measured time), like day and night with its *muhūrta*s and *pauruṣī*s[33] (532b–533b), (2) *ah'āunivvatti-kāla* (the time measuring a being's quantity of life), (3) *maraṇa-kāla* (the time of death) and finally (4) *addhā-kāla*, which DELEU translates as 'abstract time', which, of course, could be 'time of the way', especially when thinking that this particular meaning of *kāla* is described as divided in *samaya*s, defined as the distance or the way from one *padesa* to another.[34] Or one could maybe more appropriately and on a more abstract level speak of 'time defined as the stretch of time', i.e., in relation to the past, present and future, of 'dimensional time.' Surprisingly, as DELEU pointed out,[35] Abhayadeva's *Vṛtti* running *addhāḥ samayâdayo viśeṣas tad-rūpaḥ kālo 'ddhā-kālaḥ* has the feminine *addhā* and that despite the fact that there is *adhvan* in Sanskrit. The form *addhā* seems to have been artificially preserved in commentarial language as a *terminus technicus*. However, the question whether *addhā* may still carry the semantic value of way or, like in canonical Pāli, may have a strong, often exclusive temporal meaning, is difficult to decide. Many passages in Viy support a similar development like in the

---

[33] Equated by JACOBI (1884: 257, n. 4) with *yāma*, dominant in Buddhist texts (e.g. Nidd I 377 or Nidd II 631), but with a more restricted semantic field.

[34] *esa ṇaṁ Sudaṁsaṇa addhā dohāracchedeṇaṁ chijjamāṇī jāhe vibhāgaṁ no havvam āgacchai se ttaṁ samae*, 534b.

[35] DELEU (1970: 178).

Pāli texts, where it is normally used in a standardised way when speaking of past, present and future objects.

An interesting passage recalling this usage, common in Buddhist temporal description, is Viy 25.5 where *addhā-samaya* is defined by the number of *samaya*s relative to its dimensional division in past and future and the whole of time. We have *ananta samaya* in *tīy'addhā*, (the past stretch of time) as well as in *aṇāgay'addhā* (the not-yet-come, i.e. future, stretch of time) as well as in *savv'addhā* (all stretches of time), 887b. The same is said of the *āvaliyā*s (888a) and to even greater periods (888b). *aṇāgay'addhā* is said to have one *samaya* more than the *tīy'addhā*, *tīy'addhā* one less than *aṇāgay'addhā*, *savv'addhā* being twice *tīy'addhā* plus one *samaya*[36] or twice the future minus one *samaya*[37], *tīy'addhā* is half *savv'addhā* minus one *samaya*, *aṇāgay'addhā* is half *savv'addhā* plus one *samaya*, the one *samaya* being the one which constitutes the present.[38]

Nevertheless, the terminology never acquires the strictness of the Buddhist. Viy 1.1 mentions hell-beings who attract, transform, accumulate, make effective, perceptible and annihilate karmic substance in the three time stretches (23a). They are said to attract particles to build their karmic bodies only *paḍuppanna-kāla-samaya* (in the present *samaya* of time), whereas only particles which are attracted *aīya-kāla-samaya* (in the past *samaya* of time) are made effective (25b). This is one prominent example that also *kāla* is used to denote tridimensional temporal objects. There seems at this stage much less reluctance to interchange terms and freely use *kāla* in contexts where early Buddhist temporal description is much more cautious, trying to avoid the use of *kāla* because of its substantialist connotations.

On the other hand there are contexts which remind us very much of the discussions concerning *dravya* in Jaina dogmatics where of course *kāla* is mentioned, but where Viy has *addha-samaya*. Viy 149b as well as 492b state that *log'āgāsa* or *disi* consists of *jīva*s and *ajīva*s. Of these the *ajīva*s are *rūvi* (having form), i.e. *paramâṇu-poggala*s, or are *arūvi* (formless), in which case they are to be classified as (1) *dhamma* or (2) *adhamma* or (3) *addhā-samaya* (149b).[39] Indicative

[36] *savv'addhā ṇaṁ tīy'addhāo sāiregaduṇā*, 889a.

[37] *aṇāgay'addhāo thov'ūṇagaduguṇā*, 889a.

[38] GJK 578–579 formulates an analogous conception using *āvalī* (cf. *āvaliyā*) instead of *samaya*, the definition of *āvalī* being given in 574a as *āvalī-asaṁkha-samayā*.

[39] The use of *addhā-samaya* as an alternative to *kāla* is still common in the Uttar 36.7 where it is used as one of the 10 *arūvi*s and being defined as *saṁtatiṁ pappa* (Uttar 36.6). Here we have one interesting example of one of the many possible beginnings of the *niścaya-* / *vyavahāra-kāla* distinction, *dharma*, *adharma* and *ākāśa*

for an early phase of the doctrinal development[40] is the fact that in these passages neither *addhā-samaya* nor *kāla* are mentioned as being *dravya*.[41]

Another indicator of *addhā*'s early dominant usage is the already mentioned and typically Jaina expression *savv'addhā*. Viy 244a says that the total number of *jīva*s neither grows nor diminishes (*jīvā no vaḍḍhanti no hāyanti avaṭṭhiyā*), but remains the same *savv'addhā* (all the time). DELEU has 'eternally', which in view of the clearly enumerative character conferred on *addhā* by the endless number of *samaya*s seems a slightly too strong, if not even foreign concept.[42] Later texts from Umāsvāti to Kundakunda onwards exclusively use *savva-kāla/sarva-kāla*.[43]

The term *kāla* here being so conspicuously absent in many contexts where one finds it denoting important doctrinal aspects in later literature, seems to have acquired its predominance as an abstract notion only later, maybe beginning with the quadruple distinction of Viy 11.11 which is assumed to be a relatively late section.[44] Judging from its negligible role in early Buddhist texts which use *kāla* only in a very few and specific senses, one could assume that the competitive contact of the Jainas with schools and systems with a Brahmanic background like Vaiśeṣika and Nyāya may have supported a strong endorsement of this expression and its systematic development into a concept of relevance. Returning once more to the quadruple scheme of Viy 11.11, *pamāṇa-kāla* and *addhā-samaya*, correspond roughly to the *niścaya- / vyavahāra-* distinction, though there is no trace of epistemological hierarchy here. Rather, the quadruple distinction seems to be an example of a much more heterogeneous classification, including time of death and duration of life span. This could indicate that at this point or in this particular strand of the development of Jaina doctrine, ontological speculation about 'what time is' was still much more closely connected to soteriological questions as the effects of

being termed as both beginning- and endless, *addhā-samaya*, however, being *saṁtatiṁ prāpya* and having beginning and end regarding an individual existence (Uttar 36.9).

[40] OHIRA (1994: 102–109) places this phase in the latest canonical stages.

[41] Instead, Viy 356a has *kāla* as a separate entity in a series of terms running *davvao khettao kālao bhāvao*.

[42] For the problem of applying the concept of eternity to non-Christian religious contexts see ASSMANN (1983: 202–205) and COLPE (1983: 247, n. 57).

[43] The three time divisions and the expression *savva-kāla* are of particular relevance for the theory of omniscience (*kevala-jñāna*) as in Āyār 2.15.2 and 5. Also PSā 1.39–40. For further reading see SINGH (1974).

[44] OHIRA (1994: 235–236).

karman on life span or on the time of death.[45] Moreover, we find here a style of classification which apparently is not yet instrumental to finding a solution to the monistic conception of the term *kāla* vis-à-vis its multiple manifestations. Instead of an ontologically strong concept which is expected to link mutually incompatible modes of time, we here have a relatively weak term whose function seems rather to encompass and subsume temporal plurality, more apt for description and categorisation rather than answering questions of ontological hierarchy.

– 4 –

Finally, in looking at temporal description, one may push the textual and chronological horizon one step further. One may not go so far as to search for proto-philosophy in the *Āyāraṁga-sutta* like MALVANIA (1981), but one may give just a glimpse on the complex and multifaceted way in which time matters are treated here and see whether it is possible to trace back just a few notions and expressions by outlining a perspective and pointing at some features.[46]

Āyār 1.2.1.1–5 is a text where one finds some temporal descriptions concentrated just in a couple of lines:

> Āyār 1.2.1.1–2: *icc atthaṁ gaḍhie loe vase pamatte aho ya rāo paritappamāṇe kālākāla-samuṭṭhāī saṁjogaṭṭhī aṭṭhālobhī āluṁpe sahasākāre viṇiviṭṭha-citte ttha satthe puṇo puṇo. appaṁ ca khalu āuṁ iham egesiṁ māṇavāṇaṁ,*

[45] Two further important temporal expressions, which in Viy appear frequently in this context and would require further examination regarding their descriptive and theoretical implications, are (1) *aṇtara* (e.g. Viy 234b, 583a), often as *aṇtara-kāla*, being in many instances functionally comparable to *samaya*, or as *an-aṇtara*, notion crucial to the Jaina concept of simultaneity, and (2) *āuya* (*āyu*, e.g. Viy 214a, esp. 304ab) which is considered in connection with *karman*, rebirth and body and consequently with a more quantitative, material concept of duration, rather than with structure or dimension of time.

[46] As ALSDORF (1965) and ALSDORF (1977) has shown, what makes the task of systematically considering the Āyār corpus as a whole under a certain heading extremely problematic is its immensely heterogeneous constitution. Following ALSDORF's approach when isolating and comparing individual lines and verses, it is best to avoid drawing any conclusions which may refer to the text as a whole.

—'In this way the world is bound: One is careless, suffers day and night, acts at the right and at the wrong time, longs for union and possessions, wastes and is violent, directs the mind again and again on these harmful acts. The life of men is made short.'

It later continues:

> Āyār 1.2.1.3: *icc evaṁ samutthie aho vihārāe aṁtaraṁ ca khalu imaṁ sa pehāe dhīre muhuttam avi no pamāyae. vao acceti jovvaṇaṁ ca jīviṭe,*
>
> —'[…] Oh, there is a way: To go forth for religious practice! As to the short interval, truly favourable, the wise may not even for a *muhūrta* be careless. Stages in life pass as well as youth in life.'

And finally:

> Āyār 1.2.1.5: *jāṇittu dukkhaṁ patteyaṁ sāyaṁ aṇabhikkhaṁtaṁ ca khalu vayaṁ sa pehāe khaṇaṁ jāṇāhi paṁḍie,*
>
> —'He shall know each pleasure to be discomfort and as to the fact that this stage in life has not yet ended, the wise shall know *kṣaṇa*,[47] […].'

We find here some familiar and some new temporal expressions, though even the familiar ones appear to have a new meaning. *Kāla* in composition with *akāla* is not time in general but a certain time, the right time, in this case the time for action. Recalling the knowledge of *kāla* and *deśa* or *kṣetra* of successful kings in epic[48] and *subhāṣita* literature[49], it reminds especially him who strives for success and perfection on the religious level (1) when in life to make the decision for entering religious life and (2) to know what to do and what not to do on which times of the fourfold day, referring to the huge field of temporally determined prescriptions

---

[47] JACOBI (1884: 16) has 'the proper moment' and adds, in brackets, 'for entering religious life' which stands in accord with the admonition to renounce before coming to age, found here and in several other passages. Buddhist texts also stress the fact that the *bhikṣu* should be 'black-haired' when entering the *saṁgha* (e.g. SN IV 110.24–28). For all bibliographical abbreviations of Buddhist texts see Heinz BECHERT (1990).

[48] E.g. MBh 6.4 ff. on *kāla-vid*.

[49] E.g. BÖHTLINGK (1870–73: 898, 1812, 3098). See also YT 3.81 where the three times relevant to the king are those of superiority, equality and inferiority:

> *udayaḥ samatā hānis trayāḥ kālā mahī-bhujāṁ /*
> *tatrâdya eva yoddhavyaṁ sthātavyam ubhayoḥ punaḥ //*

followed by the ordained monk.[50] Another basic aspect of auspicious time throughout the canonical literature and especially regarding the hierographical description of certain events[51] is of course its cosmological and astrological setting.[52] Another term is *appam āuṁ* which we may relate to *ah'āunivvatti-kāla* from the Viy 11.11 classification (see above, p. 78), but which here too acquires the quality of reminder and admonition. This is not some fixed life span which we may categorise in terms of specific duration; this is the life span of man which is generally so short as to admonish him constantly not to lose time and resort to moral conduct and religious life. Even a *muhūrta*, here used as a relatively short period of time, is too long to let it pass without proper decision and action. The thought of the inexorable passing of youth intends to call to mind the image of decay which is so conspicuously absent in all the previous temporal descriptions. A field which can only be pointed at on this occasion is the way in which the tripartition of tenses is treated in the four 'seniors' which comes also very close to their treatment in the Buddhist *Nikāyas*, referring (1) to their role concerning the soteriological process[53] and (2) to omniscience and religious truth claims[54].

Yet, in the statement *khaṇam jānāhi* we find the expression which may surprise one most, namely, that temporal idea of discrete time in which—in view of all these shortcomings of human existence—right action shall take place before old age is reached and which takes no longer than a moment. Here Āyār uses, as do the Buddhist canonical texts for this purpose,[55] the expression *khaṇa* to designate short duration which becomes decisive due to the soteriologically crucial action which is

---

[50] E.g. concerning a prolonged stay at one place: *ayam āuso kālātikkaṁta-kiriyā bhavati*, Āyār 2.2.2.6; or concerning the begging round: *se tattha kāleṇaṁ aṇupavisejjā ttā tatth' itarehiṁ kulehiṁ samudāṇiyaṁ esiyaṁ vesiyaṁ piṇḍavāyam esittā āhāram āhārejjā. se paro kālena* [...], Āyār 2.1.9.2. It is placed, as is well-known, in the third or occasionally in the first *paurusī*. The *Piṇḍ'esaṇā* (Piṇḍ 165.) of the *Oha-nijutti* has:

duvihaṁ hoi pamāṇaṁ—kālo bhikkhā-pavesa-māṇaṁ ca /
sannā bhikkhāyariyā bhikkhe do: kāla, paḍham'addhā //

As to the interpretation of *addhā,* see Piṇḍ 47, n. 7 where Mette would equate its use to that of *kāla*. See also N.K. PRASAD (1972: 15–16).

[51] E.g. Āyār 2.3.15.1–6.

[52] For a discussion of Jaina astrology see KAPADIA (1952).

[53] Sūy 1.2.2.5. Āyār 1.3.3.2–3.

[54] Āyār 1.4.1.1, Āyār 2.4.1.3; Sūy 1.2.2.5.

[55] E.g. DN III 185.6–14; Th 1004–1105; Dhp 315.

supposed to take place within this window of opportunity.[56] Interestingly, the texts here do not have *samaya*, the term in its temporal meaning, as METTE (1991) notes, being rarely used in the 'seniors'.[57] Neither has *khaṇa* evolved into a concept of Jaina terminology like in Buddhism where it rose to prominence with the establishment of the *kṣaṇa-bhaṅga-vāda*. Here, it is often explained as the right time, the time of youth when enough time remains to start and make progress on the path to salvation, to enter the religious life or, as in *khaṇaṁsi mukkhe* (Āyār 1.2.2.1), the time of final liberation: *aratiṁ āuṭṭe se mahāvī khaṇaṁsi mukke*—'A great man should put away all obstinacy, he is liberated instantly.'[58]

Very similar passages can be found in Sūy.[59] As both Āyār and Sūy are traditionally defined as texts dealing with right conduct, the relevance of time is diffusely and even poignantly present, but rather implicit and part of a general everyday knowledge, accessible to anyone who hears the doctrine, or as an appeal to one's religious awareness or as a clear-cut schedule for the convert's ritual timing. It is pre-scriptive rather than de-scriptive. The temporal constellation implied by the need to reach salvation encompasses a range of relevant expressions which cannot be summarised under one or more concepts of time, resisting as they do systematic definition and thereby retain their powerful religious appeal. As in the following statement, Āyār 1.7.6.6, with which I close, these texts show that we do not always need to know what time it is in order to know the time: *tattha vi tassa kāla-pariyāe se tattha viaṁtakārae*—'So will he put an end in the course of time.'

---

[56] A passage which very nicely brings together *kāla* and *khaṇa* under both their cognitive and practical aspect is: *je saṁnihāṇasathassa kheyyanne se bhikkhū kālanne balanne māyanna khaṇanne viṇayanne samayanne pariggahaṁ amamāyamīṇe kāle 'ṇuṭṭhāī apaḍiṇṇe duhno chettā niyati*, Āyār 1.7.3.3. Cf. Āyār 1.2.5.3.

[57] METTE (1991: 75). In her short but pioneering work on temporal questions in Pāli and Prakrit, including early Jainism, concerning *samaya* METTE investigates the relationship of its double meaning as both 'convention' and 'occasion,' 'fixed time' or generally 'time' defined, in contrast to *kāla*, by its 'conventional' and limited character (METTE (1991: 70)) or showing in which cases *samaya* must be understood as devoid of any temporal content (METTE (1991: 72–74)). METTE refers to Āyār 2.4.1.5 on *bhāsā-visuddhi* as a clearly temporal usage where *samaya* is used in an objective and, in contrast to *khaṇa,* not soteriological and adhortative context.

[58] JACOBI (1884: 17) 'in the proper time' stresses too unilaterally the kairologial aspect, which, of course, is also quite present.

[59] E.g. in the famous first verses: *no hūvaṇamanti rāiyo*, Sūy 1.2.1.1.

BIBLIOGRAPHY

ALSDORF 1965 = Alsdorf, Ludwig: *Les Études Jaina*. Collége de France, Paris 1965.

ALSDORF 1977 = Alsdorf, Ludwig: 'Jaina Exegetical Literature and the History of the Jaina Canon.' In: A.N. Upadhye, Nathmal Tatia, Dalsukh Malvania, Mohanlal Mehta, Nemichand Shastri, Kailashchandra Shastri (eds.): *Mahāvīra and His Teachings*. Bhagavān Mahāvīra 2,500 Nirvāṇa Mahotsava Samiti, Bombay 1977: 1–8.

AṇD = *Aṇuoga-dāra* [*Anuyoga-dvāra-sūtra*]. Ed. by Venicand Surcand, Agamodaya-Samiti, Bombay 1924.

ASSMANN 1983 = Assmann, Jan: 'Das Doppelgesicht der Zeit im altägyptischen Denken.' In: PEISL–MOHLER (1983: 189–223).

Āyār = *Āyāraṁga-sutta* [Ācārâṅga-*sūtra*]. *The Âyârâmga Sutta of Çvetāmbara Jains*. Ed. by Hermann Jacobi, Part I, Pāli Text Society, London 1882.

BALSEV 1983 = Balsev, Anidita Niyogi: *A Study of Time in Indian Philosophy*. Otto Harrassowitz, Wiesbaden 1983.

BECHERT 1990 = Bechert, Heinz (ed.): *Abkürzungsverzeichnis zur buddhistischen Literatur in Indien und Südostasien*. Göttingen 1990.

BHARUCHA 1984 = Bharucha, Filita: *The Role of Space–Time in Jaina Syadvada and Quantum Theory*. Delhi 1984.

BHATTACHARYA 1992 = Bhattacharya, Harisatya: 'The Theory of Time in Jaina Philosophy.' In: PRASAD (1992: 531–539).

BÖHTLINGK 1870–73 = Böhtlingk, Otto: *Indische Sprüche. Sanskrit und Deutsch. Zweite vermehrte und verbesserte Ausgabe*. St. Petersburg 1870–1873.

COLPE 1983 = Colpe, Carsten: 'Die Zeit in den drei asiatischen Hochkulturen (Babylon—Iran—Indien).' In: PEISL–MOHLER (1983: 225–256).

DELEU 1970 = Deleu, Jozef: *Viyāhapannatti* (*Bhagavaī*): *The Fifth Anga of the Jaina Canon*. Introduction, critical analysis, commentary & indexes. "De Tempel", Brugge 1970.

Dhp = *Dhammapada*. Ed. Suriyagoḍa Sumaṅgala Thera, Pāli Text Society, London 1914.

Dīv = *Dīva-sāgara-paṇṇatti*. see: JA.

DN = *Dīgha-nikāya*. Ed. by T.W. and C.A.F. Rhys Davids and J.E. Carpenter, 3 Vols., Pāli Text Society, London I: 1890, II: 1903, III: 1911.

DS = Nemicandra: *Dravya-saṅgrāha. Dravyasaṁgrāha of Nemicandra Siddhānta-Chakravarttī* [with *Dravya-saṅgraha-vṛtti* by Brahmadeva] edited by S.C. Ghoshal. *Sacred Books of the Jainas* 1, Arrah 1917. [Reprinted: Motilal Banarsidass, Delhi 1989].

EMMRICH 2001 = Emmrich, Christoph: 'Some Remarks on the Terminological Construction of *kāla* in Kundakunda.' In: Jayandra SONI (ed.): *Vasantagauravam. Felicitating Professor M.D. Vasantha Raj of*

Mysore On the Occasion of his Seventy-fifth Birthday. Vakils, Feffer & Simons, Mumbai 2001: 73–85.

FRAUWALLNER 1953–56 = Frauwallner, Erich: *Geschichte der indischen Philosophie*, 1. und 2. Band, Salzburg 1953–1956

GJK = *Gommaṭa-sāra-jīva-kāṇḍa* of Nemicandra. Ed. by Rai Bahadur Jagmandar Lal Jaini, Central Jaina Publishing House, Lucknow 1937.

von GLASENAPP 1964 = Glasenapp, Helmuth von: *Der Jainismus. Eine indische Erlösungsreligion*. Hager, Berlin 1964. [First edition: 1925].

JA = *Jīvâbhigama*. Bombay 1919.

JACOBI 1884 = Jacobi, Hermann: *Jaina Sûtras. Part I: Âcârâṅga Sûtra, Kalpa Sûtra*. Translated from Prâkrit by … . *Sacred Books of the East* 22, Oxford University Press, Oxford 1884.

JAIN 1992 = Jain, Jagdishchandra: *Studies in Early Jainism. Selected Research Articles*. Navrang, Delhi 1992.

JDP = *Jambuddīva-paṇṇatti*. Devcand Lālbhāi Jaina Pustakoddhara, Bombay 1920.

JSK = *Jainendra Siddhānta Kośa*. ed. by Jinendra Varṇī, Vols. 1–4, *Jñānapīṭha Mūrtidevī Jaina Granthamālā, Saṁskṛta Granthâṅka* 40, Delhi 1971; s.v. *kāla*, Vol. II (k–n).

KAPADIA 1952 = Kapadia, Hirarlal R.: 'Horoscopic Data of the Jaina Literature.' *Journal of the Oriental Institute of Baroda* 2 (1952) 41–49.

KIRFEL 1920 = Kirfel, Willibald: *Die Kosmographie der Inder nach Quellen dargestellt*. Schroeder, Bonn–Leipzig 1920.

MALVANIA 1981 = Malvania, Dalsukh, D.: 'Beginnings of Jaina philosophy in the *Ācārāṅga*.' In: *Studien zum Jainismus und Buddhismus. Gedenkschrift für Ludwig Alsdorf*. Ed. Klaus Bruhn and Albrecht Wezler. *Alt- und Neu-Indische Studien* 23, Franz Steiner Verlag, Wiesbaden 1981: 151–153.

MBh = *The Mahā-bhārata*. Critically ed. by V.S. Sukthankar and others. Bhandarkar Oriental Research Institute, Poona 1933–66.

METTE 1973 = Mette, Adelheid: *Indische Kulturstiftungsberichte und ihr Verhältnis zur Zeitaltersage*. Akademie der Wissenschaften und der Literatur. Abhandlungen der Geistes- und Sozialwissenschaftlichen Klasse. Verlag der Akademie der Wissenschaften und der Literatur, Mainz–Wiesbaden 1973.

METTE 1991 = Mette, Adelheid: 'Notes on samaya "convention" in Pali and Prakrit.' In: Colette CAILLAT (ed.): *Middle Indo- Aryan and Jaina Studies*. Panels of the VIIth World Sanskrit Conference Vol. VI/VII, Leiden 1991: 69–80.

MOOKERJEE 1961 = Mookerjee, Satkari: 'The Jaina Concept of Time.' *Vishvabharati Quarterly* 27,2 (1961) 122–139.

Nidd I = *Mahāniddesa*. Ed. by Louis de la Vallée Poussin and E.J. Thomas, Pāli Text Society, London 1916.

Nidd II = *Cullaniddesa*. Ed. by William Stede, Pāli Text Society, London 1918.

OHIRA 1994 = Ohira, Suzuko: *A Study of the Bhagavatīsūtra. A Chronological Analysis*. Prakrit Text Society, Ahmedabad 1994.

PADMARAJIAH 1946 = Padmarajiah, Y.J.: 'Theory of Time in Jainism.' *Journal of Mysore University* 37 (1946) 111–115.

PSSā = Kundakunda: *Pañcâstikāya-samaya-sāra*. Ed. and trans. by A. Chakravartinayanar, *Sacred Books of the Jainas* 3, Arrah 1920.

PEISL–MOHLER 1983 = Peisl, Anton; Mohler, Armin (eds.): *Die Zeit*. Schriften der C.F. von Siemens-Stiftung, Vol. 6. München 1983.

Piṇḍ = Mette, Adelheid (ed., trsl. &. comm.): *Piṇḍ'esaṇā – Das Kapitel der Oha-nijjutti über den Bettelgang übersetzt und kommentiert*. Abhandlungen der Mainzer Akademie der Wissenschaften und der Literatur, Abhandlungen der Geistes- und Sozialwissenschaftlichen, Nr. 11, Franz Steiner Verlag, Wiesbaden 1974.

PRASAD 1972 = Prasad, Nand Kishore: *Studies in Buddhist and Jaina Monachism*. Research Institute of Prakrit, Jainology and Ahimsa, Vaishali 1972.

PRASAD 1982 = Prasad, Hari Shankar: *The Concept of Time in Buddhism*. Dissertation, Australian National University, Canberra 1982.

PRASAD 1992 = Prasad, Hari Shankar (Ed.): *Time in Indian Philosophy. A Collection of Essays*. Sri Satguru Publications, Delhi 1992.

PSā = Kundakunda: *Pavayaṇa-sāra* [*Pravacana-sāra*]. *Śrī Kundakundācārya's Pravacanasāra (Pavayaṇasāra), a Pro-Canonical Text of the Jainas, the Prakrit Text critically edited with the Sanskrit Commentaries of Amṛtacandra and Jayasena*. Ed. by A.N. Upadhye, Parama-Śruta-Prabhāvaka Mandal, Shrimad Rajachandra Ashrama, Agās–Gujarat 1984. [First edition: Bombay 1935].

RVār = *Tattvârtha-vārttika* (*Rāja-vārttika*) *of Śrī Akalaṅkadeva*. Edited with Hindi Translation, Introduction, appendices, variant readings, comparative notes etc. by Prof. Mahendra Kumar Jain. Parts I–II. First edition, *Jñānapīṭha Mūrtidevī Jaina Granthamālā: Sanskrit Grantha* No. 10, 20, Bhāratīya Jñānapīṭha, Delhi 1953–1957. [Second edition: Delhi 1982].

SCHRADER 1902 = Schrader, F. Otto: *Über den Stand der indischen Philosophie zur Zeit Mahāvīras und Buddhas*. Friedrich, Strassburg 1902.

SCHUBRING 1935 = Schubring, Walther: *Die Lehre der Jainas—Nach den alten Quellen dargestellt*. Walter de Gruyter, Leipzig 1935.

SHAH 1968 = Shah, Nagin J.: 'Nature of Time.' *Shri Mahavir Jaina Vidyalaya Golden Jubilee*, Bombay 1968: 63–87.

SHAH 1977–78 = Shah, Nagin J.: 'Jaina Conception of Space and Time.' *Sambodhi* 6, 3/4 (1977–78): 12–31.

SINGH 1974 = Singh, Ram Jee: *The Jaina Concept of Omniscience*. L.D. Institute of Indology, Ahmedabad 1974.

SP = *Sūrya-prajñapti*. Sri Agama Prakasana Samiti, Byavara/Rajasthan 1989.

SSi = *Sarvârtha-siddhi* of Pūjyapāda Devanandin, ed. with *Tattvârtha-sūtra* of Umāsvāti. Sanskrit text with Hindi translation by Phoolchandra Siddhāntaśāstrī. *Jñānapīṭha Mūrtidevī Jaina Granthamālā, Sanskrit Grantha* 13, Bhāratīya Jñānapīṭha, Varanasi 1971.

STCHERBATSKY 1926 = Stcherbatsky, Fëdor I.: 'Le temps (*kāla*).' In: Fëdor I. Stcherbatsky: *La théorie de la connaissance et la logique chez les bouddhistes tardifs*. Geuthner, Paris 1926.

Sūy = *Sūyagaḍaṁga* [*Sūtrakṛtâṅga-sūtra*]. Āgamodaya-samiti, Bombay 1917.

TATIA 1994 = Tatia, Nathmal (tr.): *Tattvārtha Sūtra: That Which Is. Umāsvāti / Umāsvāmī; with the combined commentaries of Umāsvāti / Umāsvāmī, Pūjyapāda and Siddhasensgaṇi*. Harper Collins Publishers, San Francisco—London—Australia 1994.

Th = *Theragāthā* ed. by Hermann Oldenberg and *Therīgāthā* ed. by. Richard Pischel, rev. K.R. Norman, L. Alsdorf. 2nd ed., Pāli Text Society, London 1966.

Ṭhāṇ = *Ṭhāṇaṁga-sutta* [*Sthānâṅga-sūtra*]. Āgamodaya-samiti, Mehesana 1918–20.

TrD = *Trailokya-dīpikā*. Surat 1916.

TrS = *Trailokya-sāra*. Bombay 1918.

TS = Umāsvāti: *Tattvârtha-sūtra*. Hermann Jacobi (ed.): *Eine Jaina-Dogmatik—Umāsvāti's Tattvārthādigama Sūtra. Zeitschrift der Deutschen Morgenländischen Gesellschaft* 60. Leipzig 1906.

TSṬ = Siddhasenagaṇi: *Tattvârthâdhigama-sūtra-svopajña-bhāṣya-ṭīkā. Tattvārthādhigamasūtra (A Treatise on the Fundamental Principles of Jainism) by His Holiness Śrī Umāsvāti Vācaka, together with his Connective Verses Commented upon by Śrī Devaguptasūri and Śrī Siddhasenagaṇi*. ed. by H.R. Kapadia, 2 vols., Jivanachand Sakerchand Javeri, Bombay 1926, 1930.

Uttar = *Uttarajjhayaṇa-sutta* [*Uttarâdhyayana-sūtra*]. *The Uttarādhyayanasūtra*. An introduction, text, critical notes and a commentary, by Jarl Charpentier, *Archives d'Etudes Orientales*, Vol. 18:1–2, Uppsala 1921–1922.

Viy = *Viyāha-pannatti* [*Bhagavatī Vyākhyā-prajñapti = Bhagavatī-sūtra*]. Bombay 1918–1921.

YT = Handiqui, Krishna Kanta (ed. & transl.): *Yaśastilaka and Indian Culture or Somadeva's Yaśastilaka and Aspects of Jainism and Indian Thought and Culture in the Tenth Century*. Jaina Saṁskriti Saṁrakshaka Saṅgha, Sholapur 1949.

Extrasensory Perception and Knowledge in Jainism

KRISTI L. WILEY

The capacity for attaining various supernatural powers through yogic concentration or advanced forms of meditation is recognised in a number of religious traditions and philosophical schools of ancient India. Among these is the ability to attain extrasensory perception and knowledge. For example, the supernatural powers (*vibhūti*), which are discussed in Chapter Three of Patañjali's *Yoga-sūtra*, include knowledge of subtle, concealed, or obscure objects, including the arrangement of cosmic space, and also knowledge of the mind (*citta*) of others.[1] It is not surprising, therefore, that the subject of extrasensory perception has been discussed by a number of Jaina *ācārya*s as well. Like other subjects associated with their detailed explanations of the workings of *karman*, there is an in-depth discussion in Jaina texts about the nature of such knowledge and how it may be attained.

1. Introduction

According to Jaina sources, the quality (*guṇa*) of awareness or consciousness (*caitanya*) is the characteristic of the soul (*jīva*) that distinguishes it from all other existents. It is because of this quality that souls are knowers of objects. Cognition (*upayoga*), or the application of consciousness, normally operates sequentially. First there is perception (*darśana*), or an indistinct awareness of the general qualities of an object. This is followed by knowledge (*jñāna*), or an awareness of the details or specific qualities of that object.[2] Because of the sequential nature of cognition, *darśana* and *jñāna* are often considered to be two distinct qualities of the soul.[3]

Awareness can be seen as a continuum; from varying degrees of limited sensory perception, to varying degrees of limited extrasensory perception and knowledge, to

---

[1] Patañjali's *Yoga-sūtra* 3.25 and 3.19, respectively; see: WOODS (1914).

[2] These terms are also translated as 'indeterminate' and 'determinate' knowledge. For a detailed discussion of these terms, see TATIA (1951: 70 ff.).

[3] JAINI (1979: 104).

Essays in Jaina Philosophy and Religion.
Warsaw Indological Studies, Volume 2 (2002), pp. 89–109.

absolute unlimited perception and knowledge. Such perfect knowledge was attained by the twenty-fourth Tīrthaṅkara of our era, Lord Mahāvīra.

> 'When the Venerable Ascetic Mahāvīra had become a Jina and an Arhat, he was a *kevalin*, omniscient, comprehending all objects. He saw and knew whence they had come, where they would go, and whether they would be reborn as men, animals, gods, or hell-beings. He knew the ideas and thoughts, the food, doings, desires, and deeds of all the living beings in the world.'[4]

Omniscient knowledge is not restricted to the Jinas. It is experienced by all who, through their own spiritual efforts, have eliminated all passion (*kaṣāya*s) and who have brought to an end the bondage of the soul in the cycle of death and rebirth (*saṁsāra*).

Although omniscience is inherent in all souls, it remains unmanifested in most because of the effects produced by the operation of karmic matter. In Jainism, *karman* is understood to be an extremely subtle type of matter, which is attracted to the soul by actions of the body, speech, and mind. It is bound with the soul whenever passions (*kaṣāya*s) are present. There are numerous varieties of karmic matter, each of which produces a specific effect when coming to fruition. For instance, there are certain *karman*s that determine life-span (*āyus-karman*s) and others that cause the formation of the body (*nāma-karman*s). *Mohanīya-karman*s cause false views of reality (*mithyātva*) and give rise to passions (*kaṣāya*s) in the form of anger (*krodha*), pride (*māna*), deceitfulness (*māyā*) and greed (*lobha*).

It is sub-varieties (*uttara-prakṛti*s) of obscuring (*āvaraṇīya*) *karman*s that affect the perception and knowledge qualities of the soul. One of the *āvaraṇīya-karman*s obstructs the perception of the soul that is conditional upon the eye (*cakṣur-darśana-āvaraṇīya-karman*), another obstructs the perception conditional upon the other sense-organs including the mind (*acakṣur-darśana-āvaraṇīya-karman*), and yet another obstructs knowledge transmitted through the sense-organs (*mati-jñāna-āvaraṇīya-karman*). If the obscuring *karman*s associated with the sense-organs were to rise without any impediment whatsoever, there would be no cognition by the soul at all. However, in all souls there is enough energy (*vīrya*) available to partially destroy and partially suppress (*kṣayôpaśama*) the rise of those obscuring *karman*s associated with the sense-organs to some degree. Thus, even the most rudimentary one-sensed beings with only the sense of touch have some awareness of their environment, however minimal it might be.

---

[4] *Kalpa-sūtra* [KS] 121, as translated in JAINI (1979: 28). See also *Ācārâṅga-sūtra* [Āyār] 2.15.26.

This is not the case, however, for all of the *āvaraṇīya-karmans*. One is prevented from realising omniscience on account of the unimpeded rise (*udaya*) of the varieties of *karman* that obstruct perfect perception (*kevala-darśana-āvaraṇīya-karman*) and perfect knowledge, or omniscience (*kevala-jñāna-āvaraṇīya-karman*). Unlike sensory perception and knowledge, which vary in accordance with the destruction-cum-suppression of the corresponding *karman*s, it is not possible to experience omniscient perception and knowledge in anything but its absolute degree because it is not possible to partially destroy and partially suppress (*kṣayôpaśama*) the rise of the two sub-varieties of *karman*s that obscure perfect perception and knowledge. Instead, realisation of perfect awareness coincides with the elimination of all sub-varieties of *āvaraṇīya-karman*s from the soul, including the two that are directly associated with absolute perception and knowledge.[5]

In addition to sensory perception and knowledge as well as 'scriptural' knowledge (*śruta-jñāna*, i.e. that knowledge acquired from interpreting words, writing, and gestures) it is possible on occasion for a non-omniscient being to have cognition that is not associated with the sense-organs or with the mind. Like the various types of sensory knowledge, cognition through clairvoyant perception and knowledge (*avadhi-darśana* and *avadhi-jñāna*) and telepathic knowledge (*manaḥ-paryaya-jñāna*) are obscured by the rise of corresponding sub-varieties of *āvaraṇīya-karmans*.[6] It is often the case that the rise of these obscuring *karman*s is totally

[5] I use the term 'perfect awareness' rather than perfect perception and knowledge in light of the debate among the commentators regarding these two terms in the state of omniscience. Some commentators (e.g., Jinabhadra) understand *darśana* and *jñāna* to operate sequentially as they did in the pre-omniscient state; other Śvetāmbara commentators and all Digambara commentators understand them to operate simultaneously; and still other Śvetāmbara commentators (e.g., Siddhasena Divākara and Yaśovijaya) do not believe that a distinction between *darśana* and *jñāna* is valid in the omniscient state. For further details, see TATIA (1951: 74–80).
There is also a disagreement about whether all five types of knowledge can be present in the same soul. It is generally accepted that four types can coexist, namely *mati*, *śruti*, *avadhi*, and *manaḥ-paryaya*. However, some maintain that with the realisation of perfect knowledge (*kevala-jñāna*), the remaining ones cease to exist in that soul. Others believe that they continue to exist but no longer serve any purpose as they are overshadowed by *kevala-jñāna*. In any case, only one type of knowledge is active at any given time. See J.L. JAINI (1920: 43).

[6] There is no *manaḥ-paryaya-darśana* because mind-reading recognises only the details or particular features of the objects in the minds of others, not their general features. Thus, there is no *manaḥ-paryaya-darśana-āvaraṇīya-karman*. See TATIA (1951: 77).

unimpeded; thus, there is no extrasensory cognition whatsoever. However, there are some who are capable of experiencing such knowledge. Why might one person experience such knowledge while others do not? Or, expressed in karmic terms, what might cause the partial destruction and partial suppression (*kṣayôpaśama*) of *avadhi-darśaṇa-* and *avadhi-jñāna-* or of *manaḥ-paryaya-jñāna-āvaraṇīya-karmans*? What can be known through these types of non-omniscient extrasensory cognition, and what are the limits of such knowledge?

2. *Avadhi-jñāna*, or Clairvoyance

Let us first examine *avadhi-jñāna*, which is often translated as 'clairvoyance,' or 'the power or faculty of discerning objects not present to the senses,' or 'the ability to perceive matters beyond the range of ordinary perception.'[7] The word *avadhi*, when used as an adjective, means 'limited' or 'bounded,' thus, *avadhi-jñāna* is knowledge that is limited in certain respects. Unlike the first two types of knowledge, *mati-* and *śruta-jñāna*, this knowledge is not indirect or mediate (*parokṣa*) because it is not acquired by means of the senses (*mati*) or the scriptures (*śruta*). Instead, like *kevala-jñāna*, it is direct or immediate (*pratyakṣa*), but as its name implies, it is partial or incomplete (*deśa-pratyakṣa*).[8] *Avadhi-jñāna* is also called *sīmā-jñāna* because it is limited with respect to the subject matter (*dravya*), location (*kṣetra*), duration of time (*kāla*) and modes or aspects (*bhāva*).[9] It is knowledge of that which is material (*pratirūpi*), that is, of *pudgala*.[10] Only *kevala-jñāna* is complete direct knowledge (*sakala-pratyakṣa*) because the scope of this knowledge includes non-material existents (*arūpi-dravya*) as well, such as souls (*jīva*), time (*kāla*), and motion and rest (*dharma* and *adharma*).

Although there are innumerable degrees of *avadhi-jñāna* that are manifested in accordance with the level of destruction and suppression of the corresponding varieties of karmic matter, it is conventionally understood as having three main divisions. The lower degrees of the first division is called *deśâvadhi-jñāna*, or

---

[7] *Webster's Collegiate Dictionary*, sv. For translations, see TATIA (1994: 12) and S.A. JAIN (1960: 16).

[8] *Tattvârtha-sūtra* [TS] 11–12 and 22 (J. L. JAINI's translation and commentary) and *Gommaṭa-sāra-jīva-kāṇḍa* [GJK] 369. It should be noted here that in Jainism *pratyakṣa* does not mean 'apprehension by the senses' as it does in other philosophical systems but rather 'apprehension directly by the soul.'

[9] GJK 370.

[10] GJK 376.

partial clairvoyant knowledge. It arises automatically in heavenly beings and hell-beings at birth (*bhava-pratyaya*), without any effort or external efficient causes. It can be acquired by humans and five-sensed rational womb-born animals through exertion or merit (*guṇa-pratyaya*). Higher degrees of *deśâvadhi* can be realised only by those who are self-controlled (*saṁyama*), in other words, by those who have taken the mendicant vows (*mahā-vrata*s).[11] Depending on the extent and duration of *kṣayôpaśama* of the *āvaraṇīya-karman*s, a person may experience this knowledge while in a particular place, but it ceases when moving to a different place. For others, there is clairvoyance in various locations, but it does not last for the rest of one's life. It may gradually expand in range, it may gradually contract in range, or it may fluctuate repeatedly. Naturally, the lower degrees of clairvoyant knowledge are more limited with respect to the distance of an object. With increased partial destruction and partial suppression of these *āvaraṇīya-karman*s, a person can know objects in increasingly distant locations and can remain focused on them for longer periods of time.

On occasion, *avadhi-jñāna* may continue until death, into the next life, or until attaining omniscience.[12] In the latter instance, the extent of this knowledge would continue to expand, and the person would be capable of experiencing the second and third degrees of clairvoyant knowledge, called *paramâvadhi-jñāna* and *sarvâvadhi-jñāna*. These two can be acquired only by those in their final human birth (*carama-śarīra*), in other words, by those who will attain *mokṣa* in that very life.[13] Thus, in our location of the universe at this time no one can realise the second and third degrees of *avadhi-jñāna*. This possibility ended with the death of Jambū, the last person in our location of the universe to attain *mokṣa* in the current half-cycle of time.[14]

There are two types of *deśâvadhi-jñāna*. When it arises in a person with a false view of reality (*mithyātva*), clairvoyant knowledge is false (*viparyaya*). Such incorrect knowledge is called *vibhaṅga-jñāna*. False clairvoyant knowledge should not be understood as an error in the ascertainment of an object, for 'just as the man of right attitude ascertains matter through clairvoyance, so also does the man of wrong attitude through erroneous clairvoyance.' However, because it co-exists with wrong belief (*mithyātva*), it has false qualities, like 'milk kept in a bitter gourd. Now

[11] GJK 371 and 373–374.

[12] TS 1.23 (= SSi 1.22) and commentary as translated by TATIA (1994: 19).

[13] GJK 374. Some sources only understand two types: *āhohiya* (= *ādho-avadhi-jñāna*) and *paramâvadhi-jñāna*. See, for example, *Bhagavatī-sūtra*, *śataka* 1, *uddeśaka* 4 (66a) and *Sthānāṅga-sūtra* 61a, as cited in SCHUBRING (1962: 169).

[14] *Viśeṣâvaśyaka-bhāṣya* 2593, as cited in MAHĀPRAJÑA (1996 I: 553).

the taste of the milk becomes different on account of the defect of the receptacle in which it is kept.'[15] In the *Bhagavatī-sūtra* there is a story about a king of Hastinapūra named Śiva who wanted to renounce the world. At this time, there were many groups of ascetics living on the banks of the Ganges practising various kinds of austerities (*tapas*), and the king became a Disāpokkhī ascetic. It was customary for these ascetics to observe a fast, which was broken on the sixth meal (*chaṭṭhama*) by gathering fruits and flowers, by purifying the cardinal directions with water, by worshipping deities such as Vaissadeva (Vaiśvānara = Kubera), Soma, and Varuṇa, and by making oblations in the fire. On account of these practices and by observing chastity (*brahma-çarya*) and self-restraint, the *rājarṣi* Śiva acquired *vibhaṅga-jñāna*. He saw (*paśyati*) seven continents and seven oceans in the universe (*loka*). Because he did not know anything beyond this, he assumed that this was the extent of the universe. He went to Hastinapūra, declared that he had acquired extraordinary supernatural knowledge and perception (*aisesa* = *atiśeṣa-jñāna* and *darśana*), and related what he had seen. The people there were quite impressed with his knowledge. Indrabhūti Gautama, Mahāvīra's chief disciple (*gaṇadhara*), questioned the Tīrthaṅkara about this. Through his omniscient knowledge (*kevala-jñāna*), Mahāvīra knew that there were many more continents and oceans, and he described to Gautama the nature of substances therein. After being informed of Mahāvīra's statements, Śiva approached Mahāvīra and became a Jaina mendicant (*nirgrantha*), ultimately attaining *mokṣa*.[16]

There is another example of *vibhaṅgâvadhi-jñāna* also found in the *Bhagavatī-sūtra*. There are mendicants (*anagāra*s) whose souls are pure but nonetheless have a false view of reality (*mithyātva*) and deceit (*māyā*) and therefore would acquire only *vibhaṅgâvadhi-jñāna*. If such a mendicant were to create, by means of special powers, the cities of Vāraṇāsī and Rājagṛha, and vast clusters of towns in between them, he could perceive all of them, but he would not know them as they really are (i.e. to be created by special powers and therefore not real cities) because his perception is perverted (*viparīta*). However, if his *avadhi-jñāna* were not accompanied by *mithyātva* and *māyā*, he would have 'a feeling that neither is it the city of Rājagṛha, nor is it the city of Vāraṇāsī, nor a vast cluster of towns in between.'[17] Thus, in both of these examples, objects were perceived by *vibhaṅga avadhi-jñāna*, but there was a mistake in ascertaining the true nature or characteristics of these objects (*svarūpa viparyaya*). Other examples of *vibhaṅga avadhi-jñāna* are associated with arriving at incorrect conclusions about the nature

---

[15] SSi commentary to TS 1.31, as translated by S.A. JAIN (1960: 39–40).

[16] *Bhagavatī-sūtra*, *śataka* 11, *uddeśaka* 9; see DELEU (1970: 175–76).

[17] *Bhagavatī-sūtra*, *śataka* 3, *uddeśaka* 6, as translated by LALWANI (1974: 101–106).

of reality and on the basis of this rejecting the teachings of the Arhants, such as the existence of a non-material soul, and so forth.[18] As in the case of *rājarṣi* Śiva, false clairvoyant knowledge is said to be acquired as the fruit of *bāla-tapas*, i.e. those forms of austerities or religious practices that are associated with violence (*hiṁsā*) or those that do not emphasise non-possession (*aparigraha*).[19]

When *avadhi-jñāna* arises in a person who has a proper view of reality (*samyag-darśana*), clairvoyant knowledge is also correct. Although lower degrees of partial clairvoyant knowledge (*deśâvadhi-jñāna*) can be either correct or incorrect, higher degrees of clairvoyant knowledge arise only in a person with *samyaktva*. Thus, there can be no *vibhaṅgâvadhi-jñāna* in the case of the second and third degrees of clairvoyant knowledge, namely *paramâvadhi-jñāna* and *sarvâvadhi-jñāna*.

There are numerous accounts of mendicants who have attained *avadhi-jñāna* accompanied by *samyag-darśana*. In the *Kalpa-sūtra* it is said that among the mendicant followers of Mahāvīra one thousand three hundred had *avadhi-jñāna*, and [some among them had] the highest degree (*utkṛṣṭa*) of *avadhi-jñāna*. There are similar statements regarding the mendicant followers of the other Tīrthaṅkaras here as well as in Hemacandra's *Tri-ṣaṣṭi-śalākā-puruṣa-caritra* ('Life-Stories of the Sixty-Three Illustrious Persons'), and in various Digambara sources such as Jinasena's *Hari-vaṁśa-purāṇa*.[20]

All of the examples of *avadhi-jñāna* mentioned so far have arisen in those who have renounced the household life. However, on occasion, *deśâvadhi-jñāna* is possible for a lay person as well. An illustration of this is found in the life-story of the pious householder Ānanda related in the *Upāsaka-daśāḥ* (UvD).[21] Ānanda had formally taken the vows of a lay follower (*aṇu-vrata*s) under Mahāvīra, and he regularly practised severe forms of fasting. He decided to undertake the fast ending

[18] For seven types of false knowledge about the nature of soul, matter, and so forth gained by *vibhaṅgâvadhi-jñāna*, see *Sthānâṅga-sūtra* (Ṭhāṇ), *sthāna* 7, *sūtra* 542.

[19] See the editor's notes to Hindi edition of the *Bhagavatī-sūtra* (Viy) on *śataka* 9, *uddeśaka* 31, verse 14. (vol. II: 443).

[20] KS 139. Mahāvīra had a total of fourteen thousand male and thirty-six thousand female mendicant followers. The twenty-second Tīrthaṅkara, Neminātha, had fifteen hundred mendicant followers with *avadhi-jñāna*, and the first Tīrthaṅkara, Ṛṣabha, nine thousand (KS 181 and 219). These numbers agree with Digambara sources. See JSK II: 386 (entry 42).

[21] The story of Ānanda is the first of the ten lectures in the *Upāsaka-daśāḥ*. It is summarised in JAINI (1979: 233–40). The portion of the story that relates to *avadhi-jñāna* is found at UvD 1.12–1.15. The entire text has been translated by A.F.R. HOERNLE (1888–1890).

in death (*sallekhanā*) and renounced all food and drink. 'Then one day on account of auspicious mental effort (*śubhâdhyavasāya*), auspicious transformation (*śubha-pariṇāma*), and mental coloration (*leśyā*) that had become pure, bright, or clear (*viśuddha*), there arose in Ānanda *avadhi-jñāna* from the partial destruction and partial suppression of *avadhi-jñāna-āvaraṇīya karman*.' With this knowledge, he could 'see' five hundred *yojana*s (1 *yojana* = approximately 8 miles) to the east, west, and south; he could see up to five hundred *yojana*s in the area of the Salt Sea (Lavaṇasamudra, the ocean that encircles Jambūdvīpa, the continent where Bharatakṣetra is located); to the north he could see the Himalayas up to Varṣadhara Mountain. In an upward direction, he could see as far as the Saudharmakalpa (the first or lowest of the heavenly abodes) and downwards he could see as far as the Ratnaprabhā (the first or uppermost of the hell regions), to the level within this region where hell-beings have a life-span of 84,000 years (Lolupācyuta Hell). Thus, according to this account, the attainment of *avadhi-jñāna* in humans is associated with auspicious mental effort (*adhyavasāya*), which in turn would cause auspicious transformations of the soul, including auspicious mental colorations, or *leśyā*s. In his notes to his Hindi translation of this text, Dr. Chaganlal Shastri adds, '*avadhi-jñāna* is obtained by the *kṣayôpaśama* of *avadhi-jñāna āvaraṇīya* karmic matter through austerities (*tapas*), vows (*vrata*), and restraint (*pratyākhyāna*), all of which are rooted in the wearing off or disassociation of karmic matter from the soul (*nirjarā*).'[22]

Returning to our narrative, it is evident from a conversation between Ānanda and Indrabhūti Gautama that clairvoyant knowledge of this extent was considered to be quite unusual for a lay person. Ānanda asked Gautama if it was true that a householder could attain *avadhi-jñāna*. When Gautama answered in the affirmative, Ānanda related to him what he had seen. Indrabhūti Gautama told him that a householder could not possibly have such extensive clairvoyant knowledge and asked him to confess his sin and perform penances. Ānanda then inquired if a person needed to confess and perform penances if what he had said was true. When Indrabhūti told him that it was not necessary, Ānanda said that it was Indrabhūti Gautama himself who should confess and perform penances. Confused, Indrabhūti Gautama went to Mahāvīra and told him all that had transpired. Mahāvīra replied that indeed Gautama should confess his sin, perform penances, and forgive the rudeness of the layman Ānanda for contradicting him in this matter.

In addition to heavenly beings, hell-beings and humans, it is believed that five-sensed rational animals can also acquire *deśâvadhi-jñāna*. According to Jaina sources, animals like lions and elephants can practice austerities equivalent to those

---

[22] UvD, p. 74.

of a lay person by fasting and by observing restraint with respect to harming. It also is believed that such animals may acquire a proper view of reality (*samyaktva*) and even may informally assume the lay vows (*aṇuvrata*s). However, I have found only a single reference to this in Hemacandra's *Tri-ṣaṣṭi-śalākā-puruṣa-caritra*, where it mentions that an elephant named Secanaka knew his former birth from clairvoyance.[23]

2. *Manaḥ-paryaya-jñāna*, or Mind-Reading

Although Jaina *ācārya*s are in close agreement regarding *avadhi-jñāna*, this is not the case with *manaḥ-paryaya-jñāna*, knowledge of the states (*paryāyas*) of the mind of others, or direct knowledge (*pratyakṣa*) of the objects in the minds (*manas*) of others.[24] I will examine here the view supported by the majority of commentators that *manaḥ-paryaya-jñāna* is a distinct type of direct knowledge (*pratyakṣa*), different from *avadhi-jñāna*, that is obstructed by a specific type of karmic matter, namely, *manaḥ-paryaya-jñānâvaraṇīya-karman*.[25]

According to *Tattvârtha-sūtra* 1.26 (= SSi 1.25), 'Mind-reading (*manaḥ-paryaya*) and clairvoyance (*avadhi*) differ with regards to purity (*viśuddhi*), space (*kṣetra*), knower (*svāmi*), and objects (*viṣaya*).' With respect to objects, a person who has clairvoyance can apprehend objects composed of matter that is more subtle than that which forms the gross physical body (*audārika-śarīra*) of humans and animals. For example, the transformational body (*vaikriyaka-śarīra*) of a heavenly being or a hell-being can be 'seen' by some who have *avadhi-jñāna*. Except for karmic matter that comprises the karmic body, matter that forms the mind is the most subtle matter in any body. It is by perceiving the modifications of this matter itself that one 'knows the objects thought of by the minds of others.'[26] In his notes on this *sūtra*,

---

[23] JOHNSON (1931–1962 VI: 161).

[24] *Manaḥ-paryaya* is also written as *manaḥ-paryāya* and *manaḥ-paryava*. See TATIA (1951: 65, n. 1). I do not intend to examine here the view held by Jinabhadra and certain other commentators that follow him that *manaḥ-paryaya* is a type of direct knowledge (*pratyakṣa*) but that it is restricted to intuition of the states of the mind engaged in thinking, and that the external objects that are thought of are known only by inference (*anumāna*). For a discussion of the various commentators on this subject, see TATIA (1951: 65–68).

[25] The opposing view is held by Siddhasena Divākara, who understands *manaḥ-paryaya* to be a specific type of *avadhi-jñāna*. For details, see TATIA (1951: 69).

[26] S.A. JAIN (1960: 34).

TATIA explains that 'Mind-reading knows the thinking expressed by the modes of the material clusters which constitute the mind. Mind-reading knows the finer modes of the material clusters which are beyond the reach of clairvoyance.'[27] In his notes on *Tattvârtha-sūtra* 1.29 (= SSi 1.28), which reads: 'Mind-reading is an infinitesimal part of that [which is ascertained by clairvoyance],' TATIA explains that mind-reading is narrower because 'it can only identify the modes of the material clusters that constitute mind, while clairvoyance can identify all kinds of material clusters in cosmic space. However, clairvoyance cannot read the mind, that is, it cannot identify the modes of the mind's material clusters because these are too subtle.'[28]

There are two types of mind-reading according to *Tattvârtha-sūtra* 1.24 (= SSi 1.23): *ṛju-mati-manaḥ-paryaya*, 'straight' or 'simple' mind-reading, and *vipula-mati-manaḥ-paryaya*, 'complex' mind-reading. TATIA states that simple mind-reading knows only a few general modes of the mind and relates to thoughts about an object or an action, while complex mind-reading knows many different modes and is related to the deeper motivation or beliefs that underlie simple thoughts. 'Simple modes relate to thoughts about an object or action and the complex to the deeper motivation and beliefs that lie behind these thoughts.' According to *Gommaṭa-sāra*, by directing one's attention to the material object located in the mind of another, a person directly knows the thoughts of another through simple mind-reading.[29] In his translation of this text, J.L. JAINI mentions that 'simple mental-knowledge directly sees the thing upon which the mind of another is exercising at the present. For example, a man is thinking of establishing a library. Simple mental knowledge will see this fact ... If he has forgotten some of the details, simple knowledge will see the present desire and also the forgotten details.'[30] He explains complex mental knowledge using the example of Mahāvīra's renunciation: 'There is no historic record of a particular action done by Lord Mahāvīra, when preparing for his renunciation. Complex knowledge can even today see his mental activity corresponding to that preparation. Simple knowledge cannot see this fact because there is nothing in the mind of another, at the present moment, to link up that past with the present.'[31] Among these two, 'complex mind-reading (*vipula-mati-manaḥ-paryaya*) is more pure than simple mind reading (*ṛju-mati-manaḥ-paryaya*) because the conduct of the person who has it is increasing in

[27] TATIA (1994: 20).

[28] TATIA (1994: 21).

[29] GJK 448.

[30] J.L. JAINI's commentary on GJK 441 (1927: 230–31).

[31] J.L. JAINI's commentary on GJK 441 (1927: 230–31).

purity. However, *ṛju-mati* is subject to downfall (*pratipāta*) because in the person who has it there is the destruction of [good] conduct from the rise of *kaṣāyas*.'

Regarding space, although it is possible for clairvoyant knowledge to reach to the limits of the occupied universe (*lokâkāśa*), mind-reading extends only to the most distant regions of the universe where humans live (two and one-half continents and oceans in the centre of the universe). The *Sarvârtha-siddhi* explains that simple mind-reading can extend from a distance of one *krośa* (two miles) up to one *yojana* (eight miles) and complex mind-reading up to the mountain range that forms the boundary of human habitation (Mānuṣôttara).[32] However, *Gommaṭa-sāra* 456 understands this to be the area of a square, not the circumference of the Mānuṣôttara. According to J.L. JAINI, the spatial range of complex mind-reading therefore would include the thoughts of those five-sensed rational animals and heavenly beings living in this area as well.[33] This contradicts the view found in the *Āvaśyaka-niryukti* that that mind-reading is limited to the minds of humans (*jaṇa-maṇa*).[34] With respect to time, simple mind-reading extends from a minimum of two or three past or future births to a maximum of seven or eight births, while complex mind-reading extends from a minimum of seven or eight births to innumerable births.[35] Thus, when compared with clairvoyant knowledge, mind-reading is more restricted in its scope of objects as well as its spatial range.

In comparison to the number of beings who attain *avadhi-jñāna* either by birth or through merit, there are only a few who will attain *manaḥ-paryaya*. Commenting on who can attain it, Akalaṅka quotes a lengthy passage from an unidentified source stating

> '*Manaḥ-paryaya* is manifested only among humans, not among heavenly beings (*devas*), hell-beings (*nārakis*), or animals (*tiryañcas*). Among humans, it arises only among those capable of complete development (*paryāptas*), not among those born through coagulation (*sammūrcchana*). Among womb-born humans, it arises only in those

[32] TS 1.23 and commentary, as translated by S.A. JAIN (1960: 34–35). GJK 445 uses the term '*pṛthaktva*,' for the minimum and maximum. This is glossed in the commentary as 2 or 3 *krośas* minimum and 7 or 8 *yojanas* maximum.

[33] J.L. JAINI (1927: 235).

[34] TATIA (1951: 69), quoting *Āvaśyaka-niryukti* 76. However, some Śvetāmbara commentators understand this to include all five-sensed beings living in the *manuṣya-loka*, see Siddhasenagaṇi's commentary on TS 1.24.

[35] This same statement is found at GJK 457. Unfortunately neither Pūjyapāda nor the commentators on *Gommaṭa-sāra* discuss how mind-reading in past and future births is to be understood.

born in the *karma-bhūmis*, not among those in the *akarma-bhūmis*. Among those *karma-bhūmi* born humans, it arises only in those whose development is completed, who have attained *samyag-dṛṣṭi*, and who are restrained. It does not arise in one who is not restrained (*asaṁyata*) or who is partially restrained (*saṁyatâsaṁyata*). It arises in those from the sixth *guṇa-sthāna* (*pramatta*) through the twelfth *guṇa-sthāna* (*kṣīṇa-kaṣāya*) whose purity of conduct is increasing (*pravardhamāna-cāritra*), not among those whose purity of conduct is decreasing (*hīyamāna-cāritra*).[36] Among them, it arises only in those who have attained at least one of the seven *ṛddhis*, or supernatural powers, and among them, it arises only in some, not in all.'[37]

Likewise, the *Ṣaṭ-khaṇḍâgama* (ṢKhĀ) states that *manaḥ-paryaya* is possible from the sixth (*pramatta-saṁyata*) through the twelfth (*kṣīṇa-kaṣāya vīta-rāga chadmastha*) *guṇa-sthānas*. And there is a similar passage in *Gommaṭa-sāra-jīva-kāṇḍa* 445 that reads 'And mental knowledge appears in saints with one or more of the seven supernatural powers (*ṛddhis*), and with ever increasing lofty conduct, in the seven,' namely, from the sixth through the twelfth *guṇa-sthānas*.

In spite of these statements, there is some disagreement regarding the attainment of *manaḥ-paryaya* in the sixth *guṇa-sthāna*. In the edition of *Sarvârtha-siddhi* edited by Phoolchandra Siddhanta Sastri, there is a note that other manuscripts read *apramatta* (seventh *guṇa-sthāna*).[38] S.A. JAIN translates this as 'from the seventh stage of perfection of vows to the twelfth stage of destroyed delusion.'[39] It is possible that this difference may be the result of scribal differences in eliding the initial 'a' of the word '*apramatta*.' However, this is not the case in Śvetāmbara sources, which apparently understand the attainment of *manaḥ-paryaya* in the seventh *guṇa-sthāna* and not the sixth. In his commentary on *Tattvârtha-sūtra* 1.24, Siddhasenagaṇi glosses Umāsvāti's term *saṁyata* as 'excluding the (first) six (*guṇa-sthānas*), *mithyā-dṛṣṭi* through *pramatta*.' Likewise, there is a passage in the *Nandī-sūtra*, similar to that quoted in Akalaṅka's commentary mentioned above, stating

[36] SSi 222 on TS 1.25.

[37] RVār 1.25. See also SSi 222 and GJK 445. The *ṛddhis* listed here are *buddhi*, *pasa*, *vikriyā*, *auṣadha*, *rasa*, *bala* and *akṣina*.

[38] See Bhāratīya Jñānapīṭha edition of SSi, p. 94, note 2. He provides few details regarding these alternate readings. The references are to 'mu' = Mudrita copy (*Sarvārthasiddhi*) and 'di 1,2' = Dilli copy 1,2. The Bhāratīya Jñānapīṭha edition of Rājavārttika reads *pramatta*, with no alternate readings given.

[39] S.A. JAIN (1992: 36).

that persons who are 'self-controlled and free from passions (*apramatta*) and who are possessed of *ṛddhis* are entitled to possess this *manaḥ-paryaya*.'[40]

There is yet another alternative offered in the Digambara *Pañcâstikāya*. Here it states that both *ṛju-mati* and *vipula-mati* arise only in a muni who is *apramatta*, without the fifteen types of carelessness (*pramāda*), and who has proper faith, knowledge, and conduct. Although it is a rule that at the time of its arising, the muni must be *apramatta*, after this, it can exist in the state of *pramatta*.[41] This opinion regarding the attainment of *manaḥ-paryaya* is similar to the rule associated with the *karman* that forms the translocational body of a muni (*āhāraka-śarīra-nāma-karman*). This *karman* can be bound only while the muni is in the seventh *guṇa-sthāna* but it must come into rise forming the body in the sixth *guṇa-sthāna*. GLASENAPP (1942: 83, n. 1) explains that 'if a *yati* manifests in himself the translocation-body, he exhibits a certain impatience (*autsukya*) and is therefore *pramatta*.' Perhaps there is a similar notion regarding *manaḥ-paryaya*, that while a muni is in such a state of purity and is practising various forms of meditation (*dhyāna*), he would not choose to employ his ability to know the thoughts of others, although this power would be in existence at this level of spiritual purity.

There is no good explanation offered by the commentators as to why it is not possible for those in the lower *guṇa-sthānas* to attain *manaḥ-paryaya*. In Vīrasena's *Dhavalā-ṭīkā* to ṢKhĀ, the question is raised, 'Why is *manaḥ-paryaya* not possible for beings in the lower *guṇa-sthānas*, *deśa-virati*, etc.' As is often the case, Vīrasena's response merely states, 'It is not possible because there is a prohibition in its arising in those who are partially restrained (*saṁyamâsaṁyama*) and not restrained (*asaṁyama*).'[42] Nor is there an explanation offered as to why not everyone who attains the sixth *guṇa-sthāna* will acquire *manaḥ-paryaya*. Vīrasena states, 'if it were the case that restraint was the only cause of this, then this would be a valid assumption. However, there are some additional causes, namely, excellent (*vasiṣṭha*) location, and time, and so forth.'[43]

In accordance with the degree to which *manaḥ-paryaya-jñāna-āvaraṇīya-karman* is partially destroyed and partially suppressed (*kṣayôpaśama*) at any given time, the extent of this knowledge will increase or decrease, and it may even be lost altogether (*pratipātī*) if *kṣayôpaśama* of this *karman* ceases. However, complex mind-reading is characterised by increasing partial destruction and partial suppression of *manaḥ-paryaya-āvaraṇīya-karman*, and once attained, it is never lost

[40] *Nandī-sūtra* 17, as quoted in TATIA (1951: 68).

[41] *Pañcâstikāya*, as quoted in JSK III: 269.

[42] See JSK III: 269 (entry 4).

[43] See JSK III: 269.

(*apratipātī*). 'A saint with complex mental knowledge must attain liberation from the same body. That very knowledge is enlarged to omniscience.'[44]

While it is certain that male mendicants may sometimes acquire *manaḥ-paryaya*, this may not be the case for female mendicants. For Digambaras, of course, the question of a woman attaining *manaḥ-paryaya* does not arise because they maintain that it is not possible for a woman to take the mendicant vow of non-possession (*aparigraha*); thus their highest spiritual attainment is that of the fifth *guṇa-sthāna*. However, there is a discussion of this subject in *Strī-nirvāṇa-prakaraṇa* (c. 814–867), a text of an extinct sect called Yāpanīya. This text says '[The opponent (i.e. Digambaras)] may say that women do not attain *nirvāṇa* [for the following reasons] (2) because they lack supernatural powers (*labdhi*s) such as that of winning debates and so on and (5) because they lack the direct awareness of the thought forms of others (*manaḥ-paryaya-jñāna*).'[45] The Yāpanīya response is as follows: 'There is no non-attainment of *siddhi* [i.e. *mokṣa*] even in cases where there is non-attainment of such supernatural powers as skill in debate or transformation of the body and so forth … or [if one does not have] direct mental perception [which are all points agreed upon by both sides].'[46] In his *Svopajña-vṛtti* on the *Strī-nirvāṇa-prakaraṇa*, Ācārya Śākaṭāyana explains that

> '"transformation of the body" is the power that enables one to assume the form of Indra and other [gods]; it is also known as the supernatural power to transform oneself. The words "and so forth" include such supernatural powers as walking in the air; women do not have these powers … . "Direct mental perception" is divided into a "straightforward" type [which is restricted in both time and space] and a "curved" type [which can extend through innumerable births and into all human abodes]. [Direct mental perception] is possible only to a monk who has taken the total vows of a mendicant; it is the knowledge of objects that are within the minds of animals and human beings who reside within the confines of the Mānuṣottara range of mountains. Women do not possess it. Thus, even though women are incapable of these powers that are produced through excellence in knowledge, conduct, and austerities, this does not mean that they are incapable of *mokṣa*. *Mokṣa* is not dependent on these alone.'[47]

---

[44] GJK 447 and J.L. JAINI's commentary (1927: 222–23).

[45] *Strī-nirvāṇa-prakaraṇa* #12 [4], as translated by JAINI (1991: 51).

[46] *Strī-nirvāṇa-prakaraṇa* #21 [7], as translated by JAINI (1991: 53).

[47] *Strī-nirvāṇa-prakaraṇa* #21 [7], as translated by JAINI (1991: 53–54).

Although Śvetāmbaras concur with the Yāpanīyas on the ability of women to attain *mokṣa* and the eating of morsel-food by *kevalin*s, I am not certain whether Śvetāmbaras agree with the Yāpanīyas on this matter. In her translation of Hemacandra's *Tri-ṣaṣṭi-śalākā-puruṣa-caritra*,[48] Helen JOHNSON provides a long note on the subject of *labdhi*s. She states that all *labdhi*s can be acquired by *bhavya* men; but there are ten that are not possible to *bhavya* women. She does not include either *ṛju-mati-jñāna* or *vipula-mati-jñāna* in her list of those that cannot be acquired by women. She then states, 'These ten exceptions, plus no. 8 (*ṛjumati jñāna*), no. 9 (*vipulamati jñāna*), and no. 12 (*kevali*) are not possible to *abhavya*-men. This is according to *Pravacana-sārôddhāra*.'[49] Unfortunately, I do not have access to this text to verify her statement. If she is correct, it would appear that there were some Śvetāmbara *ācārya*s who disagreed with the Yāpanīyas in this regard and maintained that it is possible for both men and women to acquire *manaḥ-paryaya* after taking the mendicant vows.

There is at least one woman who according to Śvetāmbaras attained *manaḥ-paryaya*: the nineteenth Tīrthaṅkara, Malli.[50] In her life-story in Hemacandra's *Tri-ṣaṣṭi-śalākā-puruṣa-caritra*, it is mentioned that 'After a three-day fast Lord Malli became a mendicant … Malli's mind-reading knowledge arose just then, and on the same day omniscience arose.'[51] I have found no other mention in Śvetāmbara sources of a woman attaining *manaḥ-paryaya*. It is difficult to decide whether this might be interpreted as an extraordinary event (*āścarya*) associated with the special circumstances of Malli's birth as female or whether *manaḥ-paryaya* might arise in other mendicant women as well.

Although there are many stories in Jaina texts that mention the application of clairvoyant and omniscient knowledge, I have been unable to locate any narratives describing the details of what was perceived via *manaḥ-paryaya*. Hemacandra's *Tri-ṣaṣṭi-śalākā-puruṣa-caritra* relates the stories of the twenty-four Tīrthaṅkaras who attained omniscience in Bharatakṣetra during this descending half-cycle of time

---

[48] According to WINTERNITZ (1983 III: 557, n. 1) a commentary was written on this text by Siddhasenasūri in CE 1185. This Siddhasena is different from Siddhasena Divākara and Siddhasenagaṇi, who wrote a commentary on TS.

[49] JOHNSON (1931–1962 I: 75–76, n. 111). She mentions here that the *Pravacana-sārôddhāra* of Nemicandra (verses 1492–1508) is the most complete list that she has found. An *abhavya* could never have this type of knowledge because they can never attain *samyaktva* (= fourth *guṇa-sthāna*). Thus, the question of their assuming mendicant vows would not arise. For details on *abhavyatva*, see JAINI (1977).

[50] Digambaras believe that Malli was a male.

[51] JOHNSON (1931–1962 IV: 66).

(*avasarpiṇī*). In the story of *Ṛṣabha*, the first Tīrthaṅkara of our time, it is said that he renounced the world and after fasting for three days 'The Lord's *manaḥ-paryaya* knowledge, which makes clear the mind-substance of the human world, arose just as if it had an appointment with the initiation.'[52] The attainment of this knowledge immediately after renunciation is included in the life-story of most, but not all, of the Tīrthaṅkaras. There apparently is a belief that all Tīrthaṅkaras have *avadhi-jñāna* from the time of conception and that all attain *manaḥ-paryaya-jñāna* soon after renunciation.[53]

It is not surprising that there is no further mention of *manaḥ-paryaya* between the time of renunciation and the attainment of omniscience in the narratives of the lives of most of the twenty-four Tīrthaṅkaras because the accounts often are quite abbreviated. However, even for those Tīrthaṅkaras whose life-stories are more detailed, the treatment of *manaḥ-paryaya* is quite cursory. For example, in the *Tri-ṣaṣṭi-śalākā-puruṣa-caritra*, it is said that Mahāvīra's *manaḥ-paryaya* 'became manifest at the same time as good-conduct' following a two day fast just after initiation.[54] There are references to Mahāvīra's *avadhi-jñāna* between the time of his renunciation and his attainment of omniscience some twelve and one-half years later. For instance, it is said that 'The Lord knew by clairvoyance "Today much of my *karman* must be destroyed",' and his 'religious meditation (*dharma-dhyāna*), which is especially destructive type of *karman*, burned during the night as he endured the calamity of the cold. Śrī Vīrasvāmin's clairvoyance (*avadhi-jñāna*), like that of an Anuttara-god, became very strong, beholding the entire world (i.e. it extended as far as the border of the occupied universe, the *lokâkāśa*).'[55] But oddly enough, there is almost total silence regarding his *manaḥ-paryaya*. The only reference that I have located regarding the application of his direct knowledge is a passage in the *Jñātṛ-dharma-kathāḥ* (*Nāyā-dhamma-kahāo*) where Mahāvīra knows the thoughts of Mehakumāra.[56]

---

[52] JOHNSON (1931–1962 I: 166).

[53] Charlotte KRAUSE (1952: 130, n. 6) mentions this subject in *Ancient Jaina Hymns*. Commenting on the phrase '*adya-jñāna-traya*' she states that the Tīrthaṅkaras are believed to possess the first three categories of knowledge, namely *mati-jñāna* or knowledge obtained through the senses and the process of thinking, *śruta-jñāna* or knowledge acquired by instruction, and *avadhi-jñāna*, or transcendental knowledge of material things, from their very conception. They acquire the last two, namely *manaḥ-paryāya-jñāna* or thought-reading, and *kevala-jñāna* at later stages of their lives.

[54] JOHNSON (1931–1962 VI: 39).

[55] JOHNSON (1931–1962 VI: 76 and 80).

[56] This is mentioned in DEO (1956: 200, n. 311) (Nāyā, p. 44).

Both Śvetāmbaras and Digambaras maintain that it is not possible for anyone in this location of the universe at this time to attain *manaḥ-paryaya*. In the *Viśeṣâvaśyaka-bhāṣya*, Jinabhadra lists twelve extraordinary attainments (*labdhi*s) that came to an end after the death of Jambū, including ascent of the *upaśama*- and *kṣapaka-śreṇi*s, and attainment of *paramâvadhi-jñāna* and *manaḥ-paryaya-jñāna*. There also is a passage in the *Mahā-purāṇa* of Jinasena that reads, '*muni*s of the *pañcama-kāla* will not have *avadhi-jñāna* and *manaḥ-paryaya-jñāna*.'[57] Thus, as with *paramâvadhi-jñāna* and *sarvâvadhi-jñāna*, the possibility of having any type of *manaḥ-paryaya* apparently ended some sixty-four years after Mahāvīra's *nirvāṇa* with the death of Jambū, when the possibility of attaining *mokṣa* also ended.

It is easy to understand why complex mind-reading is no longer possible because it is attained only by those who will ascend the *kṣapaka-śreṇi*, thereby attaining *mokṣa* in that very life. However, I have found no statements in the commentaries as to why this is the case with simple mind-reading as well. One might speculate that the non-attainment of *manaḥ-paryaya* would correspond with the non-attainment of the *ṛddhi*s. However, according to traditional accounts such as Hemacandra's *Pariśiṣṭa-parvan*, it was still possible to attain various supernatural powers after the time of Jambū. Here, it states that Bhadrabāhu, the last muni to know all fourteen *Pūrva*s, had taught his disciple Sthūlabhadra ten *Pūrva*s. Bhadrabāhu refused to teach him the remaining *Pūrva*s out of displeasure at Sthūlabhadra's using his magical powers to turn himself into a lion, thereby frightening his sisters who had come to see him.[58]

As illustrated by the story of Sthūlabhadra, when supernatural powers, including *avadhi-jñāna* and *manaḥ-paryaya-jñāna*, arise in a person that is subject to passions

---

[57] *Mahā-purāna* 41.76, as quoted in JSK I: 198. Regarding the loss of *avadhi-jñāna*, there is a passage in the *Tri-loka-prajñapti* (4.1510–1517, as cited in JSK I: 198) stating that two hundred seventy-five years after the loss of all those who knew the *Ācārâṅga*, King Kalki will demand taxes from the munis, and some of them will go without food. Not eating, some may get *avadhi-jñāna*. Every thousand years or so, there may be someone who will have it.

[58] FYNES (1998: 194–95). See also Canto 12, where the magical powers of Vajra are described. It should be noted that not all magical powers are acquired directly by asceticism. It is believed that there are certain supernatural powers (*vidyā*s) that are gifts from the gods and some that could be learned from the *Pūrva*s. See, for example, FYNES (1998: 226, verse 157) and (: 237, verses 307–08). In Vajra's life-story, there is also the following statement: 'Vajra knew what the citizens were thinking and saying through his excellent powers of perception;' FYNES (1998: 235, verse 285). Since I do not have access to the original text, I would hesitate to speculate about the intended meaning of this passage.

(*kaṣāyas*) of stronger degrees of intensity, they can pose a threat to spiritual progress, because there is always the danger of attachment to these powers. This would be the case for lower degrees of clairvoyant knowledge (*deśâvadhi-jñāna*) and for simple mind-reading (*ṛju-mati-manaḥ-paryaya*). With clairvoyant knowledge, if a person has a false view of reality (*mithyātva*), there is the additional danger that such knowledge is false; therefore, it could mislead others and could contradict Jaina *dharma*. Even when such powers are associated with a correct view of reality (*samyag-darśana*) attachment to these powers is detrimental to a mendicant's continued spiritual progress. Therefore, those mendicants who make a living through occult powers, including clairvoyance and mind-reading, are considered to be the lowest among the five classes of ascetics.[59] There is, however, apparently little danger associated with the higher levels of clairvoyance and mind-reading, for those who have *paramâvadhi-jñāna*, *sarvâvadhi-jñāna*, and *vipula-mati-manaḥ-paryaya* do not fall to the lower states of spiritual purity and thus are never subjected to stronger degrees of passions that would be associated with attachment to these powers. In a sense, these three advanced levels of direct knowledge are precursors of perfect knowledge (*kevala-jñāna*), which arises only after the *mohanīya-karman* that causes attachment or pride has been totally destroyed. Thus, it would be correct to say that among the three types of direct knowledge 'only omniscience is perfectly innate because it alone arises out of the total elimination of knowledge-covering *karma*.'[60] It is never accompanied by ignorance nor is it ever associated with impure transformations of the soul caused by the rise of the destructive *karman*s. Unlike knowledge attained through lower levels of clairvoyance and mind-reading, that which is known through omniscient knowledge can never lead to actions that are harmful to the soul in any way because there can never be the binding of any new *karman* that would lead to future births, be they pleasant or unpleasant, that would prolong the soul's beginningless, but not necessarily endless, journey in *saṁsāra*.

---

[59] Such mendicants are called *pulāka* because they are like husks, or empty or shrivelled grain. For the five classes of mendicants, see TS 9.48 (= SSi 9.46).

[60] TATIA (1994: 13).

BIBLIOGRAPHY

Āyār = *Āyāraṁga-sutta* [*Ācārâṅga-sūtra*]. See: JACOBI (1884).

DELEU 1970 = Deleu, Jozef: *Viyāhapannatti* (*Bhagavaī*): *The Fifth Anga of the Jaina Canon*. Introduction, critical analysis, commentary & indexes. 'De Tempel', Brugge 1970. [Reprinted: *Lala Sundar Lal Jain Research Series* 10, Motilal Banarsidass, Delhi 1996].

DEO 1956 = Deo, S. B.: *History of Jaina Monachism from Inscriptions and Literature*. *Deccan College Dissertation Series* 17, Deccan College Postgraduate and Research Institute, Poona 1956.

FYNES 1998 = Fynes, R.C.C. (tr.): *The Lives of the Jain Elders*. Oxford University Press, Oxford – New York 1998.

GJK = *Gommaṭa-sāra-jīva-kāṇḍa* of Nemicandra (with the *Karṇāṭāka-vṛtti* of Keśavaṇṇa, the Sanskrit *ṭīkā* of Jīvatattvapradīpikā, and Hindi translation). 2 vols. Eds. Ādinātha Neminātha Upādhye and Pt. Kailāśacandra Śāstrī. Jñānapīṭha Mūrtidevī Jaina Granthamālā, Prakrit Grantha, nos. 14 and 15. Bhāratīya Jñānapīṭha, Delhi 1978.

von GLASENAPP 1942 = Glasenapp, Helmuth von: *The Doctrine of Karman in Jain Philosophy*. English translation from the Original German by G. Barry Gifford, ed. H.R. Kapadia, Bai Vijibhai Jivanlal Pannalal Charity Fund, Bombay 1942.

HOERNLE 1888–1890 = Hoernle, A.F. Rudolf: *The Uvāsagadasāo or the Religious Profession of an Uvāsaga expounded in ten lectures, being the Seventh Anga of the Jains*. Prakrit text ed. and transl., 2 vols., *Bibliotheca Indica* 105, Calcutta 1888–1890.

JACOBI 1884 = Jacobi, Hermann: *Jaina Sûtras. Part I: Âcârâṅga Sûtra, Kalpa Sûtra*. Translated from Prâkrit by … . *Sacred Books of the East* 22, Oxford University Press, Oxford 1884. [Reprinted: Motilal Banarsidass, Delhi 1989].

JAIN 1960 = Jain, S.A. (tr.): *Reality: English Translation of Pūjyapāda's Sarvārthasiddhi*. Vira Sasana Sangha, Calcutta 1960. [Reprinted: Jwalamalini Trust, Madras 1992].

JAINI 1920 = Jaini, J.L. (tr.): *Tattvarthadhigama Sutra. A Treatise on the Essential Principles of Jainism. The Sacred Books of the Jains* 2. The Central Jaina Publishing House, Arrah1920.

JAINI 1927 = Jaini, J. L.: *Gommatsara Jiva-Kanda* of Nemicandra. The Sacred Books of the Jainas, vol. 5. The Central Jaina Publishing House, Lucknow 1927. [Reprinted: Today & Tomorrow's Printers & Publishers, New Delhi 1990].

JAINI 1977 = Jaini, Padmanabh S.: 'Bhavyatva and Abhavyatva: A Jain Doctrine of "Predestination".' In: A.N. Upadhye, Nathmal Tatia, Dalsukh Malvania, Mohanlal Mehta, Nemichand Shastri, Kailashchandra Shastri (eds.): *Mahāvīra and His Teachings*. Bhagavān Mahāvīra 2,500 Nirvāṇa Mahotsava Samiti, Bombay 1977: 95–111.

JAINI 1979 = Jaini, Padmanabh S.: *The Jaina Path of Purification*. University of California Press, Berkeley—Los Angeles—London 1979.

JAINI 1991 = Jaini, Padmanabh S.: *Gender and Salvation: Jaina Debates on the Spiritual Liberation of Women*. University of California Press, Berkeley and Los Angeles 1991.

JOHNSON 1931–62 = Johnson, Helen M. (tr.): *Triṣaṣṭiśalākāpuruṣacarita or the Lives of Sixty-three Illustrious Persons by Ācārya Śrī Hemacandra*. 6 vols., *Gaekwad's Oriental Series*, Oriental Institute, Baroda 1931–62.

JSK = *Jainendra Siddhānta Kośa*. ed. by Jinendra Varṇī, Vols. 1–4, *Jñānapīṭha Mūrtidevī Jaina Granthamālā*, Bhāratīya Jñāna-pīṭha Publications, Delhi 1970–1973 [In Hindi].

KRAUSE 1952 = Krause, Charlotte (ed.): *Ancient Jaina Hymns*. *Scindia Oriental Series* 2. Scindia Oriental Institute, Ujjain 1952.

KS = *Kalpa-sūtra*. See: JACOBI (1884).

LALWANI 1973–80 = Lalwani, K.C. (tr.): *Bhagavatī Sūtra*. 3 vols. Jain Bhawan, Calcutta 1973–80.

MAHĀPRAJÑA 1996 = Mahāprajña, Ācārya (ed.): *Śrībhikṣu Āgama Viṣaya Kośa*. ('Cyclopaedia of Jain Canonical Texts'), Part 1, Jain Vishva Bharati Institute, Ladnun (Rajasthan) 1996.

RVār = *Tattvârtha-vārttika* (*Rāja-vārttika*) *of Śrī Akalaṅkadeva*. Edited with Hindi Translation, Introduction, appendices, variant readings, comparative notes etc. by Prof. Mahendra Kumar Jain. Parts I–II. First edition, *Jñānapīṭha Mūrtidevī Jaina Granthamālā: Sanskrit Grantha* No. 10, 20, Bhāratīya Jñānapīṭha, Delhi 1953–1957. [Second edition: Delhi 1982].

SCHUBRING 1962 = Schubring, Walther: *The Doctrine of the Jainas*. Translated from the German by Wolfgang Beurlen, Motilal Banarsidass, Delhi 1962.

ṢKhĀ = *Ṣaṭ-khaṇḍâgama* of Puṣpadanta and Bhūtabali, ed. with the *Dhavalā-ṭīkā* of Vīrasena. Prakrit and Sanskrit texts with Hindi translation by Hiralal Jain. 16 vols. Jaina Sāhityoddhāraka Fund, Amaravati 1939–1959. [Revised edition: Jaina Samskriti Samrakṣak Sangha, Solapur 1985].

SSi = *Sarvârtha-siddhi* of Pūjyapāda Devanandin, ed. with *Tattvârtha-sūtra* of Umāsvāti. Sanskrit text with Hindi translation by Phoolchandra Siddhāntaśāstrī. *Jñānapīṭha Mūrtidevī Jaina Granthamālā*, *Sanskrit Grantha* 13, Bhāratīya Jñānapīṭha, Varanasi 1971.

TATIA 1951 = Tatia, Nathmal: *Studies in Jaina Philosophy*. Jain Cultural Research Society, Varanasi 1951.

TATIA 1994 = Tatia, Nathmal (tr.): *Tattvārtha Sūtra: That Which Is. Umāsvāti / Umāsvāmī; with the combined commentaries of Umāsvāti / Umāsvāmī, Pūjyapāda and Siddhasensgaṇi*. The Sacred Literature Series, Harper Collins Publishers, San Francisco—London—Pymble 1994.

Ṭhāṇ = *Ṭhāṇaṁga-sutta* [*Sthānâṅga-sūtra*]. *Sthānâṅga-sūtram* (with Abhayadevasūri's Vṛtti) and *Samavāyâṅga-sūtram*. Ed. Muni Jambuvijaya. *Jaina-āgama-granthamālā* 3, Motilal Banarasidass Publishers, Delhi 1985.

TS = Umāsvāti: *Tattvârthâdhigama-sūtra. Tattvārthādhigamasūtra (A Treatise on the Fundamental Principles of Jainism) by His Holiness Śrī Umāsvāti Vācaka, together with his Connective Verses Commented upon by Śrī Devaguptasūri and Śrī Siddhasenagaṇi*. ed. by H.R. Kapadia, 2 vols., Devchand Lalbhai Jain Pustakoddhar Fund, series nos. 67 and 76, Jivanachand Sakerchand Javeri, Bombay 1926, 1930.

TṢŚPC = Hemacandra: *Tri-ṣaṣṭi-śalākā-puruṣa-carita*. See: JOHNSON (1931–62).

UvS = *Uvāsaga-dasāo* [*Upāsaka-daśāḥ-sūtra*]. Ed., tr., and annotated by Dr. Chaganlal Shastri. Sri Agam Prakashan Samiti, Beawar (Rajasthan) 1980 [in Hindi].

Viy = *Viyāha-pannatti* [= *Bhagavatī Vyākhyā-prajñapti*]. Tr. and annotated by Sri Amar Muni and Sri Chand Suran 'Saras'. Sri Agam Prakashan Samiti, Beawar (Rajasthan) 1983 [in Hindi].

Webster's = *Webster's Collegiate Dictionary*. Tenth Edition, 1993.

WINTERNITZ 1983 = Winternitz, Maurice: *A History of Indian Literature*. Vol. 2. Revised Edition. Motilal Banarsidass, Delhi 1933. [Reprinted: Delhi 1988].

WOODS 1914 = Woods, James H. (tr.): *The Yoga-System of Patañjali or The Ancient Hindu Doctrine of Concentration of Mind, Embracing Yoga-Sūtras, Yoga-Bhāṣya and Tattva-Vaiśaradi*. Cambridge (Mass.) 1914. [Reprinted: Motilal Banarsidass, Delhi 1988].

द्वितीयारनयविवरणम्

Early Jainism, Buddhism and Âjîvikism

The Essence and Outline of Jainism

MUNI JAMBŪVIJAYA

॥श्री ऋषभदेवस्वामिने नमः॥ ॥श्री शंखेश्वरपार्श्वनाथाय नमः॥

जैनदर्शनस्य स्वरूपमुद्देशश्च ॥

संस्कृतभाषायां जयार्थे वर्तमानाज्जिधातोः जिनशब्दो निष्पद्यते। जयतीति **जिनः**। अतिभीषणानतिदुःखदायकान् रागद्वेषमोहरूपान्नन्तरङ्गशत्रून् यो जयति यश्च अनन्यसाधारणैर्विविधैरतिशयैर्युक्तः दुःखनिमग्नस्यास्य जगत उद्धरणार्थं तीर्थस्य प्रवर्तकः अपारकरुणानिधिः तीर्थकरः सोऽत्र **जिन**शब्देन विवक्षितः। ईदृशं जिनं ये देवत्वेन स्वीकुर्वन्ति पूजयन्ति च ते **जैना** इत्युच्यन्ते। ईदृशं जैनत्वं कस्मिन्नपि देशे कस्मिंश्चिदपि काले कस्यामपि जातौ केनचिद् अपि प्राप्तुं शक्यते। जैनत्वं खलु देशकालानवच्छिन्नम्।

रागद्वेषमोहविजेतारः अनेके आत्मानः संभवन्ति। किन्तु तेषु तीर्थकरा अल्पीयांस एव। जगदुद्धर्तारो जिना यदा सर्वज्ञत्वं प्राप्नुवन्ति तदा सर्वस्य जगतो हितार्थं तीर्थं प्रवर्तयन्ति येन दुःखनिमग्ना जीवाः संसारमहोदधिं सुखेनैव तरीतुं शक्नुवन्ति। अनादिकालीनचतुर्गति-भ्रमणरूपसंसारसमुद्रतरणार्थं यं मोक्षमार्गमुपदिशन्ति यश्च तदाधारभूतः चतुर्विधः संघः स तीर्थशब्देनात्र अभिप्रेतः।

सर्वदुःखक्षयो मोक्षः। अतो मोक्षमार्गोपदेश एव उत्कृष्टो हितोपदेशः। मोक्षमार्गमुपदिश्य तन्मार्गयायिनां साधूनां साध्वीनां श्रावकाणां श्राविकाणां च संघं जिनाः स्थापयन्ति अतस्ते तीर्थकरा अप्युच्यन्ते।

Essays in Jaina Philosophy and Religion.
Warsaw Indological Studies, Volume 2 (2002), pp. 113–117.

गृहवासं परित्यज्य जैनीं दीक्षां गृहीत्वा यावज्जीवं ये पुरुषाः साध्वाचारं पालयन्ति ते साधव इत्युच्यन्ते, स्त्रियस्तु साध्व्य उच्यन्ते। ये गृहस्थिताः तेषां भूमिकानुसारेण व्रतानि पालयन्ति ते श्रावका उच्यन्ते, स्त्रियस्तु श्राविका उच्यन्ते।

रागद्वेषमोहविरहितैर्जिनैः परिपूर्णविशुद्धज्ञानबलेन यो मार्गो दृष्ट उपदिष्टश्च स एव जैनधर्मः जैनदर्शनं वा उच्यते। अस्मिन्मार्गे ये गच्छन्ति तेषां सर्वेषां तत्सम्बद्धानामन्येषां च परमसुखकरः परमकल्याणकरश्च अयं मार्गः। संसारान्मोक्षप्राप्तिः जैनधर्मस्य जैनदर्शनस्य च परम उद्देशः।

कालस्य चक्रं सततं परिवर्तते। तत्र एको भाग ऊर्ध्वगामी, अपरश्च अधोगामीति भागद्वयं वर्तते। ऊर्ध्वगामी 'उत्सर्पिणी' इत्युच्यते, अधोगामी भागस्तु 'अवसर्पिणी' इत्युच्यते। उत्सर्पिण्यां पदार्थानां शक्तयो रूपादयश्च जीवानां च आयुर्विज्ञानादयो गुणाः क्रमेण वृद्धिं प्राप्नुवन्ति, अवसर्पिण्यां तु ते क्रमेण क्रमेण हीयन्ते। उत्सर्पिण्या अवसर्पिण्याश्च योगेन एकं कालचक्रं परिपूर्णं भवति। ईदृशानि अनन्तानि कालचक्राणि अतीते काले व्यतीतानि, एष्यति च काले भविष्यन्ति। एकैकस्यामुत्सर्पिण्यामवसर्पिण्यां च चतुर्विंशतिः तीर्थंकराः पृथक् पृथक् समये प्रादुर्भवन्ति। एवं च अनन्ते काले यद्यपि अनन्ता जिना भवन्ति तथापि संसारमहोदधिं तरीतुं दुःखविनाशाय सुखप्राप्तये च यं मार्गं त उपदिशन्ति स सामान्यरूपेण एकरूप एव। अतोऽनादिरनन्तश्च जैनधर्मः (जैनदर्शनम्)। पृथक् पृथक् समये पृथक् पृथक् तीर्थंकरा इमं मार्गमुपदिशन्ति। अस्यामवसर्पिण्याम् **ऋषभदेवः** (आदिनाथः) प्रथमः तीर्थंकरः, ततः पर**मजितनाथा**दयः **पार्श्वनाथ**पर्यन्ता द्वाविंशतिः तीर्थंकराः, ततः परं चतुर्विंशतितमो भगवान् वर्धमानः **महावीरः** चरमः तीर्थंकरः।

> Dr. Hermann Jacobi: 'In conclusion let me assert my conviction that Jainism is an original system quite distinct and independent from all others, and that therefore it is of great importance for the study of philosophical thought and religious life in ancient India.'[1]
>
> Dr. Sarvepalli Radhakrishnan: 'There is nothing wonderful in my saying that Jainism was in existence long before *Vedas* were composed.'

[1] Hermann Jacobi: *Jaina Sûtras. Part I: Âcârânga Sûtra, Kalpa Sûtra*. Translated from Prâkrit by … . *Sacred Books of the East* 22, Oxford University Press, Oxford 1884.

Lokamanya Balagangadhar Tilak: 'We learn from *shastras* and commentaries that Jainism is existing from beginningless time. This fact is indisputable and free from difference of opinion. There is historical evidence on this point.'

Mrs. Annie Besant: 'Lord Mahaveera was the last and not the first of the great 24 teachers.'[2]

जैनदर्शनाभिप्रायेण लोके मौलिकं द्रव्यद्वयं वर्तते –सचेतना ये ते जीवा आत्मानो वा उच्यन्ते, अपरे अजीवाः। अजीवाः पञ्चविधाः – पुद्गलाः (matter), धर्मास्तिकायः, अधर्मास्तिकायः, आकाशम् , कालश्च। जीवानामन्यसम्बन्धेन अज्ञानाद् रागद्वेषा जायन्ते तद्वशेन जीवा नरनारकतिर्यग्देवरूपासु चतसृषु गतिषु निरन्तरं भ्राम्यन्ति, नानाविधानि भीषणानि दुःखानि च अनुभवन्ति। अतः सर्वेभ्यः सांसारिकदुःखेभ्यो मुक्त्यर्थं तत्कारणभूता रागद्वेषमोहा उन्मूलनीयाः। रागद्वेषमोहोन्मूलनाय तद्रूपाः कामक्रोधमान(अहंकार)मायालोभाज्ञानादयो दोषा अवश्यमुन्मूलनीया भवन्ति। एते दोषाः कीदृशा भीषणाः, कथं चोत्पद्यन्ते, कथं च उन्मूल्यन्ते इत्यस्य विस्तरेण वर्णनं जैनग्रन्थेषूपलभ्यते। जिनोपदेशमनुसृत्य तच्छिष्यैः गणधरैः ततः परतरैश्च आचार्यैर्विरचिताः परःशताः प्राचीना ग्रन्था उपलभ्यन्ते। प्राचीनैरर्वाचीनैश्च साधुसाध्वीश्रावकश्राविकाभिः अन्यैश्च संस्कृतप्राकृतादिभाषासु हिन्दीगुजरातीमहाराष्ट्री-English-German-आदिभाषासु च लिखिताः परःसहस्रा ग्रन्थाः सम्प्रत्युपलभ्यन्ते। न केवलं धर्मग्रन्था एव, व्याकरणकाव्यकोषच्छन्दःशास्त्रज्योतिषादिविषयेष्वपि जैनाचार्यैर्विरचितो विपुलो ग्रन्थराशिर्वर्तते।

Dr. Hertel: 'The Jainas have written great masterpieces for the benefit of the world.'

जिनैर्यो मोक्षमार्ग उपदिष्टः तत्र हिंसा-असत्यभाषण-चौर्य-मैथुन-परिग्रहत्यागादेः द्यूत-मदिरा-मांस-भक्षणादित्यागस्य च उपदेशोऽस्त्येव। तत्रापि, जगति सर्वे जीवा जीवितुमिच्छन्ति, केऽपि मर्तुं न वाञ्छन्ति। तस्माद्घोरपीडादायकः प्राणिवधः सर्वैरपि सर्वथा सन्त्याज्यः, मनसा वचसा कायेन च अहिंसाधर्मः सुखार्थिभिरवश्यं पालनीय इति

[2] *Jain Gazette* 10/1 (1914) 4.

जैनधर्मस्य महती प्रतिज्ञा। अतो जैनधर्मे मांसभक्षणस्य मदिरापानादेश्च त्यागो महता विस्तरेण विशेषत उपदिश्यते। जैनसाधवः मांसभक्षणं मदिरापानं च कदापि नैव कुर्वन्ति।

आचारे अहिंसा, विचारे अनेकान्तवादः (स्याद्वादः), जीवनपद्धतौ च कर्मवादिति जैनदर्शनस्य महद् वैशिष्ट्यं वर्तते।

> Dr. Rajendra Prasad (the first President of India): 'Jainism has contributed to the world the sublime doctrine of *ahiṁsā*. No other religion has emphasised the importance of *ahiṁsā* and carried its practice to the extent that Jainism has done. Jainism deserves to become the universal religion because of its *ahiṁsā* doctrine.'

विचारेऽपि सूक्ष्मापि हिंसा मा भूत्, सत्यग्राहित्वमेव च सदा भवेदित्येतदर्थमनेकान्तवादो जैनदर्शने स्वीक्रियते। वस्तुनः स्वरूपमेव अपेक्षया विविधं प्रतीयते। अतः सर्वदर्शनेषु यद्यत्सारभूतं सत्यं वर्तते तस्य संग्रहाय सन्मानाय च जैनैः स्याद्वादः स्वीकृतः। अस्यैव फलभूतो नयवादः सप्तभङ्गीवादश्च वर्तते। एषा खलु जैनदर्शनस्य सर्वोत्कृष्टा विचारधारा। सम्यगेतज्ज्ञानार्थं जैनग्रन्थानामध्ययनमतीवावश्यकम्, तथा जैनसाधुसाध्वीनां जीवनचर्याविलोकनमप्य॰ ॰तीवावश्यकम्।

जैनसाधवः साध्व्यश्च यदा जैनीं प्रव्रज्यां प्रतिपद्यन्ते ततः प्रभृति ते यावज्जीवं पादाभ्यामेव विचरन्ति, धनं न रक्षन्ति, भिक्षयैव जीवन्ति, रात्रै न भुञ्जते न वा जलादिकं किमपि पिबन्ति, न तेषां मठादिकं किमपि स्वकीयं निवासस्थानं भवति, गृहस्थैः स्वार्थं कृतेषु कारितेषु वा स्थानेषु ते निवासं कुर्वन्ति, प्रावृषि कुत्रापि चातुर्मासिकमवस्थानं कुर्वन्ति, शेषकाले एकस्मात्स्थानात्स्थानान्तरे विचरन्ति, निरन्तरं शास्त्राणां स्वाध्यायं तप आदि च कुर्वन्ति, लोकेभ्यश्च धर्ममुपदिशन्ति। ईदृशं जैनसाधूनां जीवनं विशिष्टमपरिग्रहित्वं च वर्तते।

कर्मवादोऽपि जैनदर्शनस्य विशिष्टं स्वरूपम्। केन केन कर्मणा जीवानां सुखदुःखादिकं भवति चतसृषु गतिषु च परिभ्रमणं भवति कथं च कर्मक्षयो जायते इत्यादिकं महता विस्तरेण कर्मशास्त्रेषु वर्णितमस्ति। अत एव कृत्स्नकर्मक्षयो मोक्ष इत्यपि वर्ण्यते। जैनानां कर्मसिद्धान्तोऽपि अवश्यमध्येतव्यः।

जैनेषु मुख्यतया श्वेताम्बरा दिगम्बराश्च इति सम्प्रदायद्वयं वर्तते। श्वेताम्बराणां साधवः श्वेतवस्त्रधारिणो भवन्ति। दिगम्बराणां तु नग्ना एव साधवो भवन्ति। अन्योऽपि कश्चन भेदो वर्तते। तथापि सिद्धान्ताः सर्वेषामपि प्राय एकरूपा एव।

उभयेऽपि श्वेताम्बरा दिगम्बराश्च जैना जिनानां मूर्तीः पूजयन्ति मन्दिराणि च कुर्वन्ति। उभयेष्वपि केचन सन्ति जैना ये मूर्तिं न पूजयन्ति न वा मन्दिराणि कुर्वन्ति। स्थानकवासिनः तेरापंथिनश्च मूर्तिं न पूजयन्ति।

भारतवर्षे श्वेताम्बराणां दिगम्बराणां च परःसहस्राणि मन्दिराणि सन्ति। तानि च विशिष्टकलाकौशलयुक्तानि रमणीयानि चित्तप्रसत्तिजनकानि अवश्यं दर्शनीयानि। भारतवर्षाद् बहिरपि जैनैः सम्प्रति कृतानि मन्दिराणि वर्तन्ते।

संक्षेपेण एतत्सर्वं निदर्शितम्। विशेषतस्तु एतत्परिज्ञानार्थं जैनानां ग्रन्था एव अध्येतव्याः। जैनसाधूनां च समीपे स्थित्वा ज्ञातव्यम्।

> Dr. Satischandra Vidyabhusana: 'The Jain Sadhu leads a life which is praised by all. He practises the Vratas and the rites strictly and shows to the world the way one has to go in order to realise the soul (the Atma). Even the life of a Jain householder is so faultless that India should be proud of him.'

शिवमस्तु सर्वजगतः परहितनिरता भवन्तु भूतगणाः। दोषाः प्रयान्तु नाशं सर्वत्र सुखी भवतु लोकः॥

अहिच्छत्रा (जिल्ला-बरेली)
उत्तरप्रदेशः, भारतवर्षम्।
पौषकृष्णदशमी, बुधवासरः
२०-१-२०००

पूज्यपादाचार्यदेवश्रीमद्विजय**सिद्धि**सूरीश्वरपट्टालंकार-
पूज्यपादाचार्यदेवश्रीमद्विजय**मेघ**सूरीश्वरशिष्य-
पूज्यपादगुरुदेवमुनिराजश्री**भुवन**विजयान्तेवासी
मुनि **जम्बू**विजयः

Cātuyāma-saṁvara in the Pāli Canon

PADMANABH S. JAINI

Although more than a hundred years have passed since Hermann JACOBI published one of his most important articles 'Mahāvīra and His Predecessors' (*Indian Antiquary* 1880), his observations on the Buddhist references to Nigaṇṭha Nāṭaputta and the *cātuyāma-saṁvara* attributed to him in the *Sāmañña-phala-sutta* (DN 2)[1] remain to this day the firm foundation upon which the historicity of Mahāvīra and the antiquity of the teaching known as the *cātuyāma-saṁvara* rests. JACOBI repeats some of his arguments in the 'Introductions' to his translation of four Jaina canonical texts, *The Jaina Sūtras*, Parts 1 and 2 (1884 and 1895). Here, he gives additional literary evidence from the Jaina scriptures, especially the *Kesi-Goyamijjaṁ*, Chapter 23, of the *Uttarâdhyayana-sūtra*.[2] He demonstrates that the Pāli text was erroneous in attributing the *cātuyāma-saṁvara* (called *cāujjāma-dhamma* in the Jaina texts) to Nāṭaputta (i.e. Mahāvīra) and that the doctrine of the Nigaṇṭhas was anterior to both the Buddha and Mahāvīra. Rather, it had been preached by the twenty-third Jina Pārśva, as evidenced in the *Uttarâdhyayana-sūtra*. The *Sāmañña-phala-sutta* does not give what the four items of the *cātuyāma-saṁvara* might be. The above-mentioned passage in the *Uttarâdhyayana-sūtra* provides the information that Pārśva taught the Four Restraints, whereas Mahāvīra laid down the Five *Mahāvrata*s; however, neither of these are enumerated here. The scriptural evidence, both the Buddhist and the Jaina texts mentioned above, apparently is the extent to which virtually all subsequent researches on the *cātuyāma* / *cāujjāma* from the time of Jacobi have been confined.[3]

---

[1] DN I: 58: *Evaṁ vutte, bhante, Nigaṇṭho Nāṭaputto maṁ etad avoca—'idha, Mahārāja, Nigaṇṭho cātuyāma-saṁvara-saṁvuto hoti ... . bhante, Nigaṇṭho Nāṭaputto sandiṭṭhikaṁ sāmañña-phalaṁ puṭṭho samāno cātuyāma-saṁvaraṁ byākāsi.*

[2] Uttar 23.23:

cāujjāmo ya jo dhammo jo imo paṁca-sikkhio /
desio Vaddhamāṇeṇa Pāseṇa ya mahāmuṇī //23// .

[3] Noteworthy among these are works by KOSAMBI (1941), MODI (1965), SANGHAVI (1989), DHAKY (1997), MALVANIA (1997), and Sagarmal JAIN (1997).

Essays in Jaina Philosophy and Religion.
Warsaw Indological Studies, Volume 2 (2002), pp. 119–135.

The five *mahā-vrata*s are evident, however, from the *Sthānâṅga* and other *sūtra*s, where they are described in detail, together with the five *bhāvanā*s to perfect each of them. They consist of refraining from all killing, from telling lies, from taking anything not given, from sexual activity, and from attachment to all possessions.[4] They are also called *pañca-jāma* to contrast with the *cāujjāma* in the *Bhagavatī-sūtra* of the Śvetāmbara canon. *Śataka* no. 25, *uddeśa* 3, of this text summarises in five *gāthā*s the five kinds of *saṁyama*s, or restraints, the first two of which are of relevance here for our study. The first *saṁyama* is called *sāmāyika-saṁyama*, which according to *Ācārâṅga-sūtra* has the meaning of refraining from all evil actions whatsoever, as Mahāvīra did: *savvaṁ me akaraṇijjaṁ pāva-kammaṁ ti kaṭṭu sāmāyiaṁ carittaṁ paṭivajjai.*[5] It is said in the first *gāthā* of the *Bhagavatī-sūtra* that this *sāmāyika* itself is the supreme *cāujjāma-dhamma*. If indeed this be the case, then it would appear that Mahāvīra himself must have assumed the *cāujjāma-dhamma* at the time of his renunciation, although no Śvetāmbara commentator has made such a statement.[6]

The second *gāthā* defines the second restraint called *cheovaṭṭhāvaṇa* (= *chedôpasthāpana*). The meaning is as follows: having given up one's former faults (infringement of the *vrata*s), a person places himself in the pure state (through confession). It is said here that this *cheovaṭṭhāvaṇa* is identical with *paṁca-jāma*, that is, the fivefold restraint also known as the five *mahāvrata*s.[7]

While the term *cāujjāma* is conspicuously absent from the Digambara tradition, the terms *sāmāyika* and *chedôpasthāpana* do appear in an ancient Digambara text called *Mūlâcāra* by Ācārya Vaṭṭakera. It is stated here that the *sāmāyika-saṁyama*, which consists of refraining from all evil acts (as above in the Śvetāmbara *Ācārâṅga-sūtra*) with confession (*pratikramaṇa*) only in the case of some infraction, is taught by twenty-two of the twenty-four Tīrthaṅkaras, excepting the

---

[4] Ṭhāṇ 5.1, sū. 389: *paṁca mahavvayā ... savvāo pāṇâtivāyāo veramaṇaṁ, ... musāvāyāo ... adinnâdāṇāo ... mehuṇāo ... savvāo pariggahāo veramaṇaṁ.*

[5] JACOBI (1884: 198). On JACOBI's translation, see JAINI (1979: 17, n. 40).

[6] Viy1.1:

sāmāiyaṁmi u kae cāujjāmaṁ aṇuttaraṁ dhammaṁ /
tiviheṇa phāsayanto sāmāiyasaṁjamo sa khalu //1//

[7] Viy1.2:

chettūṇa ya pariyāyaṁ porāṇaṁ jo ṭhavei appāṇaṁ /
dhammaṁmi paṁca-jāme cheovaṭṭhāvaṇo sa khalu //2//

The word 'former state' (*porāṇaṁ pariyāyaṁ*) also is understood by the commentators to include cases of those disciples of Pārśva who give up their *cāujjāma* in favour of the *paṁca-jāma*.

first and the last. The *chedôpasthāpana-cāritra* with obligatory daily confession is taught by only the first and the last Tīrthaṅkaras, namely Ṛṣabha and Mahāvīra.[8]

As to how the word *sāmāyika* came to be equated with *cāujjāma* in the Śvetāmbara texts remains a mystery. It is unfortunate that there is no explanation for this in either the *Āgama* texts or their commentaries. However, the term *cāujjāma* certainly must have been known to the wider Jaina tradition, as is evidenced by the Yāpanīya author Aparājitasūri's commentary called *Vijayôdayā-ṭīkā* (c. tenth century) on *Bhagavatī Ārādhanā* by Ācārya Śivārya (presumably a Digambara).[9] Commenting on the *pratikramaṇa* rules applicable to the mendicants, he states that the first and the last Jinas preached the *dharma* where daily confession (*pratikramaṇa*) is obligatory whereas in the case of the middle twenty-two Jinas, one confesses only when some infraction has occurred. In this context, he says 'this difference in the practice of confession is to be found in the *paṁca-yama-dharma* of the first and last Tīrthaṅkaras, whereas elsewhere, that is in the "caturyama," the *pratikramaṇa* applies differently.'[10]

Important as the term *cāujjāma* is in Śvetāmbara texts, it should be noted that it is not found in either the Śvetāmbara or Digambara versions of the *Tattvârtha-sūtra* of Umāsvāti, nor in its commentaries. However, the five *vrata*s are enumerated at *Tattvârtha-sūtra* which reads: 'abstinence from violence, falsehood, stealing, carnality, and possessiveness—these are the vows.'[11] Commenting on this *sūtra*, the

---

[8] MĀc 535:

bāvīsaṁ titthayarā sāmāyikasaṁjamaṁ uvadisanti /

chedovaṭṭhāṇâvaṇiyaṁ puṇa bhgavaṁ Usaho ya Vīro ya // .

Vasunandi's *Ācāra-vṛtti* on MĀc 535: *dvāviṁśati-tīrthaṅkarā Ajita-Pārśvanātha-paryantā sāmāyika-saṁyamam upadiśanti pratipādayanti; chedôpasthāpanaṁ punaḥ saṁyamaṁ Vṛṣabho Vīraś ca pratipādayataḥ.*

[9] For a discussion of Aparājitasūri's alleged affiliation with the Yāpanīya sect, see Kailashchandra Siddhāntaśāstrī's Hindi Introduction to the *Bhagavatī-Ārādhanā*. For a discussion of the doctrine, literature, and research on the Yāpanīya Jaina sect, see JAINI (1991: chap. 2).

[10] Ār (vol. I, pp. 332–33): *pratikramaṇa-sahito dharmaḥ ādya-pāścātyayoḥ jinayoḥ, jātâparādha-pratikramaṇaṁ madhya-vartino jinā upadiśanti.* There are ten kinds of *pratikramaṇa* listed in the *Vijayôdayā-ṭīkā*. At the end of this passage it states: *amī pratikramaṇa-bhedā ādyânta-tīrthakara-praṇīte paṁca-yame dharme, itaratra ca catur-yame pratikramaṇasya kāla-niyama uktaḥ.*

[11] TS 7.1: *hiṁsânṛta-steyâbrahma-parigrahebhyo viratir vratam.* Commenting on this, the Digambara *Sarvârtha-siddhi* says (SSi 664): *sarva-sāvadya-nivṛtti-lakṣaṇa-*

Digambara *Sarvârtha-siddhi* states that essentially there is a single *vrata* called *sāmāyika*, which is characterised by refraining from all evil acts. This same single *vrata* is spoken of here as fivefold when considered from viewpoint of *chedôpasthāpana*. But there is no mention of *cāujjāma* in these passages.

The terms *paṁca-yama* and *catur-yama* (employed by Aparājitasūri) seem to retain the distinction made in the Śvetāmbara *Bhagavatī-sūtra* between *sāmāyika-saṁyama* and the *cheovaṭṭhāvaṇa-saṁyama*. What is extraordinary in all of these discussions is the amazing fact that the contents of the *cāujjāma* is not spelled out either in the Śvetāmbara *Bhagavatī-sūtra* or in the Yāpanīya *Vijayôdayā-ṭīkā*. This is unfortunate because it would have given us some means of verifying the list of the four items found in the *Sthānâṅga-sūtra* and might have clarified the meaning of the fourth item.

The four items of the *cāujjāma* are enumerated in *Sthānâṅga* 4, *sūtra* 266. These are refraining from all killing, lying, taking things not given, and from '*bahiddhâdāṇa*,' the meaning of which is obscure even to this day. It says here that in the lands of Bharata and Airāvata, *cāujjāma-dhamma* is laid down (*pannaveṁti*) by the twenty-two Tīrthaṅkaras, excluding the first and the last. It adds that in all the lands of the Mahāvidehas, where Tīrthaṅkaras exist at all times, only this fourfold restraint is prescribed for a mendicant.[12]

While the meaning of the first three *cāujjāma-dhamma*s is evident, the fourth, *bahiddhâdāṇa*, is subject to more than one interpretation. The Jaina commentators are at pains to assure us that the fourth restraint of Pārśva does indeed include both the fourth and the fifth *vrata*s laid down by Mahāvīra, namely refraining from *maithuna*, i.e. practising complete celibacy (*brahma-carya*), and the renunciation of all possessions (*aparigraha*)—with the exception of things required for maintaining

---

sāmāyikâpekṣayā ekaṁ vrataṁ tad eva chedôpasthāpanâpekṣayā pañca-vidham ihôcyate.
The terms *sāmāyika* and *chedôpasthāpana* appear in TS 9.18, which lists the five kinds of mendicant conduct (*cāritras*). Here, the *Sarvârtha-siddhi* defines *chedôpasthāpana* as that conduct in which there is a proper treatment of transgressions, which have been caused by heedlessness, etc. (SSi 854). Compare this with the Śvetāmbara Siddhasenagaṇi's gloss on the same (TSṬ 9.18): *sarva-sāvadya-yoga-virati-lakṣaṇaṁ sāmāyikam, tad-viśeṣā eva chedôpasthāpyâdayaḥ viśuddhatarâdhyavasāya-viśeṣāḥ sāvadya-yoga-virater eva*.

[12] Ṭhāṇ 4.1, *sū* 266: *Bharheravaesu ṇaṁ vāsesu purima-pacchima-vajjā majjhimagā bāvīsaṁ arahaṁtā bhagavaṁtā cāujjāmaṁ dhammaṁ paṇṇaveṁti, ... savvāto pāṇâtivāyāo veramaṇaṁ, evaṁ musā-vāyāo ..., adinnâdāṇāo ..., savvāto bahiddhâdāṇāo veramaṇaṁ. savvesu ṇaṁ Mahāvidehesu ... cāujjāmaṁ dhammaṁ paṇṇavayaṁti*.

a mendicant life. Abhayadeva, for example, in his *Vṛtti* on the *Sthānâṅga-sūtra*, glosses the word *bahiddhā* as sexual conduct (*maithunaṁ parigraha-viśeṣaḥ*, a special kind of possession) and other possessions as well (*ādānaṁ ca*). Thus, by joining these two words, he understands this term to be inclusive of the fourth and the fifth *vrata*s of Mahāvīra. He explains that although not explicitly mentioned, *maithuna* is certainly included in the term *parigraha* since a woman who is not accepted as one's own is not to be sexually enjoyed and therefore is to be given up like any external object. Lest someone should think that there is a fundamental difference in teaching between the two Tīrthaṅkaras with two different standards of asceticism applicable under them, Abhayadeva makes explicit that the difference seen here is strictly on account of the status of the disciples. For in actuality, all Tīrthaṅkaras lay down all five kinds of restraints.[13]

It should be noted in this context that the *Bhagavatī-sūtra* 20.8, which gives a variety of information on the *tīrtha*, the names of the twenty-four Tīrthaṅkaras, and the duration of their teachings (i.e. scriptures) and so forth, is silent on the reason for the twofold *dharma*, namely that of the *cāujjāma* and the *pañca-vrata*. In support of his claim Abhayadeva draws upon the authority of the *Uttarâdhyayana-sūtra* (23, verse 26–27), which makes an unprecedented statement that the mendicant disciples under the first and the last Tīrthaṅkaras are distinguished by the fact that the former are simple but slow of understanding (*ujju-jaḍa*) and the latter are prevaricating and slow of understanding (*vaṅka-jaḍa*), whereas the mendicants of the (twenty-two) middle ones are simple and wise (*ujju-pannā*).[14]

The explanation given in the *Uttarâdhyayana-sūtra* that at certain periods the ascetics need to be given more explicit sets of vows than at other times is a belief that is shared by the Digambaras. The *Mulâcāra* states that during the first and the last Jina's time, *pratikramaṇa*, or confession, is obligatory, whereas during the times of the middle twenty-two Jinas, confession is made only when there is an infraction

---

[13] ṬhāṇVṛ 4.1.264–66: *iha ca maithunaṁ parigrahe 'ntar-bhavati, na hy aparigṛhītā yoṣit bhujyata iti, ... cātur-yāma-dharmasya ... pañca-yāma-dharmasya prarūpaṇā śiṣyâpekṣā, paramârthatas tu pañca-yāmasyâivôbhayeṣām apy asau ...*

[14] Uttar 23.26–27:

purimā ujju-jaḍā u vaṁka-jaḍā ya pacchimā /
majjhimā ujju-pannā u teṇa dhamme duhā kae //
purimāṇaṁ duvisojjho u carimāṇaṁ duraṇupālao /
kappo majjhima-gāṇaṁ tu suvisojjho supālao //

The *Uttarâdhyayana-sūtra* does not say anything about the disciples of the Tīrthaṅkaras of Videha-kṣetra, but elsewhere Abhayadeva includes them in the category of the middle ones (i.e. *ujju-pannā*).

of the vow of the *sāmāyika-saṁyama.*[15] The reason that the first and the last Tīrthaṅkaras teach the *chedôpasthāpana-saṁyama* is that it is difficult for the disciples of the first to identify their faults, while the disciples of the last Tīrthaṅkara find it difficult to observe their vows. The first and last disciples do not understand what is allowed (i.e. proper) and what is not allowed (i.e. not proper).[16] Commenting on this, Vasunandi says that the disciples of the first one are by nature extremely innocent whereas the disciples of the last one are for the most part of a crooked nature.[17] In her Hindi translation of the *Mūlâcāra* Āryikā Jñānamatī explains that *pratikramaṇa* was required during the time of the first Tīrthaṅkara because the idyllic social conditions of the *bhoga-bhūmi*s were coming to an end and those characteristic of the *karma-bhūmi*s were just beginning. People had no notion of infractions of the vows. Thus, they were asked to repeat all of the confessional texts even if they hadn't committed any infringement. She says that during the time of the last Tīrthaṅkara, the *pañcama-kāla* was soon approaching, and people's minds were naturally inclined to be rather devious. They do not see their faults as they should, so they must repeat all items of confession.[18]

The Yāpanīya views on this matter as expressed in the *Vijayôdayā-ṭīkā* agree well with the Digambara position. Aparājitasūri explains the rule of mandatory confession (of all possible infractions) on the analogy of a blind horse being treated with medicine. When a person wanted to cure a horse of its illness, the veterinarian instructed him to feed the horse certain herbs that could be found on a nearby hilltop. The horse's owner could not distinguish one herb from the other, so he

---

[15] MĀc 628–29:

sapaḍikkamaṇo dhammo purimassa ya pacchimassa ya jiṇassa /
avarāhe paḍikamaṇaṁ majjhima-yāṇaṁ jiṇa-varāṇaṁ //
jāvedu appaṇo vā aṇṇadare vā bhave adīcāro /
tāvedu paḍikkamaṇaṁ majjhima-yāṇaṁ jiṇa-varāṇaṁ //

[16] MĀc 536–37:

ācikkhiduṁ vibhajiduṁ viṇṇāduṁ câvi suhadaraṁ hodi /
edeṇa kāraṇeṇa du mahavvayā paṁca paṇṇattā //
ādīe duvvisodhaṇa ṇihaṇe taha suṭṭhu duraṇupāle ya /
purimā ya pacchimā vi hu kappākappaṁ ṇa jāṇaṁti //

[17] Vasunandi's commentary on MĀc 536–37 (vol. 1, p. 406): *ādi-tirthe śiṣyāḥ duḥkhena śodhyante suṣṭhu ṛju-svābhāvā yataḥ. tathā paścima-tīrthe śiṣyāḥ duḥkhena pratipālyante suṣṭhu vakra-svabhāvā yataḥ.*

[18] Āryikā Jñānamatī's notes on MĀc 536–37 (vol. 1, p. 406). We might add here that these textual statements should be understood as generalisations and are not necessarily applicable to all of the Tīrthaṅkara's disciples.

brought a bundle of herbs from there and fed them all to the horse and it was cured. The comparison with disciples of the first and the last Tīrthaṅkaras is that the confessions are like herbs. If you do not know exactly what needs to be confessed, then the best remedy is to confess for all possible infractions of body, mind, speech, etc.[19]

The explanations found in both Śvetāmbara and Digambara texts regarding the necessity of obligatory confession and the enumeration of the five restraints (*vrata*s) during the times of the first and last Tīrthaṅkaras are reasonable enough. However, one should raise two questions relating to *sāmāyika-saṁyama* and the *cāujjāma* in Śvetāmbara texts. First, why was there a need for any further elaboration of the all-encompassing vow of *sāmāyika-saṁyama*, given their stated position that the disciples of the middle twenty-two Tīrthaṅkaras properly understood the meaning of this single vow? Second, in further elaborating this vow for the disciples of the second through the twenty-third Tīrthaṅkaras, why were only four restraints listed, when five restraints had previously been enumerated for the disciples of the first Tīrthaṅkara? In other words, if there was a need to spell out the restraints in the first place, why would two restraints of the *pañca-vrata*s, namely the fourth (*brahma*) and the fifth (*parigraha*), be collapsed into the obscure *bahiddhâdāṇā-veramaṇaṁ*, the fourth item in the *cāujjāma*?

The only additional Jaina source that has been discussed in this connection is the ancient but less well-known canonical text called the *Isibhāsiyāiṁ*. In his 1942 edition of this text, SCHUBRING drew attention to the section attributed to a (seemingly non-Nigaṇṭha) sage (*ṛṣi*) called Nārada (first in the list of 45 *pratyeka-buddhas*), whose first three commandments specifically mention the giving up of violence (*pāṇâtipāta*), lying (*musā-vāda*), theft (*adattâdāṇa*), but the fourth one contracts the evils of lack of celibacy and keeping possessions (= *abbambha-pariggaha*) into one. The fact that the last one combines the two gives some support to the theory that there may have been a tradition of four mendicant restraints long before the time of Mahāvīra. In section 31 (*Pāsijjanāmajjhayaṇaṁ*), which speaks of the teaching of the *ṛṣi* Pāsa, the text has two versions (*pāḍho*). The first one speaks about such topics as *loka*, *gati*, and *karma-vipāka*. But the second version talks of refraining from 'killing of beings up to (*jāva*) possessions,' dropping reference to *maithuna* altogether, and thus leaving room for doubt if celibacy was enjoined by him. This is followed by a statement that such a person, a Nirgrantha

[19] VUṬ. vol. I. pp. 332–33: *madhyama-tīrthakara-śiṣyā dṛḍha-buddhayaḥ, ekâgra-cittāḥ, amogha-lakṣyās tasmād yad yad ācaritaṁ tad garhayā śuddhyati. itare tu calacittā na lakṣayanti svâparādhāṁs tena sarvaṁ pratikramaṇam upadiṣṭaṁ jinābhyām andha-ghoṭaka-dṛṣṭânta-nyāyena.*

(Niyaṇṭhe) who is enlightened and whose activities are all well restrained by *cāujjāme* (fourfold restraints), does not bind new sets of eightfold *karmans*.[20] SCHUBRING does not comment on the significance of this passage other than to say 'That the Isibhāsiyāiṁ have a history, follows from the recording of *bio pāḍho* in 31' ('Introduction', p. 10). But it should be noted that this is the first Jaina canonical evidence linking the *cāujjāma* (*-dhamma*) with the word Nigaṇṭha and specifically with a sage called Pāsa who may or may not have been the twenty-third Tīrthaṅkara Pārśva.

In addition to the *Sāmañña-phala-sutta* referred to above, there are two *sutta*s in the *Dīgha-nikāya* that are of some importance in our study of the *cātuyāma-saṁvara*, both of which are called *Sīha-nāda* (the Lion's Roar). The subject matter of both is *tapojeguccha*, or the merit or demerit of self-mortification in the ascetic pursuit of the goal of salvation. In the first of these *sutta*s, the *Kassapa-Sīha-nāda-sutta* (no. 7), there is no discussion of the *cātuyāma-saṁvara*, but there is a passing reference by the Buddha to an ascetic named Nigrodha, whose story is related in the *Udumbarikā-Sīha-nāda-sutta* (no. 25). In this *sutta*, there is a description of the Fourfold Restraint (*cātuyāma-saṁvara*) that closely follows that found in the *Sthānâṅga-sūtra*, but there is no mention of Nigaṇṭha Nāṭaputta or any other person. This probably explains why this *sutta* escaped the notice of Jacobi and has remained neglected for so long. The *Sāmañña-phala-sutta*, appearing as number two in the extant *Dīgha-nikāya* collection, may give the appearance of being earlier than these two subsequent *sūtra*s, but this may not be the case, for it is taking place in the context of a patricide king, Ajātaśatru, who visits the Buddha out of repentance for his crime. Such an event could have taken place only in the last ten or so years of Buddha's life.

In the first *Sīha-nāda-sutta*, an ascetic (*tapassī*) called Kassapa comes to the Buddha and asks him 'if indeed the Buddha disparages all penance, reviles and finds fault with every ascetic, with every one who lives a hard life.' Kassapa then enumerates a long list of ascetic practices that were considered by many as leading to the goal of a *śramaṇa*. These ascetic self-mortifications include such practices as going naked, plucking the hair, eating from one's hands only, and so forth. Towards

---

[20] Isibh, p. 69: *kiccā esa khalu asaṁvuḍe asaṁvuḍa-kammaṁte cāujjāme ṇiyaṇṭhe aṭṭhavihaṁ kamma-gaṇṭhiṁ pagareti ... atta-kaḍā jīvā, ṇo para-kaḍā, kiccā kiccaṁ vedinti, taṁ jahā—pāṇâtipātā veramaṇeṇaṁ jāva pariggaha-veramaṇeṇaṁ*. The traditional Jaina works dealing with this text do not raise the question whether the *ṛṣi* Pāsa is identical with the Jina Pārśva. However, on the evidence of the Buddhist and Jaina texts quoted above, modern scholars have concluded that these individuals are the same. See Sagarmal JAIN (1997).

the end of this dialogue the Buddha recalls a previous occasion when a person named Nigrodha, who was a follower of the same mode of life [as Kassapa], asked him about the higher forms of *tapojeguccha* (translated as 'austere scrupulousness of life' by Rhys-Davids), and how he expounded his opinion on that matter. The Buddha preaches to Kassapa the futility of such hardships and gives a sermon on the Āryan Eightfold Path, following which Kassapa becomes a Buddhist monk and eventually attains Arhatship. Commenting on the words of the Buddha that he had visited the ascetic Nigrodha, Buddhagosa says in the *Dīgha-nikāya-Aṭṭha-kathā* that this refers to the event recorded in the sermon called *Udumbarikā-Sīha-nāda-sutta*.[21]

According to this *sutta*, a certain ascetic wanderer (*paribbājaka*) called Nigrodha with a large following lived in a park named after the queen Udumbarikā. He called himself a practitioner of severe ascetic penances. A Buddhist layman on his way to greet the Buddha at the Vultures' Peak approached Nigrodha and praised the Buddha in the presence of his congregation. Nigrodha retorted that Gautama hides in solitude, and that if he dared to come and engage him in a debate, he surely would be exposed. Knowing about this by his supernatural knowledge, the Buddha appeared in the presence of the assembly of Nigrodha. The latter asked the Buddha about the austerities, about the ways in which he trained his disciples, and about his principle of righteousness. The Buddha's response is worth noting as it sets out the manner of his memorable exposition and is relevant to our present query:

> 'Come now, Nigrodha, ask me a question about your own doctrine, about austere scrupulousness of life: in what does the fulfilment, in what does the non-fulfilment of these self-mortifications consist?
> When he had said this, the Wanderers exclaimed loudly, with noise and clamour: Wonderful, sir! Marvellous is it, sir, the great gifts and powers of Gotama in withholding his own theories and inviting the discussion of those of others!'[22]

There follows a very long dialogue between these two in which for the most part the Buddha exposes the futility of the varieties of *tapas* that were described in the *Kassapa-Sīha-nāda-sutta*. The Buddha shows Nigrodha how full of blemishes these practices are, and speaking in a metaphorical manner, he asserts that they do not even touch the bark of the tree of the holy life, let alone its pith.

---

[21] DN I: 176: *ekam idâhaṁ, Kassapa, samaye Rājagahe viharāmi Gijjhakūṭe pabbate. ... tatra maṁ aññataro tapa-brahmacārī Nigrodho nāma adhijegucche pañhaṁ pucchi. tassâhaṁ ... byākāsiṁ.*

[22] RHYS DAVIDS (1899–1921: III, 43).

When asked by Nigrodha, 'In what way, Lord, does an austerity win topmost rank (*aggappattā*), and reach the pith (*sārappattā*),' the Buddha says:

> 'Take the case, Nigrodha, of an ascetic (*tapassī*) self-restrained by the Restraint of the Fourfold Watch (*cātuyāma-saṁvara-saṁvuto*). What is the Restraint of the Fourfold Watch? It is when an ascetic inflicts injury on no living thing, nor causes injury to be inflicted on any living thing, nor approves thereof. He takes not what is not given, nor causes another to do so, nor approves thereof. He utters no lies, nor causes lies to be uttered, nor approves thereof. He craves not for the pleasures of senses (*na bhāvitaṁ āsiṁsati*), nor leads others to crave for them, nor approves thereof. Now it is thus, Nigrodha, that the ascetic becomes self-restrained by the Restraint of the Fourfold Watch.'[23]

It may be noted here that in the Jaina list of restraints against the evil actions, the second is lying, the third is theft, whereas in the Buddhist formula as quoted above, the second is theft and the third is lying. The fourth item is singularly important because it employs an expression *bhāvitaṁ*, which we have not come across anywhere else in this context in any Jaina text.

Commenting on this rather unusual word, Buddhaghosa in his *Aṭṭha-kathā* says that according to those who believe in this kind of *cātuyāma-saṁvara*, *bhāvita* means *pañca-kāma-guṇā*, i.e. 'the five strands of sensual pleasures; collectively all sensual pleasures.'[24] Although *bhāvita* is employed by the Buddhists elsewhere in the context of 'to be in love,' 'to crave for,' and 'that which is constantly thought about,' it is not part of their technical vocabulary. Buddhagosa clearly states that the meaning of the word *bhāvita* here is according to those (*tesaṁ saññāya*) who practice *cātuyāma-saṁvara*s. This is a very significant statement. It gives us reason to assume that the commentator must have been in contact with the followers of the

---

[23] DN III: 48: *idha, Nigrodha, tapassī cātuyāma-saṁvara-saṁvuto hoti. kathaṁ ca ... hoti? idha, Nigrodha, tapassī na pāṇaṁ atipāteti, na pāṇaṁ atipātayati, na pāṇâtipātaṁ atipātayato samanuñño hoti; na adinnaṁ ādiyati, na adinnaṁ ādiyāpeti, na adinnaṁ ādiyato samanuñño hoti; na musā bhaṇati, na musā bhaṇāpeti, na musā bhaṇato samanuñño hoti; na bhāvitaṁ āsīsati, na bhāvitaṁ āsīsāpeti, na bhāvitaṁ āsīsato samanuñño hoti. evaṁ kho, Nigrodha, tapassī cātuyāma-saṁvara-saṁvuto hoti.*

[24] DNAK, III, p. 158: *tapassī cātuyāma-saṁvara-saṁvuto hotī ti catubbidhena saṁvarena pihito ... na bhāvitaṁ āsīsatī ti bhāvitaṁ nāma tesaṁ saññāya pañca kāma-guṇā, te na āsīsatī ti na sevatī ti attho*. This Buddhist meaning agrees well with the Jaina meaning given to this word in a sentence: *kāma-bhoge saṁgaṁ na karoti*. See VUṬ.1.233, *kā*. 202: *kāmaṁ svêcchayā bhujyante iti kāma-bhogāḥ. sukha-sādhanatayā saṁkalpita-bhakta-pānâdayo vāma-locanâdi-vargaś ca iti*.

cātuyāma-saṁvara, who understood the fourth vow to be, as he says, the giving up of pleasures of the five senses. It is credible because the ambiguity in the meaning of word *bahiddhâdāṇa* found in the *Sthānâṅga-sūtra*, whether it refers to *maithuna* and *parigraha* together or to only one of them, is also present in the expression *bhāvita* in the Buddhist text, since the pleasures of the senses—with an emphasis on the word *kāma*—could be thought to apply to women as well as external property. It is unfortunate that neither the original Pāli *sutta* nor the *Aṭṭha-kāthā* name the school or the person associated with this practice (such as Nigaṇṭha Nāṭaputta), as is done in the *Sāmañña-phala-sutta*. One thing is certain though, that the Buddhists saw a vast difference between a whole host of self-mortifying practices indulged in by the *paribbājakas*, or wandering ascetics, and the observance of the *cātuyāma-saṁvara*. That the Buddha did not condemn the *cātuyāma* is shown by the subsequent dialogue.

Having explained the nature of the *cātuyāma-saṁvara*, the Buddha adds further that an ascetic (*tapassī*) who proceeds on the holy path according to these restraints can indeed come to experience the meditational practices (known as the *brahma-vihāras*), namely, friendliness (*mettā*), compassion (*karuṇā*), joy in the virtues of others (*muditā*), and equanimity (*upekkhā*). But he remarks that such austerity does not win the topmost rank, it does but reach into the bark, not the pith of the tree.[25]

When asked by Nigrodha again as to when such austerities reach the topmost rank, the Buddha responds by saying that such an ascetic, observing the *cātuyāma-saṁvara*, goes even beyond the *brahma-vihāras* and arrives at the fourth *dhyāna* stage, accompanied by *upekkhā*. Being free from several mental obstacles, he may gain the supernatural power (*abhiññā*) of recalling his own past births, even hundreds of thousands of them in all their details (*pubbenivāsaṁ anussarati*). But this is no more than reaching the underlying fibre (*pheggu*) of the tree. When pressed by Nigrodha as to how this austerity can attain to the top rank and reach the pith (*sāra*), the Buddha answers that such an ascetic develops further the *abhiññā* called *dibba-cakkhu*, or 'the Divine Eye', surpassing that of men, by which he can

[25] DN III: 48–49: *yato ca kho, Nigrodha, tapassī cātuyāma-saṁvara-saṁvuto hoti, aduṁ cāssa tapassitāya. so ... pañca nīvaraṇe pahāya ... mettā-sahagatena ... karuṇā ... muditā ... upekkhā-sahagatena cetasā averena avyāpajjhena pharitvā viharati. taṁ kiṁ maññasi ... tapogigucchā parisuddhā vā aparisuddhā vā? ... no aparisuddhā, ... aggappattā ca sārappattā ca. na kho ... ettāvatā ... api ca kho tacappattā hoti. kittāvatā ... ?*

see various beings, the mean and the noble, the happy and the wretched, passing from one existence to another according to their deeds.[26]

Nigrodha is now sure that such a person has reached the topmost rank for he says:

> 'Verily, Lord, austerity by these things becomes genuinely pure, and not impure; it wins topmost rank and reaches the pith.'

The Buddha's answer, undoubtedly provisional, is rather startling, for he says:

> 'Thus, Nigrodha, does austerity win topmost rank and reach the pith.'[27]
>
> 'And so, Nigrodha, when you say to me: What, lord, is this religion of the Exalted One, wherein he trains the disciples, and which those disciples ... acknowledge to be their utmost support and the fundamental principle of righteousness? I say that it is a matter of higher and more excellent degree wherein I train my disciples ... who acknowledge ... righteousness.'[28]

On the face of it this is nothing short of an endorsement by the Buddha of a non-Buddhist path, and one must wonder if indeed the compilers of this *sutta* saw the *cātuyāma-saṁvara* so faultless as to allow it to be seen as equal to their own! What is even more puzzling is that this *sutta* ends without teaching the yet higher and unequalled path that will lead to *nirvāṇa*. Nigrodha does confess his offence of reviling the Buddha and the latter does tell him that he will 'teach the Norm and instruct any man of intelligence, who is honest, candid and straightforward ... by which to realise here and now the supreme religion and goal.' But neither Nigrodha nor one of his congregation were ready to embark on his holy path because, as the Buddha says, 'Every one of these foolish men is pervaded by the Evil One (Māra).'[29] And so the Buddha departs without even a single convert, and the *sūtra*

---

[26] DN III: 49: *idha Nigrodha, tapassī upekkhāsahagatena cetasā ... aneka-vihitaṁ pubbenivāsaṁ anussarati ... na aggappattā, api ca kho pheggupattā.*

[27] DN III: 49: *ettāvatā, kho Nigrodha, tapojigucchā aggappattā ca hoti, sārappattā ca.*

[28] DN III: 49: *kittāvatā ... aggappattā? ... so dibbena cakkhunā visuddhena atikkanta-mānusakena satte passati cavamāne uppajjamāne ... yathā kammūpage satte pajānāti. taṁ kiṁ maññasi ... ? addhā kho bhante evaṁ sante tapopjigucchā aggappattā ca sārappattā ca. ettāvatā ca kho, Nigrodha, tapojigucchā aggappattā ca hoti, sārappattā ca .... iti kho taṁ, Nigrodha, ṭhānaṁ uttaritaraṁ ca paṇītataraṁ ca yenāhaṁ sāvake vinemi ...*

[29] DN III: 49: *yathā taṁ Mārena pariyuṭṭhita-cittā. atha kho Bhagavato etad ahosi—sabbe pi me moghapurisā phuṭṭhā pāpimatā; yatra hi nāma ekassa pi na evaṁ bhavissati handa mayaṁ. ... samaṇe Gotame brahma-cariyaṁ carāma ...*

strangely ends leaving the *cātuyāma-saṁvara* as a sort of a semi-final teaching of the Buddha.

This puzzle is solved by looking at the beginning portion of this dialogue where in the manner of the '*sīha-nāda*' the Buddha had boldly said that he would answer questions pertaining to the austerities practised by others, even before expounding on his own doctrine. The Buddha's proverbial confidence is based not only on his high wisdom but also on his personal experience gained when he himself had practised quite a few of these harsh penances as a Bodhisattva and had seen their futility. The *Aṭṭha-kathā* clearly perceives this to be the Buddha's reason for such uncommon elevation of the merits of *cātuyāma-saṁvara*. Commenting on the sentence '*ettāvatā ... tapojigucchā aggappattā ca hoti sārappattā ca*,' Buddhaghosa says:

> 'This the Lord said from the point of view of the Titthiyas. The Titthiyas believe that gain and honour are like the leaves of a tree. Merely keeping the five mendicant precepts is like the splinter of a tree. The eightfold meditational practices are like the bark. The *abhiññā* called the Knowledge of Previous Births is like the underlying fibre. The Divine Eye is something, however, that they think of as Arhatship. For this reason the attainment of it is for them like the pith (*sāra*) of the tree.
>
> In the teaching (*sāsane*) of the Lord, however, the gain and honour are like leaves of a tree. The practice of precepts is like the splinters. The meditational accomplishments are like the bark and the worldly *abhiññā*s are like the underlying fibre. The true pith (*sāra*) of the tree is the Holy Path and the Fruits of the Path (*Nirvāṇa*).'[30]

The attribution of the *cātuyāma-saṁvara* to the Titthiyas in the *Aṭṭha-kathā* is highly significant. In the *Sāmañña-phala-sutta*, they are described as a group of six highly organised schools of ascetics (*śramaṇa*s) with their own doctrines. There can be no doubt that the Titthiyas in the above passage (i.e. *Udumbarikā-Sīha-nāda-*

[30] DNAK, III: 54–57: *idaṁ Bhagavā Titthiyānaṁ vasenâha. Titthiyānañ hi lābha-sakkāro rukkhassa sākhā-palāsa-sadiso. pañca-sīla-mattaṁ papaṭika-sadisaṁ. aṭṭha-samāpatti-mattaṁ taca-sadisaṁ. pubbe-nivāsa-ñāṇāvasānā abhiññā pheggu-sadisā. dibba-cakkhuṁ pan'ete arahattan ti gahetvā vicaranti. tena tesaṁ taṁ rukkhassa sāra-sadisaṁ. sāsane pana lābha-sakkāro sākhā-palāsa-sadiso, sīla-sampadā papaṭikā sadisā, jhānasamāpattiyo pheggu-sadisā magga-phalaṁ sāro. iti Bhagavatā attano sāsane aneka-vidha-phala-bhāra-bharita-rukkhûpamāya desitaṁ.* For a detailed explanation, see *Mahā-sārôpama-sutta* and the *Cūla-sārôpama-sutta* (MN, Nos. 29 and 30).

sutta) refer only to the Nigaṇṭhas, led by Nāṭaputta, the only Titthiya reported to have expounded the *cātuyāma-saṁvara*.

The Buddhist statement that the Nigaṇṭhas (i.e. the Titthiyas) considered the worldly supernatural power called the 'Divine Eye', or the ability to see the births and deaths of beings in different destinies, as the one that they allegedly understood as Arhatship would certainly have been rejected by the Nigaṇṭhas themselves, as it would be by present-day Jainas. Notwithstanding the fact that the Buddhists were describing a rival group of ascetics and were bound to see certain yogic accomplishments in light of their own doctrine, it would be appropriate to see if any Jaina text would have led them to this conclusion. A passage that comes to mind is found in the *Kalpa-sūtra* (drawing undoubtedly on *Ācārâṅga-sūtra* 2.15.26), which describes the attainment of Arhatship by the Jina Mahāvīra. It says:

> 'When the Venerable Ascetic Mahāvīra had become a Jina and Arhat, he was a Kevalin, omniscient and comprehending all objects; he knew and saw all conditions of the world, of gods, men, and demons; whence they come, whither they go, whether they are born as men or animals, or become gods or hell-beings ... he the Arhat ... knew and saw all conditions of all living beings in the world... .'[31]

Another association may be found in the words used to describe the attainment of *kevala-jñāna* by Mahāvīra in the *Kalpa-sūtra*, namely *aṇuttara-jñāṇa* and *dassaṇa*, and the Buddhist understanding of these terms as found in the *Māhā-sārôpama-sutta* (MN 29). Here the *sutta* goes as far as to say that the '*ñāṇa-dassana*' obtained by a heretic is identical with the *abhiññā* known as '*dibba-cakkhu*.' Although the *sutta* uses the expression 'a certain person' (*ekacco puggalo*) in illustrating the example of touching the pith of a tree, the *Majjhima-nikāya-Aṭṭha-kathā* maintains that the person referred to is Devadatta, after his apostasy from the *saṅgha* (for committing *saṅgha-bheda*). It is said in the *sutta* that such a *bhikkhu* even when he attains '*ñāṇa-dassana*,' is touching only the underlying fibre (*pheggu*) of the tree and not its pith (*sāra*). As is well known, the formula '*ñāṇaṁ ca me udapādi, dassanaṁ ca me udapādi*,' when spoken by the Buddha (or an Arahā) is always followed by

[31] JACOBI (1884: 185–86). KS, § 120–21: *tassa ṇaṁ bhagavaṁtassa aṇuttareṇaṁ nāṇeṇaṁ aṇuttareṇaṁ daṁsaṇeṇaṁ aṇuttareṇaṁ carittenaṁ ... appāṇaṁ bhāvemāṇassa ... aṇaṁte aṇuttare nivvāghāe nirāvaraṇe kasiṇe paḍipuṇṇē kevala-nāṇa-daṁsaṇe samuppanne. tae ṇaṁ samaṇe bhagavaṁ Mahāvīre arahā jāe, jiṇe kevalī savvaññū savvadarisī sadeva-maṇuyâsurassa loyassa pajjāe jāṇai pāsai, savva-loe savva-jīvāṇaṁ āgaiṁ gaiṁ ṭhiyiṁ cavaṇaṁ uvavāyaṁ ... savva-loe savva-jīvāṇaṁ savva-bhāve jāṇamāṇe pāsamāṇe viharati.*

claims regarding the end of *saṁsāra* expressed in such words as, '*khīṇā me jāti ... natthi dāni punabbhavo.*' The *Majjhima-nikāya-Aṭṭha-kathā* therefore deems it necessary to explain that in the present context (of Devadatta) *ñāṇa-dassana* does not refer to a supramundane achievement, but only to the *abhiññā* called *dibba-cakkhu*, the highest of the five mundane attainments (*lokiyâbhiññā*s).[32]

The emphasis laid in these short passages from the Jaina *Kalpa-sūtra* on the ability to see the births and deaths of beings, and the ability to 'know' and 'see,' which is very similar to *dibba-cakkhu-abhiññā* (identified, as above, with *ñāṇa-dassana*) of the Buddhists, might well have given the Buddhist commentators the idea that the attainment of these were considered by the Nigaṇṭhas as the attainment of the goal of Arhatship. While the rivalry between the two faiths is well known through a large number of passages in the Pāli canon, Buddhaghosa's *Aṭṭha-kathā* on the *Sāmañña-phala-sutta*, with which we started our investigation of the *cātuyāma-saṁvara*, has left for us some memorable words, which are worth noting here. Commenting on the Nigaṇṭhas, he says that although they are Titthiyas, that is heretics, there is something (in their practice) that is agreeable with the Buddhist practice. However, on account of their impure viewpoint, their entire teaching turns out to be nothing more than a false view.[33]

Passages such as these found in Pāli canonical texts and their commentaries, similar in many respects with those found in extant Jaina texts, may be indicative of actual contact between Buddhist monks and a group of Jaina mendicants. As I have demonstrated in my article of 1995, because the description of Jaina mendicants by the commentator Dhammapāla (c. sixth century) agrees with representations found in sculptures, the Buddhists must have known Jaina mendicant groups living in the area of Kanchi (Madras, Chennai) in the sixth century.[34] The fact that even as late as the time of the commentators, the Theravāda Buddhists do not talk about the *pañca-mahā-vrata*s of the Jaina but recognise only the *cātuyāma-saṁvara*, leads us to surmise that Buddhists in South India most probably were in contact with some Jaina mendicants who may still have been observing the *cātuyāma-saṁvara*.

---

[32] MN, II: 196: *so ñāṇa-dassanaṁ ārādheti... ñāṇa-dassanena majjati pamajjati ... ayaṁ bhikkhu ... pheggum aggahesi brahma-cariyassa*. Cf. MNAK (*Papañca-sūdanī*) II: 173: *ñāṇa-dassanaṁ ārādhetī ti Devadatto pañcâbhiñño, dibba-cakkhuṁ ca pañcannaṁ abhiññāṇaṁ matthake ṭhitaṁ, taṁ imasmiṁ sutte 'ñāṇa-dassanaṁ' ti vuttaṁ.*

[33] DNAK (*Sāmañña-phala-sutta-vaṇṇanā*) I: 168: *Nāṭaputta-vāde cātuyāma-saṁvara-saṁvuto ti catukoṭṭhāsena saṁvarena saṁvuto ... gatatto ti koṭippatta-citto. yatatto ti saṁyata-citto. ṭhitatto ti suppatiṭṭhita-citto. etassa hi kiñci sāsanânulomaṁ pi atthi, asuddha-laddhitāya pana sabbā diṭṭhi yeva jātā.*

[34] See JAINI (1995).

BIBLIOGRAPHY

Ār = *Bhagavatī Ārādhanā* of Śivārya with Aparājitasūri's *Vijayôdayā-ṭīkā*. 2 vols. Ed. with Hindi translation by Kailshachandra Siddhāntaśāstrī. Jivaraj Jain Granthamala, Solapur, 1978.

DHAKY 1997 = Dhaky, M.A. (ed.): *Arhat Pārśva and Dharaṇendra Nexus*. Bhogilal Leharchand Institute of Indology, Delhi 1997.

DN = *Dīgha-nikāya*. Ed. T.W. and C.A.F. Rhys Davids and J.E. Carpenter, 3 Vols., Pāli Text Society, London I: 1890, II: 1903, III: 1911.

DNAK = *Dīgha-nikāya-Aṭṭha-kathā* (*Sumaṅgala-vilāsinī*). Ed. T.W. Rhys-Davids, Pāli Text Society, London 1886–1932.

Isibh = (1) *Isibhāsiyāiṁ. Ein jaina Text der Frühzeit*. Von Walther Schubring, Nachrichten von der Akad. Wiss. in Göttingen, Philologisch-Historische Klasse, Göttingen 1942: Nr.1, S.481–576. [1952: Nr.2 S.21–52]. (2) English translation by Charlotte Krause, L.D. Institute of Indology, Ahmedabad, 1974.

JACOBI 1880 = Jacobi, Hermann: 'On Mahāvīra and his predecessors.' *The Indian Antiquary* 9 (1880) 158–161.

JACOBI 1884 = Jacobi, Hermann: *Jaina Sûtras. Part I: Âcârâṅga Sûtra, Kalpa Sûtra*. Translated from Prâkrit by … . *Sacred Books of the East* 22, Oxford University Press, Oxford 1884.

JACOBI 1895 = Jacobi, Hermann: *Jaina Sûtras, Part II: Uttarâdhyayana Sûtra and Sûtrakṛtâṅga*. Translated from Prâkrit by … . *Sacred Books of the East* 45, Oxford University Press, Oxford 1895.

JAIN 1997 = Jain, Sagarmal: 'The teachings of Arhat Pārśva and the distinctness of his sect.' In: DHAKY (1997: 15–24).

JAINI 1979 = Jaini, Padmanabh S.: *The Jaina Path of Purification*. University of California Press, Berkeley—Los Angeles—London 1979.

JAINI 1991 = Jaini, Padmanabh S.: *Gender and Salvation: Jaina Debates on the Spiritual Liberation of Women*. University of California Press, Berkeley and Los Angeles 1991.

JAINI 1995 = Jaini, Padmanabh S.: 'Jaina Monks From Mathurā: Literary evidence for their identification on Kuṣāṇa sculptures.' *Bulletin of the School of Oriental and African Studies* [University of London] 58 (1995) 479–494.

KS = *Kalpa-sūtra*. Ed. M. Vinayasagara, Prakrit Bharati, Jaipur 1977.

KOSAMBI 1949 = Kosambi, Dharmanand: *Pārśvanāthācā Cāturyāma dharma* [in Marathi], Vora & Co., Bombay 1949.

MĀc = *Mūlâcāra* of Ācārya Vaṭṭakera, ed. with Vasunandi's *Ācāra-vṛtti*. 2 vols. Ed. by Kailashchandra Sidhāntaśāstrī, with a Hindi translation by Āryikāratna Jñānamatījī. Bharatiya Jnanapith, Delhi 1984.

MALVANIA 1997 = Malvania, Dalsukh, D. 'Jina Pārśva in Jaina Canonical Literature.' In: DHAKY (1997: 25–28).

MN = *Majjhima-nikāya*. Ed. V. Trenckner and R. Chalmers. 3 Vols., The Pāli Text Society, London 1887–1902.

MNAK = *Majjhima-nikāya-Aṭṭha-kathā* (*Papañca-sūdanī*). Navanalanda Mahavihara, Nalanda 1978.

MODI 1965 = Modi, P.K. (ed.): *Pāsaṇāhacariu*. Prakrit Text Society, Varanasi 1965.

RHYS DAVIDS 1899–1921 = Rhys Davids, T.W.; Rhys Davids, C.A.F. (tr.): *Dialogues of the Buddha—translated from the Pali of the Dīgha Nikāya*. Parts 1–3, The Pāli Text Society, Oxford University Press, London I: 1899, II: 1910, III: 1921. [Reprinted: 1978].

SANGHAVI 1989 = Sanghavi, Sukhalal: *Cār Tīrthaṅkar* [in Hindi]. 2nd edition, Pārśvanāth Vidyāśram, Varanasi 1989.

SSi = *Sarvârtha-siddhi* of Pūjyapāda Devanandin, ed. with *Tattvârtha-sūtra* of Umāsvāti. Sanskrit text with Hindi translation by Phoolchandra Siddhāntaśāstrī. Bhāratīya Jñānapīṭha, Varanasi 1934.

Ṭhāṇ = *Ṭhāṇaṁga-sutta* [*Sthānâṅga-sūtra*]. *Sthānâṅga-sūtram* (with Abhayadevasūri's *Vṛtti*) and *Samavāyâṅga-sūtram*. Ed. Muni Jambuvijaya. *Jaina-āgama-granthamālā* 3, Motilal Banarasidass Publishers, Delhi 1985.

ṬhāṇVṛ = Abhayadevasūri: *Sthānâṅga-sūtra-vṛtti*. See: Ṭhāṇ.

TS = Umāsvāti: *Tattvârthâdhigama-sūtra*. *Tattvārthādhigamasūtra (A Treatise on the Fundamental Principles of Jainism) by His Holiness Śrī Umāsvāti Vācaka, together with his Connective Verses Commented upon by Śrī Devaguptasūri and Śrī Siddhasenagaṇi*. ed. by H.R. Kapadia, 2 vols., Devchand Lalbhai Jain Pustakoddhar Fund, series nos. 67 and 76, Jivanachand Sakerchand Javeri, Bombay 1926, 1930.

TSṬ = Siddhasenagaṇi: *Tattvârthâdhigama-sūtra-svopajña-bhāṣya-ṭīkā*. See: TS.

Uttar = *Uttarajjhayaṇa-sutta* [*Uttarâdhyayana-sūtra*]. *The Uttarādhyayanasūtra*. An introduction, text, critical notes and a commentary, by Jarl Charpentier, *Archives d'Etudes Orientales*, Vol. 18:1–2, Uppsala 1921–1922. [Reprinted: Ajay Book Service, New Delhi 1980.]

Viy = *Viyāha-pannatti* [*Bhagavatī Vyākhyā-prajñapti* = *Bhagavatī-sūtra*]. In 7 parts, text with Hindi translation by Ghevarchand Banthiya. Sadhumargi Jain Samskriti Rakshak Sangh, Sailana 1972.

VUṬ = Aparājitasūri: *Vijayôdayā-ṭīkā*, a commentary on *Bhagavatī Ārādhanā* of Śivārya. See: Ār.

A Comparative Study of Passages from Early Buddhist and Jaina Texts: Āyār 2.15 : Dhp 183 and Isibh 29.19 : Dhp 360, 361*

KENJI WATANABE

In her survey of comparative studies of Jaina and Buddhist texts in the field of linguistics, Colette CAILLAT makes the following observation:

> 'Jaina lexicography, especially when dealing with Pkt. terms, has often been coupled with grammatical and etymological observations. In several cases, comparisons of AMg / JM terms with their Buddhist counterparts have proved fruitful, especially when an evaluation of semantic evolutions is necessary. Many technical terms still have to be investigated.'[1]

As it is well known, Buddhism and Jainism share a number of elements in their phraseology. The Buddhist Canon contains a huge material pertaining to Jaina practice and theories, to the personality of Mahāvīra, etc., highly valuable to the student of Jainism. On the other hand, Jaina Canons contain accounts of the Buddha and his followers, of comparable value. The subject has often been investigated by several scholars so far, and their research has yielded significant results.[2]

In this short paper, I would like to indicate a few corresponding passages which seem to have been overlooked so far.

---

* The present article is based on my papers in Japanese: WATANABE (1981) and WATANABE (1986). See also WATANABE (1987) and WATANABE (1993–94).

I wish to express my thanks here to Professor Dr. Nalini Balbir, the editor of *Bulletin d'Études Indiennes*, for her kind encouragement and help.

[1] CAILLAT (1993: 49, esp. 50–51).

[2] About an investigation of the close parallels which can be traced between Pāli and AMg: NAKAMURA (1983). Most recent study on this subject is BALBIR (2000). In her excellent article, N. BALBIR states in her conclusion (p. 42): 'Although the basically polemical attitude of Theravādins has naturally restricted the power of their analyses, confrontation with available Jaina texts shows that sound and reliable evidence is clothed in literary garb, that there is a full awareness of Jain technical terminology.' N. BALBIR additionally furnishes a comprehensive bibliographic survey on the subject.

Essays in Jaina Philosophy and Religion.
Warsaw Indological Studies, Volume 2 (2002), pp. 137–152.

– 1 –

Pāli Dhp 183 reads as follows:

sabbapāpassa akaraṇaṁ kusalassa upasampadā /
sacitta-pariyodapanaṁ etaṁ Buddhāna sāsanaṁ //

—'The avoidance of all evil; the undertaking of good; the cleansing of one's mind; this is the teaching of the awakened ones.' [Tr. by K.R. NORMAN]

This famous Buddhist verse is said to have been taught by Kāśyapa Buddha, one of the seven Buddhas of the past, which would mean that the Buddhist tradition goes back to pre-Gotama Buddha's religious thought. This is what came to be regarded as the very source of all the teachings of Buddhism, from which sprang the various tenets of both Mahāyāna and Theravāda.

A parallel passage to the *pada* d was identified by Hajime NAKAMURA[3] as the saying of the first disciple of Gotama Buddha in a Jaina scripture, namely Isibh 38, one of the oldest Jaina scriptures:

evaṁ buddhāna sāsaṇaṁ (Isibh 38.4)
etaṁ Buddhāna sāsanaṁ (Dhp 183).

– 2 –

With the above *pāda*s of the *Dhamma-pada* one can compare the famous prose passage of the Āyār 2.15, where Mahāvīra expresses his vow to abstain from all sinful acts, after he has plucked out his hair in five handfuls and paid obeisance to all Liberated Souls (Siddhas):

"savvaṁ me akaraṇijjaṁ pāvakammaṁ" ti kaṭṭu sāmaiyaṁ carittaṁ paḍivajjai.[4]

[3] NAKAMURA (1966) and NAKAMURA (1969).

[4] Āyār p. 273 [Muni Jambūvijaya ed.] = Āyār 424a [Agamodaya ed.]. H. JACOBI's edition runs thus: *savvaṁ akaraṇijjaṁ pāvaṁ ti kaṭṭu sāmaiyaṁ carittaṁ paḍivajjai* (1882: 129). But according to Ernst LEUMANN's suggestion, 'Die Wörter *me* und *kammaṁ* sind in Jacobi's Ausgabe vergessen' (LEUMANN (1934: 6a)). I accept here the reading of Muni Jambūvijaya's edition.

—'He decided: "I should not commit any sinful acts," and then he adopted the *sāmayika-cāritra*.'

Sāmayika is defined as an equanimity of mind and right conduct in accordance with the great vows (*mahavvaya*s) and as the ability to concentrate on spiritual matters for 48 minutes. Its importance lies in the fact that it helps to restrain karmic influx and to exhaust past *karman*s. It is worth noting that *sāmayika-cāritra* as a pre-Mahāvīra's lore referred to the fourfold restraints (*cāujjāma*, i.e. Pārśva's lore) according to the *Viyāha-pannatti*.[5] This accords with the fact that Mahāvīra's parents were described as followers of Pārśva in Āyār 2.15.

The *Kalpa-sūtra* (=*Pajjosavaṇākappa*) is introduced by the well-known invocation formula [= ĀvN 1018 = MĀc 514]:

eso paṁca-namokkāro savva-pāva-ppaṇāsaṇo /
maṁgalāṇaṁ ca savvesiṁ paḍhamaṁ havai maṁgalaṁ // [Ed. by H. JACOBI]

—'This fivefold obeisance, destroying all sins, is of all benedictions the principal benediction.' [Tr. by H. JACOBI, p. 217].

In this important formula for the Jainas, we can also find the expression 'destroying all sins' (*savva-pāva-ppaṇāsaṇo*).

Similarly, also in Āyār 1 (=*Bambha-ceräiṁ*) there are some expressions synonymous with avoiding 'all sinful acts' (*savva-pāva-kammaṁ*), or phrases related to Dhp 183:[6]

Āyār 6.4–5 = 23.22–3: *se vasumaṁ savva-samannāgaya-pannāṇeṇaṁ appāṇeṇaṁ akaraṇijjaṁ pāvaṁ kamm'antaṁ no annesiṁ*.

—'He who has the true knowledge about all things, will commit no sinful act, nor cause others to do so, etc.' [Tr. by H. JACOBI].

Āyār 11.26 = Isibh 39–(1)ab: *se ttaṁ saṁbujjhamāṇe āyāṇīyaṁ, samuṭṭhāe-tamhā pāvaṁ kammaṁ n'eva kujjā na kārave*.

---

[5] See Jozef DELEU (1970: 289): 'For *sāmaiya-saṁjama*, the Fourfold Restraint (*cāujjāma*, i.e. Pārśva's lore) is the highest *dharma*, and, who practises it in the three ways is *sāmāiya-s*. He who adopts the Fivefold Restraint (*panca-jāma*, i.e. Mv.'s lore) after having quit his former spiritual rank is a *cheovaṭṭhāvaṇīya-saṁjama*,' and Uttar 28.32. cf. MĀc 524.

[6] The text used in this connection is W. SCHUBRING's edition [Āyār (4)]; references are to this edition. Translation is by H. JACOBI (1884).

—'He who perfectly understands (what has been said in preceding lesson) and follows the (faith) to be coveted, should therefore do no sinful act, nor cause others to do one.'

Āyār 14.11: *sammatta-daṁsī na karei pāvaṁ.*

—'He who has right intuition, commits no sin.'

Āyār 14.19: cf. Āyār 22.5 '*āyaṅka*': *āyaṅka-daṁsī na karei pāvaṁ.*

—'Aware of the punishment, commits no sin.'

Āyār 14.26: *bahuṁ ca khalu pāvaṁ kammaṁ pagaḍaṁ.*

—'Manifold, indeed, appear sinful actions.'

Āyār 14.28: *etthôvarae mehāvī savvaṁ pāvaṁ kammaṁ jhosei.*

—'Delighting in it, a wise man destroys all *karman*.'

Āyār 15.9: *nisaṇṇo pāvehi kammehiṁ.*

—'keeping off from sinful acts.'

Āyār 19.27=Āyār 33.25: *je nivvuḍā pāvehiṁ kammehiṁ aniyāṇā te viyāhiyā.*

—'Those who are free from sinful acts are called *anidāna*.'

Āyār 21.14: *ramai pāvehiṁ kammehiṁ.*

—'Also the fool, suffering (for his passion's), delights in bad acts here, …'

Āyār 22.5 cf. Āyār 14.19: *je asattā pāvehiṁ kammehiṁ uyāhu: te āyaṅkā phusanti iti, uyāhu vīre:*

—'Those who are not given to sinful acts are (nevertheless) attacked by calamities; but then the steadfast will bear them.'

Āyār 24.29: *"vai-guttĕ ajjhappa-saṁvude" parivajjae sayā pāvaṁ.*

—'Careful in his speech and guarding his mind, he should always avoid sin.'

Āyār 31.11 pāṭh. (Nāg.): *"samaṇā bhavissāmo aṇagārā akiṁcaṇā aputtā apasū avihiṁsayā suvvayā dantā paradatta-bhoiṇo; pāvaṁ kammaṁ no karissāmo" samuṭṭhāe.*

Āyār 35.9: *nihāya daṇḍaṁ pāṇehiṁ pāvaṁ kammaṁ akuvvamāṇe.*

—'A person who is without desires and does no harm unto any living beings".'

Āyār 44.4–5: *naccāna se mahāvīre no vi ya pāvagaṁ sayaṁ akāsī annehiṁ vī na kāretthā kīrantaṁ pi nânu jānitthā.*

—'Having wisdom, Mahāvīra committed no sin himself, nor did he induce others to do so, nor did he consent to the sins of others.'

– 3 –

There seems to be some parallelism between the Buddhist *kusala* and the *sāmayika-cāritra* in Jainism.

Gotama Buddha says to his last disciple Subhadda about his motive for renouncing the world:

ekūnatiṁso vayasā Subhadda, yaṁ pabbajiṁ kiṁkusalānuesī.[7]

—'But twenty-nine was I when I renounced the world, Subhadda, seeking after Good (*kusala*).'

Again, *kusala* occurs in Dhp 173ab:

yassa pāpaṁ kataṁ kammaṁ kusalena pithīyati /
so'maṁ lokaṁ pabhāseti abbhā mutto va candimā //

—'Whose evil deed when done covered up by a good one, he illuminates this world like the moon released from a cloud.' [Tr. by K.R. NORMAN].

In the above passages we observe that *kusala* refers to the stopping of karmic inflow caused by evil acts, and it has the same meaning as *sāmayika-cāritra* ('checking influx and exhausting past *kamma*') in Jainism.

---

7 *Mahā-parinibbāna-suttanta*. DN Vol. II, p. 151.

In Buddhism,[8] the word *kusala* generally means 'karmically wholesome.' All karmic volitions and the associated consciousness as well as mental factors accompanied by the absence of greed (*alobha*), of hate (*adosa*), and eventually of delusion (*amoha*), contain the seeds of happy destiny, since they are the causes of favourable *karman*-results. The Buddhist *kusala* is therefore not very much different from the *sāmayika-cāritra* of Jainism, as is attested by the following passages in the *Mūlâcāra* 23:

> *jīvida-maraṇe lābhâlābhe saṁjoya-vippaoge ya /*
> *bamdhuri-suha-dukkhâdisu samadā sāmāiyaṁ ṇāma //*
>
> —'*Sāmayika* means the equanimity [of mind] in the midst of life and death, gain and loss, friends and foes, pleasure and pain.'

Furthermore, Dhp 173ab (see above, p. 141) and MĀc 523 and 524 are not very different from each other:

> *rāga-dose ṇirohittā samadā savva-kammesu /*
> *sattesu ya pariṇāmo sāmāiyam uttamaṁ jāṇe //523//*
> *virado savva-sāvajjaṁ ti-gutto pihid'iṁdio /*
> *jīvo sāmāiyaṁ ṇāma samjamaṭṭhānaṁ uttamaṁ //524//*
>
> —'Subduing the love and hatred, equal to all acts, as final result in the Scriptures, *Sāmayika* is the best. One, who has renounced all sinful acts, protected by the mind, speech and body, the organs were covered. For him, *Sāmayika* is the best for self-restraint.'

These verses imply the avoidance of all sinful tendencies, keeping equanimity in body, speech and mind, whose organs of sense are barred against karmic inflow in all kinds of actions.

– 4 –

Another expression of Dhp 183c: *sacitta-pariyodapanaṁ* ('to purify one's mind') finds an interesting rendering in the *Bhikṣūṇi-Vinaya* of the Mahāsāṅghika–Lokottaravādins[9]:

> *sarva-pāpasyâkaraṇaṁ kuśalasyôpasaṁpadā /*
> *sva-citta-paryādamanaṁ etad Buddhânuśāsanaṁ //*

---

[8] NYANATILOKA (1950: 78).

[9] BhVin, p. 52, 67.

The expression *sva-citta-paryādamanaṁ*, meaning 'to subdue one's mind' (*pary-ā√dam*), has its variant in the *Patna–Dharmapada*, viz. *-payirodamana*, which bears close resemblance to the above mentioned general meaning of *sāmāyika* ('equanimity of mind') in Jainism. Some Chinese translations of the verse in question—such as the Sarvāstivāda *Vinaya* or *Yogâcāra-bhūmi* (*Yü-ch'ieh-shi-ti-lun*), etc.—which read *t'áofu* ('taming and subduing') or *jōbuku* ('conquest of the passion in mind'), also support this interpretation.

– 5 –

Thus, we find the following correspondences:

> *savvaṁ me akaraṇijjaṁ pāva-kammaṁ* (Āyār 2.15)
> *sabba-pāpassa akaraṇaṁ* (Dhp 183a)

and

> *sāmāiyaṁ carittaṁ paḍivajjai* [*prati√pad*] (Āyār 2.15)[10]
> *kusalassa upasaṁpadā* [*upa-saṁ√pad*] (Dhp 183b)

Although the words are different, the concepts and purpose of these two passages, especially of *kusala* and *sāmāiya-cāritta*, are very close to each other.

– 6 –

As it is well known, Buddhism came into existence in the same period and in the same area as Jainism, sharing similar social and historical background. One would therefore quite naturally expect a number of common elements, as those mentioned above. Indeed, there is more evidence which supports this[11], such as the expressions for the restraint (*saṁ√vṛ*) of sense organs in order to ward off the inflow of karmic matter. Some of the phrases found in Dhp 360, 360 are identical with those in the oldest strata of the Jaina canon.

---

[10] Cf. In Jaina expressions on *upa-sam√pad*: [1] Viy 998a: ... *cāujjāmao paṁca mahavvayāiyaṁ sa-paḍikkamaṇaṁ dhammaṁ uvasaṁpajjittāṇaṁ viharai*, [2] ĀyārCū 377: *padhame mahavvae, tassa upasaṁpajjaṇattha*[*ṁ*].

[11] See ENOMOTO (1989) and WATANABE (1987).

– 7 –

Below are some Buddhist examples, taken from Dhp 360, 361:

> *cakkunā saṁvaro sādhu, sādhu sotena saṁvaro /*
> *ghāṇena saṁvaro sādhu, sādhu jivhāya saṁvaro* //360//
>
> —'Restraint of the eye is good; restraint of the ear is good; restraint of the nose is good; restraint of the tongue is good.' [Tr. by K.R. NORMAN]
>
> *kāyena saṁvaro sādhu, sādhu vācāya saṁvaro //*
> *manasā saṁvaro sādhu sādhu sabbattha saṁvaro /*
> *sabbattha saṁvuto bhikkhu sabbadukkhā pamuccati* //361//
>
> —'Restraint of the body is good; restraint of the voice is good; restraint of the mind is good, restraint everywhere is good. A bhikkhu who is restrained everywhere is released from all misery.' [Tr. by K.R. NORMAN]
>
> *vācânurakkhī manasā susaṁvuto kāyena ca akusalaṁ na kayirā /*
> *ete tayo kammapathe visodhaye, ārādhaye maggam isippaveditaṁ* //281//
>
> —'Guarding one's speech, well restrained in mind and body, one should not do evil. Purifying these three paths of action, one would attain the path taught by the sages.' [Tr. by K.R. NORMAN]

– 8 –

There are some Jaina examples, pertaining to Mahāvīra's teaching of the five great vows (*paṁca-mahavvaya*) and found in the Āyār 2.15, titled '*Bhāvaṇa*', that illustrate the idea of restraint or warding off the karmic inflow through sense organs:

> *soteṇaṁ jīve maṇuṇṇâmaṇuṇṇāiṁ saddāiṁ suṇei, maṇuṇṇâmaṇuṇṇehiṁ saddehiṁ no sejjā, no rajjejjā, no gijjhejjā, no mujjhejjā, no ajjhovajjejjā, no viṇigghayaṁ āvajjejjā, ...*
>
> *na sakkā na souṁ saddā soyavisayaṁ āgatā /*
> *rāga-dosā u je tattha taṁ bhikkhu parivajjae //*
> *sotao jīvo maṇuṇṇâmaṇuṇṇāiṁ saddāiṁ suṇei /* [ed. Muni Jambūvijaya]

[In the subsequent portion of Mahāvīra's elucidation of the fifth vow, *sotato* is substituted with *cakkhuto, ghaṇato, jibbhato* and *phāsato*.]

> —'If a creature with ears hears agreeable and disagreeable sounds, it should not be attached to, nor delighted with, nor desiring of, nor infatuated by, nor covetous of, nor disturbed by the agreeable or disagreeable sounds. ... If it is impossible not to hear sounds, which reach the ear, the mendicant should avoid love or hate, originated by them ...' [Tr. JACOBI (1884: 209).]

In JACOBI's translation, the sequence of 'ears ... sounds' is further substituted with 'eyes ... colours,' 'nose ... smell,' 'tongue ... taste' and 'touch ... feel.'

– 9 –

The motif of restraint in Āyār 2.15, with slight verbal variations though, is also found in Isibh 29:

> *saddam sotam uvadaya manunnam va vi pavagam /*
> *manunnammi na rajjejja, na padussejja hi pavae //* [3]
> *manunnammi arajjhante adutthe iyarammi ya /*
> *asutte avirodhinam evam soe pihijjati //* [4]
> *ruvam cakkhum uvadaya ...* [5] [6]
> *gandham ghanam uvadaya ...* [7] [8]
> *rasam jibbham uvadaya ...* [9] [10]
> *phasam tayam uvadaya* [11] [12]

> —'[3] Through the ear, hearing agreeable or disagreeable sounds, one should not be attached to agreeable sounds, nor hate disagreeable ones. One who is alert among the ruffled ones at the agreeable or disagreeable sounds, his karmic inflow is blocked.'

In subsequent stanzas 5–12, the ear is replaced with the eyes, nose, tongue and the organ of feeling.

– 10 –

As regards *saṁvara* (*saṁ√vṛ*), the idea appears in the famous passage of Nigaṇṭha Nātaputta's teachings in *Sāmañña-phala-sutta*[12], the so-called 'Teachings of the Six

[12] DN 1.57.

Heretics,' which is said to allude to the words of Mahāvīra. In spite of many previous studies, its meaning still remains somewhat unclear. Nigaṇṭha Nātaputta's portion runs as follows:

> ... *idha mahārāja nigaṇṭho sabba-vārī-vārito ca hoti sabba-vārī-yuto ca, sabba-vārī-dhuto ca, sabba-vārī-phuttho ca, ...*

The reading *-vāri-*, as this is found in the *Burmese Chaṭṭha Saṅgāyana* edition, the Thai *Royal edition*, the *Sri Lankan Simon Hewavitarne Bequest Series* edition, as well as in the PTS edition of the *Sumaṅgala-vilāsinī* and in the PTS dictionary, seems preferable.

Buddhaghosa's *Aṭṭha-kathā* commenting on this passage reads:

> *nāta-putta-vāde cātu-yāma-saṁvara-saṁvuto ti cātu-koṭṭhā-sena saṁvareṇa saṁvuto. sabba-vāri-vārito cāti vārita-sabba-udako, paṭikkhitta-sītodako ti attho. so kira sītodake satta-saññī hoti, tasmā taṁ na vaḷañjeti. sabba-vāri-yuto ti sabbena pāpa-varaṇena yutto. sabba-vāri-dhuto ti sabbena pāpa-varaṇena dhuto-pāpo. sabba-vāri-puṭṭho ti sabbena pāpa-varaṇena phuṭṭho.*

The expression *sabba-vāri-* occurs here four times. The compound *cātu-yāma-saṁvara-saṁvuto* is taught to mean 'being protected / restrained (*saṁ√vṛ*) by the four kinds of restraint / rules (*saṁvara*).' Buddhaghosa goes on to explain the first *sabba-vāri-vārito* as 'restraining from all water, refusing cold water. They say that cold water contains [the consciousness of] [a] living being[s] and therefore one does not use it.'

Curiously enough, three subsequent occurrences of *sabba-vāri-* are explained differently: '*sabba-vāri-yuto* means being intent (*-yuto*) upon warding off (*vāraṇa*) all evil,' *-vāri-* being rephrased as *vāraṇa*. This 'warding off the inflow of all evil karmic matter' is a familiar expression in Jaina literature. Western Pāli dictionaries, the *Sadda-nīti*, the *Abhidhānappa-dīpikā*, and the Pāli–Burmese dictionary *Ṭipiṭaka Pālimranmā Abhidhān* have only 'water' for *vāri*. The question arises why Buddhaghosa gave two different meanings for one and the same word in the same passage?

The *Papañca-sūdanī*, the commentary on the *Majjhima-nikāya*, repeats the same explanation of the *Sumaṅgala-vilāsinī*: 'One should not use cold water, as there are living creatures in it,' after which it adds: 'or (*athavā*), *sabba-vāri-vārito* means "having all evil warded off by warding off all evil" (*sabbena pāpa-vāraṇena vārita-pāpo*).' The latter explanation in both texts conforms to the meaning expected in the Jaina context.

As *vāri* only means 'water' in Pāli, we can assume that Buddhaghosa accurately knew the proper Jaina meaning of the word. Had he read *vāraṇa* in *sabba-vāri-vārito*, this would imply that Nigaṇṭha 'was restrained, warding off all (evil).' Such interpretation is hardly compatible with the intention of a passage which aims at extolling Buddhism and refuting other religions. The precepts of early Buddhism and Jainism were extremely similar, and their precise descriptions must have been a delicate matter, especially in parts containing such idioms as *saṁvara*, common to both religions.

Among many scholars, it is only Louis RENOU who consistently interpreted *vāri* as *vāraṇa*: '… le Nigaṇṭha s'abstient de toutes choses en les écartant …'[13]

In the subsequent portion, I will give some further examples of the use of *vāri(ya)*- and cognate words in Jaina texts.

– 11 –

In the chapter called 'In Praise of Mahāvīra' (*Vīratthuī*) of *Sūyagaḍaṁga*, the ancient Śvetâmbara work, we read:

> *se vāriya itthī sa-rāi-bhattaṁ,*
> *uvahāṇavaṁ dukkha-kkhay'atthayāe* /
> *logaṁ viditā āraṁ pāraṁ ca,*
> *savvaṁ pabhū vāriya savva-vāraṁ* / [Sūy 1.6.28]
>
> —'He abstained from women, and from eating at night, he practised austerities for the removal of pain, he knew this world and that beyond: the lord renounced everything at every time.' [Tr. JACOBI (1895: 291)][14].

Savva-vāraṁ is explained by some commentators as follows:

> SūyCū: *sarva-vāri sarva-vāraṇa-śīla ity arthaḥ*: '*sarva-vāri* means the practice or warding off everything.' The explanation comes close to Buddhaghosa's *sabbena pāpa-vāraṇena vārita-pāpo*.
>
> SūyṬ (and SūyD): *sārva-vāraṁ bahuśo nivāritavān*: (Skt.) '*sārva-vāraṁ*, one who has repeatedly warded off.'

---

[13] *Canon* (1949: I /1, p. 51). See RENOU (1987: 419).

[14] JACOBI (1895: xx–xxi).

The *Nāgārjuṇīya*-recension gives no explanation on this problem. It should be noted that the *Aṅga-suttāni* edition of the Canon I, p. 304 [Āyār (5)], mentions a sixteenth-century manuscript containing the variant *vāre*.

– 12 –

In the 29th chapter of the *Isibhāsiyāiṁ*, which contains sayings attributed to Mahāvīra himself, stanza 19ab reads:

> *savvattha virae dante, savva-vārīhiṁ vārie* /

Walther SCHUBRING initially explained *vāri* as 'Absonderung' in his notes to the first edition of 1942 [Isibh (2)]. He seems to have changed his opinion in his German translation of 1969, in which he gives 'Pforte' instead, Skt. *dvāra* > *vāra*. However, Late Seiren MATSUNAMI, a student of Schubring, adopted SCHUBRING's first rendering in his Japanese translation of the text.[15]

Another possibility would be to interpret *vāri* in this passage to mean 'always' from Skt. *vāra* = 'time, turn', as in we find it in JACOBI's translation of Sūy 1.6.28 (*vide supra*, p. 147). In that context, 'every time' or 'always' (*savva-vāra-*) contrasts with 'everywhere' (*savvattha*; Skt. *sarvatra*).

In terms of the *śloka*-metre the reading *savva-vāri hi vārie* would also be possible, since the syllable preceding *vārie* should metrically be a short one. This would accord with the version of SūyC: *vāriya-savva-vārī*.

– 13 –

Thus we get the following readings:

> Isibh: *savva-vārīhiṁ vārie* or *savva-vārī hĭ vārie* [emendation for the *śloka* metre]
> SūyC: *vāriya savva-vārī*
> SūyṬ: *vāriya savva-vāraṁ* (text; v.l. *vāre*)
> SPhS: *sabba-vāri-vārito* (only PTS has *vārī*).

Phonetic confusion between *i* and *e*, and orthographic confusion between *i*, *e*, and *aṁ* in Jaina manuscripts are likely to occur. Moreover, the Burmese letter for *i* and

[15] MATSUNAMI (1966). See also MATSUNAMI (1961).

aṁ are very similar. Although it is impossible to indicate the source of Buddhaghosa's interpretation, it seems to be close to SūyC. The fact that these tenets are found in both Buddhist and Jaina sources makes it highly probable that they formed a kernel of Mahāvīra's teachings.

It thus seems that these difficult passages recorded as Nigaṇṭha's sayings in the Buddhist Canon are based on Jaina sources and can only be understood when compared with the older strata of the Jaina *Āgamas*.

– 14 –

In addition, we find the following correspondences:

Dhp 361: *kāyena saṁvaro sādhu, sādhu vācāya saṁvaro* //
mānasā saṁvaro sādhu, sādhu sabbattha saṁvaro /
sabbattha saṁvuto bhikkhu sabba-dukkhā pamuccati //

Isibh 29.19: *savvattha virae dante, savva-vārīhiṁ vārie* / [or *savva-vārī hĩ vārie*]
savva-dukkha-ppahāṇe ya siddhe bhavati ṇīraye //

– 15 –

Although the wording of Dhp and Isibh slightly differs, the concepts and purpose of the texts are very close to each other. From the comparison of these two texts we can recognise that both Buddha and Mahāvīra, having renounced the world, sought for an effective means to avoid all sinful acts and to control their minds in order to ward off the karmic inflow from the sense organs. It is quite possible that the ideas formulated by both Buddha and Mahāvīra in fact originated in the same intellectual environment, the so-called Śramaṇa–Brāhmaṇa religious thought, and were very much alike at the starting point of their religious careers.

BIBLIOGRAPHY

ĀvN = Haribhadra: *Āvaśyaka-ṭīkā* [*Āvaśyaka-vṛtti*] on *Āvaśyaka-niryukti*. *Śrīmad-Āvaśyakam, with Haribhadra's Āvaśyaka-vṛtti*. Āgamodaya-samiti, Bombay 1916–1917. [Reprinted: Bombay Saṁ. 2038).

Āyār = *Āyāraṁga-sutta* [*Ācārâṅga-sūtra*]. (1) *Āyāraṁga-suttam*. Ed. by Muni Jambūvijaya, *Jaina-Āgama-Series* No. 2 (I), Shrī Mahāvīra Jaina Vidyālaya, Bombay 1976. (2) *Āyāraṅgasuttam with Śīlāṅka's Ṭīkā*. Āgamodaya-samiti, Bombay 1917. (3) *The Âyârâmga Sutta of Çvetambara Jains*. Ed. by Hermann Jacobi, Pāli Text Society, London 1882. (4) *Ācārāṅga-Sūtram, Erster Śrutaskandha*, Text, Analyse und Glossar von Walther Schubring, F.A. Brockhaus, Leipzig 1910. (5) *Aṅga-suttāni I*. Ed. Muni Nathmal, Jain Viswa Bhārati, Ladnun 1974 (V.S. 2031). (6) Translation, see: Jacobi (1884).

ĀyārCū = *Āyāraṁga-cuṇṇi* [*Ācārâṅga-cūrṇi*]. Ṛṣabhadevaji Kesarīmalajī Śvetāmbara Saṁsthā, Ratlam 1941.

ENOMOTO 1989 = Enomoto, Fumio: 'Shoki Bukkyō ni okeru Gō nō shōmetsu' ['Extinguishing of *Kamma* in Early Buddhism']. *The Journal of the Nippon Buddhist Research Association* Vo.54 (1989) 120–125 [Tokyo].

BALBIR 2000 = Balbir, Nalini: 'Jain-Buddhist Dialogue: Material from the Pāli Scriptures.—I. B. Horner Memorial Lecture 1997.' *Journal of the Pāli Text Society* 26 (2000) 1–42.

BhVin = *Bhikṣuṇī-Vinaya*. Edited and annotated by Gustav Roth. Tibetan Sanskrit Works Series Vol. XII, Patna 1970.

CAILLAT 1993 = Caillat, Colette: 'Jainology in Western Publication II.' In: Smet–Watanabe (1993) 43–51.

Canon = Bloch, Jules; Filliozat, Jean; Renou, Louis: *Canon Bouddhique Pāli*, tome I, facs. 1, Paris, 1949.

DELEU 1970 = Deleu, Jozef: *Viyāhapannatti* (*Bhagavaī*)*: The Fifth Anga of the Jaina Canon*. Introduction, critical analysis, commentary & indexes. *Rijksuniversiteit te Gent* no. 151, "De Tempel", Brugge 1970. [Reprinted: *Lala Sundar Lal Jain Research Series* 10, Motilal Banarsidass, Delhi 1996.]

Dhp = *Dhammapada*. (1) Edited by Oskar von Hinüber and K.R. Norman, Pāli Text Society, Oxford 1994. (2) *The Word of the Doctrine* (*Dhammapada*). Translated with an introduction and notes by K.R. Norman, Pāli Text Society, Oxford 1997.

DN = *Dīgha-nikāya*. Ed. T.W. and C.A.F. Rhys Davids and J.E. Carpenter, 3 Vols., Pāli Text Society, London I: 1890, II: 1903, III: 1911. [Reprinted: London 1947].

Isibh = (1) *Isibhāsiyāiṁ. Aussprüche der Weisen aus dem Prakrit der Jainas.* Übersetzt nebst dem revidierten Text von Walther Schubring, *Alt- und Neu-Indische Studien* 14, Hamburg 1969. (2) *Isibhāsiyāiṁ. Ein jaina Text der Frühzeit.* Von Walther Schubring, Nachrichten von der Akad. Wiss. in Göttingen, Philologisch-Historische Klasse, Göttingen 1942: Nr.1, S.481–576; 1952: Nr.2 S.21–52.

JACOBI 1884 = Jacobi, Hermann: *Jaina Sûtras. Part I: Âcârâṅga Sûtra, Kalpa Sûtra.* Translated from Prâkrit by .... *Sacred Books of the East* 22, Oxford University Press, Oxford 1884.

JACOBI 1895 = Jacobi, Hermann: *Jaina Sûtras, Part II: Uttarâdhyayana Sûtra and Sûtrakṛtâṅga.* Translated from Prâkrit by .... *Sacred Books of the East* 45, Oxford University Press, Oxford 1895.

KS = *Kalpa-sūtra.* (1) *The Kalpasûtra of Bhadrabâhu.* Edited with and Introduction, Notes and a Prākṛit-Saṁskṛit Glossary by Hermann Jacobi. *Abhandlungen für die Kunde des Morgenlandes* 7/1, Leipzig 1879. (2) Translation, see: JACOBI (1884).

LEUMANN 1934 = Leumann, Ernst: *Übersicht über die Āvaśyaka-Literatur.* Aus dem Nachlass hrsg. von Walther Schubring, Hamburg 1934.

MATSUNAMI 1966 = Matsunami, Seiren: 'Seisen no Goroku' [A translation of the Jaina text *Isibhāsiyāiṁ*]. *Studies in commemoration of the fortieth Anniversary of the existence of the Department of Literature in Kyūshū University,* Hukuoka1966. [in Japanese].

MATSUNAMI 1961 = Matsunami, Seiren: 'Buddhist Variants of two Portions of the *Isibhāsiyāiṁ.*' *Indogaku Bukkyōgaku Kenkyū* [*Journal of Indian and Buddhist Studies*] 9/2 (1961) [Tokyo].

NAKAMURA 1966 = Nakamura, Hajime: 'Sāriputta ni daihyosareta Saishoki no Bukkyō.' ['The earliest Buddhism represented by Sāriputta']. *Indogaku Bukkyōgaku Kenkyū* [*Journal of Indian and Buddhist Studies*] 14/2 (March 1966) 455–466 [Tokyo].

MĀc = *Shrivaṭṭakerācharya's Mūlâcāra.* Jnanpiṭh Mūrthidevī Jaina Granthamālā: Prākrit-grantha No. 19, New Delhi 1984.

NAKAMURA 1969 = Nakamura, Hajime: 'The earliest Buddhism represented by Sāriputta.' In: *Genshi Bukkyō no Seiritu* [*The origination of Early Buddhism*], Shunjūsha, Tokyo 1969: 379–89 [in Japanese].

NAKAMURA 1983 = Nakamura, Hajime: 'Common Elements in Early Jain and Buddhist Literature.' *Proceedings of the International Symposium on Jaina Canonical and Narrative Literature, Strasbourg, 16th–19th June 1981, Indologica Taurinensia* 9 (1983) 302–330 [Turin].

NYANATILOKA 1950 = Nyanatiloka: *Buddhist Dictionary. Manual of Buddhist Terms and Doctrines.* Colombo 1950.

RENOU 1987 = Renou, Louis: 'Notes critiques ad Dīgha Nikāya sutta 1–3.' *Bulletin d'Études Indiennes* 5 (1987) 419–451 [Paris, Association Française pour les Études Sanskrites, Edité par Nalini Balbir et Georges Pinault].

SphS = *Sāmañña-phala-sutta.*

SMET–WATANABE 1993 = Smet, Rudy; Watanabe, Kenji (eds.): *Jain Studies in Honour of Jozef Deleu*. Ho-No-Tomosha, Tokyo 1993.

Sūy = *Sūyagaḍaṁga* [*Sūtra-kṛtâṅga*]. *Sūtrakṛtâṅgam with Śīlāṅka's Ṭīkā*. Āgamodaya-saṃiti, Bombay 1917.

SūyCū = *Sūyagaḍaṁga-cuṇṇi* [*Sūtra-kṛtâṅga-cūrṇi*]. *Sūtrakṛtâṅgacūrṇiḥ with Nijjuttī and Jinadāsa's Cuṇṇi*. Śri-Ṛṣabhadevaji Keśarimalajī Śvetāmbara saṁsthā, Ratlam 1950.

SūyD = *Sūyagaḍaṁga-dīpikā* [*Sūtra-kṛtâṅga-dīpikā*]. *Sūyagaḍâṅga-sūtra with Śīlāṅka's Ṭīkā, Harṣakula's Dīpikā and Pāśacandra's Gujarātī Paraphrase*. Bombay 1936.

SūyṬ = Śīlāṅka: *Sūyagaḍaṁga-ṭīkā* [*Sūtra-kṛtâṅga-ṭīkā*]. See: Suy.

Uttar = *Uttarajjhayaṇa-sutta* [*Uttarâdhyayana-sūtra*]. *The Uttarādhyayanasūtra*. An introduction, text, critical notes and a commentary, by Jarl Charpentier, *Archives d'Etudes Orientales*, Vol. 18:1–2, Uppsala 1921–1922.

WATANABE 1981 = Watanabe, Kenji: 'Nigaṇṭha Nātaputta setsu saikō.—Jainakyō bunken kara mita Shamongakyō no rokushi' ['N.N.'s Sayings Reconsidered. The Six Heretics in the *Samañña-phala-sutta* According to Jaina Literature']. *Sankō Bunka Kenkyūjo Nenpō* 13 (1981) 1–20.

WATANABE 1986 = Watanabe, Kenji: '-vāraṁ to -vārī- wo megurite' ['Some notes on *-vāraṁ* and *-vārī-*']. *Indogaku Bukkyō Kenkyū* 34/2 (1986) 917–912.

WATANABE 1987 = Watanabe, Kenji: 'Some notes on the expression *sabba-vārī- / savva-vāraṁ*.' *Bulletin d'Études Indiennes* 5 (1987) 375–386 [Paris, Association Française pour les Études Saṅskrites, Edité par Nalini Balbir et Georges Pinault].

WATANABE 1993–94 = Watanabe, Kenji: 'Avoiding all sinful acts by both Buddha and Mahāvīra.' *Bulletin d'Études Indiennes* 11–12 (1993–94) 229–232 [Paris].

Viy = *Viyāha-pannatti* [= *Bhagavatī Vyākhyā-prajñapti*]. *Viyāhapannatti with Abhayadeva's Vṛtti*. Āgamodaya-samiti, Bombay 1918–1921.

Ājīvika Doctrine Reconsidered

JOHANNES BRONKHORST

rājño vadhaṁ cikīrṣed yas tasya citro vadho bhavet
ājīvakasya stenasya varṇa-saṁkarakasya ca
Mahā-bhārata 12.86.21

One of the mysteries that confront those who study the religious context in which Buddhism arose is the religion of the Ājīvikas, called Ājīvikism by some modern scholars.[1] The Ājīvikas, like the early Jainas and Buddhists, were Śramaṇas, ascetics who left their homes in order to find some kind of highest goal by practising various forms of asceticism. Unlike the early Jainas and Buddhists, however, they left no literature that has survived until today. Worse, there are no Ājīvikas left today. The last Ājīvikas may have lived in the fifteenth century, in the south of India, after which they disappeared. What we know about them mainly derives from Buddhist and Jaina literature, neither of which felt much sympathy for the Ājīvikas, and presents its doctrines in a biased and often caricatural fashion. Ājīvikism is—as A.L. BASHAM calls it in the subtitle of his classical study—a vanished Indian religion.

The sources of information about the religion of the Ājīvikas have been collected and studied in exemplary fashion by A.L. BASHAM in his book *History and Doctrines of the Ājīvikas*. This book came out in 1951 and has been reprinted several times since then. No study has appeared during the next half century that substantially adds to its conclusions. The contribution on the Ājīvikas in Mircea ELIADE's *Encyclopedia of Religion* has been written by the same author, A.L. BASHAM, and does little beyond summing up the contents of the book; the same is

[1] In another study, BRONKHORST (2000/b), it has been argued that the term *ājīvika* (regularly *ājīvaka* in Pāli) is used in the Buddhist canon to refer to naked ascetics in general. The present article only deals with the 'real' Ājīvikas, who presumably constituted a subset of the group of all naked ascetics and shared, beside nudity, a number of beliefs and, perhaps, the habit of referring to themselves as Ājīvikas.

Essays in Jaina Philosophy and Religion.
Warsaw Indological Studies, Volume 2 (2002), pp. 153–178.

true of the article on Ājīvikas in the *Encyclopaedia of Buddhism* (EncBuddh (1961–1965: I: 331–333). More recently, Gustav ROTH (1993) has restudied the Jaina sources on Gosāla Maṅkhaliputta and arrived at the conclusion that 'the most ancient and the most primitive doctrine of the Ājīvikas which originally existed before the development of a more elaborate system' is to be found in the 'doctrine of the six "Unavoidables": Gain and Loss, Happiness and Distress, Life and Death' (p. 420); this may be true, but tells us little about the 'more elaborate system.' Some authors—most notably Claus VOGEL in his *The Teachings of the Six Heretics*—have criticised BASHAM's exclusive use of the Pāli sources and his neglect of the Tibetan and Chinese translations, but add little to our understanding of Ājīvikism.[2] What is more, a more recent study by Graeme MACQUEEN, which compares the different versions of the *Sūtra* which is our most important source (MACQUEEN (1988: 195)), arrives at the conclusion 'that [the Pāli version], of all the versions, preserved the most ancient state of the text.'[3] In other words, BASHAM's study is reliable after all, in spite of the fact that he did not take all the source material into consideration.

Does this mean that since BASHAM no more can be said about this mysterious vanished religion? Has the last word been said about it until and unless some new sources are discovered which throw new light on this particular movement? I intend to show in this article that this is not necessarily the case. There is more to philology—the study of a culture on the basis of literary sources—than the mere linguistic analysis of those sources. The task of interpreting the contents of those sources in the light of what we know about their cultural and religious contexts is at least as important. After the initial task of collecting and reading the sources comes the next one of trying to understand what those texts are telling us. This latter task, I will argue, has not been carried out to the fullest extent possible in this case.

What then did the Ājīvikas do, and what did they believe? To begin with the latter of these two questions, BASHAM (1951: 3–4) points out that '[t]he cardinal point of the doctrines of its founder, Makkhali Gosāla,[4] was a belief in the all-embracing rule

[2] VOGEL (1970: 1). See further MACQUEEN (1984: 291 f.), (1988: 164 f.). VOGEL (1970), MEISIG (1987) and MACQUEEN (1988) provide parallel passages from the other traditions.

[3] Similarly MACQUEEN (1988: 190): '[the Pāli version] stands out as the most archaic of our texts.'

[4] Perhaps the only passage in the Pāli canon that explicitly, though not directly, associates Makkhali Gosāla with the Ājīvikas is AN 3.384, where Pūraṇa Kassapa presents—out of six 'classes'—'the white class (*sukkâbhijāti*)' as being 'the male and female Ājīvikas (?; *ājīvakā ājīvakiniyo*),' and 'the supremely white class (*parama-sukkâbhijāti*)' as Nanda Vaccha, Kisa Saṅkicca and Makkhali Gosāla.

of the principle of order, Niyati, which ultimately controlled every action and all phenomena, and left no room for human volition, which was completely ineffectual. Thus Ājīvikism was founded on an unpromising basis of strict determinism, above which was developed a superstructure of complicated and fanciful cosmology, incorporating an atomic theory which was perhaps the earliest in India, if not in the world.' This is clear, and even though it is not immediately clear why anyone in ancient India should accept such a system of beliefs, it does not by itself present a major problem of understanding.

Such a problem comes up when we consider what the Ājīvikas did. It is clear from the sources that the Ājīvikas practised asceticism of a severe type which often terminated, like that of the Jainas, in voluntary death by starvation. This is peculiar. The Jainas, too, practised asceticism which might culminate in death by starvation, but in their case this made sense, as I will explain shortly. In the case of the Ājīvikas the meaning of death by starvation is by no means obvious. If it makes no difference what one does, why should one choose severe asceticism and death by starvation rather than a more agreeable form of life?[5]

BASHAM's study throws no light on this riddle. It points out that the Buddhists, too, were perplexed. BASHAM tries to make sense of the situation in the following passage (p. 228): 'The usual Buddhist criticism of the Ājīvika *Niyati* doctrine was pragmatic. ... Since there is no possibility of modifying one's destiny by good works, self-control, or asceticism, all such activity is wasted. The Ājīvika doctrines are, in fact, conducive to luxury and licentiousness. This practical criticism of the Ājīvika philosophy might have been easily countered by the Ājīvikas with the claim that ascetics performed penances and led righteous lives under the compulsion of the same all-embracing principle as determined the lives of sinners, and that they were

[5] Cp. DUNDAS (1992: 26): 'it seems doubtful whether a doctrine which genuinely advocated the lack of efficacy of individual effort could have formed the basis of a renunciatory path to spiritual liberation.' DUNDAS suspects 'that the Jains and Buddhists deliberately distorted Ajivika doctrine for their own polemical purposes.' Regarding the ascetic side of the religion of Makkhali Gosāla we have independent evidence in the following statement by the grammarian Patañjali (second century BCE): *mā kṛta karmāṇi mā kṛta karmāṇi śāntir vaḥ śreyasîty āhāto maskarī parivrājakaḥ*—'Because he said "do not perform actions, do not perform actions, peace is better for you," he is Maskarin the wandering mendicant' (MBhā III p. 96.13–14, on Pāṇ 6.1.154). Note however ROTH (1993: 422): 'A comparison of Jaina Pkt. Gosāle Maṅkhali-putte and Pāli Makkhali Gosālo with B. Skt. Maskarī Gośālī-putraḥ shows that the latter, though it is closer to the Pāli reading, is of secondary origin. In both cases the words of Jaina Pkt. Maṅkhali and of Pāli Makkhali, connected with the name of Gosāla, with the ending -li instead of -ri, characterise themselves as variants of the eastern Māgadhī type of Prākrit.'

ascetics because *Niyati* so directed it. This very obvious argument occurs nowhere in the Buddhist scriptures, though it was known to the Jaina commentator Śīlāṅka, who quoted it as one of the arguments used by the *niyativādins*.' This argument may seem obvious, yet it is unconvincing. It is and remains difficult to believe that the early Ājīvikas engaged in painful asceticism for no other reason than that they thought that fate obliged them to do so. Even if this position turns out to be correct, it remains unintelligible without additional information as to its intellectual context.

Ājīvikism and Jainism appear to have been very close to each other in the early days. Indeed, early Jaina texts present the founder of Ājīvikism, Makkhali Gosāla, as a pupil of Mahāvīra. Gosāla subsequently broke away from Mahāvīra, but it seems *a priori* not unlikely that an understanding of the fundamental doctrines and practices of early Jainism will help us to reach a better understanding of Ājīvikism. Our first task therefore is to determine in what essential respects Jainism and Ājīvikism differed from each other.

Our information about early Jainism is not perfect. The earliest Jaina texts—the canon of the Śvetāmbara Jainas—were not written down until a millennium after the death of Mahāvīra, and only very few of these texts may date from a period close to that of Mahāvīra. These earliest texts, moreover, are sometimes difficult to interpret. However, a number of early Buddhist texts refer to the Jainas—whom they call *nirgranthas*—and tell us things about their beliefs and practices that agree with what the earliest Jaina texts tell us. From a comparison of these passages the following picture emerges.

Early Jaina asceticism was an attempt to stop activity and to put an end to karmic traces acquired earlier.[6] It was a direct response to the challenge posed by the doctrine of *karman*, interpreted in a literal way: acts—i.e. physical and mental acts—produce results in this or a next life. Physical and mental immobility discards the traces left by earlier acts, and purifies the soul from all acts, with total liberation as ultimate outcome. The following passages from the Jaina canon illustrate this. The *Uttarajjhayaṇa / Uttarajhāyā*, for example, states in its 29th chapter:

> 'By being without activity the soul does not bind new *karma* and destroys the *karma* that was bound before.'[7]
>
> 'Having reached the state [of motionlessness] of the king of mountains, the homeless [monk] destroys the four parts of *karma* which [even] a

[6] BRONKHORST (1993: §§ 1–3).

[7] Uttar 29.37, 29.38, 1139: *ajogī ṇaṁ jīve navaṁ kammaṁ na baṁdhai, puvva-baddhaṁ nijjarei.* This and the following passages are also cited in BRONKHORST (1993: 37, 27).

> *kevalin* possesses. After that [the soul] becomes perfected, awakened, freed, completely emancipated, and puts an end to all suffering.'[8]

Also the Buddhist canon ascribes this belief to the Jainas. In the *Cūḷa-dukkhakkhandha-sutta* of the *Majjhima-nikāya*, for example, Nigaṇṭha Nāthaputta (or Nātaputta, i.e. Mahāvīra) is reported to present his teachings in the following words:

> 'Formerly, Nigaṇṭhas, you performed sinful activities; you must exhaust that [sinful activity] by means of this severe and difficult practice. Being here and now restrained in body, speech and mind, amounts to not performing sinful activity in the future. Thus, as a result of the annihilation of former actions by asceticism, and of the non-performing of new actions, there is no further effect in the future; as a result of no further effect in the future there is destruction of actions; as a result of the destruction of actions there is destruction of suffering; as a result of the destruction of suffering there is destruction of sensation; as a result of the destruction of sensation all suffering will be exhausted.'[9]

This brief characterisation does not of course exhaust what can be said about early Jainism. Yet it allows us to see the 'logic' (if this is an appropriate term in this context) behind the tendency of Jaina ascetics to practise immobility, in the extreme case until death. This practice has a double objective: it destroys the traces of earlier deeds, and it binds no new *karman*.

It is also clear that Jainism accepted the doctrine of *karman* in a form in which bodily movement played a central role. Bodily movement leads to results, and in order to avoid those results bodily movement has to be halted. The early Buddhists did not share this understanding of the doctrine of *karman*. For them desire, or intention, was crucial. An early Buddhist sermon—the *Upāli-sutta*[10]—contrasts the two interpretations, or attitudes. It points out that what is central for the Jainas is physical activity, whereas for the Buddhists it is mental activity. Other passages allow us to

---

[8] Uttar 29.61, 29.62, 1163: *selesiṁ paḍivanne aṇagāre cattāri kevali-kammaṁse khavei / tao pacchā sijjhai bujjhai muccai* [*parinivvāi*][a] *savva-dukkhāṇam aṁtaṁ karei.*
[a] This term is not found in Charpentier's edition.

[9] MN 1.93 l. 2–10: *atthi kkho vo nigaṇṭhā pubbe pāpaṁ kammaṁ kataṁ / taṁ imāya kaṭukāya dukkara-kārikāya nijjaretha / yaṁ pan' ettha etarahi kāyena saṁvutā vācāya saṁvutā manasā saṁvutā taṁ āyatiṁ pāpassa kammassa akaraṇaṁ / iti purāṇānaṁ kammānaṁ tapasā byanti-bhāvā navānaṁ kammānaṁ akaraṇā āyatiṁ anavassavo, āyatiṁ anavassavā kammakkhayo, kammakkhayā dukkhakkhayo, dukkhakkhayā vedanākkhayo, vedanākkhayā sabbaṁ dukkhaṁ nijjiṇṇaṁ bhavissatîti.* See BRONKHORST (1993: 29, n. 8) for further references.

[10] MN 1.371 f. (no. 56).

interpret this more precisely. The Jainas did not only try to suppress bodily but also mental activity. The Buddhists, on the other hand, did not count mental activity as such as essential, but the intention behind it. Some Buddhist texts do not hesitate to ridicule the Jaina emphasis on bodily motionlessness and its resulting extreme discomfort. In the *Devadaha-sutta* of the *Majjhima-nikāya* the Buddha is recorded to have said:

> 'If the pleasure and pain that beings feel are caused by what was done in the past, then the Nigaṇṭhas surely must have done bad deeds in the past, since they now feel such painful, racking, piercing feelings.'[11]

An early Jaina text pays back in kind by pointing out that a Buddhist who grills a child and eats it, but without knowing that he does so, is supposedly free of guilt, whereas that same Buddhist is guilty if he eats a gourd while thinking it is a baby. The passage, which occurs in the *Sūyagaḍaṁga/Sūtra-kṛtâṅga*, reads, in BOLLÉE's (1999: 411–413) translation:

> 'If someone puts a ball of oilcake on a spit and roasts it with the idea: this is a man, or a gourd, thinking it to be a baby, he becomes for us soiled / soils himself for us with killing a living being. On the other hand, however, if a non-aryan puts a man on a spit and roasts him, taking him for an oil-cake, or does the same to a child he thinks is a gourd, in our opinion he is not soiled with killing a living being. If (*ca*) someone puts a man or a child on a spit and roasts it on a fire taking it for a lump of oil-cake, it would be fit for Buddhists to end their vow of fasting with.'[12]

---

[11] MN 2.222: *sace bhikkhave sattā pubbe-kata-hetu sukha-dukkhaṁ paṭisaṁvedenti, addhā, bhikkhave, Nigaṇṭhā pubbe-dukkata-kamma-kārino, yaṁ etarahi evarūpā dukkhā tippā kaṭukā vedanā vediyanti.* Tr. ÑĀṆAMOLI–BODHI (1995: 832).

[12] Sūy 2.6.26–28:

piṇṇāga-piṇḍī-m-avi viddhā sūle, keī paejjā "purise ime" tti /
alāuyaṁ vāvi "kumārae" tti, sa lippaī pāṇi-vaheṇa amhaṁ //
ahavāvi viddhūṇa milakkhu sūle, piṇṇāga-buddhīĕ naraṁ paejjā /
kumāragaṁ vāvi alābuyaṁ ti, na lippaī pāṇi-vaheṇa amhaṁ //
purisaṁ ca viddhūṇa kumāragaṁ vā, sūlammi keī pae jāya-tee /
piṇṇāga-piṇḍaṁ sai-m-āruhettā, buddhāṇa taṁ kappai pāraṇāe //

JACOBI (1895: 414) translates: 'If (a savage) thrusts a spit through the side of a granary, mistaking it for a man; or through a gourd, mistaking it for a baby, and roasts it, he will be guilty of murder according to our views [i.e. according to the views of the Buddhists]. If a savage puts a man on a spit and roasts him, mistaking him for a fragment of the granary; or a baby, mistaking him for a gourd, he will not be guilty of murder according to our views. If anybody thrusts a spit through a man or a baby, mistaking him for a fragment of the granary, puts him on the fire, and roasts him, that will be a meal fit for Buddhas to break fast upon.'

Passages like these, by contrasting the positions of Buddhists and Jainas, allow us to arrive at a clearer picture of early Jainism.[13] Let us now turn to some of the textual passages that inform us about the doctrine of the Ājīvikas. BASHAM's *locus classicus* is the *Sāmañña-phala-sutta* of the Buddhist *Dīgha-nikāya*. In this sermon the views of the so-called six heretics are recorded. One of these is Nigaṇṭha Nātaputta, who is the same as Mahāvīra, the last Jaina *tīrthaṅkara* who was a contemporary of the Buddha. His views should correspond to at least some extent to what we know about early Jainism, but the correspondence is not immediately obvious. BASHAM (1951: 17) comments by saying: 'The teaching ascribed to Nigaṇṭha Nātaputta is very obscure, but, as JACOBI has pointed out, while it is not an accurate description of the Jaina creed it contains nothing alien to it.'[14] This may be a somewhat optimistic characterisation of the situation,[15] yet it is clear that the teaching attributed to the Jaina leader is

---

[13] Jainism does (come to) pay attention to intention. Note, however, the following remarks by John E. CORT (1999: 49): 'The Jain conception of karma is well-known for its attention to both intention and unintentional action as being of equal importance; however, in academic presentations more attention is paid to the former. Scholars tend to focus upon the way in which Jain praxis aims at the transformation of the psychological make-up of the subject, so that both consciously and unconsciously the person is acting in a way that will be karmically beneficial and in the end lead to liberation. But if all this is so much a matter of intention, then how do we account for the energy devoted for many centuries to disagreements over calendrical interpretation, disagreements concerned with ensuring that ascetic practices are performed on the proper days? If asceticism is a matter of intention, what does it matter if a person fasts or undertakes any other ascetic action on the fourth or the fifth of the lunar fortnight? The fervour with which disputants have argued their cases for many centuries indicates that it does matter on which day ascetic practices are observed.'

[14] The reference is (indirectly) to JACOBI (1880), where it is argued that the position described in the *Sāmañña-phala-sutta* can be identified as belonging to Pārśva, Mahāvīra's predecessor.

[15] There can be no doubt that *cātuyāma-saṁvara-saṁvuto* of the *Sāmañña-phala-sutta* alludes to the *cāujjāma-dhamma*, 'the Four Restraints' of the followers of Pārśva, but it has repeatedly been pointed out—e.g. RHYS DAVIDS (1899: 75, n. 1); WALSHE (1987: 545, n. 115)—that the specification of the Four Restraints in the Buddhist *Sutta* is quite different from the one found in the Jaina texts. The Jaina Ṭhāṇ 4.136, for example, states: *bharaheravaesu ṇaṁ vāsesu purima-pacchima-vajjā majjhimagā bāvīsaṁ arahaṁtā bhagavaṁto cāujjāmaṁ paṇṇavayaṁti, taṁ jayā: savvāo pāṇātivāyāo veramaṇaṁ, savvāo musā-vāyāo veramaṇaṁ, savvāo adiṇṇâdāṇāo veramaṇaṁ, savvāo bahiddhâdāṇāo veramaṇaṁ.*—'In the Bharahas and the Eravayas the Arhats in the middle, excepting the first and the last, preach the doctrine of the Four Restraints, viz.

recognisably Jaina. We may be well advised to take a similar stance with regard to the teachings supposedly characterising Ājīvikism: These teachings may not be an accurate description of the Ājīvika creed, but they may contain little that is alien to it.

The following is, in BASHAM's paraphrase (pp. 13–14), the teaching attributed to Makkhali Gosāla:

> 'There is neither cause nor basis for the sins of living beings; they become sinful without cause or basis. Neither is there cause or basis for the purity of living beings; they become pure without cause or basis. There is no deed performed either by oneself or by others, no human action,[16] no strength, no courage, no human endurance or human prowess.[17] All beings, all that have breath, all that are born, all that have life, are without power, strength, or virtue, but are developed by destiny, chance, and nature, and experience joy and sorrow in the six classes (of existence).
> There are 1,400,000 chief uterine births, 6,000 and 600; 500 *karma*s, 5 *karma*s, 3 *karma*s, a *karma*, and half a *karma*; 62 paths; 62 lesser *kalpa*s; 6 classes (of human existence); 8 stages of man; 4,900 means of livelihood (?);[18] 4,900 ascetics; 4,900 dwellings of *nāga*s; 2,000 faculties; 3,000 purgatories; 36 places covered with dust (?); 7 sentient births; 7 insentient births; 7 births from knots (?); 7 gods; 7 men; 7 *pisāca* (births?); 7 lakes; 7 knots (?), and 700; 7 precipices, and 700; 7 dreams, and 700; and 8,400,000 great *kalpa*s through which fool and wise alike will take their course, and make an end of sorrow. There is no question of bringing unripe *karma* to fruition, nor of exhausting *karma* already ripened, by virtuous conduct, by vows, by penance, or by chastity. That cannot be done. *Saṁsāra* is measured as with a bushel, with its joy and sorrow and its appointed end.[19] It can neither be lessened nor increased, nor is there any excess of deficiency of it. Just as a ball of

abstaining from killing living beings, abstaining from false speech, abstaining from taking what is not given, abstaining from sexual intercourse'—cp. DELEU (1970: 256).

[16] For the nom. sg. in *-e* (*-kāre*) see K.R. NORMAN (1976: 240 f.).

[17] I omit the additions made by BASHAM on the basis of Buddhaghosa's commentary.

[18] The Nālandā edition of this passage (as well as the PTS edition elsewhere, e.g. SN 3.211) has *ājīvaka-sate*; the translation will then be: 4,900 Ājīvikas. This fits in well with the following *paribbājaka*s.

[19] FRANKE's translation (1913: 58) may have to be preferred: 'Glück und Leid sind wie mit Scheffeln zugemessen, und die Dauer der Seelenwanderung hat ihren bestimmten Termin.'

thread will, when thrown, unwind to its full length, so fool and wise alike will take their course, and make an end of sorrow.'[20]

Beside this passage from Buddhist literature, there is a passage in the Śvetāmbara Jaina canon that informs us about the teachings of Gosāla. It occurs in the *Viyāhapannatti* (*Bhagavatī*) and reads as follows:

> 'All those who have reached or are reaching or will reach salvation must finish in order 8,400,000 *mahākappa*s, seven divine births, seven groups, seven sentient births, seven "abandonments of transmigration" (*pauṭṭa-parihāra*), 500,000 *kamma*s, and 60,000 and 600 and the three parts of *kamma*. Then, being saved, awakened, set free, and reaching *nirvāṇa* they have made or are making or will make an end of all sorrow.'[21]

---

[20] DN 1.53–54, as cited by BASHAM (14–15, n. 3): *N'atthi ... hetu, n'atthi paccayo sattānaṁ saṁkilesāya, ahetu-apaccayā sattā saṁkilissanti. N'atthi hetu, n'atthi paccayo sattānaṁ visuddhiyā, ahetu-apaccayā sattā visujjhanti. N'atthi atta-kāre n'atthi para-kāre, n'atthi purisa-kāre, n'atthi balaṁ n'atthi viriyaṁ, n'atthi purisa-thāmo n'atthi purisa-parakkamo. Sabbe sattā sabbe pāṇā sabbe bhūtā sabbe jīvā avasā abalā aviriyā niyati-saṅgati-bhāva-pariṇatā chass'evâbhijātisu sukha-dukkhaṁ paṭisaṁvedenti. Cuddasa kho pan'imāni yoni-pamukha-satasahassāni saṭṭhiñ ca satāni cha ca satāni, pañca ca kammuno satāni pañca ca kammāni tīṇi ca kammāni kamme ca aḍḍha-kamme ca, dvaṭṭhi paṭipadā, dvaṭṭh'antara-kappā, chaḷâbhhijātiyo, aṭṭha purisa-bhūmiyo, ekūna-paññāsa ājīva-sate, ekūna-paññāsa paribbājaka-sate, ekūna-paññāsa nāgâvāsa-sate, vise indriya-sate, tiṁse niriya-sate, chattiṁsa rajo-dhātuyo, satta saññi-gabbhā, satta asaññi-gabbhā, satta nigaṇṭhi-gabbhā, satta devā, satta mānusā, satta pesācā, satta sarā, satta paṭuvā, satta paṭuvā-satāni, satta papātā, satta papāta-satāni, satta supinā, satta supina-satāni, cullâsīti mahā-kappuno satasahassāni yāni bāle ca paṇḍite ca sandhāvitvā saṁsaritvā dukkhass'antaṁ karissanti. Tattha n'atthi: iminâhaṁ sīlena vā vatena vā tapena vā brahmacariyena vā aparipakkaṁ vā kammaṁ paripācessāmi, paripakkaṁ vā kammaṁ phussa phussa vyanti-karissāmîti. H'evaṁ n'atthi. Doṇa-miṭe sukha-dukkhe pariyanta-kaṭe saṁsāre, n'atthi hāyana-vaḍḍhane n'atthi ukkaṁsâvakkaṁse. Seyyathā pi nāma sutta-guḷe khitte nibbeṭhiyamānam eva phaleti, evam eva bāle ca paṇḍite ca sandhāvitvā saṁsaritvā dukkhass'antaṁ karissanti.*

[21] Viy 15.101 (Ladnun: p. 677); 15.68 (Bombay: p. 712.1–6): *kei sijjhiṁsu vā sijjhaṁti vā sijjhissaṁti vā savve te caurāsītiṁ mahā-kappa-saya-sahassāiṁ, satta divve, satta saṁjūhe, satta saṇṇugabbhe, satta pauṭṭa-parihāre, paṁca kammaṇi*[a] *sayasahassāiṁ saṭṭhiṁ ca sahassāiṁ chac ca sae tiṇṇi ya kammaṁse aṇupuvveṇaṁ khavaittā tao pacchā sijjhaṁti bujjhaṁti muccaṁti parinivvāyaṁti savva-dukkhāṇam aṁtaṁ kareṁsu vā kareṁti vā karissaṁti vā.* Tr. BASHAM (1951: 219), modified. Note that something very similar to the end of this passage (*tao pacchā sijjhai bujjhai muccai parinivvāi savva-dukkhāṇaṁ antaṁ karei*) occurs several times in Uttar 29. Cp. n. 8, above.

A comparison of these two passages leads BASHAM (1951: 219) to the no doubt correct conclusion: 'The close similarity shows that both passages are garbled borrowings from a common source.' It also constitutes an important argument to look upon the passage in the Pāli *Sāmañña-phala-sutta* as providing historical information about the Ājīvikas, even though there appear to be no precise parallels in Chinese and Tibetan.[22]

An analysis of these two passages induces BASHAM to conclude that Gosāla opposed the doctrine of free will. All and sundry are completely subject to the one principle which determines all things. He cites here once again the following words from the *Sāmañña-phala-sutta* (p. 224–225): 'Just as a ball of thread when thrown will unwind to its full length, so fool and wise alike will take their course, and make an end of sorrow.' However, according to BASHAM '[t]his absolute determinism did not preclude a belief in *karma*, but for Makkhali Gosāla the doctrine had lost its moral force. *Karma* was unaffected by virtuous conduct, by vows, by penances, or by chastity, but it was not denied. The path of transmigration was rigidly laid out, and every soul was fated to run the same course through a period of 8,400,000 *mahākalpa*s.' He cites in this connection another portion of the passage from the *Sāmañña-phala-sutta*: 'There is no question of bringing unripe *karma* to fruition, nor of exhausting *karma* already ripened, by virtuous conduct, by vows, by penance, or by chastity. That cannot be done.'

A closer consideration of this portion suggests that BASHAM may have overstated his case. The portion speaks of 'bringing unripe *karma* to fruition' and of 'exhausting *karma* already ripened.' We have seen that this is precisely what the Jainas tried to do. Asceticism in Jainism had a double function, as we have seen: 'the annihilation of former actions, and the non-performing of new actions.' Makkhali Gosāla, we now learn, maintains that the former of these two is impossible. Our two passages do not contradict the view that *karman* does determine the future condition of an individual. They, or at any rate the first one of them, reject the possibility that this process can be precipitated, but this may mean: karmic retribution takes its time, and virtuous conduct, vows, penance, and chastity do not hasten the process.[23]

[a] On *kammaṇi*, cp. LEUMANN (1889: 339 [525]); SCHUBRING (1954: 260 [472]). BASHAM, quoting an edition not accessible to me ('with the comm. of Abhayadeva, 3 vols., Bombay 1918–21'), reads *kammāṇi*.

[22] Cp. MACQUEEN (1988: 167).

[23] Cp. PANDE (1974: 344–45): 'it appears that once earned, the inheritance of Kaṁma was held to be independent of individual will and supposed to work its way out along its

In this way an interesting contrast between Ājīvikism and Jainism becomes visible. The Jaina ascetic, by practising immobility, aspired to bring about a twofold effect: the annihilation of former actions, and the non-performing of new actions. The inactivity of the Jaina ascetic was not only meant to avoid producing karmic effects in the future, but also to destroy actions carried out in the past. The Ājīvika denied that present inactivity can destroy actions carried out in the past. For him these former actions will carry fruit whatever one does. However, there is no reason to believe that he rejected the possibility of non-performance of new actions.[24] We may therefore formulate the hypothesis that both Jainism and Ājīvikism interpreted the doctrine of *karman* in the same way, believing that bodily and mental movements were responsible for rebirth. But whereas the Jainas believed that motionlessness might destroy past *karman*, the Ājīvikas did not think so.

This does not yet solve all the problems surrounding Ājīvikism. The central question remains unanswered: why did the Ājīvikas adhere to their strict determinism? We may understand this question better by studying another position known from ancient India that might be called determinism, a position which is taught in the *Bhagavad-gītā*. Let me try to put the message of this text into its historical context.

It is clear from various sources that there were people in ancient India who were neither Buddhists nor Jainas, but who shared with the Jainas the conviction that the doctrine of *karman* concerns physical and mental acts; these people had nonetheless

---

own logic. … It was considered necessary to exhaust the numerous but enumerated types of Kaṁma prior to the attainment of liberation.'
Note that something not altogether dissimilar is ascribed (perhaps incorrectly) by Herodotus to the Egyptians. See KIRK–RAVEN–SCHOFIELD (1983: 219–220), which translates Herodotus II,123: 'the Egyptians are the first to have maintained the doctrine that the soul of man is immortal, and that, when the body perishes, it enters into another animal that is being born at the time, and when it has been the complete round of the creatures of the dry land and of the sea and of the air it enters again into the body of man at birth; and its cycle is completed in 3,000 years. There are some Greeks who have adopted this doctrine, some in former times, and some in later, as if it were their own invention; their names I know but refrain from writing down.'

[24] As late an author as Kamalaśīla attributes this position to the Ājīvikas: *yac câpy ucyate / na kiṁcit kuśalâdi-karma kartavyam iti / tatrâivâivaṁ-vadatā karma-kṣayān muktir ity ājīvaka-vā*(*dâbhyupagamo*) *bhavet* / (TUCCI (1971: 20))—'Now as for the statement "No wholesome or other act need be performed," anyone who speaks like this on this point would be in agreement with the doctrine of the Ājīvikas that liberation results from the ending of karma'; tr. OLSON–ICHISHIMA (1979: 216 [42]), modified. I thank Martin Adam for drawing my attention to this passage.

found another way to reach liberation. This other way is insight into the true nature of the self. The self is here looked upon as being totally different from all that acts in a person. Knowing the true nature of the self implies: knowing that in reality one never acts. This insight separates one from the acts, which are henceforth known to belong to the body and the mind but not to the self, and leads to, or constitutes, liberation from the effects of one's acts.

This 'other way' finds variously expression in numerous texts and traditions in India, and is indeed one of the corner stones of most Brahmanical philosophies. One aspect of this solution is not very often addressed in the earliest texts, but must have confronted all those who took this solution seriously. Knowing the true nature of one's self means: no longer identifying with the activities of body and mind. What happens at that moment to the activities of body and mind? Classical Sāṁkhya—one of the Brahmanical philosophies just referred to—offers the following answer: the material world will stop being active once the self withdraws itself, just as a dancer stops dancing when the spectators lose interest. This does not however provide much help to those who look for practical guidance after obtaining the desired insight.

Some rather different answers are associated with the *Bhagavad-gītā*, from where they spread elsewhere, soon to gain widespread recognition. The position (or positions) of the *Bhagavad-gītā* deserve(s) detailed attention here, for it (they) may throw light on the religious quest of the Ājīvikas.[25]

The general theoretical background of the *Bhagavad-gītā* is close to Sāṁkhya: the self is different from material nature, and this difference is to be realised. The question presents itself how matter, and more in particular the body accompanying a self (which includes in this discussion the mind), will continue once the difference between self and material nature is realised. Is there such a thing as the own nature of the body, which determines its activity independently of the involvement of a self? For the *Bhagavad-gītā* there is. It is the own duty, the *svadharma*, of each person. Sometimes it is characterised as the own nature (*prakṛti*, 3.33; *svabhāva*, 18.41) of the person concerned. It is different for Brahmins, Kṣatriyas, Vaiśyas and Śūdras:

> 'Calm, [self-]control, austerities, purity, patience, and uprightness, theoretical and practical knowledge, and religious faith, are the natural-born actions of Brahmins. Heroism, majesty, firmness, skill, and not fleeing in battle also, generosity, and lordly nature, are the natural-born actions of warriors. Agriculture, cattle-tending, and commerce are the

[25] The following reflections also occur in BRONKHORST (forthcoming / b).

natural-born actions of artisans; action that consists of service is likewise natural-born to a serf.'[26]

What counts in the *Bhagavad-gītā* is the attitude with which these duties are to be carried out. A right attitude secures that material nature acts without involvement of the self. Non-involvement is central. It is fundamental that one dissociates oneself from one's actions, or rather from their fruits. Actions which are not inspired by the desire to obtain happiness or to avoid suffering do not produce karmic effects. They are as good as complete inactivity. The *Bhagavad-gītā* poignantly impresses its message upon the warrior (*kṣatriya*) Arjuna who is about to destroy a major part of his family, and this makes the point very clear. Arjuna must carry out this task without concern for the disturbing results. 'Holding pleasure and pain alike, gain and loss, victory and defeat, then gird thyself for battle; thus thou shalt not get evil.'[27] The trick in all this is a certain state of mind, a mental attitude, which we may call non-attachment: 'In the mental attitude seek thy [religious] refuge; wretched are those whose motive is the fruit [of action].'[28]

Obtaining this mental attitude can be facilitated in various ways. Acting as an offering to Kṛṣṇa is recommended: 'Whatever thou doest, whatever thou eatest, whatever thou offerest in oblation or givest, whatever austerity thou performest, son of Kuntī, that do as an offering to Me.'[29] Action is also depicted as a sacrifice: 'Except action for the purpose of sacrifice, this world is bound by actions; action for

[26] BhG 18.42–44 (= Mhb.6.40.42–44):

śamo damas tapaḥ śaucaṁ kṣāntir ārjavam eva ca /
jñānaṁ vijñānam āstikyam brahma-karma svabhāvajam //
śauryaṁ tejo dhṛtir dākṣyaṁ yuddhe câpy apalāyanam /
dānam īśvara-bhāvaś ca kṣātraṁ karma svabhāvajam //
kṛṣi-gaurakṣya-vāṇijyaṁ vaiśya-karma svabhāvajam /
paricaryâtmakaṁ karma śūdrasyâpi svabhāvajam //

Tr. EDGERTON (1944), modified.

[27] BhG 2.38 (= MBh 6.24.38):

sukha-duḥkhe same kṛtvā lābhâlābhau jayâjayau /
tato yuddhāya yujyasva nâivaṁ pāpam avāpsyasi //

Tr. EDGERTON (1944: 23).

[28] BhG 2.49cd (= MBh 6.24.49cd):

buddhau śaraṇam anviccha kṛpaṇāḥ phala-hetavaḥ //

Tr. EDGERTON (1944: 25).

[29] BhG 9.27 (MBh 6.31.27):

yat karoṣi yad aśnāsi yaj juhoṣi dadāsi yat /
yat tapasyasi kaunteya tat kuruṣva mad-arpaṇam //

that purpose, son of Kuntī, perform thou, free from attachment [to its fruits].'[30] Sacrifice implies giving to the gods, who in return give to the sacrificer. Devotion is a central theme of the *Bhagavad-gītā*. Related to it is the notion of casting, or depositing, one's actions on Kṛṣṇa, or on Brahman. In verse 3.30 Kṛṣṇa invites Arjuna to cast all actions onto him, then to fight, free from longing and from selfishness.[31] Verse 5.10 speaks, similarly, of 'putting [all] actions in Brahman.'[32]

In the *Bhagavad-gītā* the right mental attitude is more important than the activity actually carried out. Once the mental attitude is in order, actions will follow suit: 'Even if a very evil doer reveres Me with single devotion, he must be regarded as righteous in spite of all; for he has the right resolution. Quickly he becomes righteous (*dharmātmā*) and goes to eternal peace.'[33] This suggests that the evil doer will soon turn to his *svadharma*. Right action is clearly the result of right attitude, not vice-versa.

Though the role of devotion to the Lord should not be underestimated, the *Bhagavad-gītā* often creates the impression that this is just one means, perhaps beside others, for obtaining the right mental attitude. This right mental attitude is, we have seen it before, non-attachment to the fruit of action. The *Bhagavad-gītā* contains passages which present knowledge of the inactive nature of the soul as a means to obtain this mental attitude. 'Actions,' verse 3.27 explains, 'are, all of them, undertaken by the *guṇa*s of Original Nature (*prakṛti*). He who is deluded by egoism thinks "I am the doer".'[34] The immediately following verses then continue: 'But he,

---

[30] BhG 3.9 (= MBh 6.25.9):

yajñârthāt karmaṇo 'nyatra / loko 'yaṁ karma-bandhanaḥ /
tad-arthaṁ karma kaunteya mukta-saṅgaḥ samācara //

Tr. EDGERTON (1944), modified.

[31] BhG 3.30 (= MBh 6.25.30):

mayi sarvāṇi karmāṇi saṁnyasyâdhyātma-cetasā /
nirāśīr nirmamo bhūtvā yudhyasva vigata-jvaraḥ //

[32] BhG 5.10 (= MBh 6.27.10):

brahmaṇy ādhāya karmāṇi saṅgaṁ tyaktvā karoti yaḥ /
lipyate na sa pāpena padma-pattram ivâmbhasā //

[33] BhG 9.30–31ab (MBh 6.31.30–31ab):

api cet sudurācāro bhajate mām ananya-bhāk /
sādhur eva sa mantavyaḥ samyag vyavasito hi saḥ //
kṣipraṁ bhavati dharmâtmā śaśvac-chāntiṁ nigacchati /

[34] BhG 3.27 (= MBh 6.25.27):

prakṛteḥ kriyamāṇāni guṇaiḥ karmāṇi sarvaśaḥ /
ahaṁkāra-vimūḍhâtmā kartâham iti manyate //

This verse and the verses cited in note 35 are also quoted in BRONKHORST (1993: 55).

oh long-armed one, who knows the truth about the category *guṇa* and the category action, knowing that the *guṇa*s move about among the *guṇa*s, he does not get attached. Those who are confused by the *guṇa*s of Original Nature (*prakṛti*) get attached to the *guṇa*s and their actions. He who knows all should not disturb those dull [people] who do not know all.'[35] Here, then, the message of the *Bhagavad-gītā*—cultivating a mental attitude of non-attachment with regard to the fruit of one's actions—is no longer an appendage to the way of insight. Insight is here a means (beside others) that may help a person to cultivate this mental attitude.

The method of the *Bhagavad-gītā* is to be distinguished from other contemporary methods. The method of physical and mental immobility demanded extreme physical and mental control. Ideas and emotions played no active role, for they had to be suppressed. The method of insight into the true nature of the self, on the other hand, emphasised the intellectual element. Understanding the true composition of the world, and the place of the soul in it, was here deemed to secure liberation. The method of actions without consequences, propagated in the *Bhagavad-gītā*, finally, put almost exclusive weight on what may be called an emotional state, an attitude of devotion, or sacrifice, of non-attachment with regard to the fruit of one's actions. We have seen that insight into the true nature of the soul may help to obtain this state, and may indeed be a precondition for doing so, yet it would be a mistake to identify the two. The basically intellectual insight may help to bring about an emotional state which is not intellectual.

The *Bhagavad-gītā* addresses an important problem connected with the belief in the possibility of liberation through insight: what happens to the body and its activities once insight is obtained? or perhaps: how do bodies act of their own, when the persons identify with their real selves and no longer with their bodies? The answer of the *Bhagavad-gītā* can easily be interpreted to mean that the body, when left to its own devices, a u t o m a t i c a l l y carries out its caste duties. In other words, we are not far removed here from a fatalistic view of activity. Acts themselves, since they belong to the material world and not to the self, do not contribute to obtaining liberation. The self obtains liberation, precisely because it leaves acts to the material world, where they will take a certain direction (that of the caste duties) without affecting the self.

---

[35] BhG 3.28–29 (= MBh 6.25.28–29):

tattva-vit tu mahā-bāho guṇa-karma-vibhāgayoḥ /
guṇā guṇeṣu vartanta iti matvā na sajjate //
prakṛter guṇa-saṁmūḍhāḥ sajjante guṇa-karmasu /
tān akṛtsna-vido mandān kṛtsna-vin na vicālayet //

There is reason to believe that the Ājīvika shared certain notions with the author of the *Bhagavad-gītā*. Both, it seems, believed that bodies can act according to their own natures. For the author of the *Bhagavad-gītā* this only happens when people realise their true identity; the activity they engage in will then be in accordance with their caste. The Ājīvikas may not have believed that any special insight was called for. The real self being in any case inactive, bodies will always act according to their natures, which for them means that they will pass through all the stages specified in the passages studied earlier, and will reach, after 8,400,000 great *kalpa*s, the stage where all *karman* has run its course.

The reason to think that the Ājīvikas thought so is the following enigmatic passage, which is part of the passage from the *Sāmañña-phala-sutta* cited earlier:[36] 'There is no deed performed either by oneself or by others, no human action, no strength, no courage, no human endurance or human prowess.' The authenticity of this passage is confirmed by its parallel in the *Saṅgha-bheda-vastu*.[37] This passage stands out in comparison to its surroundings, for it does not, unlike its surroundings, speak about living beings (Skt. *sattva*; Pāli *satta*) but about the self (Skt. *ātman*, Pāli *atta*; beside the other: *para*) and the person (Skt. *puruṣa*, Pāli *purisa*). BASHAM's translation may not draw sufficient attention to this change of terminology, which may yet be vital. *Ātman* and *puruṣa* are precisely the terms used by those schools and thinkers (such as Sāṁkhya) which maintain that the self does not act, and that activity belongs to material nature.[38] What the present passage states is precisely this, that the self does not act. The following translation makes this clearer: 'There is no deed performed either by [one's own] self or by [the self] of others, no action belonging to the *puruṣa*, no strength, no courage [belonging to the *puruṣa*], no endurance connected with the *puruṣa* or prowess connected with the *puruṣa*.'[39]

---

[36] *N'atthi atta-kāre n'atthi para-kāre, n'atthi purisa-kāre, n'atthi balaṁ n'atthi viriyaṁ, n'atthi purisa-thāmo n'atthi purisa-parakkamo.*

[37] GNOLI (1978: 221–222), MEISIG (1987: 136): *nâsti puruṣa-kāraḥ, nâsti parâkramaḥ, nâsti puruṣa-kāra-parâkramaḥ, nâsty ātma-kāraḥ, na para-kāraḥ, anātma-kāra-para-kāraḥ.*

[38] Sūy 2.6.47 criticises those who believe in 'an unmanifest, great, eternal, imperishable and unchanging *puruṣa*' (BOLLÉE (1999: 426)). Śīlāṅka ascribes this verse to Ekadaṇḍins, which term—as BOLLÉE reminds us—*may* have covered the Ājīvikas, beside others (BASHAM (1951: 169 f.)). BOLLÉE (1999: 435, n. 26) adds the appropriate warning: 'our commentators are Jains who might have known hardly more of these old and vague views of religious opponents than we.'

[39] The fact that the following line states that all *satta*, all *pāṇa*, all *bhūta* and all *jīva* are without strength and without courage is no doubt meant to draw the conclusion that living beings, because their real selves have not strength and courage, do not really have them either.

It cannot be denied that the choice of terminology of the present passage is suggestive. It also supports the interpretation here proposed. According to the Ājīvikas, the real self does not act. Activity belongs to the material world, which includes body and mind. According to the *Bhagavad-gītā*, a body (and mind) left to its own devices follows its nature, which is the rules of the caste into which one is born. This very Brahmanical and caste-oriented way of looking at the nature of the material world was not shared by the Ājīvikas, who had different ideas about this issue. According to them, a body that is left to its own devices—i.e. for them, every body—will pass through a large number of *mahā-kalpa*s, specified in the passages studied above.

The comparison with the *Bhagavad-gītā* may explain another piece of information about the Ājīvikas as well. Pūraṇa Kassapa, another heretic whose views are described in the *Sāmañña-phala-sutta*, appears to have been a teacher who was held in respect by the Ājīvikas.[40] His views, as presented in the *Sāmañña-phala-sutta* and paraphrased by BASHAM, are as follows:

> 'He who performs an act or causes an act to be performed … he who destroys life, the thief, the housebreaker, the plunderer … the highway robber, the adulterer and the liar … commit no sin. Even if with a razor-sharp discus a man reduce all the life on earth to a single heap of flesh, he commits no sin … If he come down the south bank of the Ganges, slaying, maiming, and torturing, and causing others to be slain, maimed, or tortured, he commits no sin, neither does sin approach him. Likewise if a man go down the north bank of the Ganges, giving alms and sacrificing, and causing alms to be given and sacrifices to be performed, he acquires no merit, neither does merit

[40] He alone—unlike the other five heretics, including Maskarin Gośālīputra—is presented as 'chief of five hundred Ājīvikas' (*pañca-mātrāṇām ājīvika-śatānām pramukhaḥ*) in the *Saṅgha-bheda-vastu* of the Mūlasarvāstivādins—see GNOLI (1978: 217); the views here attributed to Pūraṇa Kāśyapa (GNOLI (1978: 220–221)) coincide however with those of Ajita Kesakambalī in the *Sāmañña-phala-sutta*. Pūraṇa Kāśyapa is several times presented as an Ājīvika teacher in later texts; cf. BASHAM (1951: 80 f.). He is also the one who held that Nanda Vaccha, Kisa Saṅkicca and Makkhali Gosāla constitute 'the supremely white class' (see n. 4, above). Moreover, '[SN 3.69] ascribes the first portion of Makkhali's views (as given in [DN 1.53])—that there is no cause, no reason for depravity or purity—to Pūraṇa Kassapa' (DPPN II p. 398 s.v. Makkhali-Gosāla n. 1). It is noteworthy that Maskari(n) and Pūraṇa are mentioned by Bhāskara I as earlier mathematicians (PINGREE (1981: 59)); see SHUKLA (1976: liii-lv, 7.7 [on *Āryabhaṭīya-daśa-gītikā* 1], 67.4 [on *Āryabhaṭīya-gaṇita-pāda* 9]).

approach him. From liberality, self-control, abstinence, and honesty is derived neither merit, nor the approach of merit.'[41]

It is more than probable that Pūraṇa's position is not here presented in the most favourable light. Moreover, we have seen that the Jainas did not shy away from accusing the Buddhists of being able to eat babies without incurring sin. The Jainas had a point there, which they however exaggerated beyond all reasonable proportions. It makes sense to assume that the Buddhist texts that describe the position of Pūraṇa Kassapa do the same. They exaggerate beyond reasonable proportion a position, or the consequences of a position, which yet belonged, in this or in a closely similar form, to Pūraṇa Kassapa, and therefore probably to the Ājīvikas.

Let us now draw the *Bhagavad-gītā* into the picture. Kṛṣṇa encourages Arjuna not to avoid battle and the killing of his relatives, and says:

---

[41] DN 1.52–53 (partly cited by BASHAM (1951: 13, n. 1): *Karato kho mahā-rāja kārayato chindato chedāpayato pacato pācayato socayato kilamayato phandato phandāpayato pāṇaṁ atimāpayato, adinnaṁ ādiyato, sandhiṁ chindato, nillopaṁ harato ekāgārikaṁ karoto paripanthe tiṭṭhato, paradāraṁ gacchato, musā bhaṇato, karoto na karīyati pāpaṁ. Khura-pariyantena ce pi cakkena yo imissā paṭhaviyā pāṇe eka-maṁsa-khalaṁ eka-maṁsa-puñjaṁ kareyya, n'atthi tato-nidānaṁ pāpaṁ, n'atthi pāpassa āgamo. Dakkhinañ ce pi Gaṅgā-tīraṁ āgaccheyya hananto ghātento chindanto chedāpento pacanto pācento, n'attho tato-nidānaṁ pāpaṁ, n'atthi pāpassa āgamo. Uttarañ ce pi Gaṅgā-tīraṁ gaccheyya dadanto dāpento yajanto yajāpento n'atthi tato-nidānaṁ puññaṁ, n'atthi puññassa āgamo. Dānena damena saṁyamena sacca-vajjena n'atthi puññaṁ, n'atthi puññassa āgamo*. A résumé of this position in verse is given in SN 1.66. Essentially the same position is attributed to Sañjayī Vairaṭṭīputra in the Mūlasarvāstivādin *Saṅgha-bheda-vastu*, see GNOLI (1978: 222–223); MEISIG (1987: 144): *kurvataḥ, kārayataḥ, chindataḥ, chedayataḥ, pacataḥ, pācayataḥ, hiṁsato, ghātayataḥ, prāṇino hiṁsataḥ, adattam ādadataḥ, kāmeṣu mithyā carataḥ, saṁprajānan mṛṣā-vādam bhāṣamāṇasya, madya-pānam pibataḥ, sandhiṁ chindataḥ, granthiṁ muñcataḥ, nirlopaṁ harataḥ, paripanthaṁ tiṣṭhataḥ, grāma-ghātaṁ kurvataḥ, nagara-ghātam, jana-pada-ghātam, kṣura-paryantī-kṛtena vā cakreṇa ye 'syāṁ mahā-pṛthivyāṁ prāṇinas tān sarvān saṁchindataḥ, saṁbhindataḥ, saṁkuṭṭayataḥ, saṁpradālayataḥ, tān sarvān saṁchindya, saṁbhindya, saṁkuṭṭya, saṁpradālya, eka-māṁsa-khalaṁ kurvataḥ, māṁsa-piṇḍaṁ, māṁsa-puñjam, māṁsa-rāśim; idaṁ pratisaṁśikṣato nâsty ato-nidānaṁ pāpam; nâsty ato-nidānam pāpasyâgamaḥ; dakṣiṇena nadīṁ gaṁgāṁ chindan bhindan vâgacchet, uttareṇa vā nadyā gaṁgāyā dadat yajamānaḥ āgacchet, nâsty ato-nidānam puṇya-pāpam; nâsty ato-nidānaṁ puṇya-pāpasyâgamaḥ; yad uta dānena, damena, saṁyamena, artha-caryayā samānârthatayā iti kurvatā na kriyate eva puṇyam iti.*

'He who thinks of him (i.e., the soul inhabiting the body) as killer, he who deems him killed, both of these possess no knowledge; he does not kill and is not killed. Never is he born or dies; he has not come to be, nor will he come to be; unborn, permanent, eternal, ancient, he is not killed when the body is killed.'[42]

Here we meet with a statement—not this time from a critic but from the author of the *Bhagavad-gītā* himself—to the extent that killing is allowed in certain circumstances, or more appropriately, that killing has no karmic consequences—is no sin—in Arjuna's situation.

It would seem, then, that both Ājīvikism and the *Bhagavad-gītā* allow for the possibility that the body, when left to its own devices, will kill its fellow human beings. For both there is nothing wrong with this; the *Bhagavad-gītā* goes to the extent of warning Arjuna not to try to stop this process. Pūraṇa may have thought that there was no way this process c o u l d be stopped. The parallelism appears to go further. The *Bhagavad-gītā*, as we have seen, denies that actions are carried out by the self; they 'are, all of them, undertaken by the *guṇa*s of Original Nature (*prakṛti*). He who is deluded by egoism thinks "I am the doer".' The account of Pūraṇa is, similarly, resumed in the one word *akiriyā* 'non-action.'[43]

What is the place of asceticism in the Ājīvika vision of the world? If our reflections so far are correct, the answer must now be evident. Asceticism cannot destroy the traces of acts committed in earlier lives, or even earlier in the present life. But asceticism in Jainism had a double function: 'the annihilation of former actions, and the non-performing of new actions.' Annihilating former actions is not recognised as possible by the Ājīvikas, but non-performing new actions is possible. It is even essential at the end of the long series of lives during which, at last, all former actions have borne fruit. The Ājīvika takes longer, much much longer, than his Jaina confrère to annihilate former actions, because he does not recognise asceticism as a means to accomplish this. He has to live through 8,400,000 great *kalpa*s to bring this about. But at the end he too, like the Jaina monk, has to abstain

[42] BhG 2.19–20 (MBh 6.24.19–20):

ya enaṁ vetti hantāraṁ yaś câinaṁ manyate hatam /
ubhau tau na vijānīto nâyaṁ hanti na hanyate //
na jāyate mriyate vā kadācin, nâyaṁ bhūtvā bhavitā vā na bhūyaḥ /
ajo nityaḥ śāśvato 'yaṁ purāṇo, na hanyate hanyamāne śarīre //

On the interpretation of verse 20b, see BRONKHORST (1991: 303).

[43] DN 1.53 (§ 18): ... *Pūraṇo Kassapo sandiṭṭhikaṁ sāmañña-phalaṁ puṭṭho samāno akiriyaṁ vyākāsi.* The Gilgit *Saṅgha-bheda-vastu* attributes this position (*akriyā*) to Sañjayī Vairaṭṭīputra, see GNOLI (1978: 223).

from further activity. Like the Jaina ascetic who is close to his goal, also the Ājīvika who is close to it must starve himself to death, without doing anything whatsoever.

* * *

The above considerations, it is hoped, have made Ājīvika doctrine somewhat more comprehensible in its historical context than it has been so far. BASHAM's excellent study had left us with the idea that a fatalistic doctrine—whose links with other contemporary doctrines and with the ascetic practices of the Ājīvikas themselves remained unclear—had somehow been able to establish itself as the core of a new religion. BASHAM may not be blamed for this, for the textual evidence is incomplete, biased, and far from perfect. Yet it is to be kept in mind that religious currents do not normally crystallise around just any idea. More often than not religious doctrine—especially the doctrines of 'new religions'—shares features with other contemporary religious currents, or addresses issues that are somehow felt to be important in the society concerned. Ājīvikism, it now appears, shared a concern for the doctrine of *karman* with the other religious currents known to have existed in its time: Buddhism, Jainism, and even some of the contemporary developments of Vedic religion. From among these religious currents it was closest by far to Jainism, which is hardly remarkable in view of the fact that the Jaina tradition presents Makkhali Gosāla as a one-time pupil of Mahāvīra. The most important difference between Ājīvikism and Jainism appears to have been the Ājīvika view that asceticism cannot annihilate former *karman*. The automatic consequence of this position is that the Ājīvikas, in order to reach liberation, will have to wait for former *karman* to run its own course. This takes long, but not forever: the Ājīvikas somehow arrived at a total duration of 8,400,000 great *kalpa*s. Once arrived at the end of this period, the Ājīvikas, like their Jaina counterparts, will have to engage in asceticism, more precisely: in the non-performing of new actions. They, like the Jaina ascetics, will choose a way of dying that is as inactive as possible: the Jainas through starvation, the Ājīvikas, it appears, through thirst.

Linked to this particular notion as to how liberation can be attained, the Ājīvikas appear to have believed in the inactive nature of the self. This, if true, would point to a resemblance between the main message of the *Bhagavad-gītā* and the doctrine of the Ājīvikas. Both would then recognise in each individual a self that does not act, and a bodily part (which includes the mind) that does act. Knowing that one's self is essentially different from one's body induces people to let the body follow its own nature; this own nature of the body is in the *Bhagavad-gītā* one's *svadharma*, one's caste duties, and for the Ājīvikas something else, most probably expressed in the long list of incarnations one has to pass through.

The main reason for believing that the self, for the Ājīvikas, was by its nature inactive, is the phrase preserved in the *Sāmañña-phala-sutta* describing their position: 'There is no deed performed either by [one's own] self or by [the self] of others, no action belonging to the *puruṣa*, no strength, no courage [belonging to the *puruṣa*], no endurance connected with the *puruṣa* or prowess connected with the *puruṣa*.' However, it is not impossible that earliest Jainism, too, had a similar conception of the self. Classical, i.e. later, Jainism has a different conception of the soul, as is well known. This classical conception, however, appears to have developed at a later time.[44]

Dalsukh D. MALVANIA (1981) and others have pointed out that the early Jaina concept of the soul was indeed very different from the classical concept which developed in the course of time. Āyār 176, he points out, describes the soul in the following terms:[45]

> 'It is not long nor small nor round nor triangular nor quadrangular nor circular; it is not black nor blue nor red nor green nor white; neither of good nor bad smell; not bitter nor pungent nor astringent nor sweet; neither rough nor soft; neither heavy nor light; neither cold nor hot; neither harsh nor smooth. It does not have a body, is not born again, has no attachment and is without sexual gender. While having knowledge and sentience, there is nonetheless nothing with which it can be compared. Its being is without form, there is no condition of the unconditioned. It is not sound nor form nor smell nor flavour nor touch or anything like that.'

Āyār 171, moreover, states:

---

[44] On the development of this concept, see BRONKHORST (2000/a).

[45] Āyār 1.5.6.176 (B: p. 56–57) = 1.5.6.170 (D: p. 153 f.) = 1.5.6.4 (S: p. 26) = 1.5.6.127 f. (L: p. 47): *se na dīhe na hasse na vaṭṭe na taṁse na cauraṁse na parimaṇḍale na kiṇhe na nīle na lohie na hālidde na sukkile na surabhi-gandhe na durabhi-gandhe na titte na kaḍue na kasāe na ambile na mahure na kakkhaḍe na maue na garue na lahue na sīe na uṇhe na niddhe na lukkhe na kāū na ruhe na saṅge na itthī na purise na annahā parinne sanne uvamā na vijjai, arūvī sattā, apayassa payaṁ n'atthi, se na sadde na rūve na gandhe na rase na phāse icc-eyāvanti.* (the reading follows ed. Schubring). Tr. JACOBI (1884: 52), emended as in DUNDAS (1992: 38).

'That which is the soul is that which knows, that which is the knower is the soul, that by which one knows is the soul.'[46]

It is not therefore impossible that the soul at this early period was not believed to participate in the activity of the body. A passage in Āyār 3 which describes the Jaina as *ātma-vādin*, *loka-vādin*, *karma-vādin* and *kriyā-vādin* is not necessarily in conflict with this.[47]

MALVANIA draws attention to the similarity with Upaniṣadic ideas, and believes that the *Āyāraṁga-sutta* 'is not free from the influence of the Upaniṣads.' This may or may not be true. It may not however be superfluous to recall that these Vedic texts themselves appear to have borrowed[48]—and adjusted[49]—these ideas from others. Unfortunately we have no precise information about the religious movements from which these Upaniṣads borrowed. Could it be that the Ājīvikas and the Jainas (which both appear to have existed well before Buddhism came into being) were among them?

---

[46] Āyāra 1.5.5.171 (B: p. 55) = 1.5.5.165 (D: p. 151) = I.5.5.5 (S: p. 25) = 1.5.5.104 (L: p. 45): *je āyā se vinnāyā, je vinnāyā se āyā, jeṇa vijāṇai se āyā* (the reading follows ed. Schubring). Tr. DUNDAS (1992: 38).

[47] Āyāra 1.1.1.3–5 (B: p. 3) = 1.1.1.5–7 (D: p. 15–16) = 1.1.1.5 (S: p. 1) = 1.1.1.5–7 (L: p. 4): *se āyā-vāī logā-vāī kammā-vāī kiriyā-vāī. "karissaṁ c'ahaṁ, kārāvessaṁ c'ahaṁ karao yāvi samaṇunne bhavissāmi"—eyāvantī savvāvantī logaṁsi kamma-samārambhā parijāṇiyavvā bhavanti* (the reading follows ed. Schubring). JACOBI (1884: 2) translates: 'He believes in soul, believes in the world, believes in reward, believes in action (acknowledged to be our own doing in such judgements as these): "I did it;"—"I shall cause another to do it;"—"I shall allow another to do it." In the world, these are all the causes of sin, which must be comprehended and renounced.' SCHUBRING's translation (1926: 67) shows that no activity of the soul is necessarily thought of: 'Er glaubt [also] an ein Ich, an eine Welt, an die [Rückwirkung aller] Handlungen und an die Willensfreiheit. [Weil er an diese glaubt, sagt er:] 'ich will handeln, ich will zu handeln veranlassen, und ich will dem zustimmen, der da handelt.' Alle diese Betätigungen durch Handlung in der Welt müssen [als schädlich] erkannt werden.'

[48] BRONKHORST (1998: § 7).

[49] Cp. BRONKHORST (forthcoming / a).

BIBLIOGRAPHY

AN = *Aṅguttara-nikāya*. 5 Vols., ed. R. Morris & E. Hardy, Pāli Text Society, London 1885–1900.

Āyār = *Āyāraṁga-sutta* [*Ācārâṅga-sūtra*]. **B** = *Āyāraṅga-Suttam*. Ed. Muni Jambūvijaya, *Jaina-Āgama-Series*. No. 2 (I), Shrī Mahāvīra Jaina Vidyālaya, Bombay 1976. **D** = *Ācārāṅgasūtram and Sūtrakṛtāṅgasūtram, with the Niryukti of Bhadrabhāhu and the commentary of Śīlāṅka*. Ed. Sāgarānandasūri, re-edited with appendices etc. by Muni Jambūvijayajī, *Lālā Sundarlāl Jain Āgamagranthamālā* I, Motilal Banarsidass, Delhi 1978. **L** = *Aṅga-suttāni I*. Ed. Muni Nathmal, Jain Viswa Bhārati, Ladnun 1974 (V.S. 2031). **S** = *Ācārāṅga-Sūtram, Erster Śrutaskandha, Text, Analyse und Glossar* von Walther Schubring. F.A. Brockhaus, Leipzig 1910.

BASHAM 1951 = Basham, A.L.: *History and Doctrines of the Ājīvikas. A Vanished Indian Religion*. London 1951. [Reprinted: Motilal Banarsidass, Delhi 1981].

BhG = *Bhagavad-gītā*. See: EDGERTON (1944) [tr.].

BOLLÉE 1999 = Bollée, W.B.: 'Adda or the oldest extant dispute between Jains and heretics (*Sūyagaḍa* 2,6), Part two.' *Journal of Indian Philosophy* 27/5 (1999) 411–437. [Dordrecht].

BRONKHORST 1991 = Bronkhorst, Johannes: 'Pāṇini and the nominal sentence. *Annals of the Bhandarkar Oriental Research Institute* 71 [(1990) 1991] 301–304.

BRONKHORST 1993 = Bronkhorst, Johannes: *The Two Traditions of Meditation in Ancient India*. Second edition. Motilal Banarsidass, Delhi 1993.

BRONKHORST 1998 = Bronkhorst, Johannes: *The Two Sources of Indian Asceticism*. Second edition. Motilal Banarsidass, Delhi 1998.

BRONKHORST 2000/a = Bronkhorst, Johannes: 'Abhidharma and Jainism.' In: *Abhidharma and Indian Thought. Essays in honor of Professor Doctor Junsho Kato on his sixtieth birthday*. Ed. Committee for the Felicitation of Professor Doctor Junsho Kato's Sixtieth Birthday, Nagoya. Shuju-sha, Tokyo 2000: 598–581 ([13]–[30]).

BRONKHORST 2000/b = Bronkhorst, Johannes: 'The riddle of the Jainas and Ājīvikas in early Buddhist literature.' *Journal of Indian Philosophy* 28 (2000) 511–529.

BRONKHORST (forthcoming / a) = Bronkhorst, Johannes: 'Discipliné par le débat.' In: *Volume d'hommages pour Charles Malamoud*.

BRONKHORST (forthcoming / b) = Bronkhorst, Johannes: 'Śramaṇa.' In: *The Hindu World*. Edited by Sushil Mittal and Gene R. Thursby. Routledge, London.

CORT 1999 = Cort, John E.: 'Fistfights in the monastery: calendars, conflict and *karma* among the Jains.' In: *Approaches to Jaina Studies: Philosophy, Logic, Rituals and Symbols*. [Proceedings of the

International Conference on Approaches to Jaina Studies: Philosophy, Logic, Rituals and Symbols, 31.03–2.04.1995 Toronto]. Ed. N.K. Wagle and Olle Qvarnström. Centre for South Asian Studies, University of Toronto. *South Asian Studies Papers* 11, Toronto 1999: 36–59.

DELEU 1970 = Deleu, Jozef: *Viyāhapannatti* (*Bhagavaī*): *The Fifth Anga of the Jaina Canon*. Introduction, critical analysis, commentary & indexes. "De Tempel", Brugge 1970. [Reprinted: *Lala Sundar Lal Jain Research Series* 10, Motilal Banarsidass, Delhi 1996].

DPPN = *Dictionary of Pāli Proper Names*, Pāli Text Society, 2 vols., London 1937.

DN = *Dīgha-nikāya*. Ed. by T.W. and C.A.F. Rhys Davids and J.E. Carpenter, 3 Vols., Pāli Text Society, London I: 1890, II: 1903, III: 1911.

DUNDAS 1992 = Dundas, Paul: *The Jains*. The Library of Religious Beliefs and Practices, Routledge, London – New York 1992.

EDGERTON 1944 = Edgerton, Franklin (tr.): *The Bhagavadgītā*. New York 1944.

ELIADE 1987 = Eliade, Mircea (ed.): *Encyclopedia of Religion*. Macmillan, New York and London 1987.

EncBuddh = *Encyclopaedia of Buddhism*. Ed. G.P. Malalasekera, vol. 1 ff., Colombo 1961 ff.

FRANKE 1913 = Franke, R. Otto: *Dīghanikāya. Das Buch der langen Texte des buddhistischen Kanons in Auswahl übersetzt*. Vandenhoeck & Ruprecht, Göttingen 1913.

GNOLI 1978 = Gnoli, Raniero: *The Gilgit manuscript of the Saṅghabhedavastu, being the 17th and last section of the Vinaya of the Mūlasarvāstivādin, Part II*. Edited, with the assistance of T. Venkatacharya. Istituto italiano per il medio ed estremo Oriente, *Serie Orientale Roma* 49/2, Roma 1978.

HOERNLE 1888–1890 = Hoernle, A.F. Rudolf: *The Uvāsagadasāo or the Religious Profession of an Uvāsaga expounded in ten lectures, being the Seventh Anga of the Jains*. Prakrit text ed. and transl., 2 vols,, *Bibliotheca Indica* 105, Calcutta 1888–1890.

JACOBI 1880 = Jacobi, Hermann: 'On Mahâvîra and his predecessors.' *Indian Antiquary* (June 1880): 158–163. [Reprinted: *Kleine Schriften II*: *Glasenapp-Stiftung*, Wiesbaden, Stuttgart 1970: 797–802].

JACOBI 1884 = Jacobi, Hermann: *Jaina Sûtras. Part I: Âcârâṅga Sûtra, Kalpa Sûtra*. Translated from Prâkrit by … . *Sacred Books of the East* 22, Oxford University Press, Oxford 1884. [Reprinted: Motilal Banarsidass, Delhi, 1980].

JACOBI 1895 = Jacobi, Hermann: *Jaina Sûtras, Part II: Uttarâdhyayana Sûtra and Sûtrakṛtâṅga*. Translated from Prâkrit by … . *Sacred Books of the East* 45, Oxford University Press, Oxford 1895. [Reprinted: Motilal Banarsidass, Delhi, 1968].

KIRK–RAVEN–SCHOFIELD 1983 = Kirk, G.S.; Raven, J.E.; and Schofield, J.: *The Presocratic Philosophers. A critical history with a selection of texts*. Second edition. Cambridge University Press, Cambridge 1983.

LEUMANN 1889 = Leumann, Ernst: 'Review of Hoernle, 1885–1888.' *Wiener Zeitschrift für die Kunde Morgenlandes* 3 (1889) 328–350 [Wien]. [Reprinted: *Kleine Schriften*, *Glasenapp-Stiftung*, Wiesbaden, Stuttgart 1998: 514–536].

MACQUEEN 1984 = MacQueen, Graeme: 'The doctrines of the six heretics according to the *Śrāmaṇyaphala Sūtra*.' *Indo-Iranian Journal* 27 (1984) 291–307.

MACQUEEN 1988 = MacQueen, Graeme: *A Study of the Śrāmaṇyaphala-Sūtra*. *Freiburger Beiträge zur Indologie* 21, Otto Harrassowitz, Wiesbaden 1988.

MALVANIA 1981 = Malvania, Dalsukh D.: 'Beginnings of Jaina philosophy in the *Ācārāṅga*.' In: *Studien zum Jainismus und Buddhismus. Gedenkschrift für Ludwig Alsdorf*. Ed. Klaus Bruhn and Albrecht Wezler. *Alt- und Neu-Indische Studien* 23, Franz Steiner Verlag, Wiesbaden 1981: 151–153.

MEISIG 1987 = Meisig, Konrad: *Das Śrāmaṇyaphala-Sūtra. Synoptische Übersetzung und Glossar der chinesischen Fassungen verglichen mit dem Sanskrit und Pāli. Freiburger Beiträge zur Indologie* 19, Otto Harrassowitz, Wiesbaden 1987.

MBhā = *The Vyākaraṇa-Mahābhāṣya of Patañjali*. Ed. by F. Kielhorn, 3 Vols., The Department of Public Instruction, Bombay 1880–1885.

MBh = *The Mahābhārata for the first time critically edited*, by V.S. Sukthankar et al., Bhandarkar Oriental Research Institute, Poona 1933–66.

MN = *Majjhima-nikāya*. Ed. V. Trenckner & R. Chalmers, 3 vols., Pāli Text Society, London 1888–1899.

ÑĀṆAMOLI–BODHI 1995 = Bhikkhu Ñāṇamoli and Bhikkhu Bodhi: *The Middle Length Discourses of the Buddha*. A new translation of the Majjhima Nikāya. Wisdom Publications, Boston 1995.

NORMAN 1976 = Norman, K.R.: 'Pāli and the language of the heretics.' In: *Collected Papers I*. The Pāli Text Society, Oxford 1990: 238–246. [Appeared originally in: *Acta Orientalia* 37 (1976) 117–126.]

OLSON–ICHISHIMA 1979 = Olson, Robert F.; Ichishima, Masao: 'The Third Process of Meditative Actualization by Kamalaśīla.' *Taishō Daigaku Sōgō Bukkyō Kenkyūjo Nempō* 1 (1979) 241–205 (= (17)-(53)).

Pāṇ = Pāṇini: *Aṣṭâdhyāyī*.

PANDE 1974 = Pande, Govind Chandra: *Studies in the Origins of Buddhism*. Second revised edition. Motilal Banarsidass Delhi 1974. [First edition: 1957].

PINGREE 1981 = Pingree, David: *Jyotiḥśāstra. Astral and mathematical literature*. A History of Indian Literature vol. 6 fasc. 4. Otto Harrassowitz, Wiesbaden 1981.

RHYS DAVIDS 1899 = Rhys Davids, T.W.: *Dialogues of the Buddha, translated from the Pali.* Part I, Oxford University Press, London 1899. [Reprinted: *Sacred Books of the Buddhists Series* 2, Pāli Text Society, London. 1977].

ROTH 1993 = Roth, Gustav: 'Gosāla Mankhaliputta's birth in a cow-stall, including notes on a parallel in the Gospel of Luke 2.' In: *Jain Studies in Honour of Jozef Deleu*, ed. by Rudy Smet and Kenji Watanabe, *Hon-no-Tomosha*, Tokyo 1993: 413–455.

SCHUBRING 1926 = Schubring, Walther: *Worte Mahāvīras. Kritische Übersetzungen aus dem Kanon der Jaina*. Vandenhoeck & Ruprecht, Göttingen 1926.

SCHUBRING 1954 = Schubring, Walther: 'Review of Basham, 1951.' *Zeitschrift der Deutschen Morgenländischen Gesellschaft* 104 (1954) 256–263. [Reprinted: *Kleine Schriften*: *Glasenapp-Stiftung*, Wiesbaden, Stuttgart 1977: 468–475].

SHUKLA 1976 = Shukla, Kripa Shaṅkar: *Āryabhaṭīya of Āryabhaṭa, with the commentary of Bhāskara I and Someśvara*. Indian National Science Academy, New Delhi 1976.

Sūy = *Sūyagaḍaṅga-sutta* [*Sūtra-kr̥tâṅga-sūtra*]. See: BOLLÉE 1999.

Ṭhāṇ = *Ṭhāṇaṁga-sutta* [*Sthānâṅga-sūtra*]. *Aṅga-suttāni I*. Ed. Muni Nathmal, Jain Viswa Bhārati, Ladnun 1974 (V.S. 2031).

TUCCI 1971 = Tucci, Giuseppe (ed.): *Minor Buddhist Texts, Part III: Third Bhāvanākrama*. Istituto italiano per il medio ed estremo Oriente, *Serie Orientale Roma* 43, Roma 1971.

Uttar = *Uttarajjhayaṇa-sutta* [*Uttarâdhyayana-sūtra*]. (1) *The Uttarādhyayanasūtra*. An introduction, text, critical notes and a commentary, by Jarl Charpentier, *Archives d'Etudes Orientales*, Vol. 18:1–2, Uppsala 1921–1922. [Reprinted: Ajay Book Service, New Delhi 1980.] (2) *Nava-suttāṇi V*. Ed. Yuvācārya Mahāprajña, Jain Vishva Bharati, Ladnun 1987. (3) *Dasaveyāliyasuttaṁ, Uttarajhayaṇāiṁ and Āvassayasuttaṁ*. Ed. Muni Puṇyavijayaji and Pt. Amritlāl Mohanlāl Bhojak, Shri Mahāvīra Jaina Vidyālaya, *Jaina-Āgama-Series* No. 15, Bombay 1977.(4) Tr. in JACOBI 1895.

Viy = *Viyāha-pannatti* [= *Bhagavatī Vyākhyā-prajñapti*]. (1) *Bhagavaī Viāhapaṇṇattī*. Ed. Muni Nathamal, Jain Viswa Bhārati, Ladnun 1974 (V.S. 2031). (2) *Viyāhapaṇṇattisuttaṁ*. Ed. Bechardas J. Doshi and Amritlal Mohanlal Bhojak, *Shrī Mahāvīra Jaina Vidyālaya*, 3 parts, *Jaina-Āgama-Series* 4, Bombay 1974–1982.

VOGEL 1970 = Vogel, Claus: *The Teachings of the Six Heretics according to the Pravrajyāvastu of the Tibetan Mūlasarvāstivāda Vinaya edited and rendered into English. Abhandlungen für die Kunde des Morgenlandes* 39, Franz Steiner Verlag, Wiesbaden 1970.

WALSHE 1987 = Walshe, Maurice: *The Long Discourses of the Buddha. A translation of the Dīgha Nikāya*. Wisdom Publications, Boston 1987.

तृतीयारनयविवरणम्

Ethics and Monastic Discipline

Paradigms of Protection in Early Indian Religious Texts or an Essay on What to Do with Your Demons

PHYLLIS GRANOFF

1. Introduction

Buddhism shares with its contemporary and rival religions, Hinduism and Jainism, a concern for protecting its believers. Protection can be of many types and from many dangers. In this paper I would like to explore how some Buddhist and Hindu texts dealt with one particular category of dangers, the dangers that were thought to beset children, born and unborn. I will then turn to Jaina texts as an illustration of a totally different paradigm. My focus is on the early centuries of our era, on the religions of Gandhāra and Mathurā. Literary and archaeological evidence tells us that people in both Gandhāra and Mathurā were concerned for the welfare of their children. Among the images that have been discovered in both centres are numerous images of deities associated with childhood illnesses and miscarriage. Texts of the period reinforce the contention that protection of children was a major preoccupation.

In Gandhāra the numerous images of Hārītī, protectress of children, attest to the desire to secure protection for the very young. The story of Hārītī seems to have been a popular one; it was told in slightly different versions in numerous Buddhist texts.[1] In addition the *Mūla-sarvāsti-vāda-vinaya* includes many similar stories of the Buddha subduing and converting demons and demonnesses who prey on children.[2] Another story that tells of a child-eating demon, the story of the *yakṣa* Āṭavika, was also represented in Gandhāran art.[3] From Mathurā there are numerous

[1] For details see the exhaustive article by Noel PÉRI (1918). On Hārītī and other demonnesses popular in early Indian religion, see Rām Nath MISRA (1981).

[2] Gregory SCHOPEN has argued convincingly for considering this text as a source of information in Gandhāran Buddhism in a paper presented at *the McMaster University — University of Toronto conference on Gandhāran Buddhism, June 1999.*

[3] See INGHOLT (1957: 87, n. 126). See also the references in Rām Nath MISRA (1981: 137). The story of Āṭavika is told in a number of places. There is a *sutta* in the

Essays in Jaina Philosophy and Religion.
Warsaw Indological Studies, Volume 2 (2002), pp. 181–212.

a deity who, we shall see in a moment, was intimately associated with childhood disease. There are also images of Ṣaṣṭhī, another figure connected with sickness.[4] There seems ample evidence to argue that protecting children was at least one of the concerns that citizens of Gandhāra and Mathurā shared, and that transcended differences in religious affiliation.

Texts of the period betray a similar concern for the welfare of the unborn and newly born. In addition to the many instances in which the Buddha stops a demonic figure from killing children, there is the evidence of the *Hari-vaṁśa*, the earliest account of the life of Kṛṣṇa. In the *Viṣṇu-parvan* Kaṁsa learns that the unborn child of Devakī and Vasudeva will bring about his end. In response to the news, he immediately orders his people to summon the various supernatural agents who are capable of killing the unborn. The list includes many of the creatures whom the child Kṛṣṇa will later battle, Pūtanā, Dhenuka, and others (46). Vasudeva, in an effort to save the baby Kṛṣṇa from Kaṁsa, hands him to the cowherd Nanda. Time and time again he tells Nanda that he must take care to protect the new-born Kṛṣṇa and his brother Bālarāma, for 'Demonic creatures attack the very young' (48.4: *bālye mūrcchanty amānuṣāh*) and 'many agents of harm violently disturb the young in this world' (48.7: *vighnā hi bahavo loke bālān uttrāsayanti hi*). The world of the village in which Kṛṣṇa and Balarāma live out their childhood is a world in which constant vigilance is required in order to protect the children.

This concern for the protection of children, particularly from supernatural agents of harm, is not confined to religious texts. In fact all of the early medical texts contain sections on the protection of children and pregnant women. Some provide long lists of the different creatures who were thought to be capable of harming children, born and unborn.[5] One text, the *Kāśyapa-saṁhitā* was entirely devoted to the subject of the treatment of diseases of children and women.[6] Among the many

---

Dīgha-nikāya, the *Āṭanāṭiya-suttanta* (DN 32, III: 194–206). The sutta does not give Āṭavika's history. That is left to the commentaries to the *Sutta-nipāta* and *Aṅguttara-nikāya*. Below I will translate the version in the *Manoratha-pūraṇī,* the commentary to the *Aṅguttara-nikāya*. See also HOFFMANN (1987).

[4] See H. HÄRTEL (1976). See also HÄRTEL (1987).

[5] A convenient summary of the relevant passages in the medical texts can be found in Māheśvara Umānātha BAHĀDUR (1996). See also Jean FILLIOZAT (1937). The relevant passages in the texts include the following: *Suśruta-saṁhitā* (SuśrS: *Uttara-tantra* chapters xxvii-xxxviii) and Vāgbhaṭa's *Aṣṭāṅga-hṛdaya* (AHṛ: *Uttara-tantra* chapter 3). See also WUJASTYK (1999).

[6] Part of the section on the *graha* or seizers of children has been translated by WUJASTYK (1998: 207–236). While it is difficult to date the *Kāśyapa Saṁhitā,*

creatures thought to harm children were Skanda, Skandâpasmāra, Viśākha, Naigameṣa, Śakuni, Revatī, and Pūtanā. Skanda, Pūtanā, Viśākha and Naigameṣa are familiar from many other texts of the early period and from early iconography. For example, in addition to the lists in the medical texts, the *Mahā-bhārata* supplies a long list of demonic creatures who harm children in the *Āraṇyaka-parvan* 3.217, when it describes the many followers of Skanda. As the text tells us,

> 'Listen to me tell of the horrific retinue of Skanda. Some boys were born when Skanda was struck by the thunderbolt; they are terrifying and carry off children in the womb or after they have been born.'[7]

Indeed in the medical texts and the *Mahā-bhārata* accounts of Skanda it is primarily as a threat to children that Skanda is known.[8] The numerous images of Skanda that have been found in many places in early India, in Gandhāra and Mathurā as well as Nāgārjunakoṇḍa, might well reflect this concern for children and their welfare.

There is ample evidence, then, from texts of different genres, and from archaeological remains, that protecting the unborn and the very young from supernatural agents of harm was a major concern in early India. Buddhists and devotees of Kṛṣṇa all sought to protect their children from the hordes of demonic creatures who threatened them. Despite this common concern, and common understanding of the causes of childhood death and miscarriage, the stories that Buddhists and non-Buddhists told of subduing the demons of child illness exhibit important differences. These differences are the subject of this paper. I will argue that the *Hari-vaṁśa* follows a very ancient and well-established pattern of dealing with the demonic that can be found in the *Ṛg-veda* and the *Brāhmaṇa*s. Essentially evil is driven away, banished from sacred ground and from the village and the home. The evil creature who brings disease may be petitioned, but the request is still that the evil one stay away from the petitioner. By contrast, the Buddhist stories keep the evil one as close as is possible to the home and to the sacred space of the monastery. I also examine Jaina treatment of the demonic. I argue that the Jainas offer yet a

---

WUJASTYK argues for an early date for the section dealing with the childhood demons. On the history of Indian medical texts see Jan G. MEULENBELD (1999). On the *Kāśyapa-saṁhitā* see P.V. TEWARI (1997).

[7] MBh, *Āraṇyaka-parvan* 3.217.1:
skandasya pārśvadān ghorāñ śṛṇuṣvâdbhuta-darśanān //
vajra-prahārāt skandasya jajñus tatra kumārakāḥ /
ye haranti śiśūñ jātān garbhasthāṁś câiva dāruṇāḥ //

[8] My student, Richard Mann, is preparing an exhaustive study of the early Skanda and the development of his cult.

different paradigm that is at the same time revealing of their religious preoccupations. Jaina stories of dealing with the demonic emphasise other dangers, the danger of *karman* and relationships, into the tangled net of which the demon is drawn in the story. In concluding I will speculate further on the meaning and the implications of these differences in dealing with the demonic.

2. Chasing away the demons: From the Vedas to the *Hari-vaṁśa*

Vedic texts, from the *Ṛg-veda* and *Atharva-veda* through the *Brāhmaṇa*s give ample evidence that the concern for warding off disease and disasters was by no means new to the period under discussion here. While it would take us too far afield to discuss in any detail this early material, a few examples will make clear the important role that protection in general, and protection from disease in particular, plays in these texts.[9]

Rudra in the *Ṛg-veda* is above all a god of disease. He has the power to make humans and animals sick and the power to heal them (RV.1.43.4; RV.7.35; RV.6.74). Again and again the petitioner prays that the bad aspects of Rudra that can kill men and beasts stay far away (RV.1.114.10; RV.2.33.4;11). In the *Atharva-veda* similar prayers are heard; thus 4.8 plaintively urges Bhava, another name for Rudra, to stay away from the hymnist. Perhaps the best known prayer to Rudra and his cohorts is that found in the *Taittirīya-saṁhitā* 4.5 and the Paippalāda recension of the *Atharva-veda* 14.29. Known to later traditions as the *Śata-rudrīya*, the prayer is above all an effort to keep the disease-bringing Rudra far from the petitioner's cattle and loved ones (4.5.10). The hymnist prays for the well-being of the village, asking that Rudra not harm the elders, the children, and the unborn. Rudra is called the killer of cattle and men (*go-ghna*; *puruṣa-ghna*), and the petitioner begs him to stay far away. His dangerous weapons are to be directed to the petitioner's enemy (4.5.10). In a similar vein, the *Kauśika-sūtra* (KauśS) contains long sections on rituals to drive away demons, particularly demons that cause disease.[10]

This preoccupation with protection against evil is by no means limited either to these Vedic hymns cited or to the *Atharva-veda* and its ritual *sūtra*, the *Kauśika-sūtra* cited here. In the ritual discussions of the *Brāhmaṇa*s repeatedly ritual measures are described as necessary to keep evil away from the sacred ground or to ward off the potentially dangerous consequences of any single ritual act. Thus, for

[9] A few relevant works with emphasis on sickness include Ernst ARBMAN (1922), Kenneth G. ZYSK (1985), Dr. V.W. KARAMBELKAR (1961).

[10] See also Kenenth G. ZYSK (1985).

example, in the consecration rituals for the Jyotiṣṭhoma sacrifice in the *Śata-patha-brāhmaṇa* 3.1.2.7, when the sacrificer prepares himself by having his nails and beard cut, the ritual actions are accompanied by a prayer to keep away the harmful effects of the razor. Even the ointment placed on his eyes is described as a protection against the demon who has entered the eye (3.1.3.11). The girdle that the sacrificer wears is made of reed, for reeds come from the weapon of Indra, the *vajra*, and are therefore capable of warding off evil in the form of the *rakṣas* who threaten the sacrifice (3.2.1.1.3). The staff that the sacrificer is given is also a thunderbolt to ward off the *rakṣas* (3.2.1.32). As we move further into the ritual the text tells us often that certain actions are done to prevent the *rakṣas* from coming near the sacrifice and its offerings; thus the *soma* is covered over to prevent the *rakṣas* from touching it (3.3.3.4.6). It would not be an exaggeration to say that keeping harm and danger away from the sacrifice and the sacrificer is a leitmotif of the text. Evil is banished, sent far away from the ritual ground and from every ritual act. Every step is taken to be certain that evil cannot come near the sacrifice.

The *Śata-patha-brāhmaṇa* does know a second strategy to contain evil, and that is to propitiate the agent of evil with a sacrificial offering that is clearly distinguished from other offerings. Rudra, identified in part as the destructive, devouring fire, and the strongest threat to the sacrifice, thus receives a portion of the offerings, for example the Sviṣṭakṛt in the *Śata-patha-brāhmaṇa* 1.7.3.1. In 9.1.1.10 he is the beneficient of the *Śata-rudrīya homa*, as the officiant pleads with Rudra to do no harm. The intent of the sacrifice is to pacify and propitiate the harmful *rudra*s and thus keep their harmful acts away from the sacrificer. The two strategies, the plea for the harmful agent to keep at a distance and the offering, are here combined, as the ritual includes the recitation of verses from the *Śata-rudrīya*. It should be noted, however, that the destructive agent, though propitiated, is not converted into a permanent agent for good. The sacrifice must be regularly repeated to keep the evil contained. Rudra and his cohorts do not become permanently benign forces, but are temporarily persuaded to unstring their dangerous bows and not fire their arrows at the sacrificer. This will be an important distinction between the *Brāhmaṇa* strategies for warding off evil and the Buddhist transformation of the rituals and stories dealing with protection from dangers. But before we move on to the Buddhist accounts, we will examine what I would consider to be a close parallel to Vedic and Brāhmanic treatments of harmful beings. This is the *Hari-vaṁśa.* When we look at the *Hari-vaṁśa* and its treatment of the harms that beset the infant Kṛṣṇa, we will see that the text treats evil or dangerous threats more in line with the first strategy of the earlier texts; the agent of harm is to be kept away and if necessary eliminated entirely. There is no question in these cases of offerings or propitiation.

3. Destroying the demons of childhood disease: Kr̥ṣṇa's early exploits

The *Hari-vaṁśa, Viṣṇu-parvan,* describes in detail the circumstances surrounding the birth of Kr̥ṣṇa, who among other things is destined to destroy evil in the form of the king Kaṁsa. Kaṁsa is warned by the sage Nārada that a child born to Devakī and Vasudeva will bring about his end. To protect himself and to destroy the child who is to be born, he summons a motley crew of beings to aid him. This is what the text says:

> 'Command the horse, Keśin, Pralamba and Dhenuka, too; Ariṣṭa the bull, Pūtanā and Kāliya, saying, "Take whatever form you wish and roam entire earth. Strike at those who are our enemies." You must know the whereabouts of every unborn child on this earth, for Nārada has said that it is the unborn that I must fear".'[11]

At least two of the names in this motley list alert us immediately to the kinds of creatures it is that Kaṁsa calls to his aid. We may start with Keśin, the hairy one. In the *Atharva-veda,* Keśin is an *asura* who attacks the unborn. Thus we read in AV.8.6.5 *yaḥ kr̥ṣṇaḥ keśy asura stambaja uta tuṇḍikaḥ arāyān asyā muṣkābhyaṁ bhaṁsasopa hanmasi*—'Let us keep the black *asura* Keśin, born in the reed clump, snout-mouthed, and all other harmful creatures, away from her genitals and from her loins.' The epithet '*stambaja*', 'born in the reeds', reminds us at once of another danger to children, Skanda, who is born in a clump of reeds. The name Pūtanā also confirms that among the creatures Kaṁsa calls to his aid are demonic beings known as killers of the unborn or newly born. Pūtanā is well known in the medical texts both as a specific figure who attacks the unborn or newly born and as the name of a class of beings who are responsible for the death of children in the womb and immediately after birth. Thus the sections on *graha*s or demons who afflict children in the *Suśruta-saṁhitā* includes several chapters on different Pūtanās. In addition to

---

[11] HV 46.25–27:

ājñāpyatāṁ hayaḥ keśī pralambo dhenukas tathā /
ariṣṭo vr̥ṣabhaś câiva pūtanā kāliyas tathā //
aṭadhvaṁ pr̥thivīṁ kr̥tsnāṁ yathêṣṭaṁ kāma-rūpiṇaḥ /
praharadhvaṁ ca sarveṣu ye 'smākaṁ pakṣa-dūṣakāḥ //
garbha-sthānām api gatir vijñeyā bhuvi dehinām /
nāradena hi garbhebhyo bhayaṁ naḥ samudâhr̥tam //

the demonness named simply Pūtanā, there are Andhapūtanā and Śītapūtanā.[12] In Vagbhaṭa's *Aṣṭâṅga-hṛdaya,* there are also several Pūtanās.[13] The *Cikitsā-sthāna* of the *Kāśyapa-saṁhitā* in its section on childhood diseases also includes Pūtanā in its list.[14] The *Hari-vaṁśa* itself calls Pūtanā a Śakuni, another familiar demonness who attacks children (50.24).[15] The *Bhāgavata-purāṇa* in its depiction of the slaying of Pūtanā calls Pūtanā a '*bāla-graha*' or 'child-seizer', the name given to demonic beings who prey on children:

> 'That child killer, looking for children, by chance came upon the child in the house of Nanda; his majesty was concealed, like the blaze of a fire hidden in ashes.'[16]

Pūtanā in the next verse is called '*bāla-māraka-graha*', 'a seizer who kills children.' In an episode that is absent from the earlier *Hari-vaṁśa*, when the women of the village recite protective spells over the baby Kṛṣṇa, the name of Pūtaṇā appears in a list of demonic figures well known from the medical texts as child killers: *Koṭarā-Revatī-Jyeṣṭhā-Pūtanā-mātṛkâdayaḥ* (10.6.28). There is no question, then, that the Pūtanā whom Kaṁsa sends to kill Kṛṣṇa is one of the many demonnesses thought to be capable of killing children.

The fate of Pūtanā is equally well known. Kṛṣṇa sucks out her life as he sucks her breasts. The episode in the *Hari-vaṁśa* ends here. Yaśodā expresses her total bewilderment at the course of events, while Nanda conceals his growing fear of Kaṁsa. The dangerous Pūtanā has been destroyed and the danger that had threatened has been removed.

It is interesting to contrast this almost peremptory treatment of Pūtanā in the *Hari-vaṁśa* with later versions of the same episode. The *Bhāgavata-pūraṇa* seems uncomfortable with this way of treating evil; it is almost as if the death of the child-seizer is no guarantee that she cannot still harm Kṛṣṇa. The women recite

---

[12] SuśrS: *Uttara-tantra*, chap. 32–34. While the identity of Pūtanā as a demonness of childhood disease is without question, Keśin is a more complex figure. After I wrote this paper, Gerard Colas referred me to the work of Charlotte SCHMID (1999). Her paper is an in depth study of Keśin, which does not mention the possibility that Keśin is a demon of childhood disease, but traces a wealth of his symbolic associations.

[13] AHṛ, *Uttara-tantra* 3.2.

[14] See KāśS, p. 67.

[15] SuśrS, *Uttaratantra* chapter 30.

[16] BhāgP 10.6.7:

bāla-grahas tatra vicinvatī śiśūn yadṛcchayā nanda-gṛhe 'sadantakam /
bālam praticchananijôro-tejasaṁ dadarśa talpe 'gnim ivâhitam bhasi //

propitiatory spells and bathe the child in cow's urine. They call upon the gods to protect the child, touching his body and reciting mantras. The men cut up the corpse of Pūtanā and fling the dismembered remains far from the village. Only then do they burn the corpse. A fragrant smoke rises from the cremation pyre, indicating that that the evil demonness has been freed from her sin by her encounter with Kṛṣṇa (10.6.34). The *Garga-saṁhitā* (GarS 13) similarly describes the rituals of protection that the cowherdesses perform for Kṛṣṇa and the cremation of the dismembered corpse. This text includes an account of Pūtanā's past birth.

The change in the story of Kṛṣṇa's encounter with Pūtanā is instructive. The earlier text is satisfied with the story as a story of Kṛṣṇa's power to banish or destroy evil forces. The later texts embellish the story with rituals to protect the child against further harm and a description of the transformation of Pūtanā; the evil demonness is freed from sin and gains release, or *mokṣa*. We shall see below that this later understanding of what happens to wicked forces corresponds more closely with the Buddhist stories that are probably contemporary to the *Hari-vaṁśa* than to the *Hari-vaṁśa* itself. I will suggest that the Buddhist stories are distinctive in their treatment of demons and demonnesses and that the paradigm they offer for dealing with the demonic may well have had influences that stretched beyond Buddhism itself.

The treatment of Pūtanā in the *Hari-vaṁśa* is typical of the treatment of the threats, human and demonic, that Kṛṣṇa faces in this early text. Thus Kṛṣṇa chastises the serpent Kālīya and banishes him from the borders of the settlement (56). Kṛṣṇa tells the serpent,

> 'I will not give you a place here in the waters of the Yamunā; go, with your wife and your relatives, to the waters of the ocean. And if ever I see any one of your servants or your sons here again, whether it be on land or in the waters, then I will kill him then and there.'[17]

As in the Vedic texts like the *Śata-rudrīya* or the *Śata-patha-brāhmaṇa*, evil is dealt with by keeping it far away from its intended victims. Similarly other demons, like Pralamba or Dhenuka, are killed by Kṛṣṇa or Balarāma.

I would argue that many of the demons Kṛṣṇa kills are indeed to be understood like Pūtanā and Keśin as demons of childhood disease or miscarriage, even when the identification is not explicit. In chapter 52, for example, the village is attacked

[17] HV 56.36–37:
tavâsmin yamunā-toye nâiva sthānaṁ dadāmy aham /
gacchârṇava-jalaṁ sarpa sabhāryaḥ sahabāndhavaḥ //
yaś cêha bhūyo dṛśyeta sthale vā yadi vā jale /
tava bhṛtyas tanūjo vā kṣipraṁ vadhyaḥ sa me bhavet //

by wolves. We learn that the wolves particularly prey on the children, carrying them off at night (52.34). The demons of childhood disease are often described as either animals or having animal heads.[18] The *Bhāgavata-purāṇa* suggests that behind the episode of the cart that Kṛṣṇa overturns is an encounter with a childhood disease demon. When Yaśodā hears her son crying after he has overturned the cart, she immediately fears that he has been seized by a *graha* and she instructs the Brahmins to say prayers for his well-being. The cowherds put the cart back in its former position and then the Brahmins offer oblations of curds, rice, grass and water, perhaps as they did after the death of Pūtanā, to insure that the evil demon can wreak no further harm.

While not all of the threats to Kṛṣṇa come from supernatural beings, there is no question that at least some of the threats are demons and that some of these demons belong to the general category of demons who were thought to bring harm to young children and the unborn. What is consistent in all of the stories in the *Hari-vaṁśa*, whatever the source of harm, is the fate that the agent of harm meets. Kṛṣṇa kills or banishes all evil from the cowherd village. In the case of the wolves, the village itself moves to keep its distance from the aggressors. While this may seem a natural course of events, and one that is well in keeping with Vedic models for dealing with demons and their dangerous potential, it was radically transformed in Buddhist stories as we shall now see.

4. Demons as resident patrons of the faith: Buddhist stories of the conversion of demons

The *Mūla-sarvâsti-vāda-vinaya* tells numerous stories of the Buddha converting a *yakṣa* or *yakṣiṇī* as the first thing he does when he comes to a new place. Interestingly, the Buddha and Kṛṣṇa meet the same *yakṣa* in Mathurā. This is Gardabha, whom Kṛṣṇa meets in a forest on the outskirts of Mathurā in chapter 57, and whom the Buddha also encounters just outside the city. In the *Hari-vaṁśa* Balarāma kills the *yakṣa* and his entourage, making the forest safe for the cowherds

[18] MBh 3.216. There is a text dealing with childhood diseases that exists only in a Chinese translation of the 6th century CE. The text, *Bussetsugoshodōjidaranikyō*, Taishō 1028a, gives spells to ward off demons of childhood disease. It also describes the symptoms of the afflicted children and gives a description of the demons themselves. Most have animal forms. In the *Hari-vaṁśa*, although the wolves are created by Kṛṣṇa himself, it is clear to what class of beings they belong: they prey particularly on the children.

and their cows. In the *Mūla-sarvâsti-vāda-vinaya-vastu* when the Buddha comes to Mathurā he is first met by the guardian goddess of Mathurā, who appears before him naked. The Buddha shames her by reminding her that it is unseemly for women to run around unclothed.[19] After detailing for the monks the five flaws that Mathurā has, the Buddha goes to the temple of the *yakṣa* Gardabha, which is situated just outside the city. The townspeople learn that the Buddha has gone to the *yakṣa* temple and they set out with a cart loaded with food. They sit down near the Buddha and listen to his edifying sermon. When the sermon is over they offer the Buddha the food they have brought. The Buddha sends Ānanda into the *yakṣa* temple to bring the monks who are resting there so that they can partake of the food. When the monks and the Buddha have eaten, the townspeople tell the Buddha,

> 'O Blessed One, you have tamed many a wicked *nāga* and many a wicked *yakṣa*. This Gardabha *yakṣa* has long been our enemy, although we have done him no wrong. He is our foe, although we bear him no ill will. He is hostile to us, although we are not hostile to him. He takes our children as soon as they are born. Please, Blessed One, be compassionate and subdue the *yakṣa* Gardabha.
>
> Now at that time the *yakṣa* Gardabha was present in that assembly. The Blessed One called out to him, "Did you hear that, Gardabha?"—"I heard, Blessed One."—"Did you hear that, Gardabha?"—"I heard, Sugata."—"Cease doing such a wicked sinful thing."—"Blessed One, I will, on one condition. If they make a *vihāra* for the *saṁgha* of the four quarters in my name." At that the Blessed One addressed the householders and Brāhmins of Mathurā. "Did you hear that, O householders and Brāhmins?"—"We heard, Blessed One. We will do that." In that way the *yakṣa* along with five hundred of his retinue was subdued. The Brāhmins and householders, all devotees of the Buddha, had five hundred *vihāra*s made in their names. In the same way the *yakṣa*s Śara and Vana and the *yakṣiṇī*s Ālikāvendā and Maghā, also were subdued".'[20]

The difference between the *Hari-vaṁśa* depiction of the 'subduing' of Gardabha and that given in the *Mūla-sarvâsti-vāda-vinaya* is clear. Whereas the *Hari-vaṁśa* episode ends in the death of Gardabha and the take over by Kṛṣṇa and Balarāma of the palm forest that the *yakṣa* had controlled, the Buddhist story makes the *yakṣa*

[19] MSVin, p. 17.

[20] MSVin, p. 18 (*Bhaiṣajya-vastu*).

into a permanent patron of the faith. The *yakṣa* is made to promise that he will no longer eat the children of Mathurā and in turn the citizens of Mathurā make *vihāra*s for the monks in the name of the *yakṣa* and his retinue. The *yakṣa* becomes a part of the Buddhist community and engages in merit-making activity. It is worth noting that the *yakṣa* is described in the *vinaya* story as a demonic being who preys on children. He is thus analogous to Pūtanā or the wolves in the *Hari-vaṁśa*. Further, the Buddhist story suggests that Gardabha of Mathurā may well belong in both accounts to the large category of demons who cause harm to children.

The Buddha does not always make the demons he conquers into faithful followers, although I would suggest that the conversion of the evil being into a faithful follower becomes the dominant paradigm for dealing with the demonic in Buddhist stories. In the well-known account of the conversion of the Kāśyapas, which appears in the Pāli *Mahā-vagga*, I.15, the Buddha simply defeats the *nāga* and brings it out and shows the Brahmins. However, in the *Mahā-vastu* something more does happen. The *nāga* is said to be filled with love for the Buddha. It assumes a human form and follows the Buddha for some distance. But then, having worshipped the Buddha, the *nāga* slinks off.[21] The evil being is both banished and converted into a faithful follower of the Buddha in the *Mahā-vastu* account. Nonetheless, the *Mahā-vagga* version suggests that there was more than one way in which these stories dealt with hostile forces.

It would seem nonetheless that accounts in which the *yakṣa* or *nāga* remained somehow connected with the Buddhist community had an extraordinary appeal. Images of Hāritī, a child-stealing *yakṣiṇī,* are familiar from Gandhāra as are accounts of her conversion in the Buddhist texts.[22] In some of the accounts Hāritī becomes a lay disciple of the Buddha; in others her incorporation into the Buddhist community is more thoroughgoing. Hāritī is given a place to reside in the Buddhist monastery and the monks are instructed to provide her with food to replace the child victims she vows never to harm again.[23] Hāritī becomes the protecting deity of the monastery. The story of Hāritī takes the account of subduing the demonic being and turning that evil doer into a faithful Buddhist a step further than what we have seen either in the story of the conversion of Gardabha or in the vanquishing of the *nāga* who lived in the fire hall of the Brahmin Kāśyapa. In the story of Hāritī, the demonness is not only turned into a Buddhist devotee or donor; she is given a permanent place in the community as an active protecting force. A cult is

[21] See the translation of JONES (1956: III: 430).

[22] See PÉRI (1918).

[23] See PÉRI (1918: 11), a translation into French of the Chinese translation of the *Saṁyukta-vastu* of MSVin.

established to her and she is given regular offerings by the monks. Other texts describe her as the giver of children, and women are instructed to pray to her for children, while her sister is said to help women in childbirth.[24]

Hāritī was not the only demonic figure who would achieve the status of 'protector', either of the monastic community or a special segment of the community. The *yakṣa* Āṭavika (Āḷavika) appears in a Pāli *sutta* that bears his name.[25] In that *sutta* we are told that Vaiśravana taught the Buddha a spell in order to protect monks who are meditating in lonely places from supernatural agents who might cause them harm. If the demons will not be pacified, then the monk is instructed to call upon their army generals, or *senā-pati*s, who will subdue the recalcitrant demon.[26] Āṭavika's history is told in the commentary to the *Aṅguttara-nikāya*. There we learn that Āṭavika, like Hāritī, was once a *yakṣa* who killed children. I translate from the *Manoratha-pūraṇī*:[27]

> 'One day King Āḷavaka had gone to the forest to hunt. He shot a deer and killed it; having cut it up he hung the pieces of the deer on the tip of his bow and set out for home. On the way he was oppressed by hunger and thirst and totally exhausted. He stopped under a fig tree with spreading shade. He rested there for a moment, but as he was about to get on his way again, the deity living in the tree grabbed him by the hand, saying, "Stop! Stop! I am going to eat you." Because the deity held him so tightly he had no other recourse but to say, "Every day I promise to send you one human being along with a pot of rice." And with those words, he returned to the city.
>
> From that time on he sent a pot of rice and one criminal whom he released from prison. When in this way the prison had been emptied of prisoners, he thought to himself, "If I send adults there will be a revolt in my kingdom." And so it was that he began to seize children. The mothers who had small children and the pregnant women in the kingdom all fled to another kingdom.

---

[24] PÉRI (1918: 15).

[25] The *Āṭanāṭiya-suttanta* (DN 32, III: 194–206). For further references see the note above 24.

[26] It is interesting to note that a Chinese text on demons who plague children, Taishō 1028b, describes rituals that force the *senā-pati*s to tie up the demons who are causing children harm.

[27] *Hatthakâḷavaka-vatthu* (MPū, p. 408–412). The story was also told in the *Yakkha-vaṇṇanā*, commentary to SN, vol.1, pp. 316 ff.

One evening the Buddha was looking around the world and he saw that the prince Āḷavaka possessed the necessary conditions for attaining the three of the fruits of the path. This is what the Buddha thought: "This prince has wandered for thousands of aeons and has now fallen from heaven to take birth in the palace of King Āḷavaka." The Buddha also reasoned that the king, not finding any other child, would take his own child along with the pot of rice to offer to the deity of the tree. And so in the evening the Buddha disguised himself and went to the gate of the dwelling of the *yakkha* Āḷavaka. There he asked the gatekeeper, a *yakkha* named Gaddabha, to let him in. He said, "Blessed One, come in. But it would not be right for me not to inform Āḷavaka that you have come." And so he went to Mt. Himavat where Āḷavaka was attending a conference of the *yakkha*s. The Teacher went into Āḷavaka's home and sat right down on Āḷavaka's own couch.

At that very moment some other *yakkha*s were on their way to the *yakkha* conference and were passing over Āḷavaka's house. They got stuck and wondered what could possibly be the reason for their inability to go any further. They investigated and saw the Teacher sitting there in Āḷavaka's house. They went right in and bowed to the Teacher and then hurried off to tell Āḷavaka how lucky he was, "Āḷavaka, fortunate indeed are you. You have everything one could desire. For in your house sits the foremost being in the world of gods and of men. Go now and listen to the teaching from the Teacher." Āḷavaka, hearing their words, thought, "They are telling me that some shaven-headed ascetic is sitting on my very own couch." He was extremely displeased and angry as he proclaimed, "Today I will fight that ascetic. Come and be my allies." He stretched out his right foot and with that traversed the peak of the mountain, a distance of some sixty *yojana*s. At this point the teller of the story is to give an elaborate description of the battle with Āḷavaka. Āḷavaka wrestled with the Tathāgata all night long but was unable to do anything to him. He approached the Tathāgata and asked him eight questions. The person who wants to elaborate on these should consult the *Āḷavaka-sutta* (*Sutta-nipāta*).

The next day when the sun rose and it was time to bring the pot of rice, they could not find a suitable child and they told the king. The king asked, "Is there any child at all, even one you might think unsuitable?" They replied, "There is, my lord. Today a son has been born to the king." "Go then, and take that child. As long as I survive, I can have other children. Send the new-born along with the pot of rice." Those servants then took the baby from his mother, who was weeping loudly,

> and took him with the pot of rice to the home of the *yakkha* Āḷavaka. They called out, "Kind sir, come and get your food for today." Āḷavaka, having become a disciple of the Buddha, was ashamed when he heard their words, and he sat there, his head bent low. But the Teacher said to him, "Āḷavaka, you have nothing to be ashamed of. Take the child and put him in my hand." The king's servants then placed the prince Āḷavaka in the hand of the *yakkha* Āḷavaka. Āḷavaka took the child and put him in the hands of the Buddha. The Buddha took the child and gave him again to Āḷavaka. Āḷavaka took him and gave him to the king's men. Thus the child went from hand to hand and so they named him Āḷavaka.
>
> The king's men were pleased and took the child back to the king. When the king saw them, he thought to himself, "Today he has not accepted the food," and he asked them, "Why have you come back like this?"—"Lord, fortune shines on this royal house. The Teacher sat in Āḷavaka's house and converted him. He made him into a disciple and instructed him to give the child back to us." The Teacher then had Āḷavaka take a robe and begging bowl and they set out for the city Āḷavaka. As they neared the city, Āḷavaka was ashamed and stepped back. The Teacher saw him and asked, "Are you ashamed, Āḷavaka?"—"Yes, Blessed One," he replied. "All because of me the inhabitants of this city have seen their mothers, their fathers and their children die. If they see me they will come after me with sticks and cudgels. That is why I stepped back, Blessed One."—"Āḷavaka, you do not have to be afraid, since you are with me. Do not worry." Saying this, the Blessed One stopped in a forest grove not far from the city. Āḷavaka and the townspeople came out to meet the Teacher. The Buddha then preached to the gathered assembly. At the end of his sermon, eighty-four thousand living beings had drunk the drink of immortality. They made a place right there for Āḷavaka to live and once a year they make offerings to him.'

In this story we learn how Āṭavika is made to desist from his practice of eating children and how a cult is established for him. Āṭavika, like Hāritī, is given a place to live in the community, and offerings are made to him once a year. While we cannot identify any cult images from Gandhāra as Āṭavika, there are reliefs that tell the story of Āṭavika's conversion. There was a cult of Āṭavika in China, and the evidence of the Pāli stories indicates that it may well have had Indian roots.[28]

[28] See the entry on 'Daigensui (myōō)' in the *Hōbōgirin*, 1983: 610 ff.

Hāritī and Āṭavika are by no means unique in the world of these stories about *yakṣas* and their encounters with the Buddha. The *Mahā-samāja-sutta* of the *Dīgha-nikāya* tells of many *yakṣas*, including Hāritī. In the *Yakkha-saṁyutta-vaṇṇanā*, we hear of a *yakkhinī,* who with her son and daughter are converted by the words of the Buddha. The *yakkhinī* then takes up permanent residence in a tree near the *gandha-kūti.*[29]

These and other stories reveal a different pattern of dealing with the demonic forces that were a threat to the community, the demons who threatened the meditating monks, and the many demons of childhood diseases. I would argue that the paradigm of making the aggressor into an active protector who stays permanently in the community is something distinctive if not new with these texts. It is worth noting that in the case of the demonic beings who cause children to die or become ill, the idea of turning the demon into an object of worship may be suggested by what we find in a medical text like the *Suśruta-saṁhitā*. In the *Suśruta-saṁhitā, Uttara-tantra* 27, we are given a list of demons or *graha*s who attack children. Immediately following the list we are told on what occasions and why they prey on children; the precise conditions for the attack differ, but only one reason is given for the attack. Demons attack children so that they can secure worship for themselves:

> 'These beings, in order to be worshipped, attack children whose mother and nursemaids have committed some transgression; they attack children who are impure and for whose welfare no rituals have been performed; they attack children who are terrified or excited, and those who have been scolded and beaten.'[30]

It is difficult, however, to determine from this bare statement if propitiatory offerings are meant or if there was to be a regular and ongoing cult to the offending demon.

There is an interesting indication from the *Mahā-bhārata* that the subduing of demons of childhood disease and the establishment of a permanent cult for them, if it did originate in the Buddhist texts, was not confined to them for very long. The *Mahā-bhārata* tells the story of the birth of Jarāsaṁdha in 2.16–17. There we learn that the king Bṛhadratha had no children and propitiated a sage, who gave the king a mango fruit. The king split the fruit between his two wives. They conceived, but

---

[29] Spk I: 311. Nepal offers us several other examples of this motif and the establishment of cults to formerly cannibalistic *yakṣas*. See the cults of Gurumāpā and Bhāṭbhāṭinī in Mary SLUSSER (1982: 364).

[30] SuśrS, *Uttara-tantra* 27.6:

> *dhātrī-mātroḥ prāk-pradiṣṭâpacārāc chauca-bhraṣṭān maṅgalâcāra-hīnān /*
> *trastān hṛṣṭāṁs tarjitān tāḍitān vā pūjā-hetor hiṁsyur ete kumārān //*

having received only half a fruit, each gave birth to only half a child. The nursemaids tied the two halves together and abandoned them at the cross-roads. There the demonness or *rākṣasī* named Jarā, who was given to eating blood and flesh, found the two half-children. When she put them together to make it easier for her to eat them, a whole child was formed. Jarā decided that if she ate the king's only child, she would not be able to stay in the kingdom. And so she took on human form and told the king what had happened. In answer to his questions she explained that she was the *rākṣasī* Jarā and that she had lived happily in the king's palace, being worshipped by him. The king was delighted and ordered that a festival to the *rākṣasī* be celebrated in his kingdom, the kingdom of Māgadha (17.5).

There are many intriguing features to the story. Jarā is clearly a demonness who preys on children in the womb. The two half-children are called abortions, *garbha-saṁplave* (2.16.37). Hāritī is associated in the texts with Māgadha; in some accounts she is said to have been originally from Māgadha and married into a family in Gandhāra.[31] But what is most interesting in the story of Jarāsaṁdha's birth is an interpolation into the text that appears immediately after 2.17.1:

> 'I am the *rākṣasī* named Jarā, good sir, and I can take any form I wish. For a long time I have lived happily in your home, receiving worship. A *rākṣasī*, divinely beautiful, I stay in the homes of men, properly installed in an image for the purpose of vanquishing the demons; I was created a long time ago by Brahmā as the Goddess of the Household. Whoever paints me on the wall of his house, in the full bloom of my youth, surrounded by my children, will see prosperity in his home. If one does not paint me on the wall, he will go to ruin. O lord, I was always worshipped in your home, with flowers and fragrances, with incense and fine things to eat. I have long been wondering how I could repay your kindness. And then I saw these two halves of your children, O righteous one. I put the two halves together and fate would have it that they turned into a fine boy. That was the result of your merit, O great king. I was just the instrument that brought it about.'[32]

---

[31] See PÉRI (1918).

[32] MBh 2.17.1–7:

jarā nāmāsmi bhadraṁ te rākṣasī kāma-rūpiṇī /
tava veśmani rājendra pūjitā nyavasaṁ sukham //
gṛhe gṛhe manuṣyāṇāṁ nityaṁ tiṣṭhāmi rākṣasī /
gṛha-devîti nāmnā vai purā sṛṣṭā svayaṁ-bhuvā //
dāna-vānāṁ vināśāya sthāpitā divya-rūpiṇī /
yo māṁ bhaktyā likhet kuḍye saputrāṁ yauvanânvitām //

This interpolation recalls in fact what the Chinese pilgrim Yi-tsing observed in Gandhāra, namely that Hāritī was painted on the walls of the monastery.[33] There is no indication in an early Hindu text like the *Hari-vaṁśa* that demonnesses or demons, once subdued, were given a permanent position in the community and offerings were designated for them. I would prefer to see in the *Mahā-bhārata* interpolation the influence from Buddhist stories like those of Hāritī and Āṭavika. There is no question that it was an influence that was far-reaching, as my next story, a story about Śiva from the *Matsya-purāṇa* indicates.[34]

5. Śiva vanquishes Andhaka

The story of Śiva destroying Andhaka was frequently represented in medieval art and was widely told in the various *purāṇas*. It seems to be a later story and is not told in full until the *Purāṇas*.[35] In the version in the *Matsya-purāṇa* 179, the account of Śiva's destruction of Andhaka is almost overshadowed by the dramatic story of a demonic female figure who assists Śiva. She is known as Śuṣkarevatī, and she is created in fact twice, by Viṣṇu when Śiva turns to Viṣṇu for assistance. Śiva has set

---

gṛhe tasya bhaved vṛddhir anyathā kṣayam āpnuyāt /
tvad-gṛhe tiṣṭhamānâhaṁ pūjitâhaṁ sadā vibho //
likhitā câiva kuḍyeṣu putrair bahubhir āvṛtā /
gandha-puṣpais tathā dhūpair bhakṣya-bhojyaiḥ supūjitā //
sāhaṁ pratyupakārârthaṁ cintayāmy aniśaṁ tava /
tavême putra-śakale dṛṣṭavaty asmi dhārmika //
saṁśleṣite mayā daivāt kumāraḥ samapadyata /
tava bhāgyān mahā-rāja hetu-mātram ahaṁ tv iha //

[33] Cited by PÉRI (1918: 46).

[34] A *Śrāvaṇa-māsa-māhātmya*, chapter 9, tells the story of a woman who worshipped the goddess Jīvantikā. Her own child had been stolen at birth by the childless queen, but she nonetheless worshipped the goddess for his welfare. She painted an image of the goddess on the wall, surrounded by many children (vs. 19). This recalls the worship of Jarā described here. The goddess Jīvantikā protects the stolen youngster, prince and then king, so efficiently, that when he is a guest in someone's home, Ṣaṣṭhī is unable to enter to steal the new-born children of the host. The text is undoubtedly late, but shows the persistence of patterns of worship.

[35] I have written about this story and about the development of the early Śaiva cult in a paper, 'Śiva and his Gaṇas: Techniques of Narrative Distancing in Purāṇic Stories'—GRANOFF (forthcoming).

out to destroy Andhaka, but with each drop of blood that falls from the demon, yet another Andhaka arises. Śiva is overwhelmed. At first he creates his own host of female figures to drink the blood, but they are not up to the task. He then turns to Viṣṇu. Viṣṇu creates a female figure in answer to Śiva's pleas. The goddess / demon Śuṣkarevatī, whom Viṣṇu creates, is in fact well-known in the early medical texts as a demonness who kills children.[36] Śuṣkarevatī drinks the blood that is falling and kills the Andhakas as they are being born, an act which seems well in keeping with her identity in the medical texts as a creature who preys on the unborn and the new-born. At the end of the story, where we might expect a fulsome glorification of Śiva, we are told how Śiva was again in difficulty and needed the help of this Śuṣkarevatī. The first group of wild females he had created has run amok and is destroying the world. Śiva must again ask the help of Viṣṇu, who this time creates another group of wild women, including Śuṣkarevatī. The first group of females, now out of control, is immediately subdued by the mere sight of this second group. Viṣṇu then makes them promise that they will protect people and restrain from causing them harm. Here is what he says:

> 'Just as men and beasts protect their young and prosper like the gods in doing so, so must you protect all creatures in the world, as I now command you. Join men and gods in worshipping Śiva, the Destroyer of the Three Cities. You must never cause any trouble for those who are devoted to the Destroyer of the Three Cities, and you must protect those who call on me. You must grant all wishes to those men who regularly offer you bali offerings. And to those who desirous of children worship the goddess Śuṣkā, she will grant children. Of this there can be no doubt.'[37]

---

[36] Thus she is listed in the *Bāla-graha-cikitsā* of KāśS and in the *Uttara-sthāna* 3.3, 3.29 of AHr̥. Other names in the *Matsya-purāṇa* list of *mātr̥ka*s are also known from the medical texts on demons who kill children, for example Revatī and Mukhamaṇḍikā.

[37] MtsP 179.77–85:

... yathā manuṣyāḥ paśavaḥ pālayanti cirāt sutān /
jayanti te tathâiva āśu yathā vai devatā-gaṇāḥ // 77 //
bhavantyas tu tathā lokān pālayantu mayêritāḥ /
manujaiś ca tathā devair yajadhvaṁ tri-purântakam // 78 //
na ca bādhā prakartavyā ye bhaktās tri-purântake /
ye ca māṁ saṁsmarantîha te ca rakṣyāḥ sadā narāḥ // 79 //
bali-karma kariṣyanti yuṣmākaṁ ye sadā narāḥ /
sarva-kāma-pradās teṣāṁ bhaviṣyadhvaṁ tathâiva ca // 80 //
śuṣkāṁ saṁpūjayiṣyanti ye putrârthino janāḥ /
teṣāṁ putra-pradā devī bhaviṣyati na saṁśayaḥ // 85 //

In this story, a story ostensibly about the destruction of a troublesome demon by Śiva, we are introduced to destructive goddesses, who are very much like Hārītī or Pūtanā, preying particularly on children. All are made to stop their destructive behaviour and they are promised offerings. In addition, one, Śuṣkarevatī, in return for the worship offered her is said to grant children to the petitioners. In this story destructive goddesses have become protectresses to whom a cult is dedicated; the child-eater has become the child-giver.

I would like to suggest that this story, closer to the Buddhist paradigm than to that in the *Hari-vaṁśa,* reflects a later stage in the development of Hindu stories about childhood disease goddesses. No longer banished and destroyed, the demons have become protectors of the faithful.

I turn now to offer some interpretation of these differences that I have highlighted between these Buddhist and Hindu stories thus far.

6. Buddhist and Hindu differences

Scholars have always interpreted the stories about conversion of the demons as examples of Buddhism incorporating local deities. As Buddhism spread, the argument goes, it encountered popular cults of *nāga*s and *yakṣa*s. Buddhism took over these local deities by converting them to Buddhism and then incorporating them into the ritual cycle of the monastery. There is no question that this theory is in part correct, but I would like to supplement it from the evidence discussed in this paper. We know that the cult of Kṛṣṇa was also spreading in the same areas in which Buddhism was spreading. There are early images of Kṛṣṇa and Balarāma on coins that come from the Northwest (the coins of Agathocles in the 2nd century BCE), and there are early depictions of the two gods from Chilas in the far Northwest. And yet we see that despite the fact that the nascent Kṛṣṇa cult must also have encountered local deities, the treatment of *yakṣa*s and *nāga*s in the *Hari-vaṁśa* is strikingly different from that in the Buddhist stories. In the *Hari-vaṁśa* demons are killed or chased off. When that fails, the cowherds and their families abandon the demon-infested place for a more salubrious environment. Can this difference help us to understand something about these two early religions?

I have argued that protection, particularly the protection of the unborn and the new-born, was a major concern for both groups. The Buddhists sought to provide for that need with the converted demons; the followers of Kṛṣṇa, on the other hand, I would argue sought their protection in Kṛṣṇa himself. Thus after Kṛṣṇa has killed the serpent Kālīya, we are told,

> 'From today on, O faultless one, the long-eyed Lord Kṛṣṇa is the refuge for the cowherds, the cows and the village at times of danger.'[38]

I have argued elsewhere that Buddhists in their stories were reluctant to see the Buddha as the one who could grant children or cure disease. Indeed the *avadānas* ridicule the notion that supernatural beings of any kind can grant children.[39] I would like to propose as an hypothesis that it was because the community was reluctant to accord the Buddha these important protective functions that they 'adopted' local deities as protectors in their stories of conversion. That this was not just a matter of the stories is, of course, suggested by the archaeological remains in India. To this we must add the Chinese evidence for cults of some of these protectors for which we no longer have evidence in India. The difference then between the *Hari-vaṁśa* and the Buddhist stories is not, or at least not only, in the area of converting local deities as the religion spread, but in the need to provide protecting deities, particularly against the illnesses of childhood which were so feared. Converting the demons who cause the disease was a perfect strategy. It was common belief that the agents who cause diseases can also cure them; thus Rudra in the *Ṛg-veda* was both the agent of disease and the one with the healing herb. In the *Kathā-sarit-sāgara* hilarious tales are told of *rākṣasī*s or *piśācī*s who both cause disease and can cure it.[40] Buddhist stories thus use old themes to create new understandings of dealing with the demonic, understandings that the Jarāsaṁdha story indicates had far-reaching influence. I turn now to what I would consider another area which these Buddhist stories eventually influenced, and that is Jaina story literature.

---

[38] HV 56.43:

adya-prabhṛti gopānāṁ gavāṁ ghoṣasya cânagha /
āpatsu śaraṇaṁ Kṛṣṇaḥ prabhuś câyata-locanaḥ //

[39] See GRANOFF (1998) and GRANOFF (2001). In the earlier article I suggested that *avadāna* stories about healing often place the Buddha at a distance from the cure, allowing another figure, sometimes the god Śakra to perform the cure. I do not mean to suggest that the Buddha or the monks were never accorded such a role. Indeed there are some tantalising stories that suggest the contrary. The *Culla-vagga* (CuV, p. 216) has a rule that a monk may step on the cloth offered by a woman who has just had a miscarriage. I suspect that behind this might lie a belief in the fructifying power of the monk's touch. In addition, in a recent article, Hubert DURT (1998) cites a number of stories in which the Buddha himself effects the cure.

[40] KSS, *Madana-mañjukâlambaka* 6, chap. 28.

7. The Jaina case

While I have dealt thus far with a few Buddhist and Hindu stories, it seems natural to want to ask how the third major religion of classical India, Jainism, dealt with the non-Jaina deities with which it was confronted, particularly the deities that were thought to cause childhood illness and the death of the unborn. An exhaustive study of the question is not possible here; nonetheless I will discuss a few illustrative examples. There is no question that medieval Jainism speaks of *yakṣa*s and *yakṣiṇī*s who protect holy places and images of the Tīrthaṁkaras. The stories of the *yakṣa* Kappardin and the *yakṣiṇī* Ambikā are well known.[41] In the biographies of medieval monks, subduing hostile *yakṣa*s or *yoginī*s is not an unfamiliar topos.[42] Nonetheless, the case with the earlier literature is more complicated.

Jaina *sūtra* literature regularly describes the Tīrthaṁkara as stopping at a local *yakṣa* shrine. We hear often how the Blessed One Mahāvīra or his disciples stopped outside the city Campā at a *ceiya* of a certain *yakṣa,* Puṇṇabhadda.[43] The Tīrthaṁkara Ariṣṭanemi stops at the *jakkhâyatana* or shrine to the *yakṣa* Surappiya, 'Fond of Drink.'[44] In brief references like these there is no hint of conflict between the Tīrthaṁkara and the *yakṣa* to whom the shrine is dedicated. In contrast to the Buddha, whose first act when he comes to town according to the *Mūla-sarvâsti-vāda-vinaya* is to subjugate a hostile *yakṣa*, Mahāvīra and the other Tīrthaṁkaras simply rest at the *yakṣa* shrines, untroubled by the *yakṣa*s and not troubling them in turn.

This by no means implies that there are no hostile encounters between the Tīrthaṁkaras and supernatural beings in their biographies, but it does suggest that these encounters were perhaps not entirely at home in the Jaina literary tradition. There is an interesting episode in the biography of Mahāvīra that describes his encounter with a vicious snake.[45] The snake had been an ascetic of particularly cruel temperament in its previous life. It has now taken over a forest and kills anyone who

---

[41] See their stories from the *Vividha-tīrtha-kalpa* that I have translated in GRANOFF (1990: 182–186).

[42] See for example the biography of Vīragaṇi told in the 14th century *Prabhāvaka-carita* (PrabhC, pp. 127–132). The *yakṣa* called Virūpānātha and Vallabhīnātha boasts that he has subdued Śiva at Somanātha.

[43] See for example the *Jñātṛ-dharma-kathāḥ* (Nāy) in the opening chapter.

[44] *Jñātṛ-dharma-kathāḥ* (Nāy, chap. 5).

[45] The story is told in the *Āvaśyaka-niryukti*. See Haribhadra's ĀvṬī, p. 131. U.P. SHAH (1997) suggested that it was modelled on the story of the Buddha encountering the *nāga* among the Kāśyapas discussed above.

comes near. Mahāvīra is undeterred by the warnings he receives and marches into the forest. The snake tries to burn him to death, but is moved when he sees that Mahāvīra is unafraid. The snake remembers its past births and begins a fast. The cowherds and their wives arrive on the scene and vent their anger on the poor snake. But then they begin to worship it. They smear the snake with milk and ghee, but this only brings an army of ants who eat the snake alive. It dies and is born among the gods. This odd story seems different from either Buddhist stories of the subjugation of *nāga*s or stories like the subjugation of Kālīya in the *Hari-vaṁśa*. In the Buddhist story of the subjugation of the *nāga* that is living in the fire shed of the Kāśyapas, conquering the *nāga* is a part of a broader conquest, the conquest of the Brahmin Kāśyapas and their followers. There is no question in the Jaina story of Brahmin ascetics; they have been pushed back into a past birth that explains why the *nāga* was born as a *nāga*. This is also not a story of a local deity who resents the intrusion of the Jina, who is pacified in order that the faith may spread. We might compare Mahāvīra's encounter with the *nāga* with this statement from the *Mūla-sarvâsti-vāda-vinaya*[46]:

> 'One hundred years after my death, there will be a monk named Mādhyaṁdina, companion to the monk Ānanda. He will subdue the wicked *nāga* Huluṭa. Then, sitting in the position of meditation, he will cause my teaching to spread throughout the territory of Kashmir.'

In the Jaina story the only cult that spreads is one dedicated to the snake itself and it has disastrous consequences. When the cowherds and their wives pour milk over the snake, the milk attracts ants who eat the snake and eventually cause his death. While the story may well serve as a commentary on the foolishness and dangerousness of a snake cult, it is not a story of the Jina facing down a rival religious group.

In the expanded biography of Mahāvīra in later medieval sources, for example the *Tri-ṣaṣṭi-śalākā-puruṣa-carita* of Hemacandra, Mahāvīra does encounter some hostile *yakṣa*s whom he subdues.[47] Immediately before the episode of the snake told here, Mahāvīra must deal with the *yakṣa* Śūlapāṇi.[48] Śūlapāṇi had been a bull in his

---

[46] MSVin, p. 8: *mama varṣa-śata-parinirvṛtasya mādhyandino nāma bhikṣur bhaviṣyaty ānandasya bhikṣoḥ sārdhaṁ vihārī. sa huluṭaṁ duṣṭa-nāgaṁ vineṣyati / atha paryaṅkaṁ baddhvā samagre kāśmīra-maṇḍale śāsanaṁ praveśayiṣyati.*

[47] Translated by Helen M. JOHNSON (1962).

[48] The story of Śūlapāṇi is also told in Haribhadra's ĀvṬī, p. 127. Haribhadra notes that the verses which describe it are not found in all the manuscripts. This may well suggest its later date. See also the article by U.P. SHAH (1961); for more information about Jain *yakṣa*s and their late appearance in both the texts and art.

past life and the villagers had abused him. He had died in anger and been reborn as a *yakṣa*, or *vyantara*. In revenge he had caused a plague in the village. The plague is eventually stopped when the villagers agree to erect a temple over his bones.[49] Mahāvīra stops at the temple and the non-believing god—*miccha-ddiṭṭiṇā sureṇa* as the text calls him—tries to terrify Mahāvīra by creating apparitions of various sorts, from goblins to snakes and elephants. When Mahāvīra does not react, the unbeliever calms down and begins to praise Mahāvīra. We are told that from that time on he became known under the name of Brahmaśānti and that he abides in the temple to Mahāvīra in the town of Satyapura.

This is definitely a conversion story of a non-Jaina deity. The name Śūlapāṇi and the bull both recall Śiva. In this story Śiva has become a *yakṣa* and his bull has become his former birth. The story is late and no doubt modelled on earlier stories, that I would argue were probably not Jaina at all. Indeed, the story of Brahmaśānti is unusual in the group of stories told about Jaina protective deities. Jaina protective deities, like Ambikā and Kappardin, for example, are more often pious men and women, particularly those who have died an unusual death.[50] I would stress another point, and that is the attention given in the story of Brahmaśānti to the past birth. Mahāvīra in the later biographies has many encounters with supernatural beings and these encounters often emphasise through the tale of the past birth how the supernatural being and Mahāvīra are connected to each other. Through the Jaina emphasis on *karman* and the persistence of emotions over a series of births, these stories of defeating demons are transformed into accounts of a personal contest between two individuals, each with his own complicated past history; they are not abstract battles between the objects of worship of different religious cults.[51] It is also

---

[49] TṢŚPC VI: 47. JOHNSON has them erect a shrine over the bones of the dead villagers. The text is unavailable to me. There is another version of the story of Śūlapāṇi in the *Vividha-tīrtha-kalpa* of Jinaprabhasūri (VTīK, p. 29). There it is clear that the bones over which the shrine is erected are the bones of the dead bull. My following comments rely upon the version in the *Vividha-tīrtha-kalpa*.

[50] See GRANOFF (1990: 182–186).

[51] Perhaps the best known example of enmity that persists over a series of births is the biography of the Tīrthankara Pārśvanātha. I do not mean to imply here that only Jainas told such stories. MISRA (1981: 75) cites a story from the commentary to the *Dhamma-pada* in which a *yakṣiṇī* devours the children of her enemy from a former birth. The *Jayaddissa-jātaka* (*Jātaka*, vol. 5, pp. 21–36) explains that the *yakkhinī* who eats the queen's new-born babies was her co-wife in her past birth, who had died hating her and vowing to kill her children. On account of this vow she had become a *yakkhinī*. Despite these examples, I would argue that such stories are in the minority in Buddhist accounts, while they predominate in the Jain texts.

worth noting that the story of Mahāvīra's encounter with the *yakṣa* Śūlapāṇi seems to have developed gradually. In the version by Haribhadra, which precedes that of Hemacandra, Mahāvīra withstands the assaults of Śūlapāṇi's magic displays. At this point, Siddhārtha, the demi-god assigned by Indra, king of the gods, to protect Mahāvīra, intervenes to explain to Śūlapāṇi Mahāvīra's greatness and to teach him the Jaina *dharma*. The episode ends with an account of Mahāvīra's ten dreams that are explained as foretelling his eventual achievement of Omniscience and expounding of the Jaina teachings.[52]

Another of Mahāvīra's encounters is with another *nāga*.[53] Mahāvīra boards a boat, and the *nāga*, motivated by his hatred for Mahāvīra from a past birth, creates a violent storm to sink the boat. Interestingly, it is not Mahāvīra who defeats the *nāga*, but two demi-gods, who have come to his rescue. These demi-gods are described as *nāga-kumāra*s, 'nāga princes', here a class of supernatural beings. We are given a full account of how they had come to be demi-gods. They were once bulls who had come to know the Jaina teachings from a pious merchant, but who were then stolen and badly mistreated. Having returned to the pious Jaina merchant, they had died by fasting, while the merchant recited to them the Jaina mantra of praise. From the merit they had thereby gained, they had been reborn in a semi-divine realm. With their supernatural knowledge they came to know of Mahāvīra's distress and hastened to his rescue.

Nothing could be further from either a Buddhist story of the subjugation of a *nāga* or the *Hari-vaṁśa*'s account of Kṛṣṇa's defeat of the hostile serpent Kālīya. Here Mahāvīra remains entirely passive, while demi-gods come to his aid. Indeed in the episode of Mahāvīra and the *yakṣa* Śūlapāṇi, discussed above, Mahāvīra had also conquered the *yakṣa* merely by remaining unmoved, while in the story of the snake who had been the ascetic Caṇḍakauśika, Mahāvīra had also remained unaffected by the assault. In addition he called the snake by his name from his previous birth. This in turn stimulated the snake to remember his past birth and with it realise the truth of the Jaina doctrine.[54] In all of these episodes, then, the story teller seems to take pains to remove Mahāvīra from any active role in the conflict. The future Tīrthaṅkara does not engage in any act that could be remotely construed as an act of violence. This may be one of the reasons behind the reluctance of these biographical texts to privilege accounts of the defeat of supernatural agents of harm. These episodes are in fact mixed in with accounts of the torments Mahāvīra receives at human hands; there is little to distinguish stories about supernatural agents of harm from those

[52] ĀvṬī, pp. 128–129.

[53] TṢŚPC VI: 58–59, and ĀvṬī, p. 132.

[54] On the importance of remembering past births see GRANOFF (1994).

dealing with human agents of harm. In both, Mahāvīra remains unmoved and unmoving. These stories, then, are not so much dramatic accounts of Mahāvīra's conquest of evil as they are testimonies of his steadfastness and resolve.

Mahāvīra's supernatural adversaries also include one figure who closely recalls the child-killing demons of our other texts, and the Jaina treatment of this figure is particularly instructive. This is the *vyantarī* called Kaṭapūtanā.[55] Despite her name, Pūtanā, which we have seen is the name given to an entire class of child-killing demonnesses in the medical texts and which is the name of the child-killing demonness in the *Hari-vaṁśa*, there is nothing in the account that suggests any relationship to these better-known Pūtanās. All we are told is that this Kaṭapūtanā came upon Mahāvīra while he was standing in meditation and was unable to bear the strength of his power (*tejas*). She turned herself into a female ascetic, cloaked in a garment made of bark and wearing matted locks. She made herself wet all over and then shook the water onto Mahāvīra. As if that were not enough, she caused a fierce wind to blow. The pain that Mahāvīra endured caused him to gain higher degrees of supersensuous knowledge. In the end the *vyantarī* gave up and worshipped Mahāvīra. In the later version of Hemacandra this *vyantarī* is provided with a past life that turns the demonness Pūtanā into a close relative of Mahāvīra, as we have seen in other accounts. We are told that this Kaṭapūtanā had been the wife of Mahāvīra in a previous birth but had died in anger. Having been reborn as a human being, she had practised a false religion, as a result of which she had become a *vyantarī*. It was the hatred that she bore Mahāvīra from her previous birth that had motivated her attack on him.[56] What is remarkable in this episode is the transformation of a member of a well-known class of dangerous supernatural beings into an angry wife; the story of the subjugation of a dangerous demonness has been turned into something of a domestic quarrel. When a *vyantarī* does seem to have anything to do with granting or harming children, the story is told in a summary fashion, divorced from the drama of Mahāvīra's wanderings. Thus we read of a merchant and his barren wife. In their efforts to have a child, the couple have exhausted themselves with pleas to all kinds of gods. One day they happen upon a dilapidated temple of the Jina Mallīnātha. They pray to Mallīnātha and vow that if they are given a child they will repair the temple and become devotees of the Tīrthaṅkara. A *vyantarī*, whose name is not even given, overhears them and causes the wife to conceive. The couple fulfil their promise, we are told, and Mahāvīra, who had no role in the story, then proceeds to the next village.[57]

---

[55] ĀvṬī, p. 139.

[56] TṢŚPC VI: 80.

[57] ĀvṬī, p. 140.

If we turn to the Jaina versions of the Kṛṣṇa story to see how they deal with accounts of Kṛṣṇa's defeat of the child-slaying demons that we had found in the *Hari-vaṁśa*, we see the same tendencies observed thus far, both to turn hostile supernatural creatures into relatives, friends and old enemies, and to reduce the violence on the part of the main actor. Thus in one version, the child-killing demon Pūtanā is not a child-killing demon at all, but is the daughter of an old enemy of Vasudeva, the father of Kṛṣṇa.[58] In the *Hari-vaṁśa* of Jinasena, Putanā is also not a Śakuni, a child-killing demon. There she is one of a group of minor gods who have been won over by Kaṁsa through the power of his austerities. They take various forms and attack Kṛṣṇa.[59] In addition, in some cases it is not Kṛṣṇa at all who defeats these enemies, but minor gods who come to his rescue, just as we have seen them come to rescue the Tīrthaṅkara Mahāvīra in his biography.[60] I have argued elsewhere that Jainas sought to distinguish themselves from other religious groups, particularly Hinduism, by rejecting certain complexes of religious beliefs. One of the clusters of religious beliefs that they rejected had to do with children, their birth and their death.[61] Jaina stories deny that the birth or death of children is caused by a supernatural agent. According to the stories, it is due to *karman*, the *karman* of the child and of the mother. I would suggest here that one reason the child-killing demons are transformed into enemies from a past birth or minor gods who aid Kṛṣṇa's enemy is to be sought in part in Jaina discomfort with beliefs in a host of demi-gods and goddesses thought to be responsible for child welfare. The same explanation might be offered for what I have described as a lack of interest in the Tīrthaṅkara biographies in accounts of the subduing of *yakṣa*s and *yakṣiṇī*s, who are, after all, best known as killers and granters of children. Even a medieval Jaina medical text when it treats the subject of childhood illnesses reinterprets the well-known attackers of children as enemies from a prior birth. Thus it has this gloss on the standard demons thought to be responsible for childhood illnesses:

> '*Vyantara*s live on earth, constantly oppressing people with their magic displays. They do this either because they are angry at their victims who were their enemies in another birth or sometimes they desire to do harm just for the fun of it.'[62]

---

58 TṢŚPC V: 160.

59 HVP, chap. 25.

60 For example in the biography of Neminātha in TṢŚPC V: 160, and HVP 25.44.

61 See GRANOFF (2001).

62 KK 66:

vyantarā bhuvi vasanti saṁtataṁ pīḍayaṁty api narān samāyayā /
pūrva-janma-kṛta-śatru-roṣataḥ krīḍanârtham athavā jighāṁsayā //

There then follows a description of the symptoms of children who are oppressed by different kinds of beings, many of whom are recognisable from non-Jaina medical texts. What is different here, however, is something we have seen in the medieval Jaina stories themselves. Supernatural beings do not wantonly attack people; one need not subdue supernatural beings and make offerings to them to pacify them. The terror in the Jaina world is something else; it is *karman* and what *karman* entails, a beginningless history of hates and enmities that can only be stopped when the cycle of rebirths itself is stopped.[63] Ultimately the Tīrthaṅkara conquers oppressive *yakṣa*s or *vyantara*s by achieving release. Meeting and subduing supernatural enemies in these stories is thus less important than pursuing a life of asceticism and restraint. This understanding surely distinguishes the accounts of the life of Mahāvīra from accounts of the deeds of either the Buddha or Kṛṣṇa, reviewed briefly above. I turn now to some final suggestions.

8. Concluding remarks

In this paper I have put forward the hypothesis that dealing with the demonic was something that different religions did differently in early Indian religious texts. I have tried to show that Buddhist stories describe the Buddha as confronting directly *yakṣa*s and *yakṣiṇī*s, *nāga*s and *nāginī*s. In addition these supernatural beings are not simply vanquished; in many cases they are made a permanent part of the monastic community and given a cult and a role to play. Given the fact that many of these creatures are described as preying on children, it is not surprising that their role includes the protection or granting of children. We have seen how it was commonly believed that the demons who wreak havoc also possessed the means to remedy the disaster they cause. Converting child-eating *yakṣa*s into protectors of children accords with well-established beliefs. I further argued that the Buddhist eagerness to accord these deities or demons a place in the monastic community may well have been related to a reluctance to grant the Buddha himself the roles that are ultimately

---

[63] As is the case with all general statements, it is not difficult to find examples that contradict this one too. Thus in the *Pañca-śati-prabandha-sambandha* (PŚPS, p. 347) we read of a plague in the city of Delhi (Yoginīpura) which is caused by the sixty-four *yoginī*s. A Jain layman takes offerings to the *yoginī*s and the plague stops. It is worth noting, however, that the disease causing agents are a group of goddesses / demonnesses thought to be generally hostile to the Jainas. The text depicts a Jain laymen propitiating them, but there is no hint that the *yoginī*s have been made part of the Jain religious community in any way.

given to these creatures. By contrast I suggested that a new and growing Hindu cult like that of Kṛṣṇa, was quick to dispatch the evil beings rather than convert them into something good. Kṛṣṇa himself is all the protection that his worshippers need. The Śaiva story I discussed is closer to the Buddhist paradigm in describing how the child-killing demonness Śuṣkarevatī was subdued and promised a cult. Here, however, the child-killing demonness was not depicted as a total outsider, as was the *yakṣa* in Buddhist stories. Here in the Śaiva story she is a figure intimately related to the great gods, Viṣṇu and Śiva. They do not chance upon her; she is their creation. Nonetheless she has a distinctive place in their cults and retains her distinctive individuality. The conclusion seems inescapable that at least this creation of the great gods once was her own creature.[64] Finally I have suggested that the lack of interest at least in earlier Jaina sources in the conquest of *yakṣa*s and *yakṣiṇī*s can also tell us something about Jaina attitudes towards the sickness and death of children. I have suggested that Jainas preferred to see behind the untimely death of children or the inability to have children not a supernatural explanation in the form of a demon or some god, but the hand of *karman*. Admittedly these are broad hypotheses based on an analysis of a small sample of stories from each of the three traditions. It is anticipated that further work will challenge and refine them.

[64] I have argued that purāṇic stories of Śiva in fact can tell us much of how the cult of Śiva developed, precisely by appropriating to itself the stories and personalities of once independent demons or deities. See GRANOFF (forthcoming).

BIBLIOGRAPHY

AHr̥ = *Aṣṭâṅga-hr̥daya* of Vāgbhaṭa. Ed. Rahul Peter Das and Ronald Eric Emmerick, Egbert Forsten, Groningen 1998.

ARBMAN 1922 = Arbman, Ernst: *Untersuchungen zum altindischen Glauben und Kultus*. Uppsala 1922.

ĀvNi = *Āvaśyaka-niryukti*. See: ĀvṬī.

AV-P = The Paippalāda recension of the *Atharva-veda*. Ed. by Raghu Vira, Ārṣa Sāhitya Pracāra, New Delhi 1976.

ĀvṬī = Haribhadra's *Āvaśyaka-ṭīkā*. Sri Bherulāl Kanailāl Kotharī Trust, Bombay 1981.

BAHĀDUR 1996 = Bahādur, Māheśvara Umānātha: *Bhūta vidyā*. K.S. Foundation, Delhi 1996.

BhāgP = *Bhāgavata-purāṇa*. Nag Publishers, Delhi 1087.

CuV = *Culla-vagga*. Nālandā Pāli edition, 1956.

DN = *Dīgha-nikāya*. Ed. T.W. and C.A.F. Rhys Davids and J.E. Carpenter, 3 Vols., Pāli Text Society, London I: 1890, II: 1903, III: 1911.

DURT 1998 = Durt, Hubert: 'Two Interpretations of Human-Flesh Offering: Misdeed or Supreme Sacrifice.' *Journal of the International College for Advanced Buddhist Studies*, vol. 1 (March 1998) 236–254.

FILLIOZAT 1937 = Filliozat, Jean: *Etude de démonologie indienne: le Kumāratantra de Rāvaṇa*. Imprimerie Nationale, Paris 1937.

GarS = *Garga-saṁhitā*. Ed. Pandit Ramtej Pandeya, Chaukhamba Sanskrit Pratisthan, Delhi 1987.

GRANOFF (forthcoming) = Granoff, Phyllis: 'Śiva and his Gaṇas: Techniques of Narrative Distancing in Purāṇic Stories.' [A paper delivered at the Nelson–Atkins Gallery in Kansas City *Symposium on the Pre-kushan Era*, November, 2000].

GRANOFF 2001 = Granoff, Phyllis: 'My Rituals, My Gods: Ritual Exclusivism in Medieval India.' *Journal of Indian Philosophy* 29/1–2 (2001) 109–134.

GRANOFF 1990 = Granoff, Phyllis (ed.): *The Clever Adulteress and other stories. A Treasury of Jaina Literature*. Mosaic Press, Oakville, Ontario 1990.

GRANOFF 1994 = Granoff, Phyllis: 'Life as Ritual Process.' In: Phyllis Granoff and Koichi Shinohara (eds.): *Other Selves. Autobiography and Biography in Cross-cultural Perspective*, Mosaic Press, Oakville, Ontario 1994: 16–35.

GRANOFF 1998 = Granoff, Phyllis: 'Cures and Karma II: Attitudes Towards Healing in Buddhist Story Literature.' *Bulletin de l'École Français d'Extrême Orient* 85 (1998) 285–305.

Hōbōgirin = *Hōbōgirin. Dictionnaire encyclopédique du buddhisme d'après les sources chinoises et japonaires.* Sixième fascicule: DA – DAIJIZAITEN. Paris–Tōkyō 1983.

HÄRTEL 1976 = Härtel, H.: 'Some Results of the Excavations at Sonkh.' In: *German Scholars on India: Contributions to Indian Studies.* Ed. by the Cultural Department of the Embassy of the Federal Republic of Germany, Nachiketa Publications, Bombay 1976: Vol. II: 69–100.

HÄRTEL 1987 = Härtel, H.: 'Die Kuṣāṇa-Göttin Ṣaṣṭhī: Über Zwei Neuerwerbungen des Museum für Indische Kunst Berlin.' In: Harry Falk (ed.): *Hinduismus und Buddhismus: Festschrift für Ulrich Schneider.* Freiburg 1987: 152–163.

HOFFMANN 1987 = Hoffmann, Helmuit: *Bruchstücke des Āṭanāṭikasūtra aus dem Zentralasiatischen Sanskritkanon der Buddhisten.* Fritz Steiner Verlag, Stuttgart 1987.

HV = *Hari-vaṁśa.* Critical Edition, Poona 1969.

HVP = *Hari-vaṁśa-purāṇa* of Punnāṭa Jinasena. Sanskrit text with Hindi tr. by Pt. Pannalal Jain, *Jnānapīṭha Mūrtidevī Jaina Granthamālā* 27, Bharatiya Jnanapitha, Kashi 1962.

INGHOLT 1957 = Ingholt, H.: *Gandhāran Art in Pakistan.* Pantheon Books, New York 1957.

Jātaka = *The Jātaka together with its commentary being Tales of the anterior births of Gotama Buddha.* For the first time edited in the original Pāli by V. Fausbøll, Vols. 1–6. London 1877–96. [Reprinted: Luzac and Company, London 1963].

JOHNSON 1931–62 = Johnson, Helen M. (tr.): *Triṣaṣṭiśalākāpuruṣacarita or the Lives of Sixty-three Illustrious Persons by Ācārya Śrī Hemacandra.* 6 vols., *Gaekwad's Oriental Series*, Oriental Institute, Baroda 1931–62.

JONES 1956 = Jones, J.J. (tr.): *Mahā-vastu.* Tr. by .... Luzac and Company, London 1956.

KARAMBELKAR 1961 = Karambelkar, V.W.: *The Atharva-veda and the Āyur-Veda.* Ku.Usha Karambelkar, Nagpur 1961.

KāśS = *Kāśyapa-saṁhitā.* Ed. by Vaidya Jādavjī Trikamjī Āchārya and Somanāth Śarmā, *Nepal Sanskrit Series* 1, Nirnayasagara Press, Bombay 1938.

KauśS = *The Kauśika Sūtra of Atharva-veda.* Ed. Maurice Bloomfield. Motilal Banarsidass, Delhi 1972. [Reprinted].

KK = *Kalyāṇa-kāraka* of Ugrādityācārya. Edited by Vardhaman Parshwanath Shastri, *Sakharam Nemchand Granthamālā* 129, Sakharam Nemchand Granthamālā, Sholapur 1940.

KSS = Somadeva: *Kathā-sarit-sāgara.* Ed. Paṇḍit Jagadīśalāl Śāstrī. Motilal Banarsidass, Delhi 1970.

MBh = *The Mahā-bhārata*. Critically ed. by V.S. Sukthankar and others. Bhandarkar Oriental Research Institute, Poona 1933–66.

MEULENBELD 1999 = Meulenbeld, Jan G.: *A History of Indian Medical Literature*. Egbert Forsten, Groningen 1999.

MISRA 1981 = Misra, Rām Nath: *Yaksha Cult and Iconography*, Munshiram Manoharlal, Delhi 1981.

MPū = *Manoratha-pūraṇī* (*Aṅguttara-nikāya-Aṭṭha-kathā*). Ed. by Dr. Nand Kishore Prasad, Nava Nālandā Mahāvihāra, Nālandā 1976.

MSVin = *Mūla-sarvâsti-vāda-vinaya*. Ed. S. Bagchi, *Buddhist Sanskrit Texts Series* 16, Mithila Institute of Post-Graduate Studies and Research in Sanskrit Learning, Darbhanga 1967.

MtsP = *Matsya-purāṇa*. Ed. with Hindi *ṭikā* by Paṇḍita Daulatarāma Gauḍa Vedācārya, Ṭhākuraprasāda and Sons Bookseller, Vārāṇasī: no date.

Nāy = *Nāyā-dhamma-kahāo* [*Jñātṛ-dharma-kathāḥ*]. Āgamasudhāsindhu, 1976.

PÉRI 1918 = Péri, Noel: 'Hāritī la Mère des Démons,' *Bulletin de l'École Français d'Extrême Orient* 18 (1918) 1–102.

PrabhC = *Prabhāvaka-carita*. Ed. Jinavijaya, *Sanghi Jain Series* 13, Singhi Jaina Granthamala, Ahmedabad–Calcutta 1940.

PŚPS = *Pañca-śati-prabandha-sambandha* of Śubhaśīlagani. Ed. Muni Shri Mrugendra, Suvasti Sahitya Prakashan, Surat 1968.

SCHMID 1999 = Schmid, Charlotte: 'Representations anciennes de Kṛṣṇa luttant contre le cheval Keśin sur des halteres: l'avatāra de Viṣṇu et le dieu du Mahābhārata.' *Bulletin de l'École Français d'Extrême Orient* 86 (1999) 65–104.

SCHOPEN (forthcoming) = Schopen, Gregory: 'The Mūlasarvāstivāda Vinaya.' Paper presented at *McMaster University — University of Toronto Conference on Gandhāran Buddhism, June 1999*.

SHAH 1961 = Shah, U.P.: 'Introduction of Śāsanadevatās in Jaina Worship.' In: V. Raghavan (ed.): *Proceedings and Transactions of the All India Oriental Conference Twentieth Session, Bhubaneshwar*. Vol.II part I, Bhandarkar Oriental Research Institute, Poona 1961: 141–152.

DHAKY 1997 = Dhaky, M.A. (ed.): *Arhat Pārśva and Dharaṇendra Nexus*. L.D. Institute, Ahmedabad 1997.

SHAH 1997 = Shah, U.P.: 'The Historical Origin and Ontological Interpretation of Arhat Pārśva's Association with Dharaṇendra.' In: DHAKY (1997: 29–43).

SLUSSER 1982 = Slusser, Mary: *Nepal Mandala: A Cultural Study of the Kathmandu Valley*. Princeton University Press, Princeton 1982.

SN = *Saṁyutta-nikāya*. Ed. M.L. Feer, 6 Vols., Pāli Text Society, London 1884–1904.

Spk = *Sāratthappakāsinī*. Ed. by F.L. Woodward, 3 vols., I: 1929, II: 1932, III: 1937.

ŚMM = *Śrāvaṇa-māsa-māhātmya*.Dhakurprasād And Sons Booksellers, Varanasi, n.d.

SuśrS = *Suśruta-saṁhitā*. Ed. with the commentary of Dalhaṇa by Paṇḍit Yādava Śarmā and Nārāyaṇa Rāma Ācārya, Nirnaya Sāgara Press, Bombay 1938.

TaitT = *Taittirīya-saṁhitā*. *The Ānandāśrama Sanskrit Series* 42, Poona 1966.

TEWARI 1997 = Tewari, P.V.: *Introduction to Kāśyapa-saṁhitā*. Chaukhamba Visvabharati, Varanasī 1997.

TṢŚPC = Hemacandra: *Tri-ṣaṣṭi-śalākā-puruṣa-carita*. See: JOHNSON (1931–62).

VTīK = *Vividha-tīrtha-kalpa* of Jinaprabhasūri. Ed. Jinavijaya, *Singhi Jain Series* 10, Singhi Jaina Jnānapītha, Śāntiniketan 1934.

WUJASTYK 1998 = Wujastyk, Dominik: *The Roots of Ayurveda*. Penguin, New Delhi 1998.

WUJASTYK 1999 = Wujastyk, Dominik: 'Miscarriages of Justice: Demonic Vengeance in Classical Indian Medicine.' IN: John R. Hinnells and Roy Porter (eds.): *Religion, Health and Suffering*, Kegan Paul, London 1999: 256–276.

ZYSK 1985 = Zysk, Kenneth G.: *Religious healing in the Veda with translations and annotations of medical hymns from the Ṛgveda and the Atharvaveda and renderings from the corresponding ritual texts*. The American Philosophical Society, Philadelphia 1985.

Waste Disposal (*pariṭṭhavaṇa-vihi*) in Ancient India. Some Regulations for Protection of Life From the Rules of the Order of Jain Monks*

ADELHEID METTE

The first of the Five Great Vows of Jain monks runs as follows:

> 'I renounce all damaging of life, small and large, animal and plant life by wanting neither to harm life myself in my person nor to have any life damaged on my behalf, nor to allow that another damages life, as long as I live [this] threefold [renunciation being undertaken] in threefold manner, with my own inner mind, my speech and my body.'[1]

The lay adherents of the Jaina religion are bound to keep the same vow in a less rigorous fashion.

The strict discipline of the monastic order to which the Jaina monks submitted led even in the earliest times to the formulation of rules in which virtually all details of the ascetic life were regulated with the view of consistent adherence to the Five Great Vows.

Probably also early on, a formulary was created which systematically catalogued the questions concerning which an account (*ālocanā*) was to be given in front of a

---

* A first draft of this article, the German version of which is foreseen to be published in: Albrecht Wezler (ed.): *Die indische Idee der Gewaltlosigkeit. Zur Beziehung zwischen Mensch und Natur in Indien*, had already been quoted by Nalini BALBIR (1993, 72). It was then entitled 'Giftmüllentsorgung im alten Indien. Einige Bestimmungen zum Schutze des Lebens aus den Ordensregeln der Jainamönche.'

I want to express my sincere thanks to the editors of *Essays in Jaina Philosophy and Religion* for publishing my article here and I am grateful to Jack Chaplin Vaughan, Houston/Texas, for translating it into English.

[1] Āyār 2.15, S. 94: *Paccakkhāmi savvaṁ pāṇāivāyaṁ se suhumaṁ vā bāyaraṁ vā tasaṁ vā thāvaraṁ vā ṇeva sayaṁ pāṇāivāyaṁ karejjā ṇev' aṇṇehiṁ pāṇāivāyaṁ kāravejjā, ṇev' aṇṇaṁ pāṇāivāyaṁ karentaṁ samaṇujāṇejjā jāvajjīvāe tivihaṁ tiviheṇaṁ maṇasā vayasā kāyasā.*

Essays in Jaina Philosophy and Religion.
Warsaw Indological Studies, Volume 2 (2002), pp. 213–226.

cleric superior (*ācārya*) each evening after preparatory examination of one's conscience. It set out the regulations that are still valid in Jainism practised today.

This confessional formulary is found in the *Āvaśyaka-sūtra* (ĀvS) of the Śvetāmbara monks ('the white-robed ones'), embedded in a gradually accreted great work of commentary, the so-called *āvaśyaka* Tradition.[2] The oldest component of this is comprised of the didactic verses called *Āvaśyaka-niryukti* (ĀvNi) which were designed to be learned by heart by the monk in training, to be explained to him in instruction, and to be orally further clarified by examples and instructive stories. These didactic verses contained explanations organised by keyword rubrics, including among others the details of the didactic rule. Fortunately, these at first orally transmitted explanations and explications, indispensable for understanding the rules, were gradually more and more fixed in written form. The oldest of these prose commentaries of the *āvaśyaka* Tradition, written in Prakrit and soon thereafter also in Sanskrit, known as *cūrṇi* and *ṭīkā*, can be dated in the seventh century. Reading these commentaries we are confronted with an elaborate casuistry with the help of which all imaginable endangerments to monastic ethics were exposed and in this way averted.

In first place stood the concern for the preservation of all kinds of life of other beings. Many of the *exempla* transmitted to us may strike us as eccentric products of excessive systematising. Others seem even quite modern: the intention behind their invention reveals a sense of a sensitive approach to nature, from which the authors of such texts were evidently in no wise alienated.

The keeping of the Five Great Vows is guaranteed by the Five Points of Circumspection (*samiti*).[3] In the confessional formulary of the *Āvaśyaka-sūtra*, which arranges the objects of penitence in ascending progressive sequence, the Points of Circumspection are enumerated immediately after the Great Vows:

---

[2] For comprehensive information concerning the origin and the composition of the texts forming this *corpus* as a whole, see BALBIR (1993) and the earlier literature mentioned there; about the position of the *Āvaśyaka-sūtra* within the overall context of the commentary especially, cf. BALBIR (1993: § 3 pp. 33–38). ĀvS is a mere print of the confessional formulary, divided in its six sections. Seemingly the editors of the *Suttâgame*, belonging to the sect of the Sthānaka-vāsins, have selected the text of the formulary from its traditional embedding.

[3] *Samiti* is a Jaina technical term sanskritised from Prakrit *samii*, probably < Sanskrit *smṛti*. Ernst Leumann (AupS, Glossary, s.v. *samiya*), however, presuming the traditional etymology (Skt. *sam*√*i*), conjectured that Skt. √*śam* had influenced the meaning of *samii*, as it is used in Jaina terminology.

'I rue with respect to the Five Points of Circumspection (1) the Circumspection of Motion, (2) the Circumspection of Speech, (3) the Seeking of alms, (4) the Taking up and Laying down of tools and vessels, and (5) the Removal (i.e. disposal) of faeces, urine, saliva, perspiration, and nasal mucus [the following is understood from the context "if in these points a transgression has occurred during the day, I have wrongly committed an injustice"].'[4]

In the following we shall be concerned only with the last of the 'Five Points of circumspection,' in which the issue is the proper removal of what is impure (*pāristhāpanikī*). This point provoked the commentators to further elaborate and determine that the ascetic must not only care for his body by eliminating bodily excrement, but must also rid himself of living and dead animals and, on occasion, even human beings.

The *āvaśyaka* Tradition thus displays, inserted as an appendage to the *Sūtra*'s penitence formulary referred to immediately above, an original didactic poem, entitled *Pāristhāpanikī-niryukti* (PārNi), consisting of 83 *āryā* stanzas in Prakrit,[5] which treat the subjects of Waste Disposal in the following arrangement:

1. One-sense objects (*ekêndriya-paristhāpya-vastu*) = stanzas 2–4;
2. Non-one-sense objects (*no-ekêndriya-paristhāpya-vastu*),
2.1. Movable objects (*trasa*),
2.11. Two-, Three- and Four-sense objects (*vikalêndriya*) = stanzas 5–7,
2.12. Five-sense objects (*pañcêndriya*),

---

[4] ĀvS (1954) Nr. 4, S. 1168 = ĀvV, S. 615b: *paḍikkamāmi paṁcahiṁ samiīhiṁ, īriyā-samiīe, bhāsā-samiīe, esaṇā-samiīe, āyāṇa-bhaṇḍa-matta-ṇikkhevaṇā-samiīe, uccāra-pāsavaṇa-khela-jalla-singhāṇa-pāriṭṭhāvaṇiyā-samiīe* (*jo me devasiyo aiyāro, tassa micchā mi dukkhaḍaṁ*).

The last sentence, quoted here from ĀvV only, is formed in accordance with other penitence formulae of the text. For translation, *see* SCHUBRING (2000: §§ 159, 173), concerning the phrase *tassa micchā mi dukkhaḍam*, see CAILLAT (1965: 155 with note).

[5] The *āryā* stanzas of this section are counted separately in Haribhadra's *Āvaśyaka-vṛtti*. Additionally, some single stanzas, counted as *Mūla-bhāṣya* of the ĀvNi and some others, cited by Haribhadra in his ĀvV, belong to the same context. The whole section is compiled from various sources (cf. *infra*, note 6). About the position of the PārNi within the *āvaśyaka* corpus as a whole cf. BALBIR (1993: § 3.10 ['Conspectus de l'ĀvNi'], especially p. 72). The regulations of the section have a less complete parallel in OghNi 596–625, introduced by the phrase *etto pariṭṭhavaṇa-vihiṁ vocchāmi* (cf. *infra* notes 7, 14, 16, 17 and METTE (1974: 15).

2.121. Humans (*manuṣya*),
2.1211. Monks (*saṁyata*) = stanzas 10–65,[6]
2.1212. Non-monks (*asaṁyata*) = stanzas 66–68,
2.122. Non-humans (*no-manuja*, [i.e. animals]) = stanzas 69 f.,
2.2. Non-movable (*no-trasa*),
2.21. Food (*āhāra*) = stanzas 72–76,[7]
2.22. Non-food (*no-āhāra*),
2.221. Clothing and Tools (*upakaraṇa*) = stanzas 78 f.,
2.222. Non-tools (*no-upakaraṇa*, i.e. human excretions) = stanzas 80–82.

This quite detailed organising structure is typical of the scholastic striving for subtle systemisation evident passim in the disciplinary writings of the Jaina religion. In this particular case, however, the writer gets into trouble, because he could not (as was usually done) undertake to draw a general classification according to animate and inanimate objects (*sacitta* vs. *acitta*), but had to deal with regulations concerning 'movable' (*trasa* 2.1) as living or dead bodies, respectively. Accordingly, he had to introduce the additional concept 'Non-movable' (*no-trasa* 2.2), comprising food, tools and human excretions, even though the true opposite of *trasa* is the *sthāvara*, the 'non-locomotive' plants, which are themselves treated in section 1 as 'one-sense living beings.' As the irregular arrangement of the stanzas indicates, the separate points of this schema are weighted very unevenly. The comments are also by no means of homogeneous origin. Rather, they have been assembled and pieced together from different sources. In the assembly process the actual object of the Fifth Point of Circumspection, the removal of human excretions, was pushed to the end of the treatise (2.222) and disposed of very briefly and abruptly (*vide infra,* p. 223). The (modern) problem of disposal of hazardous materials is mentioned in section 2.21, in which poisoned or contaminated food figures as a part of the discussion.

First, however, to clarify the above enumerated points of the organising structure, the following assorted excerpts from the Prakrit prose commentary that accompanies the stanzas are instructive.[8]

Re 1. The one-sense objects are the four elements: earth, water, fire and wind (always in this order), to the extent that they are viewed as animate, as well as

---

[6] PārNi 12–30 ≈ NisBh 3605–3636; PārNi 12–19 ≈ BṛKBh 5172–5189; PārNi 31–65 ≈ BṛKBh 5500–5557.

[7] PārNi 73–76 ≈ OghBh 305. OghNi 606, 609, 597 (cf. 617).

[8] The text of Haribhadra's *Ṭīkā* (ĀvV) has a near parallel in the *Āvaśyaka-cūrṇi* (ĀvCū), Vol. II, p. 96–112.

plants. To these objects only the sense of touch (as sensory organ, the skin, accordingly the surface) is ascribed. By way of example the following case is cited: A monk, possibly as a result of a snake bite, suffered from an ulcer or boil that burst. The wound was supposed to be sprinkled with an inanimate material attributable to the element earth (e.g. ash). The monk has to be very careful now that the material that he fetches or has brought to him is really devoid of life. He has to inquire concerning its provenance, investigate its colour, smell etc. and if contrary to expectation it does after all contain life, if possible take to a place where the substance abounds. If necessary he is supposed to preserve it in a suitable container. For the container a leaf of a fig tree, a *ficus indica* or *ficus religiosa*, would be a possibility. If water is brought to the monk, he also has to inspect that in corresponding manner, and so possibly he should pour river water into a river, lake water into a lake, etc. Only water boiled without his involvement would he be permitted to use. In this connection the possibility is mentioned that one might bring the monk life-containing water (say, out of a lake) thinking that he would not notice the difference, or even with malicious intent to force him involuntarily to break his vows.

The use of fire, usually strictly forbidden for monks, is nevertheless sometimes necessary, especially for medical purposes. A swelling arising from a snake bite, a *vāta-granthi* ('hardening in consequence of a disturbance of the body wind'), a swelling of the viscera.[9] If possible, fire is carried back to the place whence it was taken, otherwise 'isolated in the pieces of wood from which it came,' or if that, too, is impossible, 'covered with the ash that resulted from it.'[10]

Re 2.11. Kind of a two-sense being, is, for instance, the leech (*jalugā*), with which swelling and similar conditions are treated. After its application one brings it back to its place.[11]

Also mentioned are *ūraṇiyā* (Skt. *ūraṇikā, ūrṇikā*), small beings that can be found in groats or grits and must be carefully plucked out. In some circumstances these little beings are to be placed with the aid of a leaf-stalk into a hole dug in the wild for this purpose (otherwise digging in the earth is altogether forbidden to Jainas!)

---

[9] Further reasons are mentioned: A snake (?, cf. *dīgha* in Pāli) might have invaded the flat or a 'bellyspear' (a kind of medical instrument?) has to be heated (*vasahīe dīha-jāio paviṭṭho poṭṭasūlaṁ vā tāveyavvaṁ*).

[10] *tehiṁ kaṭṭhehiṁ jo agaṇī tajjāio, tatth'eva vigiṁcijjai, na hojja so vi na dejja vā tāhe tajjāeṇa chāreṇa ucchāijjai* (ĀvV p. 621b, cf. PārNi 4). Here the author distinguishes between states of wood burning through-out and of being just inflamed, so that the monk would be able to extinguish the fire. Some further regulations about the handling of the four elements are added in the ĀvV.

[11] *jalugā gaṇḍ'āisu kajjesu gahiyā tatth'eva vigincijjai* (ĀvNi S. 623b on PārNi 7).

and subsequently fed with fluids. As examples of three-sense beings adduced are maggots, worms or insects that reside in sesame seeds or in cow dung (*tila-kīḍaya, chagaṇa-kimi*), also, interestingly, mosquitoes (*makkhiyā*) and beings found in rice (*pūyaraga,* Skt. *pūtaraka*); as four-sense beings, again mosquitoes, also horseflies (*āsa-makkhiyā*) and also *kotthala-gāriyā,* beings, that build their 'house' in garments or vessels (red wasps?). In this case one is to set aside the whole (that is, it would appear, the garment or vessel); if that is not possible, after one has separated (the rest, i.e. setting aside a part of the garment) or, alternatively, one should send the *kotthala-gāriyā* to another house.[12]

It is apparent to the reader that the Jainas' care for the smallest beings observed in modern times has a long tradition.

Re 2.1211. The same verbs that are used for releasing animals in the wild (*vigiñcai, vosirai*) can be used of the exclusion of people. In the chapter we are discussing the issue is not the removal of unworthy monks from the order by way of punishment. For that there are special rules. Rather, here the case is discussed that persons who are in principle ineligible for acceptance, but nevertheless have become monks (say, inadvertently or because of the king's wish or because someone was needed, e.g. as a physician), should be excluded after all.

The first and most thorough discussion is about persons with sexual defects (*klība, paṇḍaka*), mentioned even in the earliest lists of non-ordinable persons (as they were also in the Buddhist Vinaya). In the ĀvV and PārNi, as texts belonging to the younger strata of Jaina disciplinary scripture, these persons are called *napuṁsaka* ('third sex').

If they are not willing to resign from the status of monkhood and lead a householder's life, they are made recognisable to lay-persons by a lock of hair protrusively standing out from an otherwise bald head the hair of which has not been plucked out, as it would have been in the case of an ordinary monk, but shaved. Attention is directed to the question, how much, if any, knowledge of the recitals (*pāṭha-grahaṇa*) and their performance of the same (*āsevana-śikṣā*) ought to be permitted and allowed to the *napuṁsaka* (ĀvV 427a); and it is observed in this connection that a malevolent lay adherent possibly would threaten the *napuṁsaka* with murder. The *napuṁsaka* then would be forced to flee, or the result might be a legal proceeding.

After this discussion, the proposition is stated and reasons are given why persons with speech impediments should not be ordained. An exception is possible in the case of stutterers distinguished by unusual intelligence.

---

[12] *kotthala-gāriyā vā vatthe pāe vā gharaṁ karejjā. savva-vivego, asai chindittā, ahavā annammi gharae saṁkāmijjanti* (ĀvNi S. 625a on PārNi 7).

Whereas this section of the text seems to have been taken from the *Niśītha-bhāṣya* and its commentary (the *Niśītha-cūrṇi*) the following may be obtained from the *Bṛhat-kalpa-bhāṣya* (see note 6, *supra*). Its theme centres about the regulations concerning the procedure applicable to monks with members of their community deceased. The actions that may be taken there are also referred to as *vosiraṇa* ('casting out').[13]

Re 2.1212. The community of monks must on occasion relieve itself of other, non-cleric persons, both living and dead. It might happen, for example, that a mother, in a case of starvation or desperate hunger, or in order to hide from her husband the birth of a child procreated outside the marriage, counting on sympathy from the ascetics, would lay an infant child at the monks' doorstep. Four times a day the monks have to search the grounds of their residence for children exposed in this way. If a child is found and the mother is still within view, the monks are supposed to cry out loud, 'This woman exposed and abandoned her baby and has fled.' Then, according to the text, the people come out, see the woman and 'are allowed to do with her what they see fit' (*tāhe so logo jaṁ jāṇau, taṁ karau*, ĀvV, p. 640b). But if the mother is no longer to be seen, the monk must lay the child where it can be easily discovered and he must secretly observe and see that it is not killed by a dog or a crow or a cat.

A dead beggar could be brought by an enemy of the monks to their place of abode, or the beggar could have died there, or a murdered person could lie there or a suicide could have sought out this place for his deed. In these cases the rule is to call witnesses or as quickly as possible to move the bodies to a lonely deserted place.

Re 2.122. The systematic structure practically dictates that after human people the other five-sense beings are discussed. The possibility mentioned here that fish and frogs might be found as a living additional ingredient in a rice dish sounds rather fantastic, to be sure. The text advises, cleverly, to remove them with the help of water. Water frogs, we learn, will automatically jump into the water. The monk will prompt fish with his hand to move into their element. The proposition that a hostile person or a bird will allow a dead animal to fall into the bowl or into the living area of the monks is more likely. Mentioned here are fish, mouse, gecko, goose, crow and peacock (this in systematic sequence water animals, land animals and animals of the air). Their removal follows the pattern described in 2.1212.

Re 2.21. In this and the following sections, it is no longer a matter of removal of living or dead organisms, but about things, first the issue of food that may not be

---

[13] DEO (1956) in his chapter 'Death and Funeral Rites' (428–432) refers to the proceedings as they are described in the BṛKBh.

consumed. The compiler seems here to go back to the *Ogha-niryukti*. Indeed, the author of the *Āvaśyaka-cūrṇi* (ĀvCū Vol. II, p. 110) limits himself to mere reference to that work.

In the pertinent section of the OghNi (vv. 596–618), which follows the rules concerning the monk's alms round (*piṇḍ'esaṇā*), the discussion deals exclusively with the disposal of food and foodstuffs.

In food given as alms the necessity of disposal inheres (*jātā paristhāpanikā*) if in the receiving thereof a mistake has been made, if for a greedy motive too much has been received, if it contains poisonous matter or if it is poisoned through sorcery. On the other hand, disposal does not inhere (*ajātā paristhāpanikā*) if valuable foods specially suited for a cleric superior, a sick person or a guest is accepted or if unexpectedly generous donations are given whose consumption by simple monks is not allowed according to their strict regulations or of which there is simply too much at hand. The unfavourable climatic conditions of India do not allow the itinerant monks, subject as they are to changes of abode and in principle constantly on the move, to store such per se ritually and materially pure foodstuffs overnight.

These foods are laid down in a place indicated by the teacher that is solitary, not much visited and free of live (*ekānte, lokāpāta-rahite, acitta-sthaṇḍile*), but is nevertheless highly visible (the *āloe* of the regulation is explained as 'at ground level, not in a ditch or the like'). According to the nature of the respective faults the foods are organised in one, two or three piles. At the food a threefold shout is directed: 'Abandoned! Abandoned! Abandoned!' (*vyutsṛṣṭaṁ, vyutsṛṣṭaṁ, vyutsṛṣṭam*, Droṇa on OghNi 598). In the case of 'inherent disposal' the cause, i.e. the 'fault' (*dosa*) must be adduced (OghNi 607).

Danger threatens when there is an issue of foodstuffs prepared with involvement of a form of sorcery (*abhiyogena*: the commentary distinguishes here between witchcraft [*vidyā*] and magic admixture [*dravyâbhiyogacūrṇam*]) or mixed up with poison (*viṣeṇa*). If these are not carefully disposed of according to the rule, jackals can seize upon the food and die, says OghNi 604 (cf. note 17). The usually very dry *Ogha-niryukti* commentator Droṇa describes a more drastic result when in contrast with his usual style he retells here an anecdote in Prakrit:[14]

[14] The contents of the tale is summarised in two *āryā* stanzas of the *Ogha-niryukti* (OghNi 600sq.) placed in front of the Prakrit prose narrative:

vijjāe: ho' agārī aciyattā, sā ya pucchae cariyaṁ /
abhimantaṇ' oyaṇassa u, aṇukampaṇa-m ujjhaṇaṁ ca khare //
bārassa piṭṭaṇammi ya, pucchaṇa, kahaṇaṁ ca ho' agārīe /
siṭṭhe cariyā-daṇḍo. evaṁ dosā ihaṁ pi siyā //

'There was once a lay adherent [of the Jaina religion] who was not loved by her husband. So she asked an itinerant woman ascetic, "Conjure something with a magic spell so that my husband will respond to my will." Thereupon that woman gave her a conjured rice dish. The lay adherent thought, "May he [my husband] just not die from this gift!" Then moved by pity she poured the rice dish out onto the garbage heap. But it was eaten by an ass. At night the ass began to knock on the door. The couple went outside. When they saw that the door was been knocked on by the ass, the lay adherent's husband, himself a lay adherent, said, "What is happening here?" The wife told the story of what had happened up to then. He for his part had the itinerant woman ascetic thoroughly whipped.—That is the fault [of sorcery]. If such a condition is brought about in animals, it will be brought in humans to a greater degree. Therefore such a dish may not be consumed.'

Apart from the last paragraph and the purposively lean literary texture, the little story, which doubtless was not invented in circles of Jaina monks, displays the character of a burlesque. The itinerant woman ascetic (*parivrājikā*) is not an ordained nun or anyone like that, but embodies in this genre the archetypal 'old procuress'; the motif of the peculiarly erotic nature of the ass is fairly well known in India.[15]

The last sentence demonstrates that the story was first embraced by the Jainas in a context in which the issue was not the disposal, but the acceptance of foods. It is, nevertheless, clear (and this emerges from the conclusion of the strophe OghNi 601 (see note 14) why the commentator quotes it here, of all places, within the framework of the *pāriṣṭhāpanikā-vidhi*. If one focuses strictly on the didactic value of the example, not its entertainment qualities, a peculiar nuance is noteworthy inasmuch as not only the effect of negligent human action on the ass, but also the repercussive effect on the human individual, and thereby in a way the sense of the 'food chain' is brought out.

In Droṇa's commentary of the OghNi a similar, but less original story follows immediately. It is probably derived from the preceding story, in order to provide an exemplum for 'magic admixture' as a second sort of *abhiyoga*: food sprinkled with a magic powder is presented to the cleric teacher:[16]

---

15 For instance see PISCHEL-GELDNER (1889: 82 f.).

16 The keywords of this didactic example are pressed into the stanzas OghNi 602sq.:

jogammi u: aviraiyā ajjhovavannā surūva-bhikkhummi /
kaḍa-joga-m aṇicchantassa dei bhikkhaṁ. asubha-bhāve //

sankāe sa niyaṭṭo dāūṇa gurussa kāiyaṁ nisire /
tesiṁ pi asubha-bhāvo. pucchā ya, „mamaṁ pi!", ujjhaṇayā //

'There was once a lay adherent. She took a fancy to a handsome monk and fell in love. Thereupon she confronted him with entreaties. When he rejected her advances, she saw to it that in a neighbouring house he was offered alms food prepared secretly by herself with an admixture of a magic powder compound. The compound had hardly been introduced into the alms vessel of the monk when the senses of the monk were captured by her [the woman]. But he took note of it and left. He turned over the alms vessel to his superior and went to the privy. At the same time even the teacher was taken with a condition of fond attraction to her. Then the student returned and made a confession. The teacher said, "I am in the same condition! This alms vessel doubtless has been prepared by means of a magic compound powder in such manner." It was then removed. The rule applicable to its disposal is set out in the following ... '

In a third and last short narrative example (that is to say, a further remoulding of the motif fashioned for the didactic purpose) the story tells of a housewife who was in love with a monk (here she is not a lay adherent as it is to be made clear that this is a bad character). After being rebuffed in her advances she mixed poison into the alms. The monk and his teacher got headaches. The poison was recognised by the addition of salt and by the smell. The food was disposed of.[17]

The rule says that dangerous foods of the sort described here, after being taken according to the teacher's designation to a lonely uninhabited place free of life (*vide supra*, p. 220), should be sprinkled with ashes (*chāreṇa akkamittā*, OghNi 606). Thereupon ensues the threefold shout (*vide supra*, p. 220).

Safe disposal is held to be guaranteed by this procedure. A heroic attitude on the part of the monk is not demanded here. The paradigm of rigorous heroism in the matter of disposal of poison would be the famous oft told and oft cited story fixed in the canonic writings of the Jaina religion that tells of the sacrificial death of the ascetic Dhammarui:[18]

---

[17] The topic of this example is indicated slightly by one single stanza of the *Ogha-niryukti* (OgNi 604):

> *em eva visa-kayammi vi: dāūṇa gurussa kāiyaṁ nisire, /*
> *gandh'āī vinnāe ujjhaṇa, avihī siyāla-vahe //* (*siyāla-vaho*?)

At the end of this stanza the author hints that jackals would die, if the poisoned food were disposed of incorrectly. The prose author does not mention this special point here.

[18] In the *āvaśyaka* Tradition the story of Dhammarui has its place in the section entitled *jhāṇa-saṁvara-joga* ('Practice of Defending oneself [against *karman*] by Meditation') of the chapter called *Joga-saṁgaha*. See: BALBIR (1993: 72, 187). Text:

> Someone had given the monk Dhammarui, who had wanted to enjoy his first meal after a month of fasting, a food prepared from inedible pickles. As he began to remove this food on the order of his superior, he noticed by chance that it had a fatal effect on insects. Accordingly, he himself ate the food in a remote place, enduring without complaint the pain of his poisoning, and achieved deliverance with his death.

From the refraining from retelling the legend and its key motif in the depiction of the *pāriṣṭhāpanikā-vidhi*, both in the OghNi and in the pertinent chapter of the *āvaśyaka* Tradition, it is clear that the authors were not out to glorify their religion and its saints, but merely to give practical advice for the daily management of the problems of the ascetic life.

Re 2.221. The scheme of 'inherent' and 'non-inherent' disposal is extended even to the monk's vessels and garments (*upakaraṇa*). Without further explanation it is said of these objects that in consequence of an incantation or poison (*abhiyogena vā viṣeṇa vā*)—but how could one have envisioned their contamination by poison?—their disposal could become necessary. Evidently it is not possible to de-bewitch them through a rite of some kind (as one might have expected). Instead of that, the polluted objects are in such instances cut up into small pieces and removed to a lonely place. According to the type of fault attaching to them the garments are marked with spots, vessels are marked with stripes.

Re 2.222. In the shade, preferably under a tree that does not serve people's pleasure, the monk relieves his bladder (other excretions are merely enumerated). He first confirms that the place is free of plants and sweeps the place 'to protect small fauna' (*tasa-pāṇa-rakkhaṇ'aṭṭhāe*, PārNi 81). This passage does not seem to be related to the somewhat detailed treatment of the theme in the OghNi (vv. 619–625). Although it is the real object of the Fifth Point of Circumspection, it did not especially interest the author.

This overview of the *Pāriṣṭhāpanikī-niryukti* allows one to sense the effort of its author not to leave any everyday action or activity to chance or to spontaneous reaction of the individual monk, but rather to the extent possible to specify in minute detail every individual action. In this, to be sure, not the arbitrary rule of the cleric superior, but *ahiṁsā*, the principle of conscientious non-injuring of life,

ĀvV p. 732a on stanza 1318 (Haribhadra), English translation by BALBIR (1990: 65 f.); German translation by METTE (1991: 164). For the canonical version of the tale which forms a part of the introduction of Nāy 1.16 (p. 48 f.); cf. BALBIR (1983: 157).

provides the criterion. Further, the broad dissemination of the tradition with its network of citations, variants and specifications rule out altogether the hypothesis that idle monks wanted to elevate their religious accomplishments by aggrandising indifferent and self-evident things and forcing them into a cumbersome system. Evidently, to the contrary, the quite simple forms of external living conditions forced the adoption of a detail-oriented order and strict regulations of behaviour.

At the same time the last stanza of the didactic poem introduced here sounds a bit pessimistic:

> 'Those who live at the feet of gurus—but do not behave in conformance with their gurus—from what is said here they are far, far removed.'[19]

Did the good and useful doctrines not always in the case of young ascetics fall on open ears?

[19] PārNi 83:

> *guru-mūle vi vasantā aṇukūlā je na honti u gurūṇaṁ /*
> *eesiṁ tu payāṇaṁ dūraṁ-dūreṇa te honti //*

BIBLIOGRAPHY

AupS = *Aupapātika-sūtra. Das Aupapātika Sūtra*. Hg. Ernst Leumann. *Abhandlungen für die Kunde des Morgenlandes* 8.2, Harrassowitz, Leipzig 1883.

ĀvCū = *Āvaśyaka-cūrṇi. Āvaśyakasūtra* with Jinadāsa's *Āvaśyaka-cūrṇi. Śrīmad-āvaśyaka-sūtra*. Vol. I-II. Ed. by Ānandasāgara Sūri. Ṛṣabhadevajī Keśarimalajī Śvetāmbara Saṁsthā, Ratlām / Indaur 1928–1929.

ĀvNi = *Āvaśyaka-niryukti* with Haribhadra's *Āvaśyaka-ṭīkā* [*Āvaśyaka-vṛtti*]. Āgamodaya-samiti, Bombay 1916–1917.

ĀvS = *Āvaśyaka-sūtra*. In: *Suttāgame*. Vol. II. Ed. by Muni Śrī Phūlchandjī Mahārāj, Gurgaon. Nirṇaya Sāgara Press, Bombay 1954: 1165–1172.

ĀvV = Haribhadra: *Āvaśyaka-vṛtti*. See: ĀvNi.

Āyār = *Āyāraṁga-sutta* [*Ācārâṅga-sūtra*]. In: *Suttâgame*. Vol. I. Ed. by Muni Śrī Phūlchandjī Mahārāj [Pupphabhikkhū]. Nirnaya Sāgara Press, Bombay 1953: 1–99.

BALBIR 1983 = Balbir, Nalini: „The Micro-Genre of *dāna*-Stories in Jaina Literature". *Indologica Taurinensia* 11 (1983) 145–161.

BALBIR 1990 = Balbir, Nalini: „Stories from the Āvaśyaka Commentaries". In: Phyllis Granoff (ed.): *The Clever Adulteress and other stories. A Treasury of Jaina Literature*. McMaster University Mosaic Press, Oakville, Ontario 1990: 17–73.

BALBIR 1993 = Balbir, Nalini: *Āvaśyaka-Studien – Introduction générale et Traductions. Alt- u. Neu-Indische Studien* 45.1, Franz Steiner Verlag, Stuttgart 1993.

BṛKBh = *Bṛhat-kalpa-bhāṣya. Brihat Kalpa Sutra and Original Niryukti of Sthavir Arya Bhadrabahu Swami* [etc.]. Ed. by Guru Shri Chaturvijaya and his Shishya Punyavijaya. 6 Vols. Shri Atmanand Jain Sabha, Bhavnagar 1933–1942.

CAILLAT 1965 = Caillat, Colette: *Les expiations dans le rituel ancien des religieux jaina*. L.D. Series 49, Éditions E. de Boccard, Paris 1965. [= English: *Atonements in the Ancient Ritual of the Jaina Monks*. L.D. Institute of Indology, Ahmedabad 1975].

DEO 1956 = Deo, S. B.: *History of Jaina Monachism from Inscriptions and Literature. Deccan College Dissertation Series* 17, Deccan College Postgraduate and Research Institute, Poona 1956.

METTE 1974 = Mette, Adelheid: *Piṇḍ'esaṇā – Das Kapitel der Oha-nijjutti über den Bettelgang übersetzt und kommentiert*. Abhandlungen der Mainzer Akademie der Wissenschaften und der Literatur, Abhandlungen der Geistes- und Sozialwissenschaftlichen Klasse 1973, Nr. 11, Franz Steiner Verlag, Wiesbaden 1974.

METTE 1991 = Mette, Adelheid: *Durch Entsagung zum Heil. Eine Anthologie aus der Literatur der Jaina*, Benziger, Zürich 1991.

Nāy = *Nāyā-dhamma-kahāo* [*Jñātṛ-dharma-kathāḥ*]. See: SCHUBRING (1978).

NisBh = *Niśītha-bhāṣya. Nishith Sutram (With Bhashya) by Sthavir Pungava Shri Visahgani Mahattar* [etc.]. Ed. Shri Amar Chandji and Muni Shri Kanhaiya Lalji. 4 Vols. Sanmati Gyan Peeth, Agra 1957–1960.

OghBh = *Ogha-mūla-bhāṣya*. See: OghNi.

OghNi = *Ogha-niryukti* (with *Bhāṣya* Stanzas and the *Vṛtti* of Droṇācārya). Ed. Mānavijaya. Gulābcand Lallubhāī and Himmatlāl Devjībhāī, *Vijayadānasūriśvara Jaina-grantha-mālā* 56, Surat 1957.

PārNi = *Pāriṣṭhāpanikī-niryukti*. See: ĀvNi.

PISCHEL-GELDNER 1889 = Pischel, Richard und Geldner, Karl Friedrich: *Vedische Studien I.* Stuttgart 1889.

SCHUBRING 1935 = Schubring, Walther: *Die Lehre der Jainas – Nach den alten Quellen dargestellt.* Grundriß der Indo-Arischen Philologie und Altertumskunde III 7, Walter de Gruyter & Co., Berlin–Leipzig 1935. [= Engl.: *The Doctrine of the Jainas.* Translated from the German by Wolfgang Beurlen. 2nd rev. Edition, with the three indices enlarged and added by W. Bollée and Jayandra Soni. Motilal Banarsidass, Delhi 2000].

SCHUBRING 1978 = Schubring, Walter: *Nāyādhammakahāo. Das sechste Anga des Jaina Siddhānta.* Einführung, kritische Nacherzählung mit Ausgabe der wichtigeren Textpartien, Kommentar und Glossar. Hg. Jozef Deleu. Abh. d. Mainzer Ak. d. Wiss., Geistes- u. Sozialwiss. Kl., 1978, Nr. 6, Franz Steiner Verlag, Wiesbaden 1978.

Concealing and Protecting. Stories on *Upagūhana*

LUITGARD SONI

Upagūhana is one of the eight *aṅga*s or auxiliaries of *samyaktva* or *samyag-darśana* (right belief).[1] The first four of these are freedom from the obstacles of doubt (*niḥśaṅkitā*), from craving for the joys of the world (*niḥkāṅkṣita*), from repugnance (*nirvicikitsā*) and from wrong belief (*amuḍha-dṛṣṭi*). The second half of the group is described in positive terms as contributing to the growth of *samyaktva*: they are qualities that are directed outward, toward the religious community, its status in the society and the duties among the fellow believers in the faith: these are *upagūhana* or *upagūha*, sometimes called *avagūhana* (Pkt.: *uvagūhaṇa*; protecting Jainism by concealing the faults of one's fellow members), *sthiti-kāraṇa* (strengthening the faith of the fickle-minded ones), *prabhāvanā* (propagation of the faith by spectacular good deeds like alms giving, temple building, austerities, promoting learning etc.), and *vātsalya* (kind assistance to the members of the community).[2]

Among all these virtues *upagūhana* seems to be the most 'political' guideline insofar as it highlights the strategy of concealing the faults committed by fellow members of the faith, in order to protect the prestige of one's religion in public.[3] It is

---

[1] Cf. RKŚĀ 1.11–20, Kundakunda's SSā 7.228–263, YT 6.5–20 (see HANDIQUI (1968: 258)). The importance of the eight *aṅga*s is stressed in RKŚĀ 1.21: Without the *aṅga*s right belief is not able to destroy the continuity of births, just as without the letters a *mantra* does not efface the pain caused by poison:

nâṅga-hīnâlaṁ chettuṁ darśanaṁ janma-santatim /
na hi mantro 'kṣarâyūno nihani viṣa-vedanām //

[2] BhĀr 44:

uvagūhaṇa-ṭhidi-karaṇaṁ vacchalla-pabhāvaṇā guṇā bhaṇidā /
sammatta-visodhīe uvagūhaṇa-kārayā cauro //

[3] In his comment to SSā 233:

jo siddha-bhatti-jutto uvagūhaṇago du savva-dhammāṇaṁ /
so uvagūhaṇa-kārī sammādiṭhī muṇeyavvo // ,

Amṛtacandra does not use the word *upagūhana* but *upabṛṁhaṇa*, which means 'increasing' and interprets it as increasing the powers of the self (*ātma-śakti*) by

Essays in Jaina Philosophy and Religion.
Warsaw Indological Studies, Volume 2 (2002), pp. 227–236.

the explicitness of this pragmatic demand which is intriguing and especially the way in which it is dealt with didactically in the respective stories.

Samantabhadra defines *upagūhana* as the removal of the blame originating from ignorant and incompetent ones pertaining to the right path, which in itself is pure.[4]

Somadeva, in addition, also stresses the necessity of guarding the reputation of one's religion by suppressing any blemishes which may lower it in the estimation of others. If any fellow member commits an offence by accident or error 'one should conceal it with the wealth of one's own virtues as does a mother that of her children.'[5] This protectionism of one's faith is obvious in the following story, where the innocence of the culprit is established by the pious Jaina going against his better knowledge of the facts of the situation and even facing personal offence. It is the *Upagūhanâkhyānaka*, the story of Jinendrabhakta and the thief, in ĀKP (No. 10):

> 'In the country of Saurāṣṭra, in the city Pāṭaliputra reigned king Yaśodhvaja, his queen was Susīmā. Their son Suvīra was a victim of the seven evil passions, and surrounded by many similar men. Once, he got to know that a very unique, priceless cat's-eye gem crowned the threefold umbrella of an idol of Pārśvanātha, who stood, heavily protected, on the top of a seven-storeyed building. It belonged to the merchant Jinendrabhakti. He lived in the East, in the region of Gauḍa, in the city of Tāmralipta. The prince Suvīra in his greed asked his men: "Who is able to fetch this jewel?" "I'll bring even Indra's crest-gem", the thief Sūrya roared out. He disguised himself as a *kṣullaka* [novice] and made his way to Tāmralipta, causing excitement in villages and towns on account of the mortification of his body. The merchant Jinendrabhakta heard people praise him and he went to see him. They had a conversation and Jinendrabhakti praised him, deeply impressed. He led him to see the Lord Pārśvanātha and although he seemingly refused, he [the thief Sūrya] was persuaded and assigned as the guard of the jewel. One day after having consulted the *kṣullaka* the merchant

---

cultivating forbearance and the other nine qualities of *dharma*. The intension of the term *upagūhana* evident in the stories chosen for this article might allow the extension of the term to *upabṛṁhaṇa*, the increasing of the powers of the *ātman* of the right believer, but the didactic impact of the stories clearly aims at *upagūhana* as 'concealing / protecting.'

[4] RKŚĀ 1.15:
svayaṁ-śuddhasya mārgasya bālâśakta-janâśrayām /
vācyatāṁ yad pramārjanti tad vadanty upagūhanam //

[5] HANDIQUI (1968: 260).

> set out for a sea-voyage, left the town and camped outside it. The *kṣullaka*-thief who knew that the servants were busy with the transport, grasped that jewel at midnight and ran off. But due to the lustre of the jewel he was detected on the road and pursued by the watchmen. Since he was not able to escape from them he sought refuge at the merchant's and cried: "Protect me, protect me!" The merchant appeased the shouting of the watchmen, pondered and having realised that the *kṣullaka* was a thief he told the guards for the sake of concealing [the scandal] and uplifting the religion: "I myself have told him to bring me the jewel here and it would be improper to proclaim that this great ascetic were a thief." The watchmen then bowed to him and went away. That very night the thief was removed by the merchant. In this way others too, who have the true faith should conceal a fault concerning the religion brought about by a person devoid of knowledge and not endowed with devotion.'

In the *Yaśas-tilaka* version the story ends with the solemn declaration of the merchant that he himself had given the jewel to the ascetic, a noble soul who deserved their highest veneration and respect.

The most striking feature in this story is indeed that the recommended protection of the true religion is based on an explicit lie, readily uttered by the pious Jaina merchant, and obviously raising questions about double standards. If one were to analyse such didactic stories strictly in terms of models of behaviour, one could easily and, in the numerous cases, often point out obvious contradictions regarding righteous ideals. One could, however, regard the *exemplary* stories as representing rather a realistic picture of social and communal endeavours and interactions, and that they serve as an education in various facets of successful living. A closer look at the interpretation of *asatya*, as is hinted at by JAINI (1979: 173 f.), which defines *asatya* for the layman as a lie for one's own sake, would solve some double-bind situations for the lay *satya-vratin*. An untruth spoken for the sake of avoiding *hiṁsā* would then not be harmful to the soul of the liar. By extension, lying for the sake of upholding the true faith would be acceptable, since it prevents damage to the reputation of one's religion. A monk or a nun however, whose *satya-vrata* is absolute, does not have this choice; he or she would simply have to be silent, even at the risk of somebody's destruction. There are several stories illustrating such instances of keeping silent, even at the expense of the destruction of life. However, I do not know of any scenario involving *sādhus* or *sādhvīs* set up especially in this case of *upagūhana*. It seems to be a purely *vyavahāra* theme.

The following two stories are from the *Bṛhat-kathā-kośa* of Hariṣeṇa (BKK). The BKK is a representative collection of 157 stories of varying length, stretching over 12,500 *śloka*s in Sanskrit. It is dated 931 CE. All the stories are based on *gāthā*s of the *Bhagavatī-śrādhanā* (or *Mūlârādhanā*; BhĀr) of Śivārya, an early (fourth or fifth century CE) pro-canonical text of the Digambaras. There are two stories listed under the theme of *upagūhana*.

The first story is about the model behaviour of king Śreṇika which appears as story number 9 in the BKK, the *Śreṇika-nṛpa-kathānaka*. The following is a summary of the story with a few selected quotations:

> King Śreṇika was highly praised in the assembly of gods as having *samyaktva* with *kṣāyika*, i.e. the true insight due to the destruction of *darśana-mohanīya-karma*. One of the gods, being envious, wanted to test the truth of this praise. He goes to Śreṇika's town, disguised as a *muni* and fishes in the tank with nets. King Śreṇika, full of devotion, comes to him to pay him the respects due to a Jaina *muni*. He sees him gathering fish and throwing them in a basket. He immediately descends from his elephant, circumambulates the monk and greets him with reverence. As he stands in front of him bent down in humility, Śreṇika tells him: 'Someone who follows the mendicant path to liberation ought not kill fish, since that increases the course of existences (*saṁsṛti*). Therefore give me your net, I'll collect the fish for you in the basket and you, O *sādhu*, keep away!' Without a word the ascetic gives the net to the king who throws the net in the lake. At this the *muni* prevents him telling him that he did not need more fish and lauding him as a good Jaina he gives him leave. The king returns home with the *muni*, the net and the fish.
>
> After this incident criticism is voiced among Śreṇika's vassals. They say: 'How can the *muni* catch fish and how can the king be so foolish as to worship him? And how can our king, who actually rules over us follow the orders of the monk?' King Śreṇika hears this criticism directed against Jaina principles (*jina-śāsana-dūṣaṇa*) and thinks of teaching them a lesson. He smears stinking dirt and excrement on the letters with the royal edicts which the vassals have to receive. They hold the stinking leaves reverentially to their foreheads as if they were smelling of flowers. The king then asks them, how they could act in this way and they can only answer that with anything given by the king's grace there is no question of either dirt or *kumkum*. Śreṇika then draws the analogy by saying: just as you accept with devotion all that is given by me, even though it might be foul smelling, so did I, with

> devotion to the Jina, make my reverence to the fish catcher who looked like a *muni*.
>
> At these words of the king the fisherman reveals himself as a heavenly being, explains the test-situation and praises and rewards Śreṇika highly.[6]

In this story *upagūhana* has no connotation of concealing anything, on the contrary, everything is highly public. It is quite spectacular that the king venerates a fishing *muni* and then himself undertakes to perform the unroyal and, as a Jaina, even the sinful act of fishing. The king does it in a demonstrative manner, acting out the model relation between a layman and a king towards a monk. As a layman he makes good for the misbehaviour of the monk by taking the sin upon himself, albeit not without pointing out the monk's breach of behaviour and reminding him of his ascetic duties. This is in keeping with the duty of lay-people, namely, to support the ideals of the ascetics and to make it possible for them to live up to and according to theses ideals. As a king he fulfils his duty of protecting the religious principles by using his authority to eradicate the criticism against himself as a pious Jaina and against the sweeping criticism against the apparently bad monk, who actually cannot pollute the true religion taught by the Jina.

Finally, the blame on the religion and the ascetic is lifted by revealing that the whole affair was merely orchestrated to test Śreṇika's righteousness and so there

---

[6] Haribhadrasūri gives the theme of this story in two lines in his *Vṛtti* no. 5 to the *niryukti* of DVS 3 (p. 91) as an example for *upagūhana*: 'A God, doubting Śreṇika's firmness of faith, takes the form of a novice catching fish; Śreṇika hinders him.' Cf. also related passages in the *Maṇipati-carita* (MPC) by an anonymous author (eighth or ninth century) and the one by Haribhadra (twelfth century) (MPCH), translated by R. WILLIAMS (1959). The term *upagūhana*, however, is not explicitly mentioned in these texts, but the underlying message is 'to prevent a scandal of the Jina's teaching' as will be seen below (footnote 9). Stanzas 415–416 of MPC read: 'Suddenly in a pond at the edge of the road to the city he saw an acolyte catching fish and had him called to his presence, saying: "I will give you something to make up for this, cease from this evil task."' Stanzas 124–128 of the MPCH: 'At a fitting time the king set out for his own city, and by a divine illusion beheld a *muni* catching fish. The king said: "What are you doing?" The *muni* replied: "Let it be evident to you." So saying he cast his net into the water for fish. The king said: "What is this on your lap?" The other replied: "The monk's broom." When the king asked: "What is achieved by this?", the *muni* replied: "*Jīvas* are preserved." "Then why do you kill fish?" asked the king. The *muni* replied: "In the bazaar I shall buy a blanket with them." The king indicated the reason for not taking life and bestowed a blanket on him.'

never was, in fact, a really bad monk—a device which is in itself an *upagūhana*, the protection of the religion by proving the purity of its members.[7]

The other story from the BKK illustrating *upagūhana* is a peculiar contribution to the fact of the nudity of Digambara monks and their male, biophysical conditioning. In the context of the debate on *strī-mokṣa* male nudity is a prerequisite for perfect mendicancy and liberation. Women are denied the possibility of final liberation, because they cannot abandon their clothing. But unlike the categorical prohibition of female nudity under the pretext of her biophysical and social unfitness, male nudity demands protection, if needed.

In the following story the lay woman Celanā fulfils this religious virtue. The term *upagūhana* in this story is indeed to be understood as both, concealing and protecting. It is story number 8 in BKK, called the *Celanā-mahā-devī-kathānaka*.[8] This is a summary of it:

> Prince Vaiśākha was newly married when his childhood friend, now a monk, came to his house for alms. As soon as the prince saw him, he was intensely filled with joy and devotion and when it was time for the monk to leave, the prince decided to go away with him and also became a monk. His abandoned wife realised that he had become a Jaina monk practising austerities. She practised false beliefs and when she died she became a *vyantarī*. She still bore the grudge against her former husband for abandoning her and hence decided to trouble him during his austerities. When it was time for the solitary monk, weak from a month-long fast, to take some food, she caused him to have an erection. This happened when he came into Celanā's courtyard to break his fast. 'Celanā, filled with devotion, realised that the monk was in trouble and she concealed him from public view with a piece of cloth, concerned that people would speak ill of him.' The monk then finished his meal and continued his wanderings and his austerities. He eventually attained omniscience and was worshipped by gods and men. Celanā also went to bow down to the now omniscient one. There in the assembly of gods and men she asked him why he was subjected

[7] In another context Somadeva says that a religion cannot be sullied by the misdemeanour of a weakling among its adherents, just as the ocean does not become foul on account of a frog dying in its waters (HANDIQUI (1968: 261)).

[8] The story has been published and translated by GRANOFF (1989: 57–60). I acknowledge here my sincere gratitude to Phyllis Granoff for having introduced me to Jaina narratives and for her continuous generosity and encouragement.

> to such a torment. The omniscient one explained how it was that his abandoned wife had tormented him and how grateful he was that she, Celanā, firm in her right belief, had protected him.

The story ends in the stereotyped way with the gods and people being astonished and worshipping the monk who finally attained liberation. And then the teaching is added: 'Just as Celanā protected this monk, so should others protect all those who practice the true religion.'

One has to note in this story that the *upagūhana* here does not refer to any breach of conduct on the part of the monk, as in the previous case of the fishing monk. The monkhood in that case was cleansed by revealing the bad monk as just a divine delusion. Here in the Celanā story the monk practises the true religion and is actually faultless, since abandoning his wife in order to became a mendicant would only prove that he has taken up the right path. Contrary to the other story, the monk here he is a victim of the wrath of his intolerant wife. In this way again, there is no blemish on monkhood: it is not his lack of control or weakness which causes him the embarrassment, but the curse of a *vyantarī*. The resolute action of the laywoman and her concern pertains rather to preventing public contempt and discredit of the religion than to any embarrassment of the persons involved in the scene.

From all the three stories above it becomes clear that *upagūhana* is not the protection of an individual but of the reputation of the Jaina religion.

A corresponding predicament, namely the pregnancy of nuns, also comes within the context of *upagūhana*.[9]

---

[9] Cf. footnote 6 above. Haribhadrasūri relates to this theme (*Vṛtti* no. 5 to *Niryukti* 188 of DVS 3) as the second example for *upagūhana*: 'A God, doubting Śreṇika's firmness of faith ... meets him in form of a pregnant nun. He takes her to the inner apartment and himself takes care of the delivery so that no one learns of it. The God then reveals himself in his true form and lauds him: "O Śreṇika! You have reached the purpose of existence, since you have such devotion to the teaching."' Cf. also MPC 417–418: 'Then as he entered the city he saw a Jaina nun big with child roaming about the market and, calling her, he took her to his house. From fear of opprobrium falling on the Jaina religion he himself took care of her giving her employment in his household ...'; MPC 128–129: '...Then as he was going along he saw in the bazaar a female *sādhu* pregnant. Preventing scandal to the Jina's teaching, his mind undeviatingly fixed on the sacred law, the king kept her in secret and harboured her until the day of birth.' It is noteworthy that *upagūhana* is not mentioned, but the act of protecting the religion from scandal or critique as an essential feature of the right believer corresponds to the doctrinal concept.

The following instance is from Hariṣeṇa's BKK, story number 97, *Nīla-lohita-kathānaka*, as part of a longer story of rebirths and is summarised here. The term *avagūhana* is explicitly mentioned in the respective context. The nun, a novice, is Jyeṣṭā who becomes pregnant because of her association with a *muni* (Sātyaki). Her son Rudra is abandoned in a cave and then retrieved.

> Jyeṣṭā was one of the seven daughters of king Ceṭaka and she was the sister of Celanā who was abducted by Abhayakumāra, son and counsellor of king Śreṇika of Rājagṛha, to become the wife of king Śreṇika. Jyeṣṭā was supposed to accompany her sister, but she was left behind by her jealous sister by means of a trick: when leaving the town at night Celanā sent her back to the palace to fetch a necklace. Jyeṣṭā then arrived with the necklace at the appointed place but searched in vain for her sister. She was afraid to return to her father's house and in her feeling of being destitute she entered a retreat of nuns and resorted to Jaina *tapas*. Once the nuns heard that the *muni* Sātyaki (Jyeṣṭā's husband in a former life) was practising *tapas* on a mountain near Rājagṛha and went up to him to bow down to him. On the way down, the floods of an unseasonal rainstorm made the nun Jyeṣṭā seek shelter in a cave (*gūha*). Sātyaki had to interrupt his *yoga*, disturbed by the water, and he too entered the cave. When they beheld each other there in the cave their minds were filled with amorous emotions and they united in love. Sātyaki then went to his guru, confessed and undertook the prescribed penance. Jyeṣṭā on her part went to her superior and confessed. The nun accepted her with composure and entrusted her into the care of her sister Celanā in Śreṇika's palace. There she gave birth to a heavenly shining boy. Abhayadeva (Abhayakumāra) took the newly born boy away and abandoned him in a cave. On account of a dream which Celanā had the king Śreṇikā went to this cave, found the boy and entrusted him to the care of his wife who then educated him with her own son.

In this place the narration is interrupted by the reflection: (stanza 69): 'Together with Abhayakumāra the conscientious Celanā, who was firm in the right belief, performed the concealment (*avagūhana*) of Jyeṣṭā.'

This seems to be the didactic impact of this section of this *dharma-kathā*. There is no condemnation of the breach of the monastic vows. The conduct of the monk and the nun is a matter of confession and atonement and is dealt with internally. The duty of householders, however, is to ward off any blemish in public. They give shelter to the pregnant woman, something that would be quite natural since the delivery could take place in the house of a relative. And, further, they orchestrated the hiding and 'finding' of the child, who thus was not known to be the son of Jyeṣṭā but a foundling being taken care of by friendly people.

From the examples of the stories referred to above the following points can be drawn as the main features of *upagūhana*:

1. *Upagūhana* is the protection of the reputation of the Jaina religion;
2. For this purpose it is proper for laypersons to hide the faults committed by members of the religious community by concealing facts or even lying or to counteract misbehaviour publicly;
3. *Upagūhana* is not implemented for the sake of an individual but for the status of the Jaina community in society.

BIBLIOGRAPHY

ĀKP = Prabhācandra: *Śrādhanā-kathā-prabhanda or Kathā-kośa*. Ed. by A.N. Upadhye. *D. Jaina Granthamālā* 55, Bhāratīya Jñānapīṭha Māṇikacandra, New Delhi 1974.

BhĀr = Śivārya: *Bhagavatī Ārādhana* [*Mūlârādhanā*]. Hirālāla Khuśālachanda Dośī, Phaltan 1990.

BKK = Hariṣeṇa: *Bṛhat-kathā-kośa*. *Bṛhat Kathākośa of Ācharya Hariṣeṇa*, ed. by A.N. Upadhye, Bharatiya Vidya Bhavan, Bombay 1943.

DVS = *Daśa-vaikālika-sūtra*, ed. with the *Niryukti* and Haribhadrasūri's *Vṛtti*. *Āgamasuttāṇi (saṭīkaṁ)* vol. 27, Āgama Śrādhana Kendra, Ahmedabad 2000.

GRANOFF 1989 = Granoff, Phyllis: *The Forest of Thieves and the Magic Garden: An Anthology of Medieval Jain Stories*. Penguin Classics, London 1989.

HANDIQUI 1968 = Handiqui, Krishna Kanta: *Yaśastilaka and Indian Culture or Somadeva's Yaśastilaka and Aspects of Jainism and Indian Thought and Culture in the Tenth Century*. Jaina Saṁskriti Saṁrakshaka Saṅgha, Sholapur 1968. [First edition: *Jīvarāja Jaina Granthamālā* 2, Sholapur 1949].

JAINI 1979 = Jaini, Padmanabh S.: *The Jaina Path of Purification*. University of California Press, Berkeley—Los Angeles—London 1979. [Reprinted: Motilal Banarsidass, Delhi 1998].

SSā = Kundakunda: *Samaya-sāra*, Śrīmad Rājacandra Āśrama, Agāsa 1997. [First edition: 1975].

MPC = *Maṇipati-carita*. See: WILLIAMS (1959).

MPCH = Haribhadra: *Maṇipati-carita*. See: WILLIAMS (1959).

RKŚĀ = Samantabhadra: *Ratna-karaṇḍa-śrāvakâcāra*. *Śrī Ratnakaraṇḍa Śrāvakācāra*, Śrī Madhyakṣetrīya Mumukṣu Maṇḍala Saṅgha, Sagara (MP) 1985. [First edition: 1983].

YT = Somadeva: *Yaśas-tilaka*. See: HANDIQUI (1968).

WILLIAMS 1959 = Williams, Richard (ed.): *Two Prakrit Versions of the Maṇipati-Carita*, Luzac and Co., Bristol 1959.

चतुर्थारनयविवरणम्

Mediaeval Mysticism and Sectarian Divisions

A Portrait of the *Yogi* (*joi*) as Sketched by Joindu[*]

COLETTE CAILLAT

– 1 –

The author who, at the end of the *Yoga-sāra*,[1] signs *Jogicanda* [*-muṇi*], and who, at the beginning of the *Paramâtma-prakāśa*,[2] mentions his name as being *Joindu*, is clearly anxious, in these poems, to teach his disciple how to become a *yogin*, or more exactly, to quote the Apabhraṁśa form he uses, to become a *joi*. At the same time, he also emphasises that, in his eyes, most of the exercises that are commonly termed *yoga*, *joya* are spurious, or, in any case, quite insufficient. In fact, the word *joya* itself rarely occurs in the PP. It is met with twice independently, once in the instrumental, *joẽ*:[3]

> *so, vaḍha, joẽ kiṁ karai* *jāsu ṇa ehī satti?*
> —'What is the use of yoga for him who does not have this power [to crush the mind?]';

twelve *dohās* later *joya* is used in the nominative, *jou*:[4]

> *addh'ummīliya-loyaṇihĩ* *jou ki jhaṁpiyaehĩ?*
> —'To be with eyes half- or completely closed, is that yoga?'

It also occurs in two compounds, once as the first member of *joya-gai*,

> *joiya, visamī joya-gai!* *maṇu saṁthavaṇa ṇa jāi*,[5]
> —'Uneven is the path of yoga, the mind does not reach a standstill.'

The other occurrence is in the final member of the compound *divva-joo*,[6] used in the auspicious Prakrit stanza at the end of the poem, where, together with *divva-kāo* (*divya-kāyaḥ*), it qualifies omniscience:

---

[*] This paper is based on the masterful work of A.N. UPADHYE, with whom I had the great privilege to read Joindu's poems in Mysore. See UPADHYE (1973).

[1] YS 108: *Jogicanda-muṇieṇa … kayā dohā*.

[2] PP 1.8: *Siri-Joindu-jiṇāu* (Skt. *chāyā*: *Śrī-Yogīndu-jinaḥ*).

[3] PP 2.157; Skt. *chāyā*: *yogena* (Hindi *ṭīkā*: *yog-se*).

[4] PP 2.169; Skt. comm.: *yogo dhyānam*.

[5] PP 2.137; Skt. *chāyā*: *viṣamā yoga-gatiḥ, manaḥ saṁsthāpayituṁ na yāti*.

Essays in Jaina Philosophy and Religion.
Warsaw Indological Studies, Volume 2 (2002), pp. 239–252.

... *mukkha-do divva-joo* ... *jayau* ... *kevalo ko vi boho,*
—'Let the liberating divine yoga ... , omniscience be victorious!'

According to Brahmadeva's Sanskrit commentary, *divya-yoga* denotes the second *śukla-dhyāna*, 'pure concentration',[7] i.e. the second sort of auspicious (*praśasta*) *dhyāna*, described as free from passions, devoid of mental representations.'[8] It has a liberating power (*mukkha-do*).

Remarkably, the word *joya* is not used in the poem known as *Yoga-sāra*, a title that only appears at the end of the manuscripts of the text.[9] Did the author avoid the noun for fear of misinterpretation?

Corresponding verbal forms are absent in both poems, except for the present causative *jogavai*, in the (possibly interpolated) *dohā* 2.137.5:

so joiu jo jogavai *daṁsaṇu ṇāṇu carittu*
hoyavi paṁcahā̃ bāhirau *jhāyantau paramatthu,*[10]
—'He is a *joi*, he who jointly cultivates [right] view, knowledge and conduct, having eschewed the five [senses], meditating on the highest reality.'

The first line, where *samyag-darśana*, *-jñāna* and *-cāritra* are united, apparently refers to the classical Jaina *tri-ratna*. But the second line invites to go beyond this definition, and is evidently in tune with the above Prakrit stanza.[11] It implies a

[6] PP 2. 214, Skt. comm.: *divya-yogaḥ* ... *mokṣa-pradāyakaḥ*.

[7] On '*Dhyāna*, Jaina Meditational Practices,' see JAINI (1979: 251 ff.). N. TATIA (1986: xxv ff., xxviii f.) explains: 'The *śukladhyāna* is the light discovered by the individual independently from any help from outside.'

[8] Skt. comm.: *dvitīya-śukla-dhyānâbhidhāno vīta-rāga-nirvikalpa-samādhi-rūpo divya-yogaḥ*.

[9] Cf. A.N. UPADHYE's edition, p. 96 f.: *iti Yoga-sāra samāptāḥ* (Bombay ms., no date, old); *iti Yoga-sāra samāptam* (Patan ms., Saṁ. 1712); *iti śrī Joga-sāra-granṭha samāptaḥ* (Arraḥ, Saṁ. 1992).

[10] Skt. *chāyā*: *sa yogī yaḥ pālayati* (?) *darśanaṁ jñānaṁ cāritram / bhūtvā pañcabhyaḥ bāhyaḥ dhyāyan paramârtham*.—On 'additional verses,' see UPADHYE (1973: 95, 'Introduction').

[11] Brahmadeva considers two possible interpretations. He takes *YUJ samādhau iti*, thus as meaning 'adhering to, contemplation of,' so that 'what is expressed by the word *yoga* is the contemplation free of passion, devoid of mental representation; or rather the application to, transformation into, one's own pure *ātman*, consisting in infinite knowledge, etc.'—*yoga-śabdena vīta-rāga-nirvikalpa-samādhir ucyate; athavā ananta-jñānâdi-rūpe sva-śuddhâtmani yojanam pariṇamanaṁ yogaḥ; sa itthaṁ-bhūto yogo yasyâstîti sa tu yogī dhyānī tapo-dhana ity arthaḥ*.—On Jaina *dhyāna*, see TS 9.39 ff.; N. TATIA (1986).

direct, immediate understanding of the *ratna*-triad, that amounts to the realisation of *siddhi*, when the individual soul (the *jīva*) experiences its true, luminous nature which, ultimately, is identical with the Supreme Self or Absolute Paramâtman.

As for the agent noun *joi* [*ya*], it recurs in several *dohā*s of the *Paramâtma-prakāśa* and *Yoga-sāra*. In the present paper, the relevant passages will be examined, in order to determine whether Joindu's attitude towards yoga can be defined more precisely. It should be noted that the noun is often coupled with verbal forms of the Ap. verb *joi* (*infra*, p. 244), exactly as words derived from the root √*jñā* (e.g. *ṇāṇi*, etc.) are frequently associated with verbal forms of *jāṇai*; similarly, *muṇi* is more than once closely linked with forms of the root √*man* (present: *muṇai*, *muṇei*). There is little doubt that, in Joindu's poems, these three groups are closely connected and reinforce one another. Tentatively it could be suggested that, in Joindu's teaching, this association reflects the Jaina *tri-ratna*.

– 2 –

Like mystics in general, and many Indian spiritual teachers, Joindu underlines the opposition between external behaviour and internal dispositions, between bodily postures, ritual practices, even intellectual exercises or achievements, and, on the other hand, the exclusively spiritual training and pure goal on which the *joi* should concentrate. The *Yoga-sāra* mocks those simpletons who put their faith in *tīrtha*s and temples, statues, images … ,[12] or even in study (*sattha paḍhantaha te vi jaḍa* …)[13] and in religious insignia.[14] For, as stated in the *Paramâtma-prakāśa*, the

---

[12] YS 41 ff.: *tāma ku-titthaĩ paribhamai* …—'all that time he wanders from false *tīrtha*s to false *tīrthas* … '; *mūḍhā, devali deu ṇavi, ṇavi sili lippai citti*—'silly man, the god is not in the temple, neither is he in stone, in plaster, in painting … ,' etc. Compare YS 41, *Pāhuḍa-dohā* 80 (and *passim*). It has been remarked that several passages of PD remind of PP and YS.

[13] YS 53.

[14] YS 47:

dhammu ṇa paḍhiyaĩ hoi, dhammu ṇa potthā-picchiyaĩ /
dhammu ṇa matthā-lunciyaĩ, dhammu ṇa maḍhiya-paesi //

[read thus: 14 + 12 *mātrā*s]

—'*dhamma* does not result from reading, does not result from book and bunch of feathers, does not result from entering a cell, does not result from the plucking of the hair.'

Paramâtman—the real god! the divine—cannot be reached by means of yogic exercises (*dhāraṇā, dhyeya*), or of *yantra, mantra, maṇḍala, mūdrā,*[15] or of Vedas and treatises and all the senses,[16] for He transcends the ordinary, the practical, the conventional point of view (*vavahāra, vyavahāra*).[17] It should be remembered that He is the 'realm of pure concentration of mind', *ṇimmala-jhāṇahā̃ jo visau* … :[18] He consists of the highest vision and knowledge, is intrinsically the highest happiness, the highest power: He is the highest state.'[19]

In some passages, it is true, Joindu seems not to deny that help can be derived from certain corporal postures,[20] or from psycho-physiological exercises.[21] Further, more importantly, the disciple is undeniably supposed to have thoroughly grasped

---

[15] PP 1.22:

jāsu ṇa dhāraṇu dheu ṇa vi, jāsu ṇa jantu ṇa mantu /
jāsu ṇa maṇḍalu mudda ṇa vi …

[16] PP 1.23: *veyahi̇̃ satthahi̇̃ indiyahi̇̃* …

[17] On the opposition *vyavahāra-naya* / *niścaya-naya*, 'conventional / non-conventional, i.e. absolute point of view,' see A.N. UPADHYE (1973: 32 ff., 'Introduction,' PP); also P.S. JAINI (1979: 80, 311, *ubi alia*).

[18] PP 1.23c.

[19] PP 1.24:

kevala-daṁsaṇa-ṇāṇa-mau kevala-sukkha-sahāu /
kevala-vīriu so muṇahi jo ji parāvaru bhāu // (a = PP 2.203c).

[20] YS 60 a-b: *ṇās'aggi̇̃ abbhintarahā̃ je jovahi̇̃ asarīru*—'with attention fixed on the tip of their nose, those who, inside, see the immaterial … '; PP 2.162:

ṇāsa-viṇiggau sāsaḍā ambari jetthu vilāi /
tuṭṭai mohu tada tti tahi̇̃ maṇu atthavaṇahā̃ jāi //
—'the breath that escapes the nostril disappears in the sky: then delusion is smashed, the mind sets,' cf. 2.163.

[21] YS 98 mentions four 'mystical trances,' the *piṇḍastha-, padastha-, rūpastha-, rūpâtīta-dhyāna*, which, according to N. TATIA (1951: 288), are not recorded in the Jaina works earlier than in Śubhacandra's *Jñānârṇava*, eleventh century (cf. P.S. JAINI (1979: 255)). But Joindu composed his poems before that date: 'in all probability Jōīndu flourished in the 6th century A.D.,' according to UPADHYE (1973: 75), followed by JAINI (1979: 80). Because of linguistic considerations, H.C. BHAYANI (1997: 88 n. 3) would retain ca. the tenth century. As for the above four trances, A.N. UPADHYE had drawn attention to the influence of Śaiva yoga on the Jaina treatment of *dhyāna*, cf. Suzuko OHIRA (1975: 64, and n. 13) (referring to Abhinavagupta's *Tantrâloka* 10.241, etc.). Concerning this *Tantrâloka* passage, Raniero GNOLI (1999: 266, n. 3) refers to Muni Jambuvijaya, who suggests the *Malinīvijaya* as a possible source.

the fundamental Jaina teachings concerning the *tattva*s and *padârtha*s, the contents of which are even summarised in several of the *Paramârtha-prakāśa dohā*s.[22] He should also have mastered the various forms of *tapas*. But these are only preliminary exercises, they form an elementary approach to what remains an empirical form of knowledge. A radically new outlook is necessary to reach the supreme Absolute Principle, purely spiritual, who, in fact, *is* the real, fundamental essence of the *jīva*, so that 'the *ātman* sees, knows, realises himself by himself,'

pecchai jāṇai aṇucarai appiṁ appau …[23]

Among the possible aspirants mentioned by Joindu, the *joi* / *joiu* seems to be comparatively well prepared. This Middle Indo-Aryan / Apabhraṁśa noun continues the line of development of the Old Indo-Aryan *yogin*. The etymological link with the verbal root √*yuj* appears to survive, as proved by the definition of the *joi* quoted in the PP 2.137.5 (*supra*, p. 240). At the same time, the *joi* is said to be 'concentrating on the Paramârtha' (*jhāyantau paramatthu*). Similarly, addressing the *joiya*, YS 83 teaches that, 'equipped with the *ratna*-triad', the *jīva* has become "the supreme" *tīrtha*, the means of purification, the only factor of *mokṣa*,'

rayaṇattaya-saṁjutta jiu uttimu titthu pavittu
mokkhahā̃ kāraṇa, joiyā …

Finally, towards the end of the PP, when defining the competent students, Joindu quotes the judgement of the supreme Joi, viz. the Jina: He is said to have proclaimed 'well fit' (*joggu*, *yogyaḥ*) him who sees the knowledge clearly, him whose mind is pure—in short, him who unites all three *ratna*s:

ṇāṇa-viyakkhaṇu suddha-maṇu jo jaṇu …
so Paramappa-payāsayahā̃ joggu, bhaṇanti ji Joi.[24]

Thus connections between Ap. *joi* [*ya*] and the old Indo-Aryan root √*yuj* do survive and are even liable to be emphasised by Joindu.

But no word is bound by its etymology.

[22] Cf. PP 2. 16–32, etc.

[23] PP 2.13; Skt. *chāyā*: *paśyati jānāti anucarati ātmanā ātmānaṁ ya eva* …

[24] PP 209; Skt. *chāyā*:

jñāna-vicakṣaṇaḥ śuddha-manā yo jana īdṛśaḥ kaś cid api /
taṁ paramâtma-prakāśasya yogyaṁ bhaṇanti ye yoginaḥ //

– 3 –

As it often happens, especially in the Indian traditions, historically well established etymologies on the one hand, and, on the other hand, philosophical or religious concepts and reasoning do not necessarily tally. On the contrary, the latter are often seen to differ from, and prevail over, the former.[25] In the present case, due to the phonetic evolution from Old to Middle Indo-Aryan, the Apabhraṁśa substantive *joi* [*u*] (Skt. *yogin*) is henceforward easily connected with the reflex of the present stem *jo*-, that is with the reflex of the present stem *dyot*- (cf. the Vedic, etc., present *dyótate*, 'to shine'; causative Vedic, etc., *dyotayati*). The phonetic evolution of the initial cluster had begun early, as proved by Vedic *jyotati, jyótis*. According to TURNER's *Comparative Dictionary of the Indo-Aryan Languages* (6612), not only does *dyótate* survive in Middle Indo-Aryan (Pkt. *joyai, jovai, joi*, meaning 'shines, sees'), but it is also well documented in the New Indo-Aryan languages, especially in Old Marwari, *jovai* = 'watches', further in Gujarati, *jovũ* = 'to look at, consider, examine.' Thus, the verb appears to have been alive at all stages of Middle Indo-Aryan, including Apabhraṁśa. Probably it could spread all the more easily because of the defective character of the verbal roots √*dṛś* and √*paś*. In Joindu's poems, sixteen occurrences of *joi* (*jovau, joi, joijjai*, etc.) have been quoted.[26]

As far as Joindu is concerned, he evidently takes advantage of the convergence, in MIA, of the forms that reflect on the one hand OIA *yoj* [*aya*]-, and on the other hand OIA *dyot*(*aya*)-, both resulting in Ap. *jo*-. More than once, he emphatically, pathetically adjures the *joi*, or *joiya* (in the vocative), to abandon worldly passions as well as all material belongings, and to see, to contemplate ('*joi*!', 2. singular imperative) the transcendent reality. An identical or a similar pattern can be seen to recur in several *dohā*s:

> ***joiya***, *mohu* [/ *lohu* / *ṇehu*] *pariccayahi* ...
> *mohâsattau* [/ *lohâsattau* / *ṇehâsattau*] *sayalu jagu dukkhu sahantau* ***joi*** ![27]
> —'O *joi*, abandon delusion, abandon cupidity, abandon attachment!
> See the world that is enduring pain.'

---

[25] For examples from Buddhist and Jaina scriptures, see BALBIR (1991) and G. von SIMSON (1988).

[26] Cf. Nalini BALBIR (1998: 266).

[27] PP 2.111, 113, 115; Skt. *chāyā*:
yogin, mohaṁ parityaja ... /
mohâsaktaṁ sakalaṁ jagad ... *paśya*! //

Some verses later Joindu adds:

> ***joiya***, *sayalu vi kārimau … ihu paḍicchandā* ***joi***,[28]
>
> —'O yogi, everything here is artificial! It is of no use to pound the husk… Consider this image!'

and he urges the *joi*:

> ***joiya***, *dehu pariccayahi …*
> *deha-vibhiṇṇau ṇāṇa-mau so tuhũ appā* ***joi***.[29]
>
> —'O *joi*, abandon your body, consider your *ātman*, who is distinct from the body and constituted of real knowledge.'

This, in fact, is the main, the fundamental teaching that Joindu wishes to impart: the *ātman* is clairvoyance, the *ātman* is the true, the real knowledge—is the seer, as is stressed in the burden of three *dohā*s:

> *appā … ṇāṇiu, jāṇai, joi*,[30]
>
> —'being one who knows, the *ātman* knows—the *joi*.'

The preceding *dohā* had explained how, as soon as ignorance disappears, right view or faith and understanding obtain:

> *kālu laheviṇu, joiyā, jimu jimu mohu galei,*
> *timu timu daṁsaṇu lahai jiu … appu muṇei*,[31]
>
> —'Having seized the opportune time, O *joi*, when delusion dissolves, the soul (*jīva*) seizes right insight, it thinks [realises] the *ātman*.'

Right insight is luminous and comparable to brilliant light:

> ***joiya***, *ṇiya-maṇi ṇimmalae para* ***dīsai*** *siu santu*
> *ambari ṇimmali ghaṇa-rahie* ***bhāṇu*** *ji jema* ***phurantu***.[32]

---

[28] PP 2.129.

[29] PP 2.152; Skt. *chāyā*:

> *yogin, dehaṁ parityaja … /*
> *deha-vibhinnaṁ jñāna-mayaṁ taṁ tvam ātmānaṁ paśya //*

[30] PP 1.86d (v.l.), 88d, 90d; Skt. comm.: *jñānī yo 'sau yogī sa jānāty ātmānam; athavā jñānī jñāna-svarūpeṇa ātmā; ko 'sau jānāti? yogīti.*—PP 1.86 (edition) reads *jāṇẽ* [unmetrical] *joi*; Skt. *chāyā*: *jñānī … jñānena karaṇa-bhūtena paśyati*; but 1.88, 90: *jānāti yogī*.

[31] PP 1.85; Skt. *chāyā*: *… tathā tathā darśanaṁ labhate jīvaḥ*.

[32] PP 1.119; Skt. *chāyā*:

> *yogin, nija-manasi nirmale paraṁ dṛśyate śivaḥ śāntaḥ /*
> *ambare nirmale ghana-rahite bhānuḥ iva yathā sphuran //*

—'O *joi*, in your own pure mind, supremely, the Auspicious, the Saint is seen—exactly like the sun, dazzling in the pure, cloudless sky.'

This pure enlightened view is characteristic of the Siddhas, as stated in the *Yoga-sāra*:

je siddhā je sijjhihihĩ je sijjhahĩ ...
appā-daṁsaṇĩ te vi phuḍu ehau jāṇi ṇibhantu.[33]

—'Those who have become, who will become, who are becoming Siddhas do so thanks to their right view of *ātman*—know this without error.'

Potentially this right view also belongs to men, so that, if successfully trained, the elated disciple might exclaim

jo Jiṇa so haũ so ji haũ ...
mokkhahã kāraṇa, joiyā, aṇṇu ṇa tantu ṇa mantu.[34]

—'I am, I am the Jina! ... such is the cause of *mokṣa*, O *joi* ... —there is no other, neither tantra nor mantra.'

The exceptional perfection of the *joi* is also emphasised in the *Paramârtha-prakāśa* 2.160, where it is said that

bali kijjaũ tasu joiyahĩ jāsu ṇa pāu ṇa puṇṇu.[35]

—'He deserves offerings, as neither merit nor demerit accrues to him.'

In fact, the enlightened insight of the *joi* and his knowledge of the spiritual truth are correlative, concomitant, as stressed by the association of *joijjai* and *jāṇijjai*:

joijjai *tiṁ baṁbhu paru,* — ***jāṇijjai*** *tiṁ soi*
baṁbhu ***muṇeviṇu*** *jeṇa lahu gammijjai para-loi,*[36]

—'The supreme brahman is seen, this very brahman is known when, having realised the brahman, one immediately reaches the supreme world.'[37]

---

[33] YS 107, Skt. *chāyā*: *ye siddhā, ye setsyanti, ye sidhyanti ..., ātma-darśanena te api sphutaṁ, etat jānīhi nirbhrāntam.*

[34] YS 75; Skt. *chāyā*: *yaḥ Jinaḥ sa ahaṁ sa eva aham ... / mokṣasya kāraṇaṁ, yogin, anyaḥ na tantraḥ na mantraḥ.*

[35] PP 2.160; Skt. *chāyā*: *baliṁ kurve 'haṁ tasya yoginaḥ yasya na pāpaṁ na puṇyam.*

[36] PP 1.109; Skt. *chāyā*: *dṛśyate tena brahmā paraḥ, jñāyate tena sa eva / brahma matvā yena laghu gamyate para-loke.*

[37] The process thus described is the *Siddhi*, cf. SCHUBRING (1962: § 187); cf. YS 107, supra n. 33.

It will have been observed that the *jo*is do not act: they see, they know, they reflect; they practice *dhyāna* and *parama-samādhi*:[38]

ekku ji, joiya, jhāiyai *jo tailoyahā̃ sāru.*[39]
—'They meditate, exclusively, the essence of the triple world.'

Thus they approach the model set by the great Jois, viz. the Arhats and Jinas, who, in Joindu's poems, are described as having proclaimed 'the factor of *mokṣa*' (*mokkhahā̃ kāraṇa eu bhaṇai, joi—Joihiṁ bhaṇiũ*)[40], or again, as having 'taught in the Āgama' (*Āgami Joihĩ diṭṭhu*)[41].

– 4 –

The above quotations will have made it clear that, in Joindu's poems, *joi* and *joei* are often associated with various forms derived from the present *jāṇai* (*jānāti*), 'he knows', or the compound verbs *pari-* or *vi-jāṇai*, and the corresponding nouns, *ṇāṇa* (*jñāna*), *ṇāṇi*, *ṇāṇiya* (*jñānin*). These regularly continue formations that are usual in OIA, and Joindu chooses to keep the historically inherited terms. On the other hand, he abundantly favours etymological figures based on the antique root √*jñā*: around 200 such forms can bee traced, whereas some 75 only are related to *joei*, *joi*, and 150 to *maṇṇai*, *muṇai*, *muṇei*, *muṇi*. These are only rough figures, but they do point to the importance attached to knowledge (*ṇāṇa*) and to mental reflection (*muṇai*, *muṇei*) in both the *Yoga-sāra* and the *Paramâtma-prakāśa*.

It should be observed that the association of vision and knowledge is not only formal, but fundamental. It corresponds to Joindu's opinion concerning the epistemological process. He sides with those (particularly the Digambaras) who consider *daṁsaṇa* and *ṇāṇa* to be so intimately linked that the latter is always preceded by *daṁsaṇa*. Both are successively defined in *Paramâtma-prakāśa* 2.34 and 2.35. *Daṁsaṇa* is mentioned first:

sayala-payatthahā̃ jaṁ gahaṇu …
vatthu-visesa-vivajjiyau *taṁ ṇiya-daṁsaṇu joi.*[42]

---

[38] Cf. PP 1.1 ff.

[39] PP 1.96c; Skt. *chāyā*: *eka eva, yogin, dhyāyate yaḥ trailokyasya sāraḥ.*

[40] YS 38; Skt. *chāyā*: *mokṣasya kāraṇam etat bhaṇyate, yogin—Yogibhiḥ bhaṇitam.*

[41] PP 2.123d; Skt. *chāyā*: *Āgame Yogibhiḥ dṛṣṭam.*

[42] PP 2.34; Skt. *chāyā*:
sakala-padārthānāṁ yad grahaṇaṁ … /
vastu-viśeṣa-vivarjitaṁ tat nija-darśanaṁ paśya //

—'To grasp the principles clearly in their totality, excluding specific characteristics, see this as authentic *daṁsaṇa*.'

Next *ṇāṇa* is defined:

daṁsaṇa-puvvu havei phuḍu *jaṁ jīvahã viṇṇāṇu*
vatthu-visesu muṇantu, jiya, *taṁ muṇi avicalu ṇāṇu,*[43]

—'The analytical knowledge of the *jīva* preceded by the right view, with due consideration of the specific characteristics of the items—this consider as firm knowledge.'

These twin definitions serve as a sort of conclusion after the ten *dohās* in which the *Paramâtma-prakāśa* has examined the six 'substances' (*davva, dravya*). The same two *dohās* should also be read bearing in mind what has been stated shortly before, concerning 'right conduct':

jāṇavi maṇṇavi appu paru *jo para-bhāu caei*
so ṇiu suddhau bhāvaḍau *ṇāṇihĩ caraṇu havei.*[44]

—'If, having known, having reflected upon, the self and the other, one rejects the entity that is other, this is the authentic pure state, the right conduct of those who know.'

In the *Paramâtma-prakāśa* and the *Yoga-sāra*, *ṇāṇa* (*jñāna*) naturally means knowledge of *mokṣa*, and knowledge of the path leading to *mokṣa*: both texts repeat that it is via knowledge that *mokṣa* can be, and is gained: *ṇāṇiṁ mukkhu.*[45] More precisely liberation obtains thanks to knowledge of the unique Reality, that of the self (*appā, ātman*), which is the authentic aspect of the individual *jīva*, is pure *daṁsaṇa*, *ṇāṇa*, *caritta*, and, as such, is identical with the Paramâtman or Supreme Brahman. It is emphatically stated that *daṁsaṇa*, *ṇāṇa* and *caritta* 'perfectly determine the liberation of the soul,'

jīvahã mokkhahã heu varu *daṁsaṇu ṇāṇu carittu;*

The poet adds:

---

[43] PP 35; Skt. *chāyā*:

darśana-pūrvaṁ bhavati sphuṭaṁ yat jīvānāṁ vijñānam /
vastu-viśeṣaṁ jānan, jīva, tat manyasva avicalaṁ jñānam //

[44] PP 2.30; Skt. *chāyā*:

jñātvā matvā ātmānaṁ paraṁ yaḥ para-bhāvaṁ tyajati /
sa nijaḥ śuddhaḥ bhāvaḥ, jñāninām caraṇaṁ bhavati //

[45] PP 2.73; Skt. *chāyā*: *jñānena mokṣaḥ …*

te puṇu tiṇṇi vi appu muṇi *ṇicchaẽ ehau vuttu.*[46]

—'Consider this triad as the *ātman*: it is thus proclaimed from the transcendental point of view.'

In this triad, knowledge always appears as the pre-eminent factor, as it is proclaimed to be the subject, the object, the instrument of this superior knowledge: whether in the *Paramâtma-prakāśa* or in the *Yoga-sāra*, it is repeated that one knows and understands the *ātman* thanks to the *ātman*: *appiṁ appu / appau*,[47] or *appā appa*.[48] Or, again, it is stated that

appā saṁjamu sīlu tau, *appā daṁsaṇu ṇāṇu*
appā sāsaya-mokkha-pau, *jāṇantau appāṇu.*[49]

—'*Ātman* is self-control, morality, asceticism; *ātman* is right view and knowledge, *atman* is the eternal place of *mokṣa*—(*ātman*) who knows himself.'

The *Paramâtma-prakāśa* adds that

joiya, appẽ jāṇieṇa *jagu jāṇiyau havei.*[50]

—'It is thanks to the *ātman*, if known, that the world is known.'

The poem vividly underlines the central role of knowledge, which, at one and the same moment, is the subject, the object or goal, and the tool of knowledge:

ṇāṇiya, ṇāṇiu, ṇāṇieṇa *ṇāṇiũ jā ṇa muṇehi*
tā aṇṇāṇiṁ ṇāṇamaũ *kiṁ para baṁbhu lahehi?*[51]

—'O you who know, as long as you who know do not, with the help of what is known, reflect on the object of knowledge, then, how do you, via non-knowledge, reach Him who is pure knowledge?'

---

[46] PP 2.12; Skt. *chāyā*:

jīvānāṁ mokṣasya hetuḥ varaṁ darśanaṁ jñānaṁ cāritram /
tāni punaḥ trīṇy api ātmānaṁ manyasva: niścayena evam uktam //

[47] PP 1.76, 2.13.

[48] YS 11, etc.

[49] PP 1.93; Skt. *chāyā*:

ātmā saṁyamaḥ śīlaṁ tapaḥ ātmā darśanaṁ jñānam /
ātmā śāśvata-mokṣa-padaṁ jānan ātmānam //

[50] PP 1.99; Skt. *chāyā*: *yogin, ātmanā jñātena jagat jñātaṁ bhavati.*

[51] PP 1.108; Skt. *chāyā*:

jñānin, jñānī jñāninā jñāninaṁ yāvat na jānāsi /
tāvad ajñānena jñānamayaṁ kiṁ paraṁ brahma labhase? //

Thus, according to Joindu, there is no gap between the knower and the object of knowledge. Consequently, though it is clear from several developments that he explicitly accepts the pluralist doctrine taught by Jainism (*supra*, p. 243), he seems, from the transcendental point of view, to tend towards some form of monism.[52] Similarly, though in several *dohā*s he praises the usual *ratna*-triad,[53] it would appear that, from the transcendental point of view, the soteriological value of 'right conduct' can be questioned. For, whether 'good' or 'bad', all activities, in fact, result in an accumulation of *karman*. Joindu even maintains, paradoxically, that right doing, from the transcendental point of view, is worse than wrong doing. For it will normally bring pleasant rewards, will thus encourage further damageable activity, whereas perpetrators of bad actions will generally suffer, hence change their mind.[54] Instead, another triad is extolled, viz. to see, to know, to reflect upon, the supreme Brahman:[55] only such contemplation will determine the fusion of *ātman* and Paramâtman, when the essentially spiritual principle of the soul will have understood, hence recovered its true nature, thus will reach the Goal.

In spite of the emphasis that is laid on the soteriological impact of *jñāna* in Joindu's poems,[56] the Master's aim is not to teach or to impart knowledge, but to guide the disciple so that he discovers the ultimate Truth 'himself by himself.' Taking advantage of the linguistic evolution from Old Indo-Aryan to Apabhraṁśa, he invites the *joi* (Skt. *yogin*) to discover and adhere to the esoteric meaning implied in the Apabhraṁśa form, so that, in accordance with the *Paramappa-payāsa*, he sees and contemplates (*joi*, Skt. √*dyut*, *dyot*[*aya*-]) the 'radiant light of the innermost soul.'[57]

---

[52] Cf. A.N. UPADHYE (1973: 38; also 33 ff.), who points to similarities between PP, various *Upaniṣad*s, Vedānta ...

[53] Cf. PP 2.40, etc.

[54] PP 2. 56:

vara, jiya, pāvaĩ sundaraĩ ... /
jīvahā̃ dukkhaĩ jaṇivi lahu sivamaĩ jāĩ kuṇanti // ;

Skt. *chāyā*:

varaṁ, jīva, pāpāni sundarāṇi ... /
jīvānāṁ duḥkhāni janitvā laghu śiva-matiṁ yāni kurvanti //

[55] Cf. PP 1. 109, supra: *joijjai ... jāṇijjai ... muṇeviṇu ...*

[56] Compare, among others, D'SA (1982: 41–57).

[57] 'Rayonnante lumière (intérieure) de l'âme profonde,' a translation suggested by Prof. Olivier Lacombe.

ABBREVIATIONS

Ap. = Apabhraṁśa
Pkt. = Prakrit
Skt. = Sanskrit
OIA = Old Indo-Aryan
MIA = Middle Indo-Aryan[58]

BIBLIOGRAPHY

BALBIR 1991 = Balbir, Nalini, 'Le discours étymologique dans l'hétérodoxie indienne.' In: *Discours étymologiques. Actes du Colloque international organisé à l'occasion du centenaire de la naissance de Walther von Wartburg, Bâle, Freiburg i. Br., Mulhouse, 16–18 mai 1988*. Edités par J.-P. Chambon et G. Lüdi, Tübingen 1991: 121–134.

BALBIR 1998 = Balbir, Nalini: 'Glossaire du *Paramātmaprakāśa* et du *Yogasāra*.' in *Bulletin d'Études Indiennes* 18 (1998) 249–295.

BHAYANI = Bhayani, H.C.: *Some Topics in the Development of OIA, MIA,NIA*. L.D. Series 118, L.D. Institute of Indology, Ahmedabad 1997.

D'SA 1982 = D'Sa, F.X. S.J.: 'Jñāna as experience of transcendence in the Bhagavadgītā.' In: *Epiphanie des Heils. Zur Heilsgegenwart in indischer und christlicher Religion*. Arbeitsdokumentation eines Symposiums, hrsg. von Gerhard Oberhammer, Wien 1982: 41–57.

GNOLI 1999 = Gnoli, Raniero: *Abhinavagupta. Luce dei Tantra, Tantrāloka*. A cura du … , *Biblioteca Orientale* 4, Milano 1999.

JAINI 1979 = Jaini, Padmanabh S.: *The Jaina Path of Purification*. University of California Press, Berkeley—Los Angeles—London 1979.

OHIRA 1975 = Ohira, Suzuko: 'Treatment of dhyāna in the *Tattvārthādhigama-sūtra* of Umāsvāti.' *Indian Philosophical Quarterly* 3/1 (1975) 51–64.

PD = *Pāhuḍa-dohā of Ramasimha Muni*. An Apabramsa work on Jaina mysticism. Critically edited with Introduction, Translation, Glossary, Notes and Index by Hiralal Jain, Karanja Jaina Series 3, Karanja 1933.

[58] It will be remembered that in MIA (including Apabraṁśa) diphthongs have been eliminated, and hiatus is common. In the present paper, therefore, *joi* (*yogi-*), *gai*, etc., are to be read [joi], [gai] … , disyllabic.

PP = Yogīndu: *Paramâtma-prakāśa* [*Paramappa-payāsu*]. See: UPADHYE (1973).

SCHUBRING 1962 = Schubring, Walther: *The Doctrine of the Jainas*. Translated from the German by Wolfgang Beurlen, Motilal Banarsidass, Delhi 1962.

SIMSON 1988 = Simson, G. von: 'Etymologie als Mittel ideologischer Auseinandersetzung: Bemerkungen zum Aggaññasutta des Dīghanikāya.' In: *Festgabe für Werner Thomas zum 65. Geburtstag*, München 1988: 87–98.

TATIA 1951 = Tatia, Nathmal: *Studies in Jaina Philosophy*. Jain Cultural Research Society, Varanasi 1951.

TATIA 1986 = Tatia, Nathmal: *Jaina Meditation, Citta-samādhi: Jaina Yoga*. Jain Vishva Bharati, Ladnun 1986.

TATIA 1994 = Tatia, Nathmal (tr.): *Tattvārtha Sūtra: That Which Is. Umāsvāti / Umāsvāmī; with the combined commentaries of Umāsvāti / Umāsvāmī, Pūjyapāda and Siddhasensgaṇi*. The Sacred Literature Series, Harper Collins Publishers, San Francisco—London—Pymble 1994.

TS = Umāsvāti: *Tattvârthâdhigama-sūtra*. See: TATIA (1994).

TURNER 1966 = Turner, R.L.: *A Comparative Dictionary of the Indo-Aryan Languages*. London 1966.

UPADHYE 1973 = Upadhye, A.N. (ed.): *Śrī Yōgīndudēva's Paramātmaprakāśa (Paramappapayāsu). An Apabhraṁśa Work on Jain Mysticism.* The Apabhraṁśa Text edited with Brahmadeva's Sanskrit Commentary and Daulatarāma's Hindī Translation, with a Critical Introduction, Various Readings, etc., etc., and also *Yōgasāra*. Critically edited with the Sanskrit Chāyā and with the Hindi Translation of Pandit Dr. Jagdishchandra Shastri, *Śrīmad Rājachandra Jaina Śāstramālā* 3, Shrimad Rajachandra Ashrama, Agas 1973.

YS = Yogīndu: *Yoga-sāra*. See: UPADHYE (1973).

Samayasundara's *Sāmācārī-śataka* and Jain Sectarian Divisions in the Seventeenth Century

NALINI BALBIR

– 1 –

To my knowledge, attention on Samayasundara's *Sāmācārī-śataka* was first called upon a little more than a century ago by Johannes KLATT. Although this scholar (born in 1852) is not recognised as standing among the major German Indologists of the nineteenth century, he accomplished useful work in the field of history of literature, and especially of Jain literature, making good use of the post he occupied in the Indian Department of the Royal Library at Berlin, where he was held in high esteem by Albrecht Weber (1825–1901), and taking benefit from the direct access he had to manuscripts. Unfortunately, personal circumstances did not allow Klatt to produce as much as he could have done given his scientific abilities, so that his *Specimen of a literary-bibliographical Jaina Onomasticon* (Leipzig 1892) was never more than a specimen. His article on the *Sāmācārī-śataka* had a similar unlucky fate, for it could not be finished by him. Fortunately, it was revised for publication by Ernst Leumann (1859–1931), who was his friend, and appeared in the *Indian Antiquary* of 1894, together with some biographical information provided by Leumann. Although Klatt died only in 1903, this was the last contribution from his pen.[1]

[1] On J. Klatt, see KLATT (1894: 169 n. 2) (by Leumann); Leumann in PLUTAT (1998: No. 135 and 227); among Klatt's publications (listed in GUÉRINOT (1906)) are 'Eine apocryphe Paṭṭāvalī der Jainas': Festgruss an O. von Böhtlingk, Stuttgart, 1888: 54–59; 'The date of the poet Māgha': *Wiener Zeitschrift für die Kunde des Morgenlandes* 3 (1889) 121–145; 'Dhanapāla's Ṛishabhapañcāśikā': *Zeitschrift der Deutschen Morgenländischen Gesellschaft* 33 (1879) 445–483; 'Extracts from the historical Records of the Jainas': *Indian Antiquary* 11 (1882) 245–256; 'Śūrpāraka': *Indian Antiquary* 11 (1882) 293–294. Photograph in RAU (1982: 62): '31. Oktober 1852 Filehne/Posen, 27. August 1903 Berlin.' No notice in *German Indologists*.

Essays in Jaina Philosophy and Religion.
Warsaw Indological Studies, Volume 2 (2002), pp. 253–277.

The six pages he devotes to Samayasundara's work are entirely based on the reading of a manuscript which was in his possession. Later on, his wife handed it over to Ernst Leumann, so that it is now kept in the Strasbourg library together with the other Jain manuscripts collected by this scholar.[2] Since 1939 the text is available in an Indian edition, which is the document I will refer to here[3]. KLATT's analysis of the work follows the line of his usual interests and provides basic historical information. The composition of the *Sāmācārī-śataka* was spread over three years and was finished in V.S. 1672 (= 1616 CE). It took place in Rajasthan. Samayasundara, the author, was a member of the Kharatara-gaccha. His work has also the side title *Praśnôttara-śata*. 'A number of the chapters have special names,' writes KLATT (1894: 169), thereupon providing an incomplete list of such headings, whereas the rest of the investigation gives an alphabetical index of works mentioned in the *Sāmācārī-śataka*, with focus on the account of a dispute between a teacher from the Kharatara-gaccha and a rival from the Tapā-gaccha.[4] As will be seen, the learned character of Samayasundara's book is indeed one of its main characteristics and one of the main characteristics of the literary form to which it belongs. In brief, good seeds have been sown by KLATT's observations. Yet they have to be grown and reaped in order to do full justice to the author's purpose, the real literary affiliation of his book and its richness as far as the development of Jainism is concerned. This is what I shall try to do here, believing that a monographic study of such a work as Samayasundara's is not meaningless for the knowledge of history of ideas and methods of argumentation. Such an investigation takes place in a connected series of papers I have devoted either to individual works and / or topics crucial for the delineation of what Śvetāmbara Jains mean by sectarian identity (BALBIR (1999) [*Kumatāhiviṣa-jaṅgulī-mantra*]; (2000a) [monastic staff]; (2000b) [mouth-cloth]; (forthcoming) [Añcala-gaccha versus other *gaccha*s]).

– 2 –

For a correct appraisal of Samayasundara's work, it is necessary to understand the historical background where it developed. First, the Jains had had to pass through an

[2] For the history of the manuscript see TRIPATHI (1975: 121—notes on Serial No. 60).

[3] References are either to the page or to the serial number of the point in discussion ('No. X'). Unfortunately, there is no index of all the works quoted by Samayasundara. Thus KLATT's list, incomplete as it is, remains very useful.

[4] Cf. SāŚ, No. 4 (Abhayadeva's affiliation to the Kharatara-gaccha).

intense period of Moslem destruction of their patrimonial tradition, especially sacrilegious despoliation of their religious images, which could be escaped only through hiding them in underground chambers. This is implied by Samayasundara's references to contemporary rumours telling that, now that the danger had gone, in such and such village a number of old images were taken out of underground chambers and came to light.[5] Moreover, by the beginning of the seventeenth century several new monastic groups or orders supported by regional lay communities had emerged among the Śvetāmbaras. This process, which probably always existed, started anew in the eleventh–twelfth century, when the image-worshippers (the so-called Mūrtipūjaks) started to differentiate themselves in distinct well-documented *gaccha*s, such as the Tapā-gaccha, the Kharatara-gaccha, the Añcala-gaccha or the Āgama-gaccha, to name just a few of the most significant groups. This process reached its summit in the fifteenth century, when the so-called Lumpaka gaccha, the followers of Lonka Shah, came to existence. Their firm opposition to image-worship was indeed a challenge for their opponents. Such a situation created a rich ferment for discussion and also some kind of confusion, as is recognised by Samayasundara himself:

> *jainā gacchā jagati bahavo bhinna-bhinnâbhidhānā* /
> *bhinnâcārā nija-nija-mataṁ sthāpayanti pramāṇam* //
> *gacchâdhīśāḥ śruta-nigaditāṁ saṁmatiṁ darśayanti* /
> *tasyā moho na bhavati kathaṁ? yaj jinâjñâiva satyā* //[6]

This had an impact on the literary level, leading to the development of a literary form named *praśnôttara*, 'questions and answers,' or *vicāra* 'thoughts, investigations'. Such works are often authored by prominent monastic leaders of the various groups who act as spokesmen and represent a kind of spiritual authority and a guarantee: our Samayasundara, for instance, is a learned monk who was given the title *mahôpādhyāya* and as such was in the seventeenth century the third dignitary of the Kharatara-gaccha. The movement's leader was then Jinacandrasūri, who was conferred the glorious title of *Yuga-pradhāna* by Akbar, figured as one of the prominent Jain representatives at the Emperor's court, 'instituted a reform of [it] and won concessions for the Jain community from the Moslem authorities.'[7] He was

[5] SāŚ, p. 97b (see DUNDAS (1992: 188)).

[6] SāŚ, author's *praśasti* vs. 2 (p. 193a). See also the beginning of the work, vss. 2 ff.

[7] He was born in V.S. 1598, and was *sūri* from V.S. 1612 to V.S. 1670 (KLATT (1894: 169), DUNDAS (1992: 122)). On Jinacandrasūri and all the main Jain leaders who had some influence at Akbar's court see also DESAI (1941: 10 ff.) and BABB (1996: 124 ff.).

succeeded by Jinasiṁhasūri.[8] Samayasundara, who was a pupil of Sakalacandragaṇi, also visited Akbar's court. He has to his credit a number of compositions of different kinds in Sanskrit and Gujarati and could exert a great influence during his long life from 1553 to 1645 (V.S. 1610–V.S. 1702).[9] Moreover, he seems to have been fond of the *praśnôttara* genre, since, beside the *Sāmācārī-śataka*, he also wrote a *Viśeṣa-śataka*, a *Vicāra-śataka*, a *Viśeṣa-saṅgraha* and a *Visaṁvāda-śataka* which go along the same lines.[10]

Being different in their purpose from full-fledged treatises, such works are meant to discuss specific points that gave birth to different opinions within different Jain circles by referring to scriptures, with the idea to settle them according to the view in force within the order to which the author belongs. The result is a tendency to stress divergences and leave unity in the background: this is expressed linguistically by the use of *nanu* followed by the objection of imaginary or real opponents as the initial word of all hundred points discussed by Samayasundara. In a limited number of cases, the works are organised according to a clear scheme: Kīrtivijaya's *Vicāra-ratnâkara*, for instance, takes the Canonical scriptures one by one (*Aṅga*s, *Upāṅga*s, *Cheda-sūtra*s, *Prakīrṇaka*s) and successively deals only with the controversial points therein. In his so-called *Hīra-praśna* (HPr), the same author classifies the questions according to the name of the Jain teacher who put them to Hīravijayasūri, and Śubhavijaya does the same with questions asked to Vijayasenasūri in his so-called *Sena-praśna* (SPr). In a way, such a pattern reminds of the *Milinda-pañha*, except that in the last two Jain works mentioned, both the question and the

[8] Jinasiṁhasūri was the *sūri* of the Kharatara-gaccha from V.S. 1670 to V.S. 1674 (KLATT (1894: 169)).

[9] For the dates see DAVE (1998: 21); for other dates see TRIPATHI (1975: 122) following the opinion of 'Tripuṭī-mahārāj': birth in V.S. 1610 or 1620, *dīkṣā* in V.S. 1628, *gaṇi* in V.S. 1640, *upādhyāya* in V.S. 1649, *mahôpādhyāya* in V.S. 1672. For an appraisal of Samayasundara's poetic and narrative compositions in Gujarati see DAVE (1998). For a detailed study of all his literary activity, see CANDRAPRABHĀSĀGARA (1986) and SATYAVRAT (1994).

[10] For the contents of these four works, see CANDRAPRABHĀSĀGARA (1986: 96–116) (According to this author, the *Viśeṣa-śataka* is published by Muni Sukhasāgara, Lakhamīcanda Veda-Mohatā, Agra, see p. 106; the *Vicāra-śataka* is unpublished, the information given being based on a manuscript from the 'Śrī-Kuśalasūri-Jñāna-bhaṇḍāra' in Varanasi; the *Viśeṣa-saṅgraha* is 'worth publishing,' the information given being based on a manuscript from the 'Cintāmaṇi Pārśvanātha Jaina Śvetāmbara Pañcāyatī Baṛā Mandir' in Varanasi; the *Visaṁvāda-śataka* is unpublished, no detailed information on its contents being given because the only available ms., from the 'Abhaya Jain Granthālaya' in Bikaner, is very difficult to read).

corresponding answer are generally tantalisingly brief, as if they were to be considered as mere notes giving the outline of oral debates, of which they can be taken as reflexes. Note that this literary form is far from being a remnant of the past: books of this type have been written in the twentieth century and are still being written in the vernaculars for the enlightenment of monks and lay-devotees.[11]

In the great majority of cases, there does not seem to be any global organising principle: apart from small units grouped thematically, the connection is rather loose. Such is the situation with Samayasundara's *Sāmācārī-śataka*, which successively deals with a total of hundred points distributed over five *prakāśa*s in the following manner:

Prakāśa I.	No. 1–37	37 points, p. 1b–75a
Prakāśa II.	No. 38–48	11 points, p. 76a–117a
Prakāśa III.	No. 49–61	13 points, p. 118a–136a
Prakāśa IV.	No. 62–88	17 points, p. 137a–178a
Prakāśa V.	No. 89–100	12 points, p. 179a–192b.

This division, however, does not correspond to anything obvious: the only thing mentioned in the internal colophons composed by the author is the total number of points included in each chapter. If the subject discussed is the organising principle, it is not applied very systematically, since rather unexpectedly, some connected points discussed along the same lines and with the help of the same texts are found wide apart.[12] At the most, it could be observed that the second section seems to concentrate on issues put to the Sthānakvāsins, for it discusses opposition to the recognition of 45 *Āgama*s, opposition to image-worship and refusal to admit the use of a staff by the mendicant which are all characteristically their claims.[13] Unlike several authors of similar works, Samayasundara generally does not mention the name of the sectarian groups he aims at, although several of the hundred points considered are articulated according to the pattern: 'In other gacchas (it is like this, etc.), in our gaccha, in the Kharatara-gaccha (there is such and such opinion),' along with its formal variants with regard to the order or the wording.[14] The views discussed are usually clear enough to identify the target. The only group explicitly referred to is the Tapā-gaccha, whose name appears several times.[15] This might

[11] See, among many other instances, VIJAYADĀNASŪRĪŚVARJĪ (1938).

[12] E.g. No. 71 and 98, 14 and 63, etc.

[13] Points No. 38 to 48.

[14] No. 3, 6, 7, 12, 13, 27, 45, 52, 61; see also cases like No. 54 (*kecit ... pratipādayanti, tat satyam asatyaṁ vā?*).

[15] Nos. 16, 20, 21, 24, 29.

reflect a reality contemporary to the author, suggesting that the rivalry between the Kharatara- and the Tapā-gaccha was the one that mattered in the seventeenth century and that the Tapās were the most threatening: points of divergences between the two groups are the focus of many works similar to Samayasundara's.[16] Although this strong opposition was not a novelty of that time, there are hints to indicate that it was given a new impulse in the sixteenth-seventeenth centuries when important figures of the Tapā-gaccha such as Hīravijayasūri (1527–1595) or Dharmasāgara stood out. Beside cases where the aim is to oppose usages of the Kharatara-gaccha and usages of others, there are those where the aim is to establish the authenticity of one's own specific practice or to explain why it is so.[17] Finally, although present, the polemical purpose is less apparent in cases where the point is mentioned through a simple question and looks like a mere inquiry.[18]

The significance of the *Sāmācārī-śataka*, which thus finds place in a long chain of similar works, comes from its rather detailed and thoughtful manner of dealing with the topics selected. Whereas the discussions found in the *Hīra-praśna* (HPr) or the *Sena-praśna* (SPr) are so concise that they need to be supplemented by other works in order to be fully understood, Samayasundara provides the reader with all necessary material and supports his views by several quotations from the scriptures, generally accompanied by their precise reference. He obviously has a very vast and multifarious book knowledge and displays pedagogical aims. Thus, for instance, the discussion of the right procedure to be followed in order to give initiation results from his desire to render into Sanskrit what was available in one of his predecessor's books in Prakrit so that it is accessible to young monks.[19] The fact that he thinks

[16] Compare VIJAYAJAMBŪSŪRĪŚVARJĪ (1950): this booklet contains the original Gujarati texts and a paraphrase in modern Gujarati of two sets of *bols* (assertions, statements) which focus on respectively 141 and 161 points of divergences between the Kharatara- and the Tapā-gaccha. They have been edited on the basis of two manuscripts kept in the Amara Tapā-gaccha Jainaśālā library of Cambay, and could date back to the same time as Samayasundara's work. Useful recapitulation of seventeen important issues of contention in the introduction (p. 5). See also HPr, SPr, etc.

[17] E.g. No. 5, 10 (*śrī-Kharatara-gacchīyāḥ śrāddhāḥ ... gr̥hṇanti ... , tat kim?*), 15, 17 (reference to the source of authority), 18, 19, 22, 23 (*ātmanāṁ gacche ... kriyate, tat kutra tad-akṣarāṇi santi?*), 35, 69 (antiquity of a certain practice), 84, 99.

[18] E.g. No. 51, 53, 78, 88, 90, 91 (*viṁśati-sthānaka-tapasaḥ kā gāthā? tat-tapasi ca kiṁ guṇanaṁ?*), 92, 93, 95, 100.

[19] SāŚ, p. 170b (No. 86): *nanu: dīkṣā-dāna-vidhiḥ kutra pratipādito 'sti? ucyate: śrī-Vidhi-prapāyāṁ, atra śiṣyāṇāṁ sukhâvabodhârthaṁ sa eva pāṭhaḥ saṁskr̥tī-kr̥tya likhyate.*

appropriate to include in his work the original Prakrit or Sanskrit texts of the codes of conduct (*sāmācārīs*) devised by three of the most prominent Kharatara-gaccha founder leaders from the eleventh and the twelfth century (Jinavallabha, Jinadatta and Jinapati)[20] serves a similar purpose, for these texts are repeatedly referred to in the course of the book, and is a means of propaganda as well. Samayasundara's general attitude is made of a delicate balance between objectivity and in-depth analysis, on the one hand, and polemical aggressivity.[21] This sometimes gives the strange impression that, in spite of all the pages written, the divergences between rival groups cannot be smoothed and no real conclusion can be reached at (see below, p. 265). However hard Samayasundara's animosity towards the Tapā-gaccha may be, it does not prevent him from referring to books by their teachers, especially if it happens that both the Tapā- and the Kharatara-gacchas hold the same opinion, against a third group. Apart from Kulamaṇḍanasūri's *Vicārâmṛta-saṅgraha*, which is a learned and standard polemical work of the fifteenth century giving the ideas defended by the Tapās,[22] one of the most recent sources quoted by Samayasundara is the so-called *Hīra-praśna*, mentioned at least thrice.[23]

The word *sāmācārī* found in the title of Samayasundara's book clearly indicates what is his concern. He focuses on orthopraxy and ethics in its practical aspects (*rūḍhi*, e.g. p. 52b) much more than on abstract ideas or concepts, stressing the fact that divergences between the Śvetāmbara orders lie in matters of daily religious life of the mendicant as well as of the layman. Although it is a prevalent feature of the *praśnôttara*-literature, there are other works where more emphasis is put on discussions concerned with technicalities of cosmology, karma-theory, etc.[24] A rough classification of the 100 topics of Samayasundara's work gives the following picture:

---

[20] See SāŚ, No. 62–65; Jinavallabha was active in the eleventh century (DUNDAS (1992: 121)); Jinadatta between 1075–1154 (DUNDAS (1992: 122)); Jinapati: V.S. 1210–V.S. 1277 (KLATT (1894: 171)). The official foundation of the Kharatara-gaccha dates back to 1024 CE.

[21] SāŚ, vs. 5 p. 1a:

rāga-dveṣau parityajya sva-para-smṛti-hetave,
sugamaṁ sopayogaṁ ca kurve Praśnôttara-kramam,

and p. 19a (No. 4): *ke 'pi para-vighna-santoṣiṇaḥ pralapanti* ... .

[22] See BALBIR (forthcoming); SāŚ, p. 6a, 43b, 44b, 122a.

[23] See already KLATT (1894: 171); SāŚ, p. 38b corresponds to HPr ed. p. 24a-b; SāŚ, p. 46b to HPr ed. p. 16b; the passage corresponding to SāŚ, p. 65b–66a could not be traced in my edition.

—Issues pertaining to worship: especially long developments pertain to the justification of image-worship (*pūjā*) and the discussion of textual sources connected with this question (No. 39, p. 81a–95a and No. 48; No. 40: why should an image of stone or wood be worshipped; No. 41: results of image-worship; No. 42: the relationship of *pūjā* and *hiṁsā*; No. 43–44: supposed adharmic character of the gods). Importance given to this issue is to be connected with the growing influence of anti-Mūrtipūjak groups (such as the Sthānakvāsins). Measures specific to the Kharatara-gaccha are highlighted (ladies and image-worship, No. 14: see below, p. 262; main gesture of the installation of an image, i.e. *añjana-śalākā*, to be performed by an *ācārya* only, No. 26[25]). *Vidhi*s for specific rites are described (No. 80, 81, 83, 87, 91, 100 [for pacification]; No. 82: *pūjā* at home).

—Issues pertaining to the calendar, i.e. establishment of sacred days and events (No. 3, see below § 3, p. 263 ff.) and duration of festivals. Beside the vexed question of the date of Paryuṣaṇ (No. 23, 61), there are other similar discussions regarding *poṣadha* (No. 2, 27, 30), the fortnight *pratikramaṇa* (No. 8) and the concept of *tithi* (No. 28, 94; 36 [Kārttika]; 60 [Pañcamī]).[26]

—Issues pertaining to technical aspects of monastic life: procedure for giving initiation into the order (No. 73, 86), study-*curriculum* and ascetic practices (No. 45), monastic uniform (No. 46; BALBIR (2000a)), formulas to be uttered at the time of inspection (No. 20), alms-search (allowed and forbidden types of families, No. 51; No. 21: impurity due to birth or death in a house is a forbidding factor[27]), religious titles and *cursus honorum* (No. 69), co-wandering of monks and nuns (No. 6),[28] circumstances forbidding the study of religious texts (*asvadhyāya*, No. 79, 93).

—Issues pertaining to food and water: they are considered in their relationship to fasts, the point being to know which type of food is allowed or forbidden on which occasion (No. 10, 16), and especially whether it is appropriate to drink water when performing the *poṣadha* observance (No. 25) or whether its performance is authorised to one who has eaten (No. 29). This question is a common topic of the

[24] E.g. Kṣamākalyāṇa's *Praśnôttara-sārdha-śataka* in its first part.

[25] This point is discussed in connection with the place of material and mental worship (*dravya-* / *bhāva-pūjā*) in the layman's and the mendicant's religiosity in SPr, p. 96a (No. 446): although mental worship should be the prevalent mode of the mendicant, it should not exclude him from *dravya-pūjā*.

[26] See also VIJAYAJAMBŪSŪRĪŚVARJĪ (1950), introduction and passim.

[27] Compare VIJAYAJAMBŪSŪRĪŚVARJĪ (1950: No. 52 p. 40–41); HPr, p. 31a where the interdiction to use water for *pūjā* in a house where a son or daughter is born is recorded as a practice in force among the Kharatara-gaccha.

[28] See also VIJAYAJAMBŪSŪRĪŚVARJĪ (1950: No. 6 p. 4).

praśnôttara-genre and seems to have defined distinct groups[29]. Food and water are also considered in their relationship to *ahiṁsā*: the items to be counted among the so-called *abhakṣyas* are disputed and have a different status in different groups (e.g. *dvidala*, No. 7;[30] see also No. 9, 11, 12, 13, 37, 54, 55, 56 [*cūrṇa*]; 53 [differences between the four traditional types of food, *khādima, svādima, pāna, aśana*]; 88 [*vikṛtis*]). Similarly, the period of time during which foodstuff or water can be kept, how they should be kept in order to remain pure (*a-citta*, 'without living beings') is a problem subject to discussion (No. 57, 58, 99 [use of clay-pots]).

—Issues connected with the correct performance of Jain religious duties (*kriyā*, *āvaśyaka*) and with the correct utterance of formulas on these occasions. As secondary as they may look, these liturgical questions play an important part in Samayasundara's work. More generally, liturgy is one of the areas at the heart of differentiation between Jain orders. This is shown by the large numbers of points coming under this section. They specifically concern either the layman or the monk, or both together: *namaskāra* [*havai maṅgalaṁ* / *hoi maṅgalaṁ*, No. 52: cf. BALBIR (forthcoming)]; *vandana* (No. 50, 70); *sāmāyika* (No. 1, 17, 31, 78 [number of *kṣamâśramaṇas* to be uttered]; *pratikramaṇa*: No. 5, 35; No. 22, 59, 66–67, 72 [fortnight *pr.*], 84, 90, 92, 95 [morning *pr.*]; *poṣadha* (No. 19 and see above, No. 85); inspection during the morning religious duties (No. 32, 33); layman's *aticāras* (No. 74); atonements prescribed in case of accidental acts or events preventing the correct performance of religious duties (making *ghee* fall, No. 75; sneezing in *pratikramaṇa*, No. 76; unexpected coming in between of a cat, No. 77). An important question relates to the use of monastic implements by the layman during the performance of religious duties, which was forbidden by some Jain groups (No. 18 [broom], No. 49 and 68 [mouth-cloth], No. 34 and 96 [*prāvaraṇa*], No. 97 [*sthāpanâcārya*]: see BALBIR (2000b) and (forthcoming)). The Kharataras' point of view that the eleven *pratimās* are not to be adopted by laymen is also discussed at length (No. 15, p. 52b–54a): the argument is that the decline in strength has made it impossible for them to seriously observe more than the first four *pratimās*, at the most.[31] The role of deities in connection with religious duties (No. 71 and 98) will be dealt with below (§ 3, p. 270 ff.).

—Issues concerning religious texts. The main question concerns the number of *Āgamas* to be recognised as authoritative. Samayasundara of course criticises the position of the Sthānakvāsins, who count only 32 of them and not 45 like the other Śvetāmbaras (No. 38 and 47). Regarding the rejection of the *Anuyoga*, the ten

---

[29] See BALBIR (forthcoming).

[30] Compare HPr, p. 35a.

[31] See also VIJAYAJAMBŪSŪRĪŚVARJĪ (1950: 3, No. 4).

Prakīrṇakas, the *Niśītha* and the *Mahā-niśītha*, he has a rather matter of fact approach. He argues that since all the canonical texts we have date back to the Valabhī council and finally have Devarddhigaṇi as their author, there is absolutely no reason to admit some texts and reject others on account of their being apocryphal.[32] In a way they are all so, and have all been written by *chadmasthas*.[33] Hence he does not hold tight to the view, as some Jains even do today, that the scriptures go back to the Jina's mouth directly. Further, according to him, it is fully contradictory to reject thirteen texts, while admitting certain views which are precisely expressed in them. He devotes a full section to the list of such points and displays his polemical and witty eloquence on this occasion.[34] Besides, the number of recitations (*vācanās*) contained in the *Kalpa-sūtra* (No. 24) and the special status of the *Cheda-sūtras* (No. 89, see below, pp. 269–270) are also briefly dealt with.

– 3 –

There is obviously no possibility to discuss each and every issue in this paper, all the more so since a proper discussion would require a comparison of Samayasundara with other works belonging to the same tradition. I will therefore concentrate on some issues which may be regarded as representative illustrations of the methods at work and are significant for the definition of the Kharatara-gaccha's identity.

As a spokesman of the Kharatara-gaccha, one of Samayasundara's role is to justify the specific positions adopted on certain points by his group and not shared by rival groups. Among such issues are those which concern women. They are of importance since they differentiate the Kharatara-gaccha from other Śvetāmbara orders and contribute to define their identity up to the present day. One is the interdiction made to the nuns of instructing others about the *Cheda-sūtras*. According to Samayasundara, they are only permitted to study these texts for themselves (No. 89). The other concerns restrictions and interdictions applied to laywomen in the field of worship (No. 14 and, partly, 63).[35] In the rather intricate discussion, the author tries to reconcile the scriptural tradition (referring to the

---

[32] SāŚ, No. 38 (p. 77b).

[33] No. 38 (p. 77a).

[34] No. 47 (p. 114b–115b).

[35] On this striking feature, which distinguishes the Kharatara- from the Tapā-gaccha see also VIJAYAJAMBŪSŪRĪŚVARJĪ (1950: No. 34 p. 23–25).

Jñātā-dharma-kathâṅga, the sixth *Aṅga*, where worship of the Jina's image is performed by Draupadī and others[36]) and his own tradition, represented by the works of Jinadattasūri (1075–1154), who has forbidden it, not because he has rejected the tradition, as one might think, but because the contact of the hand of a 'soiled' (*dūṣitā*) young lady could endanger the power inherent in the main image of the temple. Finally, his position comes out as follows: only 'young' ladies are concerned by this restriction, and not girls and old women (*bāla-vṛddha-strī*), which clearly means that the risk of pollution comes from menstruation; moreover, only worship by anointing the Jina's image with sandal paste is forbidden, the other types of *pūjā* are accepted (but no motivation is given for the distinction).

Following the general Indian tendency, Samayasundara normally does not present these specificities as innovations, but, on the contrary, as views well-rooted in the scriptural tradition. Such an attitude implies that those who do not share these views have not properly understood the texts or have missed some important passages which they include. Source-quotations plays an essential part in the demonstration. For instance, whereas all Jain groups count five auspicious events in the lives of all the Jinas—the so-called *pañca-kalyāṇaka*s—the Kharatara-gaccha counts six of them in the case of Mahāvīra. Beside the descent on earth (*cyavana*), the birth (*janma*), the initiation (*dīkṣā*), the Omniscience (*kevala*) and the *nirvāṇa*, their followers add the transfer of the embryo from the Brahmin Devānandā's womb to the Kṣatriya lady Triśalā's womb, and this tradition is valid among them till today.[37] Samayasundara takes note of this divergence and asks the following question: 'Certain people recognise only five auspicious events in the case of Mahāvīra, but the Kharatara-gaccha recognises six, is there a testimony of the scriptures on this point'?[38] His answer is extremely clear cut: 'Since everywhere, in the *sūtra*s, in the Prakrit commentaries, in the Sanskrit commentaries, in the treatises of our own gaccha as well as in the treatises of other gacchas six auspicious events are described (and nothing else), there are indeed six auspicious events.'[39] Reading such

[36] Also quoted by the Tapā-gacchas to defend their position, e.g. SPr, p. 91b (No. 405).

[37] Cf. BABB (1996: 199 n. 7): 'I have heard this event referred to as a 'sixth *kalyāṇak*''; JAINI (1979: 8): 'The Śvetāmbaras consider it true; indeed they sometimes list the time of embryo transfer as a sixth auspicious moment in Mahāvīra's life'; see also VIJAYAJAMBŪSŪRĪŚVARJĪ (1950: No. 84 p. 71).

[38] SāŚ, p. 16a (No. 3): *śrī-mahāvīra-devasya kaiścit kalyāṇaka-pañcakam eva procyate, śrī-kharatara-gacche tu kalyāṇaka-ṣaṭkaṁ, tatra kiṁ siddhântâdi-sākṣyam?*

[39] SāŚ, p. 16a: *ucyate: sarvatra sūtra-cūrṇi-vṛtti-sva-para-gacchīya-prakaraṇâdau kalyāṇaka-ṣaṭkasya eva prarūpaṇāt kalyāṇaka-ṣaṭkam eva.*

an assertive statement one wonders how there were people who dared disagree! Anyway, this list of classes of texts is a kind of introduction announcing the quotations that follow: Samayasundara starts with the *Ācārâṅga-sūtra*, continues with the Prakrit commentary on the *Kalpa-sūtra*, with the Sanskrit commentary on the *Sthānâṅga* and with a variety of other treatises authored by Kharatara-gaccha monks as well as by monks from other groups covering a wide period of time. Thus here the scriptural tradition is considered as a whole and an identical value is attributed to all the texts adduced, independently from their literary form, their origin or their date. In the *Ācārâṅga-sūtra*, as in several of the texts quoted by Samayasundara in this discussion, the objective is to list the main events of Mahāvīra's life in connection with the astrological time when they took place. In this context, six events are mentioned: the *nirvāṇa* is separated from the rest in the wording because the constellation was Svāti, whereas the descent from heaven, the transfer of the embryo, the birth, the departure from worldly life and the attainment of Omniscience all took place under Uttaraphālgunī and are therefore listed together.[40] Since the transfer of the embryo is mentioned in such passages, it is thought sufficient by the Kharatara-gaccha to support their view, although neither the word *kalyāṇaka* which was to become a quasi-technical term, nor any other substantive occurs at this stage. This objection is considered by Samayasundara, but rejected on the basis of texts like the commentaries on *Kalpa-sūtra* where phrases such as 'the date of the six subjects concerning Lord Vardhamāna, descent on earth etc. has been explained'[41] are regarded as proofs since they imply that the transfer of the embryo is included in the list and not given a separate status. The fact that this passage speaks of 'six s u b j e c t s , ' using the word *vatthu* and not *kalyāṇaka*, is not admitted as a possible valid objection and later texts which adduce the traditional list of *kalyāṇaka*s while commenting upon the Prakrit passage are quoted in order to show that the terminological difference is irrelevant.[42] Nevertheless, the argumentation has limitations: when Samayasundara quotes a set of three verses found in Haribhadra's *Pañcāśaka* (PŚ) which explicitly list only five auspicious

---

[40] Āyār 2.15 beginning, very close to the beginning of KS, which reads: ... *paṁca-hatth'uttare yāvi hotthā, taṁ jahā: hatth'uttarāhiṁ cue caittā gabbhaṁ vakkante, hatth'uttarāhiṁ gabbhāo gabbhaṁ sāharie, hatth'uttarāhiṁ jāe, hatth'uttarāhiṁ muṇḍe bhavittā agārāo aṇagāriyaṁ pavvaie, hatth'uttarāhiṁ aṇante aṇuttare ... kevala-vara-nāṇa-daṁsaṇe samuppanne; sāiṇā parinivvue bhayavaṁ*. On the syntax see Jacobi's note in the KS, p. 99: '*paṁcahatthuttare*. I take this word to be a *madhyamapadalopī bahuvrīhi* compound: *pañca kalyāṇakāni uttaraphalgunyāṁ yasya sa*.'

[41] *Cūrṇi* on the KS quoted in SāŚ, p. 16b.

[42] SāŚ, p. 17a.

events in Mahāvīra's life and refers to the corresponding commentary by Abhayadeva which simply confirms the *mūla*,[43] he shows his objectivity since this passage goes against his view and his thought processes. But he finally brushes it aside, saying that none of these texts contains any prohibitory statement and that 'the author and the commentator or the intelligent people know the reason why they think that way.'[44] According to him there is cumulative evidence to show that the transfer of the embryo is on par with the other auspicious events, for none of the teachers has explicitly excluded it from the list. Therefore objections of those who say that it is not a *kalyāṇaka* or that it is included in the other events and needs not be mentioned separately are invalid. Further, he extensively quotes a hymn to Mahāvīra written by an author belonging to the Āgama-gaccha containing the phrase 'Princely son of King Siddhārtha, thus have thee been praised for six auspicious events.'[45] Finally, the number of Mahavira's previous incarnations up to the last being given as six in the commentary of the *Samavāyâṅga* indicates that the transfer from Devānandā's womb to Triśalā's womb counts as one.[46] Hence there is no reason why the Tapā-gacchas should not admit six auspicious events, since scriptures from their famous teachers lead to such a conclusion. The conclusion shows a kind of helplessness: 'They only would know. This is probably due to the loss of the Jina's word or to the loss of the tradition of their own teachers. How is it our fault?'[47]

---

[43] PŚ 9.30 ff. (chap. 9: *yātrā-vidhi*) deals with the subject in the context of worship:

paṁca-mahā-kallāṇā savvesiṁ jiṇāṇa honti ṇiyameṇa / [9.30ab]
gabbhe jamme ya tahā ṇikkhamaṇe ceva ṇāṇa-ṇevvāṇe //
bhuvaṇa-gurūṇa jiṇāṇaṁ kallāṇā honti ṇāyavvā // [9.31]

Samayasundara refers to PŚ 9.33–35. See especially 35bcd:

... gabbhāi-diṇā jaha-kkamaṁ ete /
hatthuttara-joeṇaṁ cauro taha sātiṇā caramo //

[44] SāŚ, p. 17b: *tad-abhiprāyaṁ tu ta eva bahu-śrutā vā jānanti.*

[45] SāŚ, p. 18a:

siddhārtha-rājâṅga-deva-rāja kalyāṇakaiḥ ṣaḍbhir iti stutas tvam,

vs. 7ab. of the sixth canto in the *Sulasācaritra* by Jayatilakasūri.

[46] These incarnations are: (1) as prince Poṭṭila; (2) as a god; (3) as prince Nandana; (4) as a god in the Puṇḍarīka heaven; (5) in the Brahmin Devānandā's womb; (6) in Triśalā's womb (SāŚ, p. 18a-b).

[47] SāŚ, p. 19a: *te eva jānanti, teṣām eva ca jina-vacana-lopasya nija-guru-pāramparya-lopasya ca doṣo bhāvī, kā hāniḥ asmākaṁ iti.* Same pattern on p. 6b (end of No. 1).

There should be an other reason than love for discussion and wish to make his order conspicuous to explain why Samayasundara defends the 'six *kalyāṇaka*s' position so vigorously. In spite of all textual evidence adduced by him, the embryo transfer of Mahāvīra is actually a disturbing point for many Śvetāmbaras.[48] For instance, one of the authorities he quotes in favour of his position takes note of the fact that 'out of sense of shame (*lajjanīyatvāt*) it should not be considered as a *kalyāṇaka* although it is mentioned in the Scriptures.'[49] The verses of Haribhadra's *Pañcāśaka* mentioned above also point in the same direction: if such an author as Haribhadra explicitly says that 'four events of Mahāvīra's life took place under the constellation Uttaraphālguṇī' and 'one under Svāti', clearly against what has been expressed in the *Ācārâṅga* and the *Kalpa-sūtra*, it reveals his intention not to include the transfer in the context of worship. As a matter of fact, even if Śvetāmbaras do not take the transfer as an easy point, which is shown by their including it in the list of ten 'wonders' (*āścarya*),[50] and sometimes ask questions about how it could have actually taken place,[51] they recognise its existence. But they differ as to the place it should have in the religious life and the religious calendar. This distinction between two fields of application is blurred by Samayasundara, his logic being that if it is recognised as an event of Mahāvīra's life it should also be regarded as a worshippable event. The problem is that this position comes up against a block called *pañca-kalyāṇaka* which, as a ritualistic term, has a distinct place in the frame of *pūjā* and forms a well-settled global concept which has been nourished in the course of time by a vast literary body of *pañca-kalyāṇaka*-hymns.[52] In view of the importance of numerical considerations and the part played by the figure 'five' in Jain thinking and religious practice (see the *pañca-parameṣṭhin*s and the *pañca-namaskāra*), the addition of a sixth unit and the fact that, in this case, all 24 Jinas cannot be considered as a globality any longer is a disturbing factor. These are no valid reasons for Samayasundara. The real motivation for his position seems to be his desire to assert the Śvetāmbaras' sectarian identity against the Digambaras. As is

---

[48] On this point see also WILLIAMS (1963: 233): '… but the notation of the *garbhāpahāra* (removal from the womb), which mirrors faithfully the *Kalpasūtra* story, seems to be rather unusual.'

[49] *Sanghapaṭṭakabṛhadvṛtti* quoted SāŚ, p. 17a.

[50] Cf. Ṭhāṇ 10 (§ 777): the transfer is No. 2.

[51] See HPr, p. 26b–27a.

[52] Cf., for instance, the hymn contained in VTīK, p. 100, vs. 1:

namivi jiṇa tāṇa kittemi kallāṇae, paṁca cui jamma vae nāṇa nivvāṇae /

well-known, the transfer of Mahāvīra's embryo is denied by the latter as 'impossible' (*asambhāvya*) because it would imply the four following risks:

1. the responsibility would be of Indra (through the command given to his messenger Hariṇaigameṣin) and not of the *karman*;
2. Mahāvīra would have two fathers;
3. It would speak in favour of Triśalā's unfaithfulness to her husband;
4. There is a physiological difficulty: the growing of an embryo in a place different from the place where it has been conceived.[53]

Under these circumstances, Samayasundara's view is that the Śvetāmbaras should stick to their own views. If they would reject the worship of the transfer as a *kalyāṇaka* on account of its being a 'wonder', they would have to reject also Mallī's femininity. In that case, as he says, it would amount to accept Digambara faith although claiming to be a Śvetāmbara.[54] On the contrary, worshipping this event as a sixth *kalyāṇaka* amounts to its full recognition and is a means to proclaim one's own faith. Although the history of the concept of the six *kalyāṇaka*s needs more investigation, there is a chance that, despite Samayasundara's arguments, it is a clearly motivated innovation of the Kharatara-gaccha explainable through the development of sectarian rivalry and idiosyncrasies, expressing the stiffening of group identity, rather than the persevering of an archaic tradition.

The preceding instance exemplifies what the Kharatara-gaccha is best known for: their insistence on displaying 'a fundamentalist adherence to the scriptures' (DUNDAS (1992: 124)), and finds a translation in cases where the question often asked by Samayasundara is: 'What are the textual references for such and such rite, usage, etc.?'[55] However, to some extent, this attitude, which was strongly attacked by Jain groups opposed to the Kharatara, albeit shared by all of them, needs qualification. Samayasundara helps to do so and to revise the clearcutness of the dichotomy between scriptures and practice. He admits that there exist various sources of authority (*pramāṇa*) and writes at the end of his book:

> *sāmācārī-śatakam idam āsūtritaṁ sūtra-gatyā /*
> *kiṁcit vṛtti-prakaraṇa-vaśāt sampradāyāc ca kiṁcit //*[56]

---

[53] This is the point of view expressed in Meghavijaya's YP, p. 177.

[54] SāŚ, p. 17b: *tathā ca sati śvetāmbara-dharme 'pi digambara-dharmatvâbhyupagamaḥ syād iti*.

[55] E.g. No. 60 (*kva proktam*?).

[56] Author's *Praśasti* vs. 1ab.

First, the distinction he makes here between what he calls *sūtra*s, on the one hand, that is the whole of the 45 *Āgama*s, and commentaries or treatises, on the other hand, shows an awareness of textual history, even if this awareness does not follow the same lines as ours. As a matter of fact, even in cases where Samayasundara finally concludes that all the evidence points to the same result—which he calls *grantha-sammati*[57]—he takes chronology into account and often mentions the dates of composition of the works he adduces for support. This carefulness is meaningful in a process where the establishment of the antiquity of a usage is of importance, and where all 'new' customs are, as such, liable to opponents' critics.[58] It also accounts for the cases where Samayasundara is not content with quoting authors whom he thinks too close to him in time (e.g. Taruṇaprabha) and prefers to refer to an 'old book' (*jīrṇa-grantha*).

Second, the word *sampradāya*. It broadly covers everything else. It means practice in the strict sense. This aspect is considered by Samayasundara, albeit seldom, for instance when he writes that 'the religious acts as performed by the laymen of his time will be taken into account..'.[59] This shows that the opponents probably lack objectivity when they underscore the Kharatara-gaccha's total lack of attention to practice. Mostly, however, *sampradāya* also refers to written sources. But whereas *siddhânta* designates any of the 45 *Āgama*s, plus their commentaries and the treatises based thereupon, *sampradāya* covers scriptures which have been written by the leaders of one's own gaccha, in this case the Kharatara.[60] Apart from the three *sāmācārī*s by Jinavallabha, Jinadatta and Jinapati (see above p. 259, n. 20), the favourite authors mentioned by Samayasundara are Jinaprabhasūri and his *Vidhi-prapā* (fourteenth century) or Taruṇaprabha and his Gujarati *Bālâvabodha* on the six *āvaśyaka*s (composed in V.S. 1411).[61] This works as an implicit and subtle way to introduce novelties without calling them so. For what would be the use of specific

---

[57] E.g. p. 62b (No. 22).

[58] See for example No. 69.

[59] SāŚ, p. 172b: *kiṁcic ca sāmpratam śrāvaka-kriyamāṇa-kriyânusāreṇa*.

[60] Compare CLÉMENTIN-OJHA (1992: 72) about the word *sampradāya*: 'La perpétuation d'une telle tradition théologique et liturgique est assurée par des spécialistes, les *guru*, qui se suivent, tels des chaînons, de génération en génération et constituent une lignée (*paramparā*, 'de l'un à l'autre'). Ce terme témoigne de l'importance accordée à la transmission, et au fait que cette transmission est ininterrompue et ordonnée. C'est de la lignée que le *sampradāya* tire sa consistance et sa stabilité. Il s'organise autour d'elle et se perpétue par elle.'

[61] ViPr, e.g. p. 59b, 63a, 67a, 72a, 73b, 155a, 167b, 170b, 183a; ṢĀBAv, e.g. p. 53a, 59b, 72a, 144b, 155a, 168a, 172b.

texts connected with a specific gaccha, if they would not bring anything different? Several of the points Samayasundara discusses in the course of his work actually start with a question which shows an awareness of this distinction: 'Is (such and such thing) rooted in the scriptures (*siddhântâdi-mūla*) or does it come from the tradition of one's own gaccha?'[62] Both criteria are of unequal value.[63] In an overwhelming number of cases scriptures are the only admissible answer. In others *siddhânta* and *sampradāya* are not exclusive of each other but complement each other, in which case the quotation of authors belonging to the order suggests a creeping evolution.[64] A last batch of much smaller size remains. It covers practices such as the custom of Kharatara-gaccha lay-followers to start studying on the occasion of *sāmāyika* after having performed eight *namaskāra*s. Samayasundara has to admit that 'there is here nothing compelling, that there is no agreement of old books, but that the teacher lineage is the only authority.'[65] He further quotes relevant passages and is content with that, not finding it necessary to explain what motivated the emergence of such a specific usage. The most significant point in this category concerns the correct procedure to be observed for installing images or *stūpa*s of the *gurus*.[66] It is not surprising that 'the authority is the procedure written in the documents transmitted from the teacher's lineage,'[67] for such a tradition is distinctly characteristic of the Kharatara-gaccha, famous for the statues and footprint images of their Dādāgurus.[68] In other words, the only label it can be given is innovation or invention.[69] There are also situations where the lack of textual evidence leads Samayasundara to admit the impossibility of any firm position and the uselessness of discussions: 'There is no basic position anywhere (regarding the number of *vācanā*s of the *Kalpa-sūtra*). Consequently, let those whose group-tradition counts nine *vācanā*s recite it with nine *vācanā*s, and those whose group-tradition counts more than nine recite it with eleven or thirteen. Those who have *dharma* as their aim

---

[62] SāŚ, p. 35b (No. 7), 44a (No. 9), 56a (No. 17).

[63] SāŚ, p. 121b: *kiṁ satyaṁ kaḥ sampradāyaḥ?*

[64] SāŚ, p. 172b.

[65] SāŚ, 71b (No. 31): *atra na kim api niyāmakaṁ, nâpi kâpi jīrṇa-śāstra-sammatiś ca, kiṁ tu guru-sampradāya eva pramāṇam.*

[66] No. 81: *gurūṇāṁ stūpasya pratimāyāś ca pratiṣṭhā kriyate, tatra ko vidhiḥ?*

[67] *atra guru-paramparā-gata-patra-likhita-vidhiḥ pramāṇam.*

[68] See, for instance, BABB (1996: 11 ff.).

[69] Compare, however, SPr, p. 24ab (No. 43) and p. 43b (No. 7) where a number of sources are quoted in support of the existence of *stūpa*s and *pratimā*s dedicated to the gurus.

should not blame anyone, because one follows the own wish of his group-tradition and of its rule.'[70] Thus, lengthy pages of argumentation do not prevent a certain amount of flexibility.

Finally, Samayasundara's awareness of the fact that a religious tradition is not immovable, that practice plays a part in making it slowly change, and that such changes are datable will be illustrated with his discussion of the following question: Does the performance of *kāyôtsarga* in front of *śruta-devatā*s ('goddesses of learning') on the occasion of *pratikramaṇa* come from scriptures (*siddhânta*) or from practice (*ācaraṇā*)?[71] The answer he gives is: 'from practice', but, as usual, this is demonstrated with recourse to… texts. The answer given is in fact not Samayasundara's but is borrowed from Haribhadra's *Pañca-vastuka* (PVa):

> *pamhaṭṭha-mera-sāraṇa viṇao u ṇa pheḍio havai evaṁ /*
> *āyaraṇā suadevaya-m-āīṇaṁ hoi ussaggo //* [491]
> *cāummāsiya varise ussaggo khitta-devayāe u /*
> *pakkhia sijja-surāe karinti caumāsie v' ege //* [492][72]

> —'[The *stutis*] help to remember the forgotten rule. Thus the proper conduct is not transgressed. The practice is to perform *kāyôtsarga* in front of the goddesses of learning and other [deities, such as the *kṣetra-* and the *bhavana*-deities].
> *Kāyôtsarga* in front of a local deity occurs in the four months or in the yearly (*pratikramaṇa*). In the fortnight (*pratikramaṇa*) in front of the deity of the *upāśraya*, some also do that for the four-month (*pratikramaṇa*).'

For Samayasundara, the conclusion is that the practice could go back to the time of the *pūrva-dhara*s and be at least anterior to Haribhadra's death, thus, according to

---

[70] SāŚ, p. 66a: *mūla-pakṣaḥ ko 'pi nāsti kvâpi, paścāt yeṣāṁ nava-vācanānāṁ gaccha-paramparā te nava-vācanābhiḥ vācayantu, atha ca yeṣāṁ gacche navâdhika-vācanānāṁ paramparā te tad ekā-daśakaṁ tat trayo-daśakaṁ vā kurvantu, na kasyâpi nindā kāryā dharmârthibhiḥ gaccha-paramparāyā vyavasthāyāś ca sva-rucy-anuyāyitvāt.*

[71] SāŚ, No. 98 (*śruta-devatâdīnāṁ kāyôtsargaḥ pratikramaṇe kriyate, sa siddhântôktyā ācaraṇayā vā kriyate? ucyate: ācaraṇayā*) and 71.

[72] Both stanzas are also quoted by Samayasundara on p. 146a (No. 71).

the traditional calculation, which he follows, before 529 CE.[73] But one sees the limits of the argumentation: the source-text itself includes an option; the wording shows that divergences are old and opens a door for discussion. This issue differs from those considered earlier in this paper insofar as the purpose is not to justify a specificity of Kharatara-gaccha practice against other groups, but to proclaim that the Kharatara shares with some the opinion that such a *kāyôtsarga* is appropriate, in contradistinction with those who deny it any value. The debate on this question was not new in Samayasundara's time. Evidence showing that it was hot already in the fifteenth century is at hand, but it probably started much earlier since it is actually at the heart of the emergence of the order called Āgama-gaccha or Tristutika-gaccha, who separated from the Pūrṇimā-gaccha in the thirteenth century.[74] This latter name precisely refers to the rejection of 'three hymns' to the *śruta-devatā*s and *kṣetra-devatā*s which had generally come to be included within the *pratikramaṇa* ritual, and are still part of it among most groups. The disputed hymns are:

(1) *sua-devayā bhagavaī, nāṇâvaraṇīya-kamma-sanghāyaṁ* /
tesiṁ khaveu sayayaṁ, jesiṁ suya-sāyare bhattī //

'May the venerable goddess of learning always annihilate the mass of knowledge-impending *karman*s of those who have devotion to the ocean of learning.'

(2) *jīse khitte sāhū daṁsaṇa-nāṇehiṁ caraṇa-sahiehiṁ* /
sāhanti mukkha-maggaṁ sā devī harau duriāiṁ //

'May the goddess in whose area monks are trying to attain the path of Emancipation through right faith and right knoweldge, as well as right conduct, remove the obstacles.'

(3) *jñānâdi-guṇa-yutānāṁ, nityaṁ svādhyāya-saṁyama-ratānāṁ* /
vidadhātu bhuvana-devī śivaṁ sarva-sādhūnāṁ //

'May the goddess of the monks' lodging (see above, p. 270: *sijja-surā*) bestow prosperity to all the monks who are endowed with qualities

---

[73] SāŚ, p. 186b–187a. This is the traditional view about Haribhadra's date, equivalent to V.S. 585 or Vīra S. 1055 (the *Pūrva*s being said to have disappeared 1000 years after Mahāvīra's *nirvāṇa*).

[74] For information collected from colophons and inscriptions, in a way usual to the author, see SHIVAPRASAD (1991); see also PP chap. 7, p. 5–6: according to Dharmasāgara, Śīlagaṇa and Devabhadra, the two leaders who founded the movement, separated from the Pūrṇimā-gaccha, joined the Añcala-gaccha and left it when they had become *ācārya*s.

such as knowledge, etc. and who are fully satisfied with study and restraint.'[75]

The importance of the debate lies in the fact that it is crucial both to the development of Jainism and to its identity. Those who argue against worshipping the *śruta-devatās* and all the associated deities—for *śruta-devatā* is a generic label—represent a kind of puritanism. They maintain that it is inappropriate to orthodox believers (*samyag-dṛś*) and might lead them on the verge of *mithyātva*. Further, they challenge the capacity of such deities to produce the required destruction of *karman* and to generate destruction of new existences which are stated in the relevant stanzas. On the other hand, the Tapā-gaccha and the Kharatara-gaccha traditionally admit that these deities protect and help the Teaching, deserve a proper worship and are not antagonistic to the context of religious duties (*āvaśyakas*, *kriyās*). This explains that Samayasundara's discussion of the issue lacks complete originality: it is an almost word-to-word repetition of what the Tapā-gaccha monk Kulamaṇḍanasūri wrote in the fifteenth century, himself more or less adjusting what one of his colleagues wrote earlier in a direct refutation of the Añcalas and the Tristutikas, and followed by other polemicists such as Dharmasāgara.[76] Thus this is a problem with a well-grounded tradition of debate involving a stock of extracts and quotations which are used by all authors[77]. The

---

[75] These three stanzas are available in all *pratikramaṇa* handbooks. There are some options: (1) is to be recited only by men and is replaced by:

> *kamala-dala-vipula-nayanā, kamala-mukhī kamala-garbha-sama-gaurī,*
> *kamalè sthitā bhagavatī, dadātu śruta-devatā siddhiṁ* —
>
> —'May the venerable goddess of learning whose eyes are as wide as the petal of a lotus, whose face is like a lotus, who is as fair as the inner part of the lotus, who is seated on the lotus give all success'—

to be recited by women; (2) is normally to be recited only by men and is replaced by a Sanskrit variant meant for women in daily *pratikramaṇa* and the same variant for men in the fortnight *pratikramaṇa*; (3) is normally reserved for the fortnight *pratikramaṇa*.

[76] SāŚ, No. 98 is to be compared with VĀS, p. 58–59, ŚVVin, fol. 17a-b of the London ms. (British Library Or. 2120 B) and fol. 18b–19a of the Ahmedabad ms. (L.D. Institute of Indology No. 4617), as well as with PPa, part 2, chap. 7, especially p. 15.

[77] The two stanzas from the *Pañca-vastuka* are quoted or referred to by Harṣabhūṣaṇagaṇi, Kulamaṇḍanasūri, Dharmasāgara (PP p. 15b on vs. 20), and Śubhavijaya's SPr (p. 91a No. 400). The first one is based on a prose sentence found in the *Āvaśyaka-vṛtti* (p. 794b). But although Harṣabhūṣaṇagaṇi, Kulamaṇḍanasūri and Dharmasāgara ascribe it to the *Āvaśyaka-niryukti*, it is not traceable as a verse in the recensions including Haribhadra's commentary or the *cūrṇi*.

Tapā- and Kharatara-gacchas refer to the scriptural tradition where such a worship is taught, were high credit is given to these deities, quote examples of great monks who where helped by them[78] and answer that destruction of *karman* will occur, provided the *kāyôtsarga* is accompanied by auspicious meditation (*śubha-dhyāna*). In short, the opposition is between a trend resisting to the growing cult of deities viewed as a kind of threat, even if *śruta-devatā*s are Jain and different from *kula-devatā*s, and the always growing inclusion of various hymns in the *pratikramaṇa*, and a trend which sees no reason for their exclusion from the realm of strictly Jain practices since they are on par with the Jinas and play a specific role in the spiritual evolution of the devotees. However, there are some difficulties: the old versions of the *āvaśyaka*-ritual transmitted by the *Āvaśyaka-niryukti* and its old commentaries (*cūrṇi* and Haribhadra), as we have them, are not as clear as the later (or modern) texts where one reads the formulas: *sua-devayāe karemi kāussaggaṁ*, *bhuvaṇa-devayāe k. k.* and *khitta-devayāe k. k.*, to be pronounced before the above mentioned stanzas.

To conclude: the examination of texts such as the *Sāmācārī-śataka* and the close study of their internal system may be helpful in defining how Jains themselves view the evolution of their practice and the various degrees of authority they ascribe to their rich textual tradition. The prevalent tendency is to see changes occurring in one's own groups as restorations, and changes made by others as lapses. This explains why in spite of numerous debates each group mostly sticks to their conclusions without really managing to convince their opponents. On the other hand, such works form a tradition of debate which shows a stage where any point could become a question, where anything in the wording of a text, especially if not totally tight, could open a road for discussion.

[78] Cf. PP p. 7 and 13 referring to the ways Hemacandra benefited from the worship of Sarasvatī.

APPENDIX

Chronology of some Śvetāmbara representatives of the *praśnôttara*-genre

date	title	author, affiliation
V.S. 1442	*Vicārâmṛta-saṅgraha* (VĀS)	Kulamaṇḍana, Tapā-gaccha
V.S. 1480	*Śrāddha-vidhi-viniścaya* (ŚVVin)	Harṣabhūṣaṇagaṇi, Tapā-gaccha [see BALBIR (forthcoming)]
?	*Sārdha-śataka-praśnôttara*	Merusundara-upādhyāya, Kharatara-gaccha
	[apparently unpublished and not easily found in standard catalogue of mss., but quoted at least twice by Samayasundara, p. 75a and 128a, with indication that the author was a contemporary of the Kharatara pontiff Jinacandrasūri (V.S. 1514–30), successor of Jinaprabhasūri (V.S. 1475–1514; see KLATT (1894: 173) for these dates)). Samayasundara quotes *praśna* No. 64 (about *dvidala*s) and No. 49 (about *abhakṣya* foodstuff) of this work. The extracts show that its language is Old Gujarati]	
?	*Hīra-praśna* (HPr)	Kīrtivijayagaṇi, Tapā-gaccha
	[no precise date of composition, but anyway prior to Samayasundara who refers to it]	
V.S. 1672	*Sāmācārī-śataka* (SāŚ)	Samayasundara, Kharatara-gaccha
[V.S. 1672	*Viśeṣa-śataka*	Samayasundara, Kharatara-gaccha]
[V.S. 1674	*Vicāra-śataka*	Samayasundara, Kharatara-gaccha]
[V.S. 1685	*Viśeṣa-saṅgraha*	Samayasundara, Kharatara-gaccha]
[V.S. 1685	*Visaṁvāda-śataka*	Samayasundara, Kharatara-gaccha
?	*Sena-praśna* (SPr)	Śubhavijayagaṇi, Tapā-gaccha
V.S. 1690	*Vicāra-ratnākara*	Kīrtivijayagaṇi, Tapā-gaccha
V.S. 1851	*Praśnôttara-sārdha-śataka* (PSŚ)	Kṣamākalyāṇa, Kharatara-gaccha
V.S. 2054	*Vividha Praśnottar*	VIJAYADĀNASŪRĪŚVARJĪ

Affiliated works

date	title	author, affiliation
V.S. 1629	*Pravacana-parīkṣā* (PPa)	Dharmasāgara, Tapā-gaccha
2nd half of 17th c.	*Yukti-prabodha* (YP)	Upādhyāya Meghavijaya, Tapā-gaccha

BIBLIOGRAPHY

ĀvVṛ = *Āvaśyaka-vṛtti*. *Agamodaya Samiti*, Bombay 1916–1917.

BABB 1996 = Babb, Lawrence A.: *Absent Lord. Ascetics and Kings in a Jain Ritual Culture*. University of California Press, Berkeley – Los Angeles – London 1996.

BALBIR 1999 = Balbir, Nalini: 'About a Jain Polemical Work of the 17th Century.' In: *Approaches to Jaina Studies: Philosophy, Logic, Rituals and Symbols*. [Proceedings of the International Conference on Approaches to Jaina Studies: Philosophy, Logic, Rituals and Symbols, 31.03–2.04.1995 Toronto]. Ed. N.K. Wagle and Olle Qvarnström. Centre for South Asian Studies, University of Toronto. *South Asian Studies Papers* 11, Toronto 1999: 1–18.

BALBIR 2000a = Balbir, Nalini: 'Le bâton monastique jaina: fonction, symbolisme, controverses.' *Vividharatna-karaṇḍaka*. Festschrift für A. Mette. Herausgegeben von Christine Chojnacki, Jens-Uwe Hartmann und Volker Tschannerl. 'Indica et Tibetica', Swisttal – Odendorf 2000: 17–56.

BALBIR 2000b = Balbir, Nalini: 'Polémiques autour du "voile buccal" des laïcs: la contribution de Vardhamānasūri.' *Bulletin d'Etudes Indiennes* 17–18 (1999–2000) 113–152.

BALBIR (forthcoming) = Balbir, Nalini: 'The Ancalagaccha viewed from inside and outside.' Prof. P.S. Jaini Felicitation Volume, Berkeley.

CANDRAPRABHĀSĀGARA 1986 = Muni Candraprabhāsāgara: *Mahopādhyāya Samayasundara: vyaktitva evaṁ kṛtitva*. Calcutta 1986 [in Hindi].

CLÉMENTIN-OJHA 1992 = Clémentin-Ojha, Catherine: 'Qu'est-ce qu'être orthodoxe? Le cas des ascètes vishnouïtes du *Catuḥ-sampradāya*.' *Ascèse et renoncement en Inde*. Textes réunis et introduction par S. Bouez. L'Harmattan, Paris 1992: 71–85.

DAVE 1998 = Dave, Vasantaray B.: *Kavi Samayasundara: ek abhyāsa*. Sharadaben Chimanbhai Educational Research Centre, Ahmedabad 1998. [in Gujarati].

DESAI 1941 = Desai, Mohanlal Dalichand (ed.): *Bhānucandra Carita by his pupil Gaṇi Siddhicandra Upādhyāya*, critically edited ... with elaborate introduction, summary, appendices, indices etc. *Singhi Jaina Series* 15, Ahmedabad – Calcutta 1941.

DUNDAS 1992 = Dundas, Paul: *The Jains*. The Library of Religious Beliefs and Practices, Routledge, London – New York 1992.

GUÉRINOT 1906 = Guérinot, Armand-Albert: *Essai de bibliographie jaina*. E. Leroux, Paris 1906.

HPr = Kīrtivijayagaṇi: *Hīra-praśna*. Mahôpādhyāya-śrī-Kīrtivijayagaṇi-samuccitaḥ *Hīra-praśnâpara-nāmā Praśnôttara-samuccayaḥ*. Hiralal Hamsaraj, Jamnagar 1917.

JAINI 1979 = Jaini, Padmanabh S.: *The Jaina Path of Purification*. University of California Press, Berkeley—Los Angeles—London 1979. [Reprinted: Motilal Banarsidass, Delhi 1998].

KLATT 1894 = Klatt, Johannes: 'The Samachari-Satakam of Samayasundara and Pattavalis of the Anchala-Gachchha and other Gachchhas.' [Revised with Additions by Ernst Leumann]. *Indian Antiquary* 23 (July 1894) 169–183. [169–174 only for Samayasundara's work].

KS = *Kalpa-sūtra. The Kalpasûtra of Bhadrabâhu*. Edited with and Introduction, Notes and a Prākṛit-Saṁskṛit Glossary by Hermann Jacobi. *Abhandlungen für die Kunde des Morgenlandes* 7/1, Leipzig 1879. [Reprinted: Nendeln, Liechtenstein 1966].

PLUTAT 1998 = Plutat, Birte: *Catalogue of the Papers of Ernst Leumann in the Institute for the Culture and History of India and Tibet, University of Hamburg. Alt- und Neu-Indische Studien* herausgegeben vom Institut für Kultur und Geschichte Indiens und Tibets an der Universität Hamburg 49, Franz Steiner Verlag, Stuttgart 1998.

PPa = Dharmasāgara: *Pravacana-parīkṣā*. Surat 1937. [Dvitīyo bhāgaḥ: chap. 7, p. 5–21 devoted to the Āgama-gaccha].

PŚ = Haribhadra: *Pañcāśaka*. Prakrit text with Hindi translation by Dinanath Sharma. *P.V. Research Institute Series* 92, P.V. Research Institute, Varanasi 1997.

PSŚ = Kṣamākalyāṇa: *Praśnôttara-sārdha-śataka*. Jinadatta Sūri Pustakoddhāra Fund Series, Surat 1930.

PVa = Haribhadra: *Pañca-vastuka*. Jinaśāsana Ārādhanā Trust, Bombay V.S. 2515.

RAU 1982 = Rau, Wilhelm: *Bilder 135 Deutscher Indologen*. [2. Auflage von 'Bilder hundert deutscher Indologen']. *Glasenapp-Stiftung Band* 23, Wiesbaden 1982.

ṢĀBAv = Taruṇaprabha: *Ṣaḍ-āvaśyaka-bālâvabodha-vṛtti*. Śrī-Taruṇaprabhâcārya-kṛta *Ṣaḍāvaśyakabālāvabodhavṛtti*. Ed. by Prabodha Becaradāsa Paṇḍita. *Singhi Jaina Series* 71, Bombay 1976.

SāŚ = Samayasundaragaṇi: *Sāmācārī-śataka*. Samayasundaragaṇi-viracitaṁ *Śrī-Sāmācārī-śatakam*. Śrī-Jinadattasūri prācīna Pustakoddhāra Fund 41, Surat 1939.

SATYAVRAT 1994 = Satyavrat: 'Samayasundara And His Contribution to Sanskrit literature,'. *Studies in Jaina Sanskrit literature*. Eastern Book Linkers, Delhi 1994: 176–189.

SHIVAPRASAD 1991 = Shivaprasad: 'Āgamika gaccha / prācīna Tristutika gaccha kā saṁkṣipta itihāsa.' *Aspects of Jainology: vol. III*. Pt. Dalsukhbhai Malvania Felicitation Volume I. P.V. Research Institute, Varanasi 1991: 241–284.

SPr = Śubhavijayagaṇi: *Sena-praśna*. Śrī-Vijayasenasūri-prāsādita-paṇḍita-Śubhavijaya-saṅkalita-praśnôttara-mayaḥ *Praśnôttara-ratnâkaraḥ (Sena-praśnaḥ)*. Jinaśāsana Ārādhanā Trust, Bombay V.S. 2045.

ŚVVin = Harṣabhūṣaṇagaṇi: *Śrāddha-vidhi-viniścaya*. See: BALBIR (forthcoming).

Ṭhāṇ = *Ṭhāṇaṁga-sutta* [*Sthānâṅga-sūtra*]. *Sthānâṅgasūtram Samavāyâṅgasūtraṁ ca*. Ed. Muni Jambuvijaya. *Jaina-āgama-granthamālā* 3, Motilal Banarasidass Publishers, Delhi 1985.

TRIPATHI 1975 = Tripathi, Candrabhal: *Catalogue of the Jaina Manuscripts at Strasbourg*. Leiden – Brill 1975.

VIJAYADĀNA-SŪRĪŚVARJĪ 1938 = Ācārya Vijayadānasūrīśvarjī: *Vividha Praśnottar*. Vibhāg 1–2. Reprinted ed. by Muni Mahābodhivijaya. Jinaśāsana Ārādhanā Trust, Bombay V.S. 2054.

VIJAYAJAMBŪ-SŪRĪŚVARJĪ 1950 = *Cirantana muni-mahattama-kṛta prācīna gujarātī bola-saṅgraha-dvaya-yukta ŚrīTapā-Kharatara-bheda*. Bhāṣākara: Āc. Śrīmad-Vijayajambūsūrīśvarjī mahārāj. *Śrī-Ātma-Kaṁala-Dāna-Prema-Jambūsūrijī Jaina Granthamālā* 16, Satya nuṁ kiraṇa 12; Śrī Muktābāi Jñānamandira, Dabhoi, V.S. 2007, Vīra S. 2477.

WILLIAMS 1963 = Williams, Richard: *Jaina Yoga*. London, 1963. [Reprinted: Motilal Banarsidass, Delhi 1983].

VĀS Kulamaṇḍanasūri: *Vicārâmṛta-saṅgraha*. *Śrī-Vicārāmṛta-sāra-saṁgrahaḥ* Jinadarśana-sūtrârtha-pākṣika-cāturmāsika-mukha-vastrikâdi-sthāpanânta-viṣaya-sūtrâlāpaka-mayaḥ. Kesharimalji, V.S. 1993, Vīra S. 2463, 1936 A.D.

ViPr = Jinaprabhasūri: *Vidhi-prapā*. *Vidhi-(mārga-)prapā*. Śrīmaj-Jinaprabhasūri-viracitā *Vidhi-mārga-prapā* nāma suvihita Sāmācārī. Ed. by Muni Jinavijaya. Śrī-Jinadattasūri prācīna Pustakoddhāra Fund 44, Bombay 1941.

YP = Meghavijaya Upādhyāya: *Yukti-prabodha*. With the author's commentary. Jinaśāsana Ārādhanā Trust, Bombay V.S. 2045 Ratlam 1928].

Dyānatrāy: An Eighteenth Century Digambara Mystical Poet*

JOHN E. CORT

1. Introduction

Dyānatrāy was a Digambara Jaina poet who composed in the Brāj language. He lived from 1676 to 1726. Dyānatrāy was born in the Goyal *gotra* of the Agravāl caste in Agra, although the family was originally from the village of Lālpur. We know that his father's name was Śyāmdās, and that he died when Dyānatrāy was only nine years old. We also know that his paternal grandfather's name was Vīrdās. He was well-trained in the traditional north Indian Digambara lay *paṇḍit* tradition. His teachers in Jainism were Paṇḍit Bihārīdās and Paṇḍit Mānsiṁh, with whom he started to study at the age of thirteen. Included in his studies were Sanskrit and Prakrit. He was married in 1691 when he was fifteen. He had seven sons and three daughters. His mother died in 1720 at Sammet Śikhar, where she had gone on pilgrimage.[1]

In a 1952 article, Paṇḍit Paramānand ŚĀSTRĪ provides some other interesting details of Dyānatrāy's life that allow us to see his personality as reflected in the Digambara religious imagination. Paṇḍit Paramānand ŚĀSTRĪ does not indicate any sources for his information; it may well come from north Indian Digambara oral traditions. According to ŚĀSTRĪ, Dyānatrāy became a devotee of the goddess Padmāvatī to fulfil his heart's desires. In return for his worship and devotion she gave him a direct vision, and asked him what he wanted. He said he did not want anything for himself, such as worldly glory or power. He just wanted that all beings in the world should become Jaina. The goddess replied that even the Jinas had been unable to accomplish this feat, and so he should instead ask for something that was within her power to give. He then asked for her help in composing the *Carcā-śataka*, a mystical text.

---

* An earlier version appeared in *Mahāvīr Jayantī Smārikā* 37 (2000), English Section 1–9. I thank the editor Gyan Chand Biltiwala for all of his assistance during research on Digambara Jain ritual cultures in 1999–2000, and for permission to reprint this material here.

[1] Basic information on Dyānatrāy's life comes from P. JAIN (1984), R. JAIN (1995), V. JAIN (1996), KĀSLĪVĀL (1965), PRACAṆḌIYĀ (1987), and P. ŚĀSTRĪ (1952). Most of this information comes from an anthology of Dyānatrāy's poetry, the *Dharmvilās*, compiled in 1727 by Paṇḍit Jagatrāy.

Essays in Jaina Philosophy and Religion.
Warsaw Indological Studies, Volume 2 (2002), pp. 279–295.

ŚĀSTRĪ (1952: 198–9) also records a curious story concerning Dyānatrāy's death:

> It is said that the poet was absorbed in meditation. The rats that lived in his seat were trapped by the poet and could not get out. They started to jump at his body and bite him, as a result of which he died. In the morning his sons opened the door to his room and found him dead.

We know that Dyānatrāy lived in both Agra and Delhi, two of the great centres of north Indian Digambara culture of his time. He met with circles of laymen who were interested in the *Adhyātma* (mystical[2]) movement in both cities; among his younger contemporaries were the important *Adhyātma* intellectuals Bhūdardās and Daulatrām.[3] The *Adhyātma* movement rose to a prominent position in north Indian Digambara society under the leadership of Banārsīdās in Agra in the 1620s.[4] This movement was the base for the current Terāpanth of the north Indian Digambara community, which started to come to prominence in the mid-seventeenth century. But it is clear that Dyānatrāy was not directly involved in this latter more conservative movement, for one of the cardinal tenets of the Terāpanth has always been a strong critique of goddess worship, whereas Dyānatrāy was clearly a devotee of both Padmāvatī and Sarasvatī. Agra and Delhi were also strongholds of the more traditional Bīspanth Digambara community, and there were seats of *bhaṭṭārak*s, the domesticated monastic leaders of the Bīspanth, in both cities.

Dyānatrāy authored the liturgies for many *pūjā*s or rites of worship of Jina images, as well as at least ninety separate *pad*s or devotional poems. While his poetry is in Braj, from his vocabulary it is evident that he also knew Gujarati and Urdu, in addition to the classical languages of Sanskrit and Prakrit. He probably also knew Apabhraṁśa; traditional sources rarely distinguish it from Prakrit.

His poetry was located at the confluence of four different streams of influence. One was that of the Digambara mystical tradition.[5] This tradition is rooted in the

---

[2] In terming Dyānatrāy a 'mystical' poet, I do not intend to enter into the on-going scholarly debates concerning the meaning and utility of 'mysticism' as a category in the study of religion; see the four volumes edited by Steven T. KATZ, most recently (2000). Rather, I simply use the term to refer to an emphasis on inner spiritual experience as the core of religious life.

[3] On Bhūdardās see N.J. ŚĀSTRĪ (1997), and on Daulatrām see KĀSLĪVĀL (1973).

[4] On Banārsīdās and the *Adhyātma* movement, see R.K. JAIN (1966) and LATH (1981). BHĀRILL (1973) is also valuable on the rise of the Terāpanth.

[5] The study of the Digambara mystical tradition has been relatively neglected in Western-language scholarship. For information on some of the most important Digambara mystics, see CAILLAT (1975–76), (1976a), (1976b), and (2002); BALBIR–CAILLAT (1999); and HARDY (1994). UPADHYE (1973) remains an indispensable source.

writings of Kundakunda, the author of a number of important Digambara texts who lived sometime in the first half millennium CE.[6] After Kundakunda, the two great representatives of this tradition are the medieval poets Yogīndu and Rāmasiṁha.[7] In the words of Paul DUNDAS (1992: 91), Kundakunda taught 'the centrality of inward experience and the reorientation of all religious practice to focus upon the self.' In particular, the Digambara mystical tradition has emphasised the need for what Dyānatrāy, following earlier authors, terms *bhed-jñān* or *bhed-vijñān*, 'knowledge of the difference.' This is a deep abiding knowledge of the fundamental difference between the innately pure soul and everything else. To quote DUNDAS again (1992: 92),

> 'For Kuṇḍakunda, the soul is the only true and ultimate category in existence which, as such, provides a particular standpoint (*naya*), the pivotal point, called either "certain" (*nishcaya*), "supreme" (*paramartha*) or "pure" (*shuddha*), with reference to which all other entities, beliefs and practices can be judged ... Everything else in the universe has a purely transactional and provisional value and is to be viewed from the perspective of a worldly (*vyavahara*) standpoint. The Jaina ascetic should therefore direct his energies to inner experience.'

In the words of Yogīndu and Rāmasiṁha, the person should realise that there is no difference between his own soul and the souls of the enlightened Tīrthaṅkaras and Siddhas. This realisation is encapsulated in the simple phrase *so 'ham*, 'I am that,' an equation that obviously echoes the Upaniṣadic *mahā-vākya* ('great utterance') of *tat tvam asi*, 'you are that,' and the Śaivite mystical utterance of *śivo 'ham*, 'I am Śiva.' At a number of places in his *pad*s Dyānatrāy explicitly tells the religious seeker that it is essential to know the difference between soul and everything else, and to meditate upon 'I am that,' i.e. 'in reality I am only soul,' if he wants to experience spiritual enlightenment and liberation.

[6] The dates for Kundakunda have been much debated, with dates as early as the first century CE and as late as the eighth century proposed. The dating of most early Digambara authors is in a state of scholarly uncertainty. The best English-language studies of the philosophy that underlies Kundakunda's mystical thought are BHATT (1974) and JOHNSON (1995).

[7] BALBIR–CAILLAT (1999: 27) give an approximate date for Yogīndu of the sixth century. Rāmasiṁha is dated to sometime between the ninth and eleventh centuries. Digambaras also read the early philosopher Samantabhadra and the third-century *Tattvârtha-sūtra* of Umāsvāti as falling within this lineage of mystics. We can be fairly certain that Dyānatrāy was familiar with all of these authors, as many of their texts received vernacular commentaries by lay Digambara scholars in North India during this time, and he composed a Braj translation of Samantabhadra's *Svayambhū-stotra*.

Dyānatrāy is also firmly within the Digambara liturgical tradition. He was the author of the texts to be sung for at least a dozen different Digambara rituals (*pūjā*) of worship of Jina images. His most popular liturgy is addressed to the worship of the fundamental triad of god, scripture and teacher (*dev, śāstra, guru*).[8] This is recited and sung by thousands of north Indian Digambara Jainas in their daily eightfold worship in the temple. It is translated below. His other liturgies include the following, each of which addresses a cardinal concept in Jaina metaphysics or sacred geography:

—the twenty Tīrthaṅkaras currently alive in various parts of the universe;
—the enlightened souls (*siddha*);
—the five Mount Merus;
—the continent of Nandīśvar;
—the three gems of right faith, knowledge, and conduct;
—the sixteen aspirations for doing good for all living beings;
—the ten characteristics of *dharma*;
—the places where the Jinas attained *nirvāṇa*;
—the goddess Sarasvatī (as scripture incarnate).

By worshipping the virtues (*guṇ*) embodied in the particular concepts, the worshiper both learns the basic of Jaina metaphysics and advances along the path to liberation. Three centuries later Dyānatrāy's liturgies remain among the most popular for Digambaras in the Hindi speaking areas of north India, and he can be said to have provided the foundation for all later Hindi Digambara liturgical poets.

A third stream is that of Jaina devotional poetry. For two thousand years Jainas have been writing devotional poems in Sanskrit, Prakrit, Apabhraṁśa, and vernacular languages. A careful reading of Dyānatrāy's poems makes it clear that he was conversant with this tradition. In his 'God, Scripture and Teacher Pūjā,' for example, the first verse in the eightfold offering describes various divine and human kings bowing to the feet of the Jina and the resulting inter-reflected lustre of the Jina's feet and the kings' crowns. This verse is influenced directly by the first verse of Mānatuṅga's Sanskrit *Bhaktâmara-stotra*, probably the most popular of all Jaina hymns, in which he employs the same visual image.

The fourth stream is that of Hindi poetry of the *sant*s or late medieval 'saints.' Literary scholars have broadly characterised Hindi poetry according to whether it is *saguṇ* or *nirguṇ*, that is, whether it characterises God as having definable characteristics or as being beyond all human attempts at portrayal. We can see elements of both strands of Hindi poetry in the songs of Dyānatrāy. His *pūjā*s are

[8] This triad is foundational for Digambara faith, and forms the structure for many oral and written presentations of the tradition. See, for example, S.L. JAIN (1994).

addressed to images, and so to physical representations of the virtues (*guṇ*) of dispassion, enlightenment, and liberation which the disembodied Jinas have realised in their state of pure soul. In the last portion of the liturgy, the 'Garland of Victory' sung during the offering of a lamp (*āratī*), the worshiper explicitly refers to the forty-six virtues of the Jinas, as well as the virtues of the three ranks within the mendicant hierarchy, the *ācārya*, *upādhyāya*, and *sādhu*. In his independent poems, Dyānatrāy strongly shows the influence of the *nirguṇ sant* poets such as Kabīr, Nānak, Dādū, and Ravidās.[9] Whereas the liturgies are directly involved in the elaborate ritual culture of temples, the *pad*s point the worshiper away from a reliance upon the external rituals of Jainism. Instead, they emphasise the need for the faithful Jaina to realise within himself the fundamental truth that in essence he is only soul. Dyānatrāy does not, however, totally reject the realm of *vyavahāra* and its emphasis on rituals. For example, he calls upon the worshiper to remember (*smaraṇ*) and recite (*jap*) the virtues of the perfect soul, and to take the five great vows (*mahā-vrat*) of the world-renouncing mendicant.[10] But he adds that these will avail the person little if he does not have a direct experience of his essential nature as pure soul. Recent scholarship on *nirguṇ* and *saguṇ* poetry in the Hindu and Sikh traditions has shown that *nirguṇ* and *saguṇ* are more modalities within a common poetic genre than they are sharply contrasting or opposing poles.[11] This is equally true of Dyānatrāy. In some poems he is more of a *saguṇ* poet, in others more a *nirguṇ* poet, and both fit together seamlessly in his total oeuvre.

[9] There may well be complicated genealogies of influence here. CAILLAT (1976b: 65), HARDY (1994: 14), S. JAIN (1996), and VAUDEVILLE (1993), among others, have commented on the many similarities between the *nirguṇ* poetry of *sant*s such as Kabīr and Nānak and the earlier Apabhraṁśa poetry of Jain poets such as Yogīndu and Rāmasiṁha. The Jain Apabhraṁśa poets bear further similarities to the Buddhist mystical poets Saraha and Kāṇha, as well as the various Siddhas and Nāth Yogīs, who also composed in Apabhraṁśa, and all of whom influenced the later Hindu *sant*s. Given the difficulties in dating authors, producing critical editions, and establishing clear lines of influence, it is perhaps best simply to agree with UPADHYE (1973: 31), that all of these poets have 'inherited a common stock of ideas and terminology which appear and re-appear in the mystical works of different religions.' At the same time, the technical vocabulary of all the Jain mystical poets makes it clear that they adhere to Jain metaphysics and conduct.

[10] Given that there were no full-fledged naked *muni*s in north India at this time, Dyānatrāy's exhortation to take the five great vows was largely rhetorical, but these devotional and liturgical descriptions of the ideal guru provided fertile ground for the twentieth century renaissance of the naked *muni* tradition in north India.

[11] See HAWLEY (1984) and HAWLEY–JUERGENSMEYER (1988).

2. A *Saguṇ* Liturgy: 'The Worship of God, Scripture and Teacher'[12]

Part One: The Establishment (*sthāpnā*)

First is the god Arhant,
then the true scripture;
the unbound guru is the third great one
on the road to liberation city.

The man of faith should meditate
on the three gems.
Devotion to these three is grace:
you will attain the supreme state.

I worship the feet of the Arhant,
I worship the feet of the guru,
I worship the goddess Sarasvatī
every day in eight ways.

(Mantra:)

Oṁ hrīṁ the collectivity of god, scripture and guru incarnate incarnate here *saṁvauṣaṭ*.
Oṁ hrīṁ the collectivity of god, scripture and guru stay stay here *ṭhah ṭhah*.
Oṁ hrīṁ the collectivity of god, scripture and guru be be near me *vaṣaṭ*.

Part Two: The Eightfold Offering (*aṣṭak*)

The kings of gods
the kings of serpents
and the kings of men
bow to venerate your glorious feet,
your feet shining
with an enchanting lustre
like radiant gold.

They bring pitchers
from the ocean of milk

[12] There are many printings of Dyānatrāy's *Dev-Śāstra-Guru Pūjā*. I have used that at D. ŚĀSTRĪ (1997: 38–46).

and dance in front of you.
Every day I worship the Arhant,
the true scripture,
and the unbound guru.

Purity is the essence of water,
so be sure all the offerings are pure.
I worship the supreme state:
god, scripture, and guru, these three.

Oṁ hrīṁ I offer water to god, scripture and guru for the destruction of birth, old age and death *svāhā*.

Creatures in all the three worlds
burn in great pain.
You speak the truth
to cure their misfortune,
to cool their pain.
This sandalwood is pure and fragrant.
I offer it to rid myself
of the desire to wander.
Every day I worship the Arhant,
the true scripture,
and the unbound guru.

Sandalwood soothes the burning.
I worship the supreme state:
god, scripture, and guru, these three.

Oṁ hrīṁ I offer sandalwood to god, scripture and guru for the destruction of the searing pain of rebirth *svāhā*.

The true rite
is the only way to cross
the uncrossable ocean of rebirth.
Devotion is a steady boat,
a supremely pure boat.
I offer unbroken white rice.
I seek the three virtues.
Every day I worship the Arhant,
the true scripture,
and the unbound guru.

The rice is white,
it smells so sweet.

I have selected only fine unbroken grains.
I worship the supreme state:
god, scripture, and guru, these three.

Oṁ hrīṁ I offer rice to god, scripture and guru to attain the permanent state *svāhā*.

You are the sun.
You shine in the lotus heart
of the virtuous man of faith.
In a clear voice
you explain the conduct
that is supreme
among the three virtues.
I seek to save myself
from the harsh suffering
of birth after birth.
I bring jasmine and lotus,
all sorts of flowers.
Every day I worship the Arhant,
the true scripture,
and the unbound guru.

Each has a unique fragrance
to captivate the bees.
I worship the supreme state:
god, scripture, and guru, these three.

Oṁ hrīṁ I offer flowers to god, scripture and guru to destroy Kāma's arrows *svāhā*.

The serpent is intoxicated
by Kāma's lustful power
and so knows no end to thirst.
But this fearsome foe
is easily vanquished by Garuḍa.
I have cooked fine food
in pure ghee
and seasoned it with all six flavours.
Every day I worship the Arhant,
the true scripture,
and the unbound guru.

The food with all its savoury flavours
tastes fresh and new.

I worship the supreme state:
god, scripture, and guru, these three.

Oṁ hrīṁ I offer food to god, scripture and guru to destroy the pangs of hunger *svāhā*.

The darkness of delusion is powerful,
it undermines all our efforts.
The flame of the lamp of knowledge
destroys all *karma*.
I bring a shining lamp
on a golden tray.
Every day I worship the Arhant,
the true scripture,
and the unbound guru.

A flame that illuminates itself,
a lamp that leaves no darkness.
I worship the supreme state:
god, scripture, and guru, these three.

Oṁ hrīṁ I offer a lamp to god, scripture and guru to destroy the darkness of ignorance *svāhā*.

The fire eagerly devours
the kindling of *karma*.
The sweet fragrance
of excellent incense
drives away all bad smells.
Every day I offer radiant incense
so I won't land in the fire of rebirth.
Every day I worship the Arhant,
the true scripture,
and the unbound guru.

The virtuous fire
of sandal and other fine woods
clears the air of all bad smells.
I worship the supreme state:
god, scripture, and guru, these three.

Oṁ hrīṁ I offer incense to the god, scripture and guru to destroy the eight *karmas* *svāhā*.

It is pleasing to the eye, the tongue,
the nose, the mind.

It is the virtuous essence of all fruit;
none is its equal.
I am full of joy
so I offer this fruit
to taste the supreme nectar.
Every day I worship the Arhant,
the true scripture,
and the unbound guru.

The five senses are absorbed
in tasting the supreme fruit.
I worship the supreme state:
god, scripture, and guru, these three.

Oṁ hrīṁ I offer fruit to god, scripture and guru to obtain the fruit of liberation *svāhā*.

I hold pure water
radiantly fragrant sandalwood
unbroken rice
flowers
food
a lamp
excellent incense
and flawless fruit
all to save myself
from the sins of my many lives.
Every day
I make this glorious offering
to reach the rank of liberation.
Every day I worship the Arhant,
the true scripture,
and the unbound guru.

With zealous mind
I bring these eight costly offerings,
I worship the supreme state:
god, scripture, and guru, these three.

Oṁ hrīṁ I make the offering to god, scripture, and guru to obtain the dispassionate state *svāhā*.

Part Three: The Victory Garland (*jaymālā*)

The auspicious gems
are god, scripture and guru.
They create the triple gem
of faith, knowledge and conduct.
I will sing the virtues of each in the *āratī*,
describing the virtues in brief and at length.

You destroy the sixty-three kinds of *karma*,
You conquer the eighteen faults.
Your forty-six profound virtues
are a supreme and eternal foundation.

You shine supreme
in the holy preaching assembly.
One hundred Indras bow their heads and honour you.
Lord of lords, Arhant, God:
I venerate you with mind, speech and body,
I serve only you.

The Jina's speech is in the form of *oṁ*.
It has no syllables. Its glory is unequalled.
It contains all the eighteen languages
and seven hundred dialects.

It is made of the seven limbs of the doctrine of maybe.
The disciples gathered the twelve-limbed scripture from it.
Neither the sun nor the moon can drive away darkness.
Bow to the scripture with great affection.

The *ācārya*, *upādhyāya* and *sādhu* are the gurus.
Their naked bodies
are treasuries of the three gems.
Feeling aversion
for their transmigrating bodies
they practice asceticism
to reach the supreme state.

Their virtues are thirty-six, twenty-five and twenty-eight.
These lords are a ship to cross the ocean of rebirth.
No one can describe the greatness of the guru,
so recite the name of the guru with mind, speech and body.

Do it as best you can.
If you are weak
then have faith.
Dyānat is such a faithful one.
He says,
you will enjoy the state
beyond old age and death.

Oṁ hrīṁ I make the great offering to god, scripture and guru *svāhā*.

All souls are happy
by the grace of the blessed lord.
The man of faith
should always serve the lord
with body, mind and speech.

2. Five *Nirguṇ Pads*[13]

1. *Guru samān dātā nahī̃ koī*

No one gives like the guru.
The light of the sun is never destroyed,
only covered by darkness.

Desiring nothing for himself
he rains on everyone
like a cloud.
He saves those souls
burning in hellish and animal births,
he gives them heaven,
he gives them liberation and happiness.

He shines like a lamp
in the temple of the three worlds
It is dark in the shadows
but his light is pure
inside and out.

People fall and sink
in the world of family.

[13] Originals found at DYĀNATRĀY (nd) and SOGĀṆĪ (1996).

The true guru
is a raft to cross over.
Dyānat says,
day and night
keep the lotus feet of the guru
in your stainless mind.

2. *Ātamrūp anupam hai*

The true form of your soul
enthroned within
is without parallel.
Remember your soul
and repeat the virtues
if you want to avoid the pains
of birth after birth.

You will find safety
in perfect faith and knowledge.
There's nothing like them
in the three worlds.

You can withstand a load of troubles
if you accept the great vows.
But without knowledge
there's no liberation,
only much *karma*.

In all the three worlds
and all the three times
there's no other cure.
Dyānat says,
you should know this:
you have to do it yourself.

3. *Ātam anubhav karnā re bhāī*

You have to experience the soul, brother.
Until you know
soul and body are different
you will carry the suffering
of birth and death.

If you want to read the soul
listen to the nine truths.
Then practice the vows,
practice austerities and equanimity.
There's no success
without knowing the self,
only the misfortune
of womb after womb.

The scriptures are a lamp, brother.
They drive away the darkness
of bad faith.
The blind man lives
and then he dies.
What will he do?

Dyānat says to the soul who wants pleasure,
this is what you must do:
recite the words 'I am that'
and cross the ocean of rebirth.

4. *Kar kar ātamhit re prāṇī*

Help everything that lives.
The transformations of *karma*
only bind you,
so give them up.

Who are you, man?
Where do you live?
Who is your partner
in pleasure?
There's a succession of bodies
all made of matter.
What makes you think this one's yours?

The flame of consciousness
blazes within you.
You forget it has no equal.
You'll find none like it,
no lamp or diamond,
moon or sun.

Dyānat says,
if you use your body, mind and speech
you can see who you really are.
Attain the state of the supreme lord—
this is the teaching of the omniscient ones.

5. *Ab ham amar bhaye na mareṅge*

Now I'm immortal.
I will not die.
This body is a source of wrong faith
so I've abandoned it.
Why should I adopt another one?

Creatures are born
and then they die
all from the workings of time.
But I have defeated time.
The world is bound by lust and anger—
I've destroyed them both.

I've overcome the body and am invincible.
I know the difference
between soul and body.
This body will perish, but I am firm.
I'm pure. I've become clear.

I did not understand
and so I died over and over again.
Now I've outwitted all sorrow.
Dyānat relies upon the words 'I am that.'
He remembers them effortlessly.

BIBLIOGRAPHY

BALBIR–CAILLAT 1999 = Balbir, Nalini; Caillat, Colette (tr.): *Yogīndu: Lumière de l'Absolu.* Traduit de l'apabhraṁśa par .... Préface de Bernard Sergent. Éditions Payot et Rivages, Paris 1999.

BHĀRILL 1973 = Bhārill, Hukamcand: *Paṇḍit Ṭoḍarmal: Vyaktitva aur Karttṛtva.* Paṇḍit Ṭoḍarmal Smārak Ṭrasṭ, Jaipur 1973.

BHATT 1974 = Bhatt, Bansidhar: 'Vyavahāra-naya and Niścaya-naya in Kundakunda's Works.' In: Wolfgang Voigt (ed.): *XVIII. Deutscher Orientalistentag vom 1. bis 5. Oktober 1972 in Lübeck, Vorträge. Zeitschrift der deutschen Morgenländischen Gesellschaft, Supplement II*, Franz Steiner Verlag, Wiesbaden 1974: 279–91.

CAILLAT 1975–76 = Caillat, Colette: 'Expressions de la Quête Spirituelle dans la Dohāpāhuḍa (Anthologie Jaina en Apabhraṁśa), et dans quelques Textes Brahmaniques.' *Indologica Taurinensia* 3–4 (1975–76) 125–38.

CAILLAT 1976a = Caillat, Colette: 'The Offering of Distichs (*Dohāpāhuḍa*).' *Sambodhi* 5/2–3 (1976) 175–200.

CAILLAT 1976b = Caillat, Colette: 'L'Offrande de Distiques (*Dohāpāhuḍa*): Traduction de l'*Apabhraṁśa*.' *Journal Asiatique* 264/1–2 (1976) 63–95.

CAILLAT 2002 = Caillat, Colette: 'A portrait of the *Yogi* (*joi*) as sketched by Joindu.' In the present volume: 239–252.

DUNDAS 1992 = Dundas, Paul: *The Jains.* The Library of Religious Beliefs and Practices, Routledge, London and New York 1992.

DYĀNATRĀY nd = Dyānatrāy. *Dyānat Pad Saṅgrah.* Jinvāṇī Pracārak Kāryalay, Calcutta: no date.

HARDY 1994 = Hardy, Friedhelm: 'Creative Corruption: Some Comments on Apabhraṁśa Literature, Particularly Yogīndu.' In: Alan W. Entwistle and Françoise Mallison (eds.): *Studies in South Asian Devotional Literature.* Manohar—École Français d'Extrême Orient, New Delhi—Paris 1994: 3–23.

HAWLEY 1984 = Hawley, John Stratton: *Sūr Dās: Poet, Singer, Saint.* University of Washington Press, Seattle 1984.

HAWLEY–JUERGENSMEYER 1988 = Hawley, John Stratton: Juergensmeyer, Mark: *Songs of the Saints of India.* Oxford University Press, New York 1988.

K. JAIN – T. JAIN 1996 = Jain, Kanchedīlāl; Jain, Tārācandra (eds.): *Adhyātma-pad-pārijāt.* Śrī Gaṇeś Varṇī Digambara Jain Saṁsthān, Varanasi 1996.

P. JAIN 1984 = Jain, Puṣpalatā: *Madhyakālīn Hindī Jain Kāvya mẽ Rahasyabhāvnā.* Sanmati Vidyāpīṭh, Nagpur 1984.

R. JAIN 1995 = Jain, Rāmakānt: *Hindī Bhārqtī ke kuch Jain Sāhityakār* (*Jain Itihās ke Prerak Vyaktitva, Bhāg 2*). Jain Vidyā Saṁsthān, Mahavirji 1995.

R. K. JAIN 1966 = Jain, Ravīndra Kumār: *Kavivar Banārsīdās (Jīvanī aur Kṛtitva)*. Bhāratīya Jñānpīṭh, Varanasi 1966.

S. L. JAIN 1994 = Jain, Sudarśan Lāl: *Dev, Śāstra aur Guru*. Akhil Bhāratvarṣīya Digambara Jain Vidvatpariṣad, Varanasi 1994.

S. JAIN 1996 = Jain, Sūrajmukhī: *Apabhraṁśa kā Jain Rahasyavād Kāvya aur Kabīr*. Kusum Prakāśan, Muzaffarnagar 1996.

V. JAIN 1996 = Jain, Vidyāvatī: 'Prastāvnā.' In: K. JAIN – T. JAIN (1996: 1–33).

JOHNSON 1995 = Johnson, W. J.: *Harmless Souls: Karmic Bondage and Religious Change in Early Jainism with Special Reference to Umāsvāti and Kundakunda*. Motilal Banarsidass, Delhi 1995.

KĀSLĪVĀL 1965 = Kāslīvāl, Kastūrcand (ed.): *Hindī Pad Saṅgrah*. Di. Jain A. Kṣetra Śrī Mahāvīrjī, Jaipur 1965.

KĀSLĪVĀL 1973 = Kāslīvāl, Kastūrcand (ed.): *Mahākavi Daulatrām Kāslīvāl: Vyaktitva evaṁ Kṛtitva*. Di. Jain A. Kṣetra Śrī Mahāvīrjī, Jaipur 1973.

KATZ 2000 = Katz, Steven T. (ed.): *Mysticism and Sacred Scripture*. Oxford University Press, New York 2000.

LATH 1981 = Lath, Mukund: *Half a Tale*. Rajasthan Prakrit Bharati Sansthan, Jaipur 1981.

PRACAṆḌIYĀ 1987 = Pracaṇḍiyā, Āditya: *Jain Hindī Pūjā Kāvya*. Jain Śodh Akādamī, Aligarh 1987.

D. ŚĀSTRĪ 1997 = Śāstrī, Devendrakumār (ed.): *Jinvar Arcana*. Bhāratīya Jñānpīṭh, New Delhi 1997.

N. J. ŚĀSTRĪ 1997 = Śāstrī, Narendrakumār Jain: *Mahākavi Bhūdhardās: Ek Samālocanātmak Adhyayan*. Śrī Vītrāg Vijñān Svādhyāy Mandir Ṭrasṭ, Ajmer 1997.

P. ŚĀSTRĪ 1952 = Śāstrī, Pt. Paramānand: 'Kavivar Dyānatrāy.' *Anekānt* 11/4–5 [June–July] (1952) 193–99.

SOGĀṆĪ 1996 = Sogāṇī, Kamal Cand (ed. and Hindi tr.): *Jain Bhajan Saurabh*. Jain Vidyā Saṁsthān, Mahāvīrjī 1996.

UPADHYE 1973 = Upadhye, A.N. (ed.): *Śrī Yogīndudeva's Paramātmaprakāśa, an Apabhraṁśa Work on Jain Mysticism, and also Yogasāra*. Shrimad Rajachandra Ashrama, Agas 1973.

VAUDEVILLE 1993 = Vaudeville, Charlotte: *A Weaver Named Kabir: Selected Verses with a Detailed Biographical and Historical Introduction*. Oxford University Press, Delhi 1993.

INDEX

A

Essays in Jaina Philosophy and Religion.
Warsaw Indological Studies, Volume 2 (2002), pp. 297–306.

E

F

G

H

I

L

M

N

O

P

Ś

T

U

V

W

Y

SOME MORE MLBD PUBLICATIONS

100 YEARS O

मोतीलाल बनारसीदास

सैद मिठा बाजार

लाहौर

1903

MOTILAL BA